THE POPULIST MOMENT
THE END OF RIGHT VS. LEFT

by

ALAIN DE BENOIST

TRANSLATED BY
F. ROGER DEVLIN

Middle Europe Books
Budapest
2025

Cover image:
Giuseppe Pellizza da Volpedo, *The Fourth Estate*, 1901
Galleria d'Arte Moderna, Milan

Cover design: Kevin I. Slaughter
Layout: Greg Johnson
Editing: Greg Johnson, John Morgan, & David Zsutty
Index & Proofing: James J. O'Meara

Published in Hungary by Middle Europe Books, Kft.
www.MiddleEuropeBooks.com

Hardcover ISBN: 978-1-64264-044-1
Paperback ISBN: 978-1-64264-045-8
E-book ISBN: 978-1-64264-046-5

To Thibault Isabel.
In memory of Paul Piccone and Costanzo Preve.

CONTENTS

INTRODUCTION

In September 2016, a poll revealed that for 85% of Frenchmen the presidential election of May 2017 would be "disappointing" no matter what the result. That figure says it all. The extraordinary distrust of ever larger layers of the population toward the "government parties" and the political class in general, to the benefit of movements of a new type called "populist," has undoubtedly been the most striking fact about the changing political landscape of at least the last two decades.

This phenomenon first affected Southern and Western Europe: Syriza in Greece, Podemos in Spain, the National Front (now the National Rally) in France, the Five Star Movement and the Northern League in Italy, and the Freedom Party in Austria. Then it reached Central Europe (Alternative for Germany, AfD), Northern Europe (Sweden Democrats), the United Kingdom ("Brexit"), and even the United States (the Trump and Sanders phenomena). Everywhere the breadth of the chasm separating the people from the incumbent political class has been confirmed. Everywhere new divides have emerged rendering the old Left-Right divide obsolete.

In France under the Fifth Republic, political life long amounted to a regular alternation between two blocs, each dominated by a major party. This system was guaranteed by a majoritarian form of election in two rounds which, by favoring a clear distinction between the majority and the opposition (the parliamentary majority superimposing itself over the governmental majority), seemed to exclude any third candidate from attaining power. But this system stops working once a third party achieves the lasting support of 25% of the electorate. This is where we are now. In the first round of the last departmental elections, the National Front, which achieves its greatest success among the young, the working class, and the lower middle class, received more than 5 million votes as compared to 3.3 for the Socialists and 3.2 for the UMP.[1] In the second round, it received an average of 35% in the 1109 cantons where it competed, rising to between 45 and 50% in 99 of the cantons. In the first round of regional elections, on December 6, 2015, it became the biggest party in France with 27.7% of the votes. So we can figure that about one voter in three votes for the National Front today, which confirms that we have entered into a new form of electoral tripartition: the political system is now structured around three principal formations, each of which attracts between a quarter and a third of voters.

In Italy, Christian Democracy and the Communist Party have practically disappeared. The same goes for the old Greek governmental parties. In Spain, the Spanish Socialist Workers' Party (PSOE) and the Popular Alliance have continually weakened to the benefit of Podemos and de Ciudadanos. In Great Britain, where bipartisanism has been a constant for three centuries (with a single change: the replacement of the Liberals by Labour), and where single-round, first-past-the-post voting gives an advantage to the large traditional parties, we have also witnessed the rise of the UK Independence Party. In Austria the two governmental parties, the Social Democrats and the Christian Social Party, received only 22% of the vote in the presidential election of 2016.

Year after year the movement accelerates. In 2016, a representative of the Five-Star Movement was elected Mayor of Rome, Britain left the European Union as Nigel Farage wished, the Austrian Freedom Party (FPÖ) barely missed electing one of its representatives to the Presidency of the Republic, the National Front passed 40% support in certain local elections, and Podemos won the mayoralties of Madrid, Barcelona, Zaragoza, La Coruña, and Cadiz. On September 4, 2016, in the regional elections of Mecklenburg-West Pomerania, Angela Merkel's home

---

[1] The Union for a Popular Movement, a mass party of the center-right. In 2015 it dissolved and was succeeded by The Republicans. — Trans.

base, the Alternative for Germany, a movement created only three years before, outdid the Christian Democratic Union (CDU) with 21% of the vote (having already achieved 24.2% in Saxony-Anhalt). Finally, in December, Matteo Renzi lost the referendum he had organized in Italy.

The great event of the American presidential election that same year, 2016, was the collapse of the old-style Republican Party, forced, beneath the blows of populist protest, to abandon its political philosophy in harmony with the business world; its most emblematic candidates, Jeb Bush, Marco Rubio, and Scott Walker, all went under. It is not the personality of Donald Trump that should occupy our attention here, but the Trump phenomenon, which must be compared to the Bernie Sanders phenomenon among Democrats. Trump (who is anti-Reagan as much as anti-Clinton) capitalized throughout his campaign on what neither his competitors nor the Republican strategists were able to see: the rise of a powerful anti-elite popular protest movement, a rejection of the *establishment* that the American political class will have to reckon with from now on. Sanders won in twenty-two states versus twenty-eight in favor of Hillary Clinton for more or less the same reasons, beginning with his denunciation of Wall Street influence. And finally, it was Trump who got elected.

Faced with this rise in populism, the establishment first tried to reassure itself with talk of a "flash in the pan." Then, when the wave continued to grow, it was explained as a mere protest vote mobilized by catch-all parties that limited themselves to exploiting discontent and anger of all sorts. Finally, they reassured themselves by alleging a glass ceiling—that has continued to rise, going from 15 to 20%, then to 25%, then from 30 to 35%, exceeding 45% in places.

To curb the phenomenon, they resorted to biomedical and epidemiological metaphors (pathology, diagnostic, remedy). Ritual denunciations multiplied: "the darkest years of our history," a "return to the 1930s." "Godwin points" could be collected by comparing populism to the "extreme Right" or "fascism," equivalencies condemned in other contexts. Concretely, this translated into an attempt to establish a *cordon sanitaire* allowing one to distinguish mentally (and at polling places) between the "decent" and "indecent" parties. But diabolization misfired. This strategy of constructing moral dikes did not amount to much, and they fell back on the republican pact of the dominant parties taking turns with one another in the name of "defending the republican values we have in common," at the risk of proving the well-foundedness of populist discourse that tends to reject all such parties on the basis that nothing really separates them — and with the consequence, for one of the big parties, of being reduced to a supporting role in favor of its adversary of yesterday, or of not being represented at all. Finally, some politicians struggled to assimilate certain populist themes by integrating them into their own discourse at the risk of legitimizing them by "banalizing" them, and without voters being convinced in any case to abandon the original in favor of the imitation.

It was also long said that populist movements disturb the political game, but could never come to power — and in any case, would be completely incapable of governing. But this is no longer true. Today, Syriza is governing Greece, as Podemos will perhaps one day govern Spain; Viktor Orbán is in charge of Hungary; the Northern League has already participated three times in a governing coalition; the FPÖ has been associated with the Austrian government since the 1980s, while the Swiss People's Party (a.k.a. the Democratic Union of the Center, UDC) is also carrying out governmental functions. Other populist formations are participating in Denmark's parliamentary majority and in the government of Finland.

In France, the founding event of the populist rise was the "no" victory in the referendum of 2005 on the projected European constitution, followed by the nullification of that vote by the adoption of the Treaty of Lisbon by the parliament without consulting the people. This "no" revealed the depth of the chasm already dug between the elites and the people, a chasm both ideological and social. It revealed the distrust of a people that no longer feels represented by those who presume to speak in their name; the latter stand accused of merely seeking to maintain their privileges and serve their own interests.

So in fact for the past several decades, the people have observed that their own daily lives are being deeply affected by developments they have never been consulted on, and that the political class of all stripes have never even tried to adjust or slow down.

First of all: immigration. In the space of two generations, through a combination of migratory influx and family reunification, what used to be temporary immigration has taken on the character of demographic replacement. Massive, rapid, badly digested, and badly controlled, it has engendered a series of social pathologies in all domains (school, daily life, employment, security, crime), created or worsened cultural or confessional divisions, affected mores, and deeply transformed the composition of the population. More than 80% of Frenchmen are concerned. The popular classes, which are the first to be confronted with these problems, have the feeling that political leaders refuse to deal with them head on, as if it were simply a matter of choosing between angelism and xenophobia. The rise of jihadism and assassinations has only poisoned the situation further.

Then there is the European Union. Since the beginning of the 1980s, the European construct has resulted in the disappearance of whole layers of state sovereignty without re-establishing it at any higher level. The rapid rise in public debt, at first due to a determination to save banks threatened by the financial crisis of 2008, has made states dependent on financial markets at the very moment the creation of the Euro deprived them of the ability to make sovereign decisions regarding monetary policy. Already militarily dependent on NATO and subject to the budgetary constraints dictated by the EU, the individual states have a mere pasteboard sovereignty. Besides, European institutions are established from the top down. The people have not been brought into the task of European construction, and the few times they have been consulted, no account has been taken of their opinion. Long presented as a solution to all problems, the building of a united Europe today appears a problem added to all the others. Debates have become increasingly technical and thus ever less comprehensible. Divided, powerless, paralyzed, the European Union has ended up discrediting the idea of a united Europe, which the dominant ideology only conceives of as a "continent asked to empty itself of all content in order to give way to the Other" (Élisabeth Lévy). "In short," notes Pierre Manent, "whereas the European Union was supposed to introduce us to the final stage of democracy, it has reconstituted a self-conscious oligarchy, sure of its prerogatives and determined to impose its views on the recalcitrant majority."[2]

Finally, there is globalization. Made possible by the collapse of the Soviet system that symbolized the division of the world into two systems, globalism represents a major symbolic revolution that has changed our relation to the world. Carrying out a switch from the normative to the cognitive register, it has put into competition not merely businesses and products but social systems and entire nations, putting an end to the slow rise of the middle classes and rendering untenable the social gains conceded to the world of work during the era of the "Thirty Glorious Years."[3] Through delocalization and by putting Europeans into competition with the underpaid masses of the Third World in a context analogous to dumping, globalization has destroyed the collective bargaining power of workers while damaging the sovereignty of states, putting them on notice not to make use of their political decision-making power.[4] Thus has

---

[2] Pierre Manent, "Les gouvernants ne nous représentent plus, ils nous surveillent" ["The Rulers no Longer Represent Us, They Monitor Us"], *Le Figaro*, August 1, 2016, 19.

[3] The thirty years of relative prosperity enjoyed by France following the Second World War. — Trans.

[4] Raoul-Marc Jennar does not hesitate to describe globalization as a

been established a world with no outside, no alternative, a world directed only toward profit. Defended by the business world in the name of the free circulation of persons, goods, and capital, globalization is defended by the Left in the name of moral cosmopolitanism and abstract humanism, both factions in agreement on the legitimization of international mass migration, the universalization of norms, downward pressure on salaries, and threats to employment. Globalization creates a lot of winners among the elites, but millions of losers among the people who, moreover, realize that economic globalization opens the way for cultural globalization — even as it dialectically elicits new forms of fragmentation.

We have also seen the near-disappearance of sociological families in which people voted the same way for generation after generation. As late as the mid-1960s, the more Catholic one was, the more likely one was to vote for the Right; and at the social level, the more one identified with the working class, the more one voted for the Left. This has no longer been the case for a long time. Electoral volatility has not stopped increasing — to the point where it is no longer rare to find people who, over the course of their lives, have voted for practically all the parties. In 1946, François Goguel calculated that between 1877 and 1936 the balance of forces between all the Right-wing and Left-wing parties in France had never varied by more than 2%. Today, we know that 17% of voters for the extreme Left at the legislative elections of 1986 voted for a Right-wing party in the first round of the 1988 presidential elections, that 60% of Mitterand voters in 1988 refused to vote socialist in 1993, and that nearly four

---

"world *coup d'Etat*," since "it amounts to a transfer of the attributes of popular sovereignty to supranational decision-making centers where everything has been done to assure that popular sovereignty cannot be exercised: the IMF, the World Bank, the World Trade Organization, the European Union" ("Left/Right: An Obsolete Divide?" at the website *Médiapart*, September 5, 2011, 3.). Cf. also Antoine Garapon, "Une gauche 'ringardisée' par la mondialization?" ["A Left Rendered Outdated by Globalization?"], *Esprit*, September 2016, 33–43.

million voters switched sides during the six months that preceded the presidential election of 2012. According to a study of the
Elabe Institute published in August 2016, the share of Frenchmen describing themselves as "with no party preference" is continually rising, especially among the young (35%), blue-collar
workers (37%), and white-collar workers (38%), while only
14.1% of those asked feel themselves close to the Socialist Party
and 16.4% to the Republicans, i.e., at total of 30.5% for the governmental parties with which, therefore, two thirds of Frenchmen no longer identify.[5]

Corresponding to this apparent loss of structure in the electorate is an enormous recentering at the level of party leadership
and government administrations, one toward which the two-
party system inherently tends. Convinced that elections "are
won at the center" — in conformity with the theory of the "average voter" developed by political scientist Anthony Downs —
and not having understood yet that the middle class is decom-
posing, the big parties continue (as they did during the Thirty
Glorious Years of the postwar era) to push their discourse toward the center in order to rally hesitant electors, leading them
to formulate programs that increasingly look alike.

In the Giscard era, some celebrated this as the benefits of
"consensus" — the consensus that Alain Minc did not hesitate to
compare to a "circle of reason." Such people were mistaken first
of all because democracy is not the extinction of conflict but the
mastering of conflict. For a political society to function normally, a consensus must obviously be established regarding the
framework and forms of debate. But if consensus makes the

---

[5] Let us remember that in the first round of the 1988 presidential election the two main candidates, François Mitterand and Jacques Chirac,
together received 54.1% of the vote. On April 21, 2002, Chirac and Lionel
Jospin already received no more than 35.8%. With 19.7% of the vote, Chirac registered the lowest score ever obtained by an incumbent president
since 1974. (François Mitterand had obtained 34.1% in the first round in
1988.)

debate itself disappear then democracy disappears by the same token, since by definition it implies, if not a plurality of parties, at least a diversity of opinions and choices, as well as recognition of the legitimacy of conflict between opinions and choices. This means that, contrary to what supporters of "nonpartisan" democracy or "good governance" maintain, democracy cannot be resolved into procedures, for it has an inevitably agonistic form. If parties are only separated by insignificant programmatic differences, if competing factions implement essentially the same policies, if neither are distinguishable in regard to their aims or the means of obtaining them—in short: if the citizens no longer see themselves presented with real alternatives and genuine choices—there is no more reason for debate, and the institutional framework that permits it to take place is merely an empty shell from which one should not be surprised to see a majority of voters turn away. The price of "consensus" is civic desertion.

But excessive consensus is antidemocratic in another way. We must not forget that, contrary to what the champions of the political marketplace assert (who assume the voter above all seeks to maximize his interests at election time), voting is above all a means of self-representation and affirmation.[6] Now, if the electorate gets the feeling no alternative is being offered to it by the parties competing for power, clearly it can only lose interest in a political game that no longer allows it to express its belonging or affiliation through voting. The end of any "democracy of identification" (Pierre Rosanvallon) will contribute to a rise in abstention, which will itself end in social anomie. There will then be a growing risk not of a society pacified by "consensus" but of

---

[6] For a critique of the theory of the political market, cf. especially Pierre Merle, "L'*Homo politicus* est-il un *Homo oeconomicus*? L'analyse économique du choix politique: approche critique" ["Is *Homo politicus* a *Homo economicus*? The Economic Analysis of Political Choice, a Critical Approach"], *Revue Française de science politique*, February 1990, 75. Cf. also Chantal Mouffe, *L'illusion du consensus* [*The Illusion of Consensus*] (Paris: Albin Michel, 2016).

a dangerous and potentially bellicose society where we should not be surprised to see the return of other forms of identitarian affirmation (religious, ethnic, national, etc.), sometimes in pathological forms. These will not result from any desire for "dangerous purity," but will be the logical consequence of the impossibility of affirming oneself as a citizen.

The principal result of recentering is in fact to disappoint those it is trying to seduce. "Nothing better displays the nature of neoliberal rationality," write Pierre Dardot and Christian Laval, "than the evolution of governmental practice, which for the past thirty years claims to be on the Left while implementing policies very similar to the Right."[7] The four alternations in power between Left and Right during the past quarter century have in fact allowed voters to take the measure of their insignificance, especially as neither camp has received decisive results, and both have proven themselves incapable of reclaiming a margin of maneuver in face of the constraints of the financial markets and European treaties. People have the feeling that the Right-wing parties are pursuing Left-wing policies while the Left-wing parties pursue Right-wing policies, or more generally that both are pursuing convergent and interchangeable policies when they come into power. This convergence has come about at the price of a double abandonment: the Right has abandoned the nation, and the Left has abandoned the people. This is what Pierre Manent observes:

> The Right has renounced the people-nation, renounced searching for justice and unity in the sense in which "the people" refers to the nation: farewell to Gaullism. The Left has renounced the people-working-class, renounced searching for justice and unity in the sense in which "the people"

---

[7] Pierre Dardot and Christian Laval, *La nouvelle raison du monde. Essai sur la société néolibérale* [*The New Reason of the World: An Essay on Neoliberal Society*] (Paris: La Decouverte, 2010), 137.

refers to "the exploited": farewell to socialism.[8]

At the same time, any genuine alternative (replaced by mere alternation) becomes impossible, and a growing number of voters have the feeling that the political system is coded in advance so that only those who can be trusted to change nothing about the system can win.

People long believed things would get better if the government were changed. Observing that nothing any longer distinguishes the big parties that still claim to oppose one another, they no longer believe this. The result is always the same, and therefore the disappointment is always the same. If one insists on analyzing the situation in market terms, political life is characterized by an ever more reduced selection in the face of an increasingly malcontented (because increasingly disorganized) demand. Consternation first favored abstention, then protest voting, then populism. The populist parties have in fact been the first to perceive a change in political and social demand that the traditional parties, whatever the goodwill of their elected officials—always concerned to be as close as possible to their electors—do not understand because they are mental prisoners of habits and schemes of thought that forbid their understanding. So the political class finds itself marked with illegitimacy because it no longer resolves any problems and offers no means of overcoming the generalized crisis of the system but seems actually to contribute to it.

*

The discrepancy between the political class and the electorate constitutes a special problem for the Left, which in the past always claimed to better represent popular aspirations than the Right. But the Left has gradually cut itself off from the people. Leftist intellectuals have abandoned the messianic hopes that

---

[8] Pierre Manent, "Les gouvernants ne nous représentent plus, ils nous surveillent," 19.

they placed in the working class not so long ago, while their political elites have gradually distanced themselves from the popular milieus by way of class contempt. Exactly like the Right, the Left has settled in the upper middle classes, if not in the state apparatus. Rallying to the market economy, privileging marginal demands to the detriment of the aspirations of those most threatened by unemployment and insecurity, and providing the spectacle of an elite wallowing in its media image, it has greatly disappointed those it was primarily supposed to address.

The people and the Left have certainly never been equivalent concepts, as was well seen during the June days of 1848 and during the Commune of 1871 when the Republican and bourgeois Left ordered the people fired upon (in his celebrated *History of the Commune*, published in 1876, Prosper-Olivier Lissagaray reminded readers that if the bourgeoisie of Versailles was able to crush the Parisian proletariat, it was thanks "to the Army, the Administration, and the Left"). We also know that during the whole twentieth century the Left showed itself largely indifferent, if not hostile, to the cooperative and mutualist movement. Still, the evolution of the Left over at least the last thirty years has something astonishing about it.

In 1979 François Mitterand and his friends presented a composite motion at the Metz Congress of the French Socialist Party affirming that "economic rigor in the sense intended by those in power constitutes a fantastic lie." But in 1992, the socialist project entitled "A New Horizon" declares: "Yes, we think the market economy constitutes the most efficient means of production and exchange. No, we do not believe in a break with capitalism." Just consider the distance travelled! This is what allowed Michel Rocard to redefine socialism as a "sort of tempered capitalism" (*sic*). In November 1999, Lionel Jospin himself declared that socialism no longer existed, either as a "doctrinal system" or "as a system of production, the superiority of the market over planning having become incontestable." Of course, one would still like to know whether socialism can be reduced to "planning" . . .

The Left's liberal turn in fact goes back to 1983, when there began a capitulation that—from privatization to subsidies for management—has continued to accelerate. So the critique of capitalism was abandoned, and along with it the idea that the state, no longer being the motor of the economy, could at least have a right of oversight over the private sector. The rehabilitation of profit, the defense of the market and "business culture," income on capital rising faster than wages: the about-face has been complete. The result is a soaring stock market, corruption everywhere, and the promotion of Bernard Tapie[9] to the rank of model economic "winner."

At the same time, the rise of a hedonistic-libertarian culture of the Left (called bobo[10]) also helped cut off Left-wing parties from the common people who watched with amazement the emergence and establishment by the media of a worldly and arrogant Left more inclined to defend homosexual adoption, the undocumented, contemporary art, minority rights, talk of gender stereotypes, political correctness, bodily phobias, and permanent surveillance of the behavior of others than to defend the interests of the working class. Cultural liberalism thus teamed up with an economic liberalism that, to allow the endless expansion of the market, seeks to destroy all traditional forms of existence beginning with the family, one of the last islands of resistance to the reign of mercantile values. The heirs of May 1968, who recently wanted to forbid forbidding and enjoy without restraint (two typically liberal slogans) quickly understood that liberal capitalism could better satisfy their desires, easily shifting from "enjoyment without restraint" to "consumption without limit" and from the utopia of the global spread of a classless society to the utopia of neoliberal globalization.

With François Hollande, the abandonment of the social for the benefit of the "societal" was confirmed and accelerated.

---

[9] Bernard Roger Tapie (1943–2021) was a French businessman, politician, and entertainer plagued by charges of corruption. —Trans.

[10] Short for "bourgeois bohemian" —Trans.

From the abandonment of any significant fiscal reform to the absence of any industrial policy, from the revision of the employment code in the sense demanded by the Movement of the Enterprises of France, France's largest employer federation, to employment blackmail aimed at lowering salaries—while those of the big bosses remained outside the "framework"—not forgetting the El Khomri law and the law on employment security that signed the death warrant of the no term contract: the social-defeatist result of François Hollande's five-year term in office gave proof of absolute submission to the demands of the financial markets.

That a leader of the Socialist Party, Dominique Strauss-Kahn as it happens, could be called to direct the International Monetary Fund to implement the same policies Christine Lagarde practices today was already highly symbolic. It is easily seen in any case that neither homosexual marriage, nor the legalization of cannabis, nor the struggle for sexual parity (except within marriage!), nor uncontrolled immigration, nor the abolition of borders, nor even the defense of the "rights of man" (pitilessly criticized by Marx) are socialist measures or themes. These are liberal themes, supposedly responding to individual desires and caprices, and which attempt to distract our attention from five or ten million unemployed. The dominant class has abandoned the social to engage in a bidding war of rights for the benefit of minority groups, each now erected into a demanding lobby. But, as Laurent Bouvet remarks, "the change in elite preoccupations from the social to the cultural is always unfavorable to the lower classes, besides being deadly for the Left."[11]

Having become a social-liberal party—ever more liberal and ever less social—the Socialist Party conceives society merely as a collection of individuals. Having rallied to the money system, it has become a party of bureaucrats, technocrats, and bobos who have long forgotten about socialism and are only interested in

---

[11] Laurent Bouvet, *L'Insécurité. Le malaise identitaire français* [*Insecurity: The French Identitarian Illness*] (Paris: Fayard, 2015), 5.

"for-everybody-ism," the "struggle against all forms of discrimination," "humanitarian" interventions, and the most emotional and lachrymose defense of "victims."[12] So one can hardly count on the party's leaders to explain that the current crisis is first of all a crisis of the capitalist mode of production, i.e., a generalized crisis of the logic of capital accumulation, and one can count on them even less to try to remedy the situation.

Thus, most voters have had leisure to observe that for at least thirty years the parties of the Left have been carrying out regressive social policies that yield in no way to those of the Right. This is what Serge Halimi has called "the great leap backwards," and Jacques Généreux "the great regression."[13] "For twenty years," observes Jean-Claude Michéa soberly, "each victory of the Left has necessarily corresponded to a defeat for socialism."[14] We are looking at the end not merely of institutional socialism, but even of social democracy, which has dissolved itself into liberalism and only serves to produce a "progressive" camouflage allowing the Left to remain in sync with the recent evolution of capitalism. The more the Left rallies to the existing system, whose wrongs the people feel, the more the people will turn away from it; the more the people turn away from the Left,

---

[12] *Cf.* Bertrand Rothé, *De l'abandon au mépris, Comment le PS a tourné le dos à la classe ouvrière* [*From Abandonment to Contempt: How the Socialist Party Turned its back on the Working Class*] (Paris: Seuil, 2013).

[13] Serge Halimi, *Le grand bond en arrière. Comment l'ordre libéral s'est imposé au monde* [*The Great Leap Backwards: How the Liberal Order Was Imposed on the World*] (Paris: Fayard, 2004); second revised edition (Marseille: Agone, 2012); Jacques Généreux, *La Grande Régression* [*The Great Regression*] (Paris: Seuil, 2010).

[14] Jean-Claude Michéa, "Pour en finir avec le XXIe siècle" ["Settling Accounts with the Twenty-First Century"] preface to the second edition of Michel Landa's French translation of Christopher Lasch's *The Culture of Narcissism: American Life in an Age of Diminishing Expectations* (Castelnau-le-Lez: Climats, 2000), 18. *Cf.* also the title of Manuel Valls' *Pour en finir avec le vieux socialism . . . et être enfin de gauche* [*To Settle Accounts with the Old Socialism . . . and Finally Be on the Left*] (Paris: Robert Laffont, 2008).

the more the Left displays its contempt for the people. This divorce, which is not peculiar to France but can be found everywhere, is now complete.

Many like to cite Berthold Brecht who, when the workers of East Berlin revolted in 1953, responded to an official tract stating "the people have by their own fault lost the confidence of the government" by ironically advising the government to "dissolve the people and elect a new one." This is more or less what the Terra Nova Foundation has proposed doing by replacing the inherited people by the addition of minorities, immigrants, young people, women, and bobos, thus following the example of America's Democratic Party.[15]

---

[15] *Cf.* the report by Bruno Jeanbar, Olivier Ferrand, and Romain Prudent, *Gauche: quelle majorité électorale pour 2012? [The Left: What Sort of Electoral Majority for 2012?]* (Paris: Terra Nova, 2011), where one can read this revealing passage: "It is not possible for the Left today to restore its historical class coalition: the working class is no longer the heart of the Left-wing electorate, is no longer in step with the Left's values as a whole, can no longer be as it once was the motor driving the constitution of a Left-wing electoral majority. For the Left to implement a class strategy based on the working class, or more broadly on the popular classes, would require it to renounce its cultural values."

Hence the embarrassment of a great part of today's Left with regard to radical Islam or anti-white racism. The memory of the anticolonial struggle has nourished the essentialist and overdetermining idea that, even after the disappearance of the old colonies, European man remains fundamentally imperialist and racist, and thus always guilty, which justifies demanding eternal "repentance" from him, while the formerly colonized and their descendants remain victims, which authorizes an empathetic response to (if not actual justification of) their most aggressive and violent behavior, since everything they do is supposed to result from their identity and their "dominated" position. So nothing is ever really their fault (such is the basis of the "culture of excuses").

Laurent Bouvet, who speaks in this context of a "colonial complex," explains:

From the 1970s, when the economic crisis and immigration

By disappointing the people, by working toward the destruction of everything to which it is attached, by taking a position of solidarity with the predators of the market society, by making a spectacle of autism, indecency, and corruption, the Left has cut itself off from the popular classes and thrown them into the arms of populist movements just waiting to receive them in order to speak in their name. Jean-Claude Michéa is correct when he writes:

> It is not in the moral darkness of one segment of the popular classes (or their "lack of education") that one must seek the true reasons for the rise of the "extreme Right." They are to be sought rather in the *indignant reaction* of these classes toward a political and intellectual movement that in the name of "science," "modernity," and the "natural" evolution of morality proposes to destroy (such, at least, is their sincere conviction) all the virtues and moral traditions to which they are attached—beginning, as Orwell

---

from formerly colonized countries began, this postcolonial way of thinking has been swallowing up the classic workers' emancipation and class struggle way of thinking. . . . A large part of the Left, in politics, non-profits, labor unions, and the intelligentsia has been orphaned by this great socialist and communist grand narrative, and will find a *raison d'être* in this fight for the new wretched of the earth by largely converting to different forms of liberalism: political liberalism with the rights of man and liberal democracy against the residues of Communist totalitarianism; economic liberalism with the law of the market and finance capitalism against statism and Keynesianism; cultural liberalism with individual emancipation according to personal rather than collective identity. . . . In such a setting, the terrorist is first and above all perceived as a victim, even if his act *per se* is condemned. ("L'Islamisme, la gauche et le complexe colonial" ["Islamism, the Left, and the Colonial Complex"] on the website *Figaro Vox*, July 22, 2016.)

The denialist Left thus nourishes the rejectionist Right.

emphasized, with their religious faith, their sense of personal effort, and their patriotism.[16]

Between the legislative elections of 1978 and the presidential elections of 2002, revealingly, the percentage of blue- and white-collar workers who voted for the Left fell from 27 to 15%. The most recent elections reveal that nearly 50% of workers now vote for the National Front. This does not mean that workers constitute the majority of the Front's voters (they represent only about 13%), but it does mean that this party is overrepresented in the world of work, something that undoubtedly contributes to its discredit among elites. The prevalence of worker support for the Left, which was regularly observed in the postwar era until the end of the 1970s, has thus disappeared. With the years, an increasing number of working people shifted to the National Front, especially those born after 1960, confronted as soon as they entered active life with problems due to immigration, unemployment, and insecurity. These generations, notes Florent Gougou, "experienced the crystallization of a mostly cultural divide produced by globalism in the dynamics of French politics, just as the interwar generations of working people experienced the crystallization of the class divide."[17] Let us also recall

---

[16] "Jean-Claude Michéa répond à dix questions" ["Jean-Claude Michéa Answers Ten Questions"], in Gilles Labelle, Eric Martin, and Stéphane Vibert, eds., *Les Racines de la liberté. Réflexions à partir de l'anarchisme tory* [*The Roots of Freedom: Reflections on Tory Anarchism*] (Montreal: Nota Bene, 2014), 359–60.

[17] In Jean-Michel De Waele and Mathieu Vieira, eds., *Une droitisation de la classe ouvrière en Europe?* [*Is the Working Class Shifting to the Right?*] (Paris: Economica, 2011). This migration of the working-class vote to the National Front, perceived as better capable of defending the structural interests of the dominated classes, accelerated the collapse of the Communist Party which, beginning with the municipal elections of 2001, lost control of one third of the towns of over 15,000 people which it had previously controlled. At the presidential election of 2007 the communist candidate Marie-George Buffet received no more than 1.9% of the vote.

that in the referendum on the European constitutional treaty 60% of young people, 80% of blue-collar workers, and 60% of white-collar workers, along with a majority of salaried employees voted *no*; the *yes* vote attracted a majority only of the upper bourgeoisie, management, the economically inactive, and retirees.

It is no different in neighboring countries. In Great Britain the majority of workers and residents of the popular neighborhoods voted in favor of Brexit, which was only able to win by mobilizing a large share of Labour Party voters (nearly 80% of districts electing a Labour Party MP voted *Leave*). In Austria at the last presidential election, the workers voted 85% for the FPÖ candidate; the working class and the unemployed are equally overrepresented in the ranks of the UDC in Switzerland and the AfD in Germany.

To speak of a "shift to the Right" would only be a lazy way of interpreting this development. It is obvious that Left and Right no longer mean anything as soon as the general opinion is that all the big parties of Right and Left are saying more or less the same thing—and confront one another at most over the means for implementing the same policies. In reality, the Left-Right divide no longer has practical value for analyzing new political phenomena, beginning with the rise of populism. The proof of this is that populist party programs often combine Left- and Right-wing themes. In Greece, Alex Tsipras, leader of Syriza, preferred to ally himself with a sovereignist party classed on the Right, the Independent Greeks (ANEL), to form his government, rather than with traditional Left-wing formations such as Pasok. In France we even saw the economist Jacques Sapir plead for an alliance between the National Front and the Left Front. Elsewhere we see voters for the big parties no longer following the directions of party leaders. Thus, it is remarkable that in Great Britain the leadership of both big parties, Conservative and Labour, were favorable to *Remain*, which means that Brexit won by combining votes from supporters of both camps. In the US, where the Left-Right scheme could barely be applied to Republicans and Democrats any longer, one also saw neocon personalities from the Republican party, and not the least of them (Paul Wolfowitz, Robert Kagan, Brent Scowcroft, Richard Armitage, James Kirchik, Max Boot, Bret Stephens, etc.), announce that they would vote for Hillary Clinton, described for the occasion as a "true conservative," the only candidate capable of resisting "systemic change"[18]—which happened anyway.

But the blurring of the Right-Left distinction could be observed not only at the base. By reaction, and in an almost symmetrical fashion, it was also found in the dominant class with the idea of a "national union" destined to prevent the rise of populism and neutralize the "recalcitrant" of both sides. There is a certain logic to this: as an electorate drawn from both Right and Left is forming at the base, populism evokes a regrouping of formerly antagonistic governmental parties at the top who today have no trouble realizing that nothing any longer really separates them.

This new strategy, which obviously favors coalition governments (in 2013 eleven of the twenty-eight countries of the European Union were governed by a coalition of Right and Left) was already present in the "third way" idea theorized by Anthony Giddens in the time of Tony Blair, whose stated object was to legitimate the "renewal" of social democracy in the sense of an assumed fusion with liberal logic.[19] This is found in France in an Emmanuel Macron, the heir of Blairism, when he assures us that "the real division in our country . . . is between progressives and conservatives," or in the Liberal Guy Sorman for

---

[18] This new rise in populism on the political scene of the United States (which is one of its countries of origin) has had its effects on party political programs. In August 2016, a poll by the Pew Research Center showed that only 32% of Republican voters are favorable to free trade, compared to 58% of Democrats, whereas in 2009 the figures were 57% of Republicans and 48% of Democrats.

[19] Anthony Giddens, *The Third Way: The Renewal of Social Democracy* (Cambridge: Polity Press, 1998).

whom "the recent British referendum on leaving the European Union did not oppose Right-wing Conservatives to Left-wing Labour, but the partisans of openness to those of closure."[20] Since "closure" is supposed to designate "withdrawal into one-self," "tribalism," and "irrational fear," we must understand that "openness" means markets transcending national boundaries and free exchange as the automatic source of growth and prosperity. "The open society" means the law of the market.

*

The end of "grand narratives," the collapse of collective projects and great struggles for liberation following the implosion of the Soviet system, spread disenchantment and disillusion. Among the popular classes this was expressed by a certain loss of orientation going well beyond the political sphere. Everything that supports identity (national belonging, social class, family, religion, relations between the sexes and the generations) is today in crisis. Education, under the influence of fashion, has abandoned its vocation in favor of utilitarian and economistic drift. Work, reduced to "employment"—Simone Weil saw in salaried employment the most important factor in uprootedness—is no longer a source of identity, and even less of dignity, but merely a painful obligation that allows one to earn a little money. Liberalism, by affirming that egoistical actions end by adding to everyone's well-being, contributes to the destruction of the foundations of morality. "Since our vices are supposed to be useful to the collective, why make an effort to be good, scrupulous, and honest?"[21] The rise of liberal individualism also crushed ancient structures of solidarity by destroying all forms of allegiance and stability. Social life has become increasingly

---

[20] Guy Sorman, "Le clivage droite/gauche est dépassé, il faudra vous y faire" ["The Right/Left Distinction is Obsolete: Get Used to It"] on the website *Contrepoints*, August 6, 2016.

[21] Thibault Isabel, "Christopher Lasch: un populiste contre le progress" ["Christopher Lasch: A Populist Against Progress"], *Krisis*, February 2008, 99.

insecure: we have reached the era of *"zapping"* and precariousness. Nothing is meant to last. The social bond is coming un-
done, and this social dissolution increases the vulnerability of
individuals in a climate of competitive pressure amounting to a
new "war of all against all."

The idea of progress, a secular form of the belief in Provi-
dence, has itself gone into crisis, and the idea that tomorrow will
necessarily be better than today is nearly dead thanks to the dynamics of permanent acceleration theorized by Hartmut Rosa.
The "sunny tomorrows" have disappeared, giving way to a diffuse fear of the future that nourishes thoughts of catastrophe
and specters of disaster. "The future is empty of promises" (André Gorz). This fear of the future, presumed to carry mainly
threats, is paradoxically accompanied by a tendency to erase the
past. "The rejection of the past, a superficially progressive and
optimistic attitude," remarks Christopher Lasch, "reveals itself
upon analysis as manifesting the despair of a society unable to
face the future."[22] All "presentism" forbids imagining the future
except as a leap into the unknown.

This disorientation is due above all to the fact that for the
dominant ideology man is not fundamentally a social being and
can construct himself out of nothing, all men being posited as
fundamentally identical ("the same") and thus substitutable for
one other. At the normative level, the goal then becomes to encourage everything that allows him to become even more "independent" of his fellows: the celebration of "nomadism," the free
circulation of men and capital, paeans to hybridization of every
sort, the denial of collective identities, the eradication of particular cultures, a programmed amnesia regarding the past, the

---

[22] Christopher Lasch, *La Culture du narcissisme* [*The Culture of Narcissism*] (Paris: Flammarion, 2006), 27. Cf. also Michaël Foessel, "Le temps
de la gauche" ["The Time of the Left"], *Esprit*, September 2016, 68–79,
who notes that the Left's view of the future "has become increasingly
disillusioned" (p. 70), whereas "faith in the future" was its principal driving force in the past.

abandonment of all concern with identity, criticism of all forms of belonging or affiliation. The "liberalization of mores" itself results from the need to submit all areas of social life to capitalist consumption; the Left defends only an indeterminate freedom (which is also the freedom of liberal anthropology) indifferent to the institutional and socio-historical conditions that allow its establishment.

But the people do not interpret the suppression of all norms as synonymous with greater freedom. Spontaneously hostile to a "counterculture" that has undertaken to deconstruct all their points of reference on the basis of an abstract conception of freedom, despoiling them of all reference to a substantial normative framework, they confusedly perceive that to be free is not to tear oneself out and refuse but to adhere and participate in (places, situations, ways of living), which involves recognizing the conditions (especially reciprocal obligations) that allow for the autonomy of human communities.[23] In a world where all forms of authority (with the single exception of the technical authority of "experts") have been delegitimized one after the other, and in which the only institutions called upon to regulate relations between men are legal contract and commercial exchange, they come to realize that this loss of meaning is bound up with the way economic relations have assumed precedence over social relations. The primacy of the economy and the "furies of private interest" have brought about a reification of human existence that puts an end to organic society, to human interdependence. "The economy transforms the world, but only into an economic world," as Guy Debord said.

The unleashing of the logic of the limitless in a world that has lost its bearings evokes in people's minds a deep identitarian and existential malaise. When we speak of populism we must take account of this malaise, aggravated by the internalization of the idea that there is no alternative to the disappearance of any

---

[23] *Cf.* Jean-Pierre Lebrun, *La condition humaine n'est pas sans conditions* [*The Human Condition Is Not Unconditional*] (Paris: Denoël, 2010).

horizon of meaning within the world of economic reproduction: "The world must be neither interpreted nor changed: it must be put up with" (Peter Sloterdijk). "Our heritage leaves us maladapted to a world that devalues what we spontaneously tend to value and that brings into the foreground what we look down upon," observes Marcel Gauchet.[24] The people are aware of this inversion of values.

They are all the more sensible to the inversion in that since the 1970s and 1980s their material situation has continually deteriorated. By the end of 2013, there were 8.5 million poor and 4 million beneficiaries of state-guaranteed social welfare payments, i.e., along with their spouses and children, 7.1 million persons (11% of the population). As of the same date, more than 40% of people consider themselves poor, as compared to 30% in 2009. Poverty has become urbanized (it is rising above all in the large urban agglomerations), younger (in the past forty years the poverty rates of those under 25 has doubled), and female (it affects mainly single-parent families, most of them headed by women).[25] As for the number of unemployed, if one takes into account low-salaried jobs, it is well over 6 million. Formerly when one made it into the middle class it was never to leave it again; today a growing number of middle-class people with modest salaries are threatened with dropping out of the middle class: for the first time, an increasing number of young people occupy a less desirable social class than their parents. The middle class is becoming impoverished, and inequality is increasing. The poor are getting poorer, the rich getting richer. The peasantry is disappearing, and farmers consume not so much what they produce as what they buy. In short, we have passed from one age — that of the "Republic of the Center" that sought to include "two Frenchmen out of three," where two thirds of citizens were satisfied with their lot — to an age when this is true only of one

---

[24] Marcel Gauchet, *Le Journal du dimanche*, September 16, 2013.

[25] Cf. Julien Damon, *Eliminer la pauvreté* [*Eliminating Poverty*] (Paris: PUF, 2010) and *L'Exclusion* [*Exclusion*] (Paris: PUF, 2014).

third of the population, the other two thirds feeling themselves excluded or threatened. Such a development necessarily has its political corollary.

In this regard, populism is also a sociological phenomenon. It is tied to the people's situation, where the predominant feeling is one of triple exclusion: political, social, and cultural. Cultural insecurity, well-studied by Laurent Bouvet,[26] begins when you start feeling, rightly or wrongly, like a foreigner in your own land, when you start perceiving, rightly or wrongly, your neighbors as a threat because of their ethnocultural origin or religion. The question of your way of life is essential here—of mores in the Hegelian sense of *Sittlichkeit* (customary ethical life as opposed to formal Kantian *Moralität*).

Christopher Guilluy has demonstrated that class divisions now conceal cultural and identitarian issues.[27] In a world become at once illegible and a source of anxiety, identitarian motivation is inseparable from the social question. Those who suffer most from the social pathologies brought on by immigration are also the very people who do not have the means of avoiding them because of poverty or the precarious situation in which they find themselves. The popular classes are suffering the consequences of austerity policies and mass immigration at the same time: those who do not have the means to live apart or go to school apart, who live far from the big cities where wealth and managerial personnel are concentrated, those who are relegated to peripheral France. At this point, the National Front becomes the middle class's party of escape. "Support for the NF expresses a real class conflict," emphasizes Christophe Guilluy.

---

[26] Laurent Bouvet, *L'Insecurité*. Cf. by the same author *Le Sens du peuple* [*The Meaning of the People*] (Paris: Gallimard, 2012).

[27] Christophe Guilluy, *Fractures françaises* [*French Fractures*] (Paris: François Bourin, 2010), second ed. (Paris: Flammarion, 2013); *La France périphérique. Comment on a sacrifié les classes populaires* [*Suburban France: How the Popular Classes Have Been Sacrificed*] (Paris: Flammarion, 2014); *Le Crépuscule de la France d'en haut* [*Twilight of the French Elites*] (Paris: Flammarion, 2016).

"The NF electorate is almost more proletarianized than the communist electorate of the 1960s."[28] He writes:

> For the first time, the majority of the popular class is not living where wealth and employment are created. This has never before happened in history. The result: the inhabitants of peripheral France are excluded from any chance of rising in society and turn towards anti-system political options. If we add white-collar workers, small farmers, and other ill-paid and threatened groups to the working class, we get most of the economically active population. Add to these the retirees and the young originating in these categories, and you have most of the French population.[29]

This is why nearly all populist movements defend both living standards and a way of life. "Parties that insist on only one or the other of these objects will not achieve great results," emphasizes political scientist Marco Tarchi.[30]

Poverty, distress, a feeling of abandonment: all this explains

---

[28] Christophe Guilluy, "L'antifascisme cache des intérêts de classe" ["Antifascism Conceals Class Interests"], *Causeur*, January 2016, 29.

[29] Guilluy, "L'antifascisme cache des intérêts de classe," 29–31. "Immigrationism, i.e., the ideology which celebrates and makes use of migratory flows, has always been the enemy of the popular classes," writes Galaad Wilgos, who recalls that "in Marx and Engels we find one of the first revolutionary critiques of immigrationism. They both use the concept of a reserve army to describe the existence of a mass of unemployed allowing the holders of capital not to raise salaries and to threaten those fortunate enough to have a job" ("Bouge de là!" ["Get Away from There!"], *Limite*, January 2016, 67–68). Marx and Engels write in particular that, "the English bourgeoisie has not only exploited Ireland's poverty to keep the English working class's standard of living low thanks to the forced immigration of poor Irishmen, but also divided the proletariat into two hostile camps" (*Ireland and the Irish Question* [New York: International Publishers, 1972]).

[30] Marco Tarchi, "Pourquoi le populisme hante l'Europe" ["Why Populism Is Haunting Europe"], *Causeur*, July–August 2016, 45.

the breadth of the crisis. As at the time of the *Cahiers de doléances*,[31] the people have the feeling they are no longer represented by the elites that form a caste "with separate interests contradicting those of the population" (Jacques Sapir). They have the feeling that their social situation is continuing to deteriorate, that the era of full employment has passed forever, and that the future will be even worse. They have the feeling that the values to which they adhere are mocked or held in contempt today, the feeling that their way of life is threatened by the presence on the national territory of a population with different mores that they perceive as foreign if not hostile. They have the feeling that the public powers have abdicated sovereignty and that the European Union, far from protecting them from the effects of globalization, constitutes an antisocial project that contributes to aggravate economic and cultural insecurity.

Ever larger segments of the people feel excluded, misunderstood, held in contempt, forgotten. They sense they have become non-existent, superfluous. They no longer support the ritual formulas and mantras of the politically correct, tools of neopuritan leagues and the interventionist state, hygienic and punitive. They are fed up with hearing that their fears are empty and the threats they face are illusory, that we are experiencing the "blessings of globalization" or that immigration is an "opportunity for France," and that in any case "one cannot stop progress." They are infuriated when the sole response to their concerns is that they result from xenophobic fantasies, optical illusions, or groundless fears. They are infuriated when told there is no problem because we have decided once and for all that there cannot be any.

A formidable crisis of confidence is affecting men, institutions, and the media. People no longer believe anyone, or believe

---

[31] On the orders of Louis XVI, the *Cahiers de doléances* (*Lists of Grievances*) were drawn up by each of the three Estates in France, between January and April 1789, the year the French Revolution began. — Trans.

in anything. Locked in a system where they can do anything as long as it does not change anything, suffering every day the effects of decisions they did not make, confronted with denial by the media and with the moral superiority claimed by elites as a monopoly, our contemporaries go mad. Then they revolt against monolithic thinking that pretends there is no alternative to the neoliberal order and that the dissolution of peoples in the global market is the only horizon of human history.

Since 2005, the same scenario has been repeated: the Right says to vote yes, the Left says to vote yes, all the big media companies say to vote yes, the international experts and foreign heads of state say to vote yes—and the people say no. Result: amazement, indignation, and anger. And on the side of the elites, contempt only grows toward an unpredictable people who think wrongly and whose reactions upset all their plans. Fear is omnipresent among them as well: fear of the people's anger, fear of losing their privileges and positions, fear of seeing the paper-mâché walls that separate them from their fellows collapse.

With the chasm that has been opened between the people and the ruling class, political legitimacy and political reality have moved farther away from one another. With the thought of the public square separated from the thought of the palace, we are seeing a new *secession of the plebs*. The "plebs" are seceding within the national community not because it wants to destroy them but because it intends to reconstitute them on a different basis. The hollowing out of politics has caused it to lose its capacity for giving institutional form to the social realm. "Without an implosion of the traditional political system," writes Christophe Guilluy, "an explosion and fragmentation of French society appear inevitable."[32]

This is the main characteristic of populism: it expresses not a horizontal (Left-Right) opposition, but a vertical one, the people against the elites, ordinary folks "down here" against the

---

[32] Guilluy, *La France périphérique*, 179.

privileged "up there." This opposition cannot be reduced to a recycling of the old Poujadist rancor of the "little people" against the "bigshots."[33] It rests on the conviction that a technocratic and financial elite established in the media and the hallways of power, based on incestuous connivance if not actual corruption, has deliberately decided to deprive the voters of their power in order to remove their own activities from all oversight. This elite, which is divided only regarding the means for arriving at the same ends, adheres to values and propounds watchwords in which the people no longer recognize themselves. It imposes tendencies the people condemn because they observe that their way of life deteriorates as a result. Cut off from social reality, it is perceived as foreign to the nation insofar as it is both indifferent to the national interests and deeply deterritorialized. As in 1793, the elites are perceived as the "foreign party" — or more precisely as the party that thinks all forms of belonging have become obsolete, so that no one is foreign any longer.

The opposition between the dominant and the dominated has thus returned in a big way. "People"[34] have replaced the people. The dominant ideology refers as always to a dominant class; but while it commands the assent of a majority within the halls of power, it has become increasingly a minority position among ordinary people. Looking for the bearings it has lost, the people manifests its disdain for a New Class[35] that thinks itself exempt from the rules to which "little people" have to submit, and whose way of life, far removed from and superior to that of the people, displays an irresistible tendency to nomadism, perpetual

---

[33] Poujadism was a French populist movement of the 1950s led by shopkeeper Pierre Poujade (1920–2003). — Trans.

[34] "Les *'people,'*" i.e., VIPs or bigshots. — Trans.

[35] The expression "New Class" goes back to Bakunin. It had a resurgence in the 1970s in the writings of the Hungarians György Konrád and Iván Szelényi who used it in their critique of the old Soviet Union. More recently it has been taken up by Paul Piccone, founder of the American journal *Telos*, in the same sense we are giving it here.

change, the rejection of roots, contempt for communitarian and popular values, a mad rush for profit, limitless permissiveness, a fascination for "winners." Elected by neocapitalist globalization, this political and media New Class formed under the effects of an intensification of mobility in a climate marked by the deregulation of markets and technological innovations that overcame the limits of space and time. It groups political leaders, businessmen, and media representatives—all intimately bound together, all convinced of the "danger" of popular aspirations—in a common elitism of wealth and appearance.

The principal characteristic of this oligarchy, writes Paul Piccone, is its claim to "possession of a superior and universally valid knowledge proper for legitimating what it envisages as a highly necessary rationalization of society." The New Class uses its cultural capital to assure itself a privileged position by disqualifying "as 'irrational' any alternative, intuitive, or more generally informal modes of existence that allow ordinary people without intellectual or specialized pretentions to give meaning and coherence to their everyday lives. The result is that we see nihilism and the gradual disintegration of society." "This social fracture," adds Piccone, "observable not merely at the local level but also on a global scale, engenders a type of inequality much deeper than anything the capitalism of old was able to create."[36]

Costanzo Preve speaks of a

> . . . global middle class characterized by ease of travel, touristic English, a moderate use of drugs, birth control, a new androgynous transsexual aesthetic, third-worldist humanism, a multiculturalism without any real cultural curiosity, and finally by a general approach to philosophy that turns it into a form of psychological group "therapy" and a gymnastics of communicational relativism where

---

[36] Paul Piccone, "De la Nouvelle Gauche au populisme postmoderne" ["From the New Left to Postmodern Populism"], *Krisis*, February 2008, 82–83.

the old, laborious Socratic dialogue becomes the babbling of the half-educated.[37]

Today, this ruling class finds itself confronted by the eternal return of the people. And this confrontation transcends all the old divisions. As Marcello Veneziani was saying as early as 1995, "It is possible that the old Left-Right opposition may be replaced or regenerated by the opposition between populism and oligarchism, or to be more exact between communitarian and liberal culture."[38] Christophe Guilluy in turn has recently observed that "the break is no longer so much between Left and Right as between the dominant class of Left or Right and the popular class." The main (but not the only) divide opposes those who profit from globalization, whether of Left or Right, and those who are its victims — those who think in terms of peoples and those who only want to recognize individuals and humanity. It is the divide that opposes peripheral France to urbanized France, the people to the globalized elites, the ordinary man to the New Class, the common people and the declining middle class to the globalist *grande bourgeoisie*, those who favor borders to the partisans of "openness," the "invisible" to the "omnipresent," in short: those below and those above. The real divide is the prohibition of the people vs. the cause of the people.

This break between the New Class and the people seems irremediable, but we must not be fooled: the rise of populism does not correspond only to a moment of crisis characterized by the decay of systems inherited from the postwar era following the

---

[37] Costanzo Preve, "Une discussion pour l'instant interminable. Considérations préliminaires sur la genèse historique passée, sur la fonction systémique présente et les perspectives futures de la dualité politico-religieuse droite/gauche" ["An Interminable (for the Moment) Discussion: Preliminary Considerations on the Past Historical Genesis, Present Systemic Function, and Future Perspectives of the Politico-Religious Duality Right/Left"], *Krisis*, May 2009, 12.

[38] Marcello Veneziani, *Sinistra e destra. Riposte a Norberto Bobbio* [*Left and Right: Response to Norberto Bobbio*] (Florence: Vallecchi, 1995), 154.

collapse of the Soviet system, the fall of the Berlin Wall, and the end of the Cold War. It also marks the end of an historical cycle that is in part the cycle of modernity. Gramsci said that the old world is dying while another is finding it hard to be born—and that between the two there exist monsters. "Political reconfiguration has itself become a political question," says Paul Piccone, "and its outcome will depend on a political struggle."[39]

"All sorts of political representation are today roundly looked down upon and sometimes even held in contempt," observes Alain Duhamel. "The parties have no prestige left. . . . Labor unions enjoy little credit. I won't even speak of the world of the media. Office-holders enjoy no prestige, and one can even speak of an adamantine contempt for representative democracy."[40] In this climate of universal organic crisis, might populist movements represent a long-term solution? This is impossible to say, and it is not the object of the pieces collected in this book to answer such a question. Some of them have been previously published, others not. They have been revised to make up the present whole, but each nevertheless preserves its autonomy and internal coherence. We have not tried to pass judgment on the value of populist movements, on their good points and faults, or on the relevance of their propositions, but rather on the political meaning of their irresistible rise insofar as it obviously corresponds to a new page in the political history of Europe. The final balance, whenever it can be drawn up, will necessarily be mixed. What we can already do now is ask about the meaning of what we are seeing.

---

[39] Paul Piccone, "Les héritiers américains de l'Ecole de Francfort" ["The American Heirs of the Frankfurt School"], *Eléments*, November 2000, 49.

[40] Alain Duhamel, "Crise des institutions ou crise de la société politique?" ["A Crisis of Institutions or a Crisis of Political Society?"], *Le Débat*, September–October 2016, 19.

CRISIS OF REPRESENTATION, CRISIS OF DEMOCRACY

Opinion democracy? Televisual democracy? Market democracy? Democracy is in crisis, and the pathologies that affect contemporary democracies increasingly occupy observers' attention. The common opinion is that these pathologies, far from being inherent in democracy itself, result from a corruption of its principles. Some attribute this corruption to external factors or phenomena, which amounts to questioning only the evolution of mores and social transformations. Others emphasize intrinsic factors to explain the more or less pronounced gap between what democracy has become and what it ought to be according to its founding principles. Still others do not hesitate to speak of "post-democracy," not in order to say that democracy is reaching its end but to suggest that it has itself adopted post-democratic forms that must, therefore, be defined and analyzed.[1] A few observers suggest we are in a situation comparable to France a few years before the Revolution.[2] The most com-

---

[1] "It cannot be ruled out that, politically, a new era is opening before us: that of post-democracy," writes Christian Savès (*Sépulture de la démocratie. Thanatos et politique* [*Burial of Democracy: Thanatos and Politics*] [Paris: L'Harmattan, 2008], 10). The thesis presented here is that democracy is "a victim of its own death instinct": "Its Freudian *thanatos* inexorably pulls it down . . . inexorably drives it to work toward its own ruin" (p. 12). But it remains to be demonstrated that democracy is inherently nihilistic. The same expression is found in the title of the little book published by Karlheinz Weißmann, *Post-Demokratie* (Schnellroda: Antaios, 2009). The author, however, is preoccupied above all with the future of the state rather than that of democracy. In passing, he notes that "the weakness of all discourse on post-democracy is due to fear of the consequences" (p. 67).

[2] This is the thesis brilliantly set out by Guy Hermet: "Like our ancestors of 1775 or 1785, we are reaching the end of a 'future *ancien régime*,' a regime coming to its conclusion, destined to give way to another political universe yet unnamed but already largely sketched out in practice. Like

mon mood is disquiet and disillusionment.

The present crisis is not the first that European democracies have known. Marcel Gauchet has published a vast four-volume fresco on this subject: *The Advent of Democracy*.[3] He summarized it in a lecture delivered at Angers in June 2006 that has itself been published in the form of a small book: *Democracy from One Crisis to Another*.[4]

The first crisis of democracy took shape in France beginning in 1880, got stronger with the shock of 1900, but only really exploded after the First World War, culminating in the 1930s. At this time, writes Gauchet, "the parliamentary regime revealed itself both deceptive and impotent; society, riven by the division of labor and class antagonism, seemed to be dislocated; historical change became broader, accelerated, was amplified, and escaped all control."[5] We entered the era of the masses, and society was torn by class struggle. Moreover, organic solidarity began to dissolve, and the countryside emptied out.

The direct consequence of this crisis would be, first of all, the rise of ideologies seeking to confer power on "experts" (planning, technocracy), and then, above all, the unleashing of totalitarian regimes that strove (as Louis Dumont—and to a lesser extent, Claude Lefort—have shown) to compensate for the solvent

---

them, we are at the gates of the Next Regime" (*L'Hiver de la démocratie ou le nouveau régime* [*The Winter of Democracy, or The New Regime*] [Paris: Armand Colin, 2007], 13). Cf. also his interview published in *Catholica* under the title "Crépuscule démocratique" ["Democratic Twilight"]: "Our present winter, our winter of democracy is already harboring a new regime" (Summer 2008, 27).

[3] Marcel Gauchet, *L'Avènement de la démocratie* [*The Advent of Democracy*], vol. I: *La Révolution moderne* [*The Modern Revolution*] (Paris: Gallimard, 2007); vol. II: *La Crise du libéralisme* [*The Crisis of Liberalism*] *(1880-1914)* (Paris: Gallimard, 2007); vol. III: *A l'épreuve des totalitarismes* [*The Totalitarian Test*] *(1914-1974)* (Paris: Gallimard, 2010); vol. IV: *Le Nouveau Monde* [*The New World*] (Paris: Gallimard, 2017). Cf. also *La démocratie contre elle-même* [*Democracy Against Itself*] (Paris: Gallimard, 2002).

[4] Marcel Gauchet, *La Démocratie d'une crise à l'autre* [*Democracy from One Crisis to Another*] (Nantes: Éditions Cécile Defaut, 2007).

[5] Gauchet, *La Démocratie d'une crise à l'autre*, 25.

effects of individualism and a loss of cultural structure by means of a holism as artificial as it was brutal. This was connected with the mobilization of the masses and the institution of a barracks regime in society as a whole based upon an appeal to pre-political notions like the "racial community" or "primitive communism." In reality, notes Gauchet, "they returned or tried to return, in a secular language, to religious society: its coherence and the convergence of its parts."[6] But the twentieth century forms of totalitarianism were also the (illegitimate) children of democratization.[7]

The end of the Second World War marked the great return of liberal democracy. At first, however, to avoid falling again into the excesses that preceded that conflict, liberal democracy draped itself in the new garments of the welfare state. In the context of triumphant Fordism, a mixed regime was in fact established that joined the classic rule of law to more essentially democratic elements, but in which democracy was conceived above all as "social democracy." Gauchet lists some of the traits of this "liberal-democratic synthesis": the reevaluation of the executive power within the representative system; the adoption of a whole series of reforms aiming to protect individuals from sickness, unemployment, old age, or poverty; and finally, the establishment of a regulatory and providential apparatus intended to

---

[6] Gauchet, *La Démocratie d'une crise à l'autre*, 27.

[7] It is under the influence of democracy's liberal conception that the classic opposition between democratic and totalitarian regimes — in which totalitarianism is considered the perfect opposite of democracy, or that which represents the farthest removed political form — was posited as final and unsurpassable. However, the most totalitarian regimes also have incontrovertibly democratic aspects. Emmanuel Todd, citing the American historian David Schoenbaum (*Hitler's Social Revolution: Class and Status in Nazi Germany, 1933–1939* [Garden City, N.Y.: Doubleday, 1966]), recalls that "Nazism, despite its nostalgic discourse on the return to blood and soil, represented for Germany a crucial stage in democratization. In a very special social sense, the National Socialist experience was the equivalent of the French Revolution, with its own version of August 4 and the abolition of privileges" (*Après la démocratie* [*After Democracy*] [Gallimard, Paris 2008], 121–22).

remedy the anarchy that the free development of market exchange involves. This system functioned more or less normally
until the end of the "Thirty Glorious Years," i.e., to the mid-
1970s.

Beginning in the period between 1975 and 1980, new tendencies appeared that once again created the conditions for a crisis — but a different crisis. Social democracy, conceived as an insurance company or benevolent organization, started to get
winded, and pure liberalism got the upper hand once again.
Civil society, henceforth immeasurably privileged, became the
engine driving a new phase of the autonomous organization of
social life. Economic liberalism made a grand comeback, while
capitalism gradually freed itself from all the obstacles that still
inhibited it, a process that culminated in the globalization that
followed the Soviet system's collapse. The ideology of the rights
of man, long restricted to the symbolic or decorative role reserved for the venerable abstractions of another era, gradually
established itself as the religion of a new age and as a culture of
good intentions.

At the same time, the nation-state proved itself increasingly
unable to face up to challenges that had become planetary, and
gradually lost all its "prestige value," while we beheld a massive
relaunching of the process of individualization in all domains.
This found expression in the *de facto* disappearance of all great
collective projects that might have provided the basis for a "we."
Whereas in the past, "it was a question only of the masses and
the classes, the individual being understood by means of his
group, mass society has been subverted from within by a mass
individualism detaching the individual from all forms of belonging."[8] This is also the era of the near-disappearance of rural society (in France, farmers today represent barely over 1% of house-
holds), a real silent revolution whose deep effects will be more
or less unperceived. And it is the era of the spread of multi-
ethnic societies resulting from mass immigration.

To understand this development, we must fully understand
what distinguishes ancient from modern democracy. The former,

---

[8] Gauchet, *La Démocratie d'une crise à l'autre*, 35.

already based on the idea of a self-constitution of human communities, can be defined as the political formation of means of autonomy through citizens' participation in public affairs. Modern democracy is intrinsically bound up with modernity, but only by way of a connection to liberalism that tends to denature democracy. The deep cause of this crisis is the unnatural alliance between democracy and liberalism, which Marcel Gauchet was able to present as "the very doctrine of the modern world."[9] The expression "liberal democracy" associates two terms as complementary when in fact they are contradictory. This contradiction, now plainly revealed, threatens the very basis of democracy. "Liberalism brings democracy into crisis," as Gauchet says.

Chantal Mouffe has very correctly observed:

> On the one hand, we have the liberal tradition constituted by the sovereignty of law, defense of the rights of man, and respect for individual freedom; on the other, the democratic tradition whose principal ideas are those of equality, identity between governors and governed, and popular sovereignty. There is no necessary relation between these two different traditions, but only a contingent historical connection.[10]

Anyone who does not see this distinction cannot understand the present systemic crisis of this "contingent historical connection." Democracy and liberalism are in no sense synonymous; on important points they are even opposed concepts. There can be illiberal democracies (democracies *simpliciter*) and liberal forms of government with absolutely nothing democratic about them. Carl Schmitt went so far as to say that the more liberal a democracy is, the less democratic it is.

In relation to ancient democracy, the great difference of modern democracy (as its principles were established beginning around 1750) is that it rests not so much on the participation of

---

[9] Gauchet, *La Crise du libéralisme*, 18.
[10] Chantal Mouffe, *The Democratic Paradox* (London: Verso, 2000), 2–3.

citizens in public affairs as on the universal right of individuals, and also that it is no longer alien, in its historical rise, to the ideology of progress. Liberalism favors a confusion of politics with morality and law. The ideology of progress confers upon the democratic dynamic an orientation that projects it constantly forward in the invention of the future. The transition to the future, a henceforth privileged historical dimension, involves a "complete reorganization of the social order."[11] In particular, it leads to an "inversion of the signs in the relations between power and society."[12] Society, and no longer power, is posited as the seat of collective movement. It follows from this that the political system must above all guarantee the freedom of the individuals who are the genuine actors of History. Thus the laws no longer determine mores, but mores gradually modify the laws.

Gauchet writes:

> Within such a framework, power can no longer be regarded as the *cause* of society, as the ultimate authority charged with bringing it into existence and ordering it. . . . Power is to be considered the *effect* of society. It can only have been secreted by society and can only have the role of fulfilling the missions society gives it. In a word, it has no meaning except insofar as it *represents* society.[13]

Of course, democracy remains classically defined as consecrating the "power of the people," but in reality, having become liberal and purely representative, it is only a political regime consecrating the rise of modern individualism and the primacy of "civil society" over political authority.

Beginning at the end of the 1980s, a decade that also saw postmodernity's emergence, the appearance of "rights-of-man democracy" is the expression of a renewed influence of liberalism on democracy. This phenomenon corresponds to what Marcel Gauchet calls the "turn of democracy against itself":

---

[11] Gauchet, *La Démocratie d'une crise à l'autre*, 21.

[12] Gauchet, *La Démocratie d'une crise à l'autre*, 21.

[13] Gauchet, *La Démocratie d'une crise à l'autre*, 22.

The concept of rule of law acquires a salience in this connection that far surpasses the technical sense to which it was formerly confined. It tends to become confused with the very idea of democracy, assimilated to a guardian of private liberties and respect for the procedures that preside over their public expression. In a revealing way, the spontaneous understanding of the word democracy has changed. . . . It used to refer to collective power, the capacity for self-government. It no longer refers to anything except personal freedoms. Anything is judged harmonious with democracy if it expands the domain and role of individual prerogative. A liberal version of democracy has supplanted its classic concept. The touchstone is no longer the sovereignty of the people, but the sovereignty of the individual, defined as his power of thwarting collective power if necessary. Because of this, the promotion of democratic law involves democracy's gradual political incapacitation.[14]

Democracy involves the existence of a democratic subject: the citizen. The atomized individual as conceived by liberal theory cannot originally be a citizen, for by nature he is alien to any form of belonging on which a will to live together is based. Doctrinaire liberals presume to defend individual freedom while unfamiliar with the demand for collective mastery inherent in democracy. Moreover, the logic of individual rights is limitless, for its vehicle is the "legal abstraction that never stops" (Gauchet). The emphasis placed on individual freedom forbids the creation of conditions of collective freedom insofar as the first is exercised at the expense of the second, thus bringing about a social disconnect. Tocqueville thought that the passion for equality would constantly threaten freedom. His mistake lay in not seeing the converse: that the passion for freedom would also threaten

---

[14] Gauchet, *La Démocratie d'une crise à l'autre*, 38–39. Christian Savès also speaks of a "veritable deconstruction of democracy by law [*droit*], law in general and the rights of man in particular" (*Sépulture de la démocratie*, 71).

democracy. Procedural democracy is based on the idea of a freedom without power, which is nothing but an oxymoron (power
simply passes elsewhere).

In a similar vein, Chantal Mouffe emphasizes that

> The inability of contemporary democratic theory to tackle
> the question of citizenship head on is the consequence of a
> concept of the subject that considers individuals anterior
> to society, the bearers of natural rights, who are either
> agents maximizing utility or rational subjects. In all cases,
> individuals are cut off from social relations and from
> power, language, culture, and the totality of practices that
> render their action possible.[15]

The prerogatives of politics are threatened not only by law
but also by the economy. In liberal society the political community, ceasing to govern itself,

> becomes a *market political society* in the strict sense. By this
> we mean not a society in which economic markets domi-
> nate political choices, but a society whose political func-
> tioning itself borrows from economics the general model
> of the market: so its overall form appears as the result of
> the initiatives and demands of different actors at the end of
> a process of self-regulated aggregation. A transformation in
> the function of the rulers follows. They are henceforth only
> there to see to it that the rules of the game are followed and
> to ensure that the process functions.[16]

The governing of men is thus reduced to administrative management. The negation of the public domain's supremacy and
the erasure of the idea of the common good, even in its degrad-
ed form as the "general interest," gives way to a multiplication
of categorial demands and particular interests, with the public
power laboring as well as it can to assure the coexistence of these

---

[15] Mouffe, *The Democratic Paradox*, 95–96.
[16] Gauchet, *La Démocratie d'une crise à l'autre*, 42–43.

conflicting demands in a state of permanent inflation. "A politics based on the addition of private interests," notes Chantal Delsol, "is more closely related to anarchy, i.e., a non-politics. Democracy on the contrary consists in allowing the defining of several versions of the general interest, which popular sovereignty alternately raises to representation."[17]

Alain Caillé observes:

> Modern democracies do not manage to conceive of themselves other than as an order based on the rational calculations of interested subjects, interested especially in their material advantage. Viewed in light of such a conception, both gifts and politics are strictly incomprehensible, and even totally invisible.[18]

This triumph of economics over politics is interpreted by liberals as a triumph of freedom, whereas it is a form of self-dispossession, since it expresses itself in the inability of collectives to have any control over their own destiny. Thus, Marcel Gauchet describes the "ravages of powerlessness" and the "festive forsakenness of last men celebrating their inability to govern."[19]

This anti-political evolution occurs in the direction of neutralization (*Neutralisierung*) mentioned by Carl Schmitt. Gauchet recalls:

> Historically, modern democracies based themselves on the appropriation of public power by members of the political body. . . . Their new idea was to neutralize power of whatever sort so as to safeguard the sovereignty of individuals from any attack. . . . Rights-of-man democracy is thus led by a powerful internal inclination to reject the

---

[17] Chantal Delsol, "La Démocratie asphyxiée" ["Suffocated Democracy"], *Valeurs actuelles*, July 10, 2008, 22.

[18] Alain Caillé, *Théorie anti-utilitariste de l'action. Fragments d'une sociologie générale* [*An Anti-utilitarian Theory of Action: Fragments of a General Sociology*] (Paris: La Découverte, 2009), 143.

[19] Gauchet, *La Révolution moderne*, 19, 25.

practical instruments it needs to become effective. Hence comes the painful discovery of the *public powerlessness* into which it constantly runs. It is democracy itself that secretes this powerlessness. . . . Here is the deep reason for the tottering of states and of the principle of their authority in today's democracy.[20]

In short: caught between economics and morality, the ideology of merchandise and that of the rights of man, present-day democracy is ever less democratic because it is ever less political.

By referring to purely abstract concepts, democracy finally relinquishes its territorial and historical dimensions. Collective beliefs formerly mobilized men because they were anchored in territories. The concept of citizenship is also directly associated with a particular territory where the citizens' lives are lived. It involves a frontier separating citizens from non-citizens. Marcel Gauchet writes:

The fundamental universalism that gnaws at democracy leads it to dissociate itself from the historical and political framework within which it was forged . . . a framework limited by definition. Ideally, it would like to be without either territory or a past. Legal logic motivates it to refuse to recognize its own inscription in space, an inscription whose limits are an insult to the universality of the principles to which it appeals. In the same way, it rejects its own insertion in a history that places it in a dependency it finds just as unbearable. Democracy is led, in other words, to being unable to accept the conditions that gave it birth.[21]

Under the influence of the rights-of-man ideology, the principle of democracy is no longer "one citizen, one vote," but "one man, one vote."

Liberal democracy gets confused with parliamentarianism and representation. It is a constitutional regime founded exclusively

---

[20] Gauchet, *La Démocratie d'une crise à l'autre*, 47–48.
[21] Gauchet, *La Démocratie d'une crise à l'autre*, 46.

on suffrage and the plurality of parties, where democracy is only the social space negotiated with a state under the rule of law. Now, as Carl Schmitt never stopped repeating, a people has less need of being represented insofar as it is politically present itself. Rousseau already said, "When the people has leaders who govern for it, whatever name these leaders have, it is always an aristocracy."[22] In liberal democracy the constitutional people is only sovereign insofar as it is able to consent to the power of those supposed to represent it. But representation is merely a last resort. "When made obligatory, the delegation of popular sovereignty to mandataries authorized in reality to appropriate such sovereignty is obviously very questionable in view of the democratic principle," Guy Hermet reminds us.[23]

This is why Althusius, according to whom society as a whole is defined as an association (*consociatio*) of mutually articulated bodies, only allows an always-revocable delegation of power (similar to what we today call an "imperative mandate"). Disconnected from all control except the vote, the representative system betrays those it is supposed to represent, the distinction between representatives and represented inevitably driving the former to make themselves into an oligarchy. This betrayal is especially marked today, what with the recentering of party programs and the disappearance of alternatives symbolized by the Left's conversion to the market society[24] and the Right's conversion to the abolition of nations, to which we may add the neutralization of universal suffrage by Brussels' directives. Everyone today is in communion with the religion of the rights of man, the dialectic of possession, and the triumph of money on the basis of *storytelling*, i.e., a spectacular commercial void.[25]

---

[22] Jean-Jacques Rousseau, *Du Contrat social*, III, 15.

[23] Guy Hermet, *L'Hiver de la démocratie ou le nouveau régime*, 185.

[24] All political polling demonstrates that Left-wing parties now get their best results in the largest cities inhabited by the new upper-middle class and no longer in the working-class neighborhoods. Christophe Guilluy, author of the *Atlas des Nouvelles fractures sociales en France* [*Atlas of New Social Fractures in France*], summarizes this in the formula: "The Left is strong where the people are weak" (*20 minutes*, March 18, 2008).

[25] English in original. — Trans. "Storytelling is the politics of distrac-

Another consistent trait of liberal democracy is that it tends to denounce as "anti-democratic" any democratic demand exceeding its own definition of democracy. Such denunciation is most often aimed at social demands, but also those that seek to give citizens any power going beyond simple suffrage. The people's participation in public affairs is thus currently rejected in the name of their "incompetence" (power must be reserved for "those who know," whether experts or governments that claim to know what is good for the people better than the people themselves), as if there were a "competence" *per se* that can be abstracted from its ends—as Aristotle already remarked. These are the same people who in the past pleaded for property qualification, meant to protect them from the "dangerous classes."[26] Representative democracy can thus be seen as a sort of process allowing popular sovereignty to be "filtered" by restricting its scope. In any case, this is a matter of presenting an oligarchy as

---

tion, of the replacement of discourse by entertainment, funny or off-color stories, political action by means of evasion, the substitution of human-interest items for political programs, the twilight of political man forced out by the entertainer, or if necessary by the subject of scandal" (Guy Hermet, "Crépuscule démocratique," 34).

[26] In 1791, 44,000 privileged electors chosen from among the biggest taxpayers, i.e., the richest, were already pre-eminent. By 1794 there would only be 25,000. Guy Hermet notes in this connection that

Medieval proto-democracy was suppressed for three reasons: the hostility of absolutist monarchs as well as enlightened despots with regard to their subjects' traditional manifestations of autonomy, the fear of the bourgeois and proprietors of any government by the little people, and the prejudices of *philosophes* and lawyers of the Enlightenment, already imagining themselves in power as mandataries obligated to the ignorant multitude. (*L'Hiver de la démocratie ou le nouveau régime*, 26).

Jacques Julliard also declares: "At least in France, representative democracy has been conceived from the beginning as a rampart against universal suffrage: once the citizens have designated their representatives, their duty is to be quiet. This is what they no longer accept" (*Le Monde*, June 1-2, 2008, 15).

naturally justified where it exists, whereas it is merely the product of a particular social history.

How can the crisis of representation be remedied? Some think we must move toward a radical extension of social democracy. This is the thesis supported by Takis Fotopoulos in a book meant to be a sort of manifesto in favor of "inclusive democracy." A partisan of localism and degrowth, Fotopoulos makes economic equality the condition for political equality and wants the *demos* to become "the authentic unity of economic life."[27] Explicitly endorsing an economy without a state, without money, and without a market, he criticizes Jürgen Habermas and denounces the "reformism" of the anti-globalist movement. His work contains a good critique of representative democracy, which he rather accurately describes as "democracy that poses no danger to the modern state." But by definition it is not the extension of social democracy that can restore to politics its proper prerogatives.

"Social democracy," which goes hand-in-hand with the welfare state, has its European origins in the reforms of Napoleon III and Bismarck. From the beginning, it involved an ambiguity. Responding to incontestably justified demands, it also made it possible to disarm the workers' revolutionary challenge even as it convinced them that "democracy" consists essentially in the granting and apportionment of quantitative benefits. It thereby erased democracy's political character and caused it to slip towards "expert" administration and pure management. Social democracy consists in "buying off the people" with increasing material benefits from one election to the other, making its practical legitimacy reside in its capacity to dispense benefits. It is an "insurance" regime, but also a suicidal one, for the public powers cannot indefinitely respond to constantly increasing demands. Moreover, this erodes the basis of the legitimacy (the capacity to "realize happiness") it has given itself and must constantly maintain by promises that are increasingly difficult to

---

[27] Takis Fotopoulos, *Vers une démocratie générale. Une démocratie directe, économique, écologique et sociale* [*Towards an Inclusive Democracy: A Direct, Economic, Ecological, and Social Democracy*] (Paris: Seuil, 2001), 205.

keep. In this light, social democracy illustrates well the confusion between extensive (superficial) democracy and deep (consistent) democracy. Extensive democracy risks ending in the dilution of democracy. Far from consolidating the desire for citizenship, it transforms the members of society into objects of assistance who dream of nothing but receiving even more assistance.

Now, one of the major contradictions of present-day rights-democracy is that, according to public opinion, it rests fundamentally on social democracy—a democracy from which one may expect everything and demand everything—while it no longer has either the will or the ability to be a social democracy. Guy Hermet observes on this point that "the obligation in which democracy as a system of government has let itself be trapped, viz. of in some sense buying support at the price of statutory and then material entitlements subject to constant renewal, affects the governments of developed societies as a whole."[28] He adds: "Pursuing this course with no defined goal," he adds, "would have meant that toward 2025 or 2030, depending on the country, the total budget of the welfare state would absorb all the wealth produced in Europe without anything left over for the commercial economy or the private expenses of its inhabitants."[29]

So a chasm continues to be dug between the people and an autistic, incestuous, and narcissistic New Class. Contrary to what gets repeated in reactionary milieus, modern democracy did not issue in ochlocracy, the power of the populace or multitude denounced by Plato, but in a new form of political, media, and financial oligarchy. To criticize liberal democracy is thus not to denounce the people, but to denounce the elites.[30] Gauchet

---

[28] Hermet, *L'Hiver de la démocratie ou le nouveau régime*, 63.

[29] Hermet, *L'Hiver de la démocratie ou le nouveau régime*, 64. On this point cf. also Danilo Zolo, *Democracy and Complexity: A Realist Approach* (Cambridge: Cambridge University Press, 1992).

[30] Cf. Emmanuel Todd, *Après la démocratie*, ch. 3, "De la démocratie à l'oligarchie" [*After Democracy*, ch. 3, "From Democracy to Oligarchy"], 67–93. "The real drama, for democracy," writes Todd, "does not so much reside in the opposition between the elites and the masses as in the lucidity of the masses and the blindness of elites" (p. 223).

mentions "the generalized sense of dispossession that haunts the democracy of rights. Its mechanism . . . inexorably erodes the people's confidence in the oligarchies to which it encourages them to entrust themselves."[31] Populism is a classic reaction to this divorce.

In liberal democracy, as we have seen, democracy does not, properly speaking, define itself by popular sovereignty, by the attribution of sovereignty to the people, but rather by a kind of state of mind that celebrates both equality of condition and the independence of individuals who perceive themselves as socially separate from one another. Under the influence of liberalism, democracy seeks to organize the freedom of individuals, not to let the people decide. But what about the people?

Grotius, Hobbes, Pufendorf, and Locke all tried to explain how it was possible for individuals to constitute themselves as a people. None of them succeeded, for one cannot arrive at a people starting from individuals. Their procedure consisted in imagining a voluntary rational act whose implementation resulted in an association of men and the formation of a society. Now, as Bruno Gnassounou remarks, "No one has ever succeeded in explaining how private individuals could contract with a collective body that is supposed to be engendered by that very contract. The whole is presupposed here. This is because it is quite simply impossible to engender a whole starting from individuals,"[32] which amounts to saying that there can be no political people if man is not both a social and a political being by nature—since the concept of contract refers to an already constituted legal order.

It is all very well for Pierre Rosanvallon to speak of a "change in the nature of citizenship"[33]—in fact, it is a disappearance of citizenship we are witnessing today, so greatly does contemporary democracy dilute the very meaning of the word "people"

---

[31] Gauchet, *La Démocratie d'une crise à l'autre*, 45.

[32] Bruno Gnassounou, "Se gouverner soi-même?" in Isabelle Koch and Norbert Lenoir, eds., *Démocratie et espace publique: quel pouvoir pour le peuple?* [*Democracy and Public Space: What Power for the People?*] (Hildesheim: Georg Olms, 2008), 119.

[33] Pierre Rosanvallon, *La Contre-démocratie* [*Counter-Democracy*] (Paris: Seuil, 2006).

by referring to a "universal people" and "citizens of the world" called upon to replace the "national people."[34] A people is not a mere sum of individuals, but neither is it interchangeable with the concept of "multitude," which also merely covers abstract singularities. A return to democracy's original spirit would be a return to the idea of a *political* people acquiring collective freedom by its participation in public affairs. Aristotle, who preferred a mixed regime, defined the democratic citizen by his capacity for "participating in deliberative and judicial power."[35] The people's power certainly can never be fully realized. It resides primarily in an aspiration, a tension.[36] But participation, even if it can never be complete,[37] is what allows us to approach most closely to the power of the people by reducing the gap between power and the people.

By participation, the people does not merely display its power and will to emancipation; it continually reinforces itself in its existence as a people. This is what Marx implies in his *Critique of Hegel's Philosophy of Right* (1843) when he locates the essence of "true" democracy in the "self-constitution of the people as subject."[38]

Today there is a desire to replace the people with "civil society." "The state," writes Marcel Gauchet, "tends to transform

---

[34] On the dialectic between *demos* and *ethnos*, cf. the fine pages Régis Debray devotes to the subject in *Le Moment fraternité* [*The Moment of Fraternity*] (Paris: Gallimard, 2009), 340–49.

[35] Aristotle, *Politics*, III, 1, 1275b 18–19.

[36] On this point, Norbert Lenoir is not mistaken to say that "democracy is at once the impossible power of the people and the attempt to create a citizens' power of political intervention" ("Démocratie: le peuple excédentaire et les voix du peuple," Koch and Lenoir, *Démocratie et espace publique*, 92). The rest of the author's views appear questionable.

[37] Aristotle also notes: "Everyone finds it more agreeable to till his own soil than to busy himself with politics and be a magistrate" (*Politics*, IV, 13, 1297b 5).

[38] On participation, cf. also Benjamin R. Barber, *Strong Democracy: Participatory Politics for a New Age* (Berkeley: University of California Press, 1984) and Volker Gerhardt, *Partizipation. Das Prinzip der Politik* [*Participation: The Principle of Politics*] (Munich: C. H. Beck, 2007).

itself into a space where civil society represents itself, without preserving any hierarchical superiority in relation to civil society or any role as historical training for it."[39] But civil society is merely a sum of group interests. By nature, it only defends general categories of interest, which prevents it from assuming the role of the state and formulating a genuine collective project or exercising an overall regulation of society.

The importance given to civil society is in fact a way of consecrating the action of interest groups and lobbies, all equally representative of this "civil society," all inclined to defend specific forms of interest or privilege. The consequence is no longer a tyranny of the majority over minorities, but a tyranny of minorities over the majority. The rise of "civil society" amounts, from this point of view, to the increasing pressure of opinion. "Opinion democracy" is one where polls have greater importance than real elections, and the images carried by television have greater importance than ideas or even acts. Régis Debray believes that

> This media-and-polling dictatorship transforms the government into a day-to-day manager, directed toward the supposed desires of public opinion, whether to anticipate or prevent them. We are witnessing, for example, the birth of a form of diplomacy where one reacts to everything instantly, the better to do nothing in the long run, where one jumps from one image to another without memory and without any plan.[40]

Debray recalls in passing that, "In the philosophic hierarchy, opinion is the lowest level of knowledge," and that it "is the very opposite of conviction, which is not a question of assent but a question of existence. No one dies for an opinion; one can die for a conviction."[41]

---

[39] Marcel Gauchet, *La Religion dans la démocratie. Parcours de la laïcité* [*Religion in Democracy: The Career of Secularism*] (Paris: Gallimard, 1998), 113.

[40] Régis Debray, *Le Monde*, June 1–2, 2008, 15.

[41] Debray, *Le Monde*, June 1–2, 2008, 15.

Participatory democracy has little in common with civil society insofar as what it needs first of all is a public space, a common
place allowing the people to exist politically and exercise its
power. The public space is the locus where *demos* and *polis* are
joined, the place—which binds insofar as it is a place—where the
crowd becomes a people. It is tied to a territorial or geographic
idea. The original sense of *demos* is "land inhabited by a people,"
which means that the people has first of all a telluric significance. Joëlle Zask writes:

> In democracy, how can union and unanimity be produced
> between different individual wills, interests, and needs?
> The sensible response is contact. But the fact is that contact
> is often conceived in terms of physical proximity. Individ-
> uals would have to touch each other on some side. Hence
> the usefulness of reasoning in terms of space. . . . In gen-
> eral, we can state that it is only when individuals are in
> contact with one another that they have a chance of forg-
> ing common ideas.[42]

As Gabriel Tarde has seen (opposing Gustave Le Bon on this
point), the despacialization of political life ends by replacing the
people with the "public," which Tarde considered the "social
group of the future."[43] Tarde is not mistaken. Modern "publics"
are characterized by dispersion and the absence of any face-to-
face relationships, and their vitality owes nothing to common
conviction or shared values. "Public" in this sense refers to nothing substantial or constant.

Another mistake is to picture the public space as purely deliberative or procedural, in the fashion of Jürgen Habermas for
example, who significantly speaks of the public sphere rather
than the public space: because respect for formal and communi-

---

[42] Joëlle Zask, "Le public est-il un espace? Réflexion sur les fonctions
des publics en démocratie"["Is the Public a Space? Reflections on the
Function of Publics in Democracy"] in Koch and Lenoir, *Démocratie et
espace publique*, 81.

[43] Gabriel Tarde, *L'Opinion et la foule* [*Opinion and the Crowd*] *(1898-
1899)* (Paris: PUF, 1989), 38.

cational rules determines nothing regarding the manner of deciding, nor regarding the value of decisions with respect to what they are meant to determine. Rules by themselves are always empty. As Bruno Gnassounou perceptively notes:

> It is obviously because they refuse, in the name of individual autonomy, to let substantive ends intervene that the adepts of "communicational spaces" appeal to procedures. But appealing to procedures . . . is above all a refusal to let the community govern itself. This is because governing oneself does not consist in imposing on oneself a law that is valid because it is in conformity with a higher law, but rather in setting an end for oneself.[44]

But setting an end for oneself already presupposes agreement on the common good.

The foregoing allows us to understand what "post-democracy" will probably be like. The two great new political phenomena are the emergence of "governance"[45] and the rise of various forms of populism.

Originally derived from "corporate governance," the whole theme of governance, in which Marc Hufty sees the triumph of "an accounting mentality,"[46] aims to transform governments into organs of management inspired by economic methods, and to reduce them to the rank of instruments subordinate to economic and especially financial imperatives. Corresponding to the "great disruption" described by Francis Fukuyama, it is based both on civil society as a substitute for the political people and on the "convergence of choices at the international level silently secreted by the connivance of governing milieus" (Marcel Gauchet).

---

[44] Gnassounou, "Se gouverner soi-même?," 124.

[45] On governance, cf. Alain de Benoist, *Le Traité transatlantique et autres menaces* [*The Transatlantic Treaty and Other Threats*] (Paris: Pierre-Guillaume de Roux, 2015), 105–48.

[46] Cf. Marc Hufty, ed., *La Pensée comptable. Etat, libéralisme, nouvelle gestion publique* [*The Accounting Mentality: The State, Liberalism, and the New Public Administration*] (Paris: PUF, 1998).

Governance breaks the classical hierarchy in the direction of public affairs. The state loses its symbolic power and finds itself restricted to a role as a regulatory agency, decisions increasingly being made by coopted actors without democratic legitimacy on the basis of interests negotiated at higher levels—and, as regards local affairs, in a simple consultatory relation with self-proclaimed representatives of civil society. Governance ends in the primacy of interest over value, of the negotiated norm over the law voted upon, and thus of the judge over the legislator. The model is that of aligning the conduct of public affairs with the management of private affairs based on the belief that "in all domains, societies and relations between countries can be directed by automated balancing mechanisms related to those of the economic market," and on the conviction "that the great questions of collective significance should be free of the whims of any majority will, so as to obey either rational choices or bargaining at the top conditioned by changing equilibria independent of the will of states."[47] Finally, of course, "governance is foreign to the accomplishment of any relatively long-term project designed to satisfy a common good now become unintelligible, or to satisfy a majority will considered potentially oppressive."[48]

Governance aims at the privatization of global society on the model of the market. But the market does not get along well with democracy. It demands the suppression of borders, whereas democracy can only be conducted within a given polity. It implies that economic mechanisms should free themselves of all political oversight directed toward the common good.[49] Moreover, the development of markets is, historically speaking, the direct consequence of the separation between the worker and his means of production—i.e., the automation of the economy—

---

[47] Hermet, *L'Hiver de la démocratie ou le nouveau régime*, 202, 212.

[48] Hermet, *L'Hiver de la démocratie ou le nouveau régime*, 204.

[49] Economist Robert Reich, author of *Supercapitalism: The Transformation of Business, Democracy, and Everyday Life* (New York: Alfred A. Knopf, 2007), reminds us that "no company can sacrifice its profit to the common good" ("La démocratie est malade du supercapitalisme" ["Democracy Is Sick From Supercapitalism"], *Sciences humaines*, March 2008, 31).

which has ended with two factors previously considered non-negotiable, man and the Earth, beginning to be considered as "economic goods" produced with a view toward selling them on the market.[50] Historical experience shows, moreover, that capitalism can very well coexist not only with a purely oligarchic regime but even with an authoritarian one (yesterday in Chile, today in China), which refutes the idea according to which the market economy automatically creates the conditions for democracy.

The increasingly repetitive use of the term "governance," Guy Hermet concludes, attests to "a will to repress the concept of government, with its political connotation of the prioritization of public authority and the general interest over what comes from private interest and private actors. Governance is the end of politics, and with it of civic democracy."[51] Obeying "an anti-political principle that commands that the people, considered ignorant and fickle, not be convened . . . the concept of governance corresponds to a system of command that would no longer be a truly political regime."[52]

The present-day crisis of democracy is above all a crisis of politics.

---

[50] Cf. Karl Polanyi, *La Grande Transformation. Aux origines politiques et économiques de notre temps* [*The Great Transformation: The Political and Economic Origins of Our Time*] (1944), trans. Catherine Malamoud and Maurice Angeno (Paris: Gallimard, 1983). Cf. also Jérôme Maucourant, "Marché, démocratie et totalitarisme" ["Market, Democracy and Totalitarianism"], in *Peut-on critiquer le capitalisme?* [*Can One Criticize Capitalism?*] (Paris: La Dispute, 2008), 107–22.

[51] Hermet, "Crépuscule démocratique," 34.

[52] Hermet, *L'Hiver de la démocratie ou le nouveau régime.*

THE ERASURE OF THE
RIGHT-LEFT DIVIDE

Everyone is familiar with Alain's frequently quoted remark: "When someone asks me if the distinction between parties of the Right and Left, men of the Right and Left, is still meaningful, my first thought is that the man asking the question is certainly not a man of the Left."[1] Alain wrote that in 1925. He might be surprised to observe that this question which he imagined could only be posed by a man of the Right is today on everyone's lips.

Natacha Polony recently declared, "When I look at the representatives of the Right, I do not feel myself part of the Right for one second. The same with the Left, where I do not find myself either." Ever more people are in this situation. In fact, for the past several years all opinion polling agrees in showing that in the eyes of a majority of Frenchmen, the Left/Right divide is increasingly devoid of meaning. In 1980, only 30% thought the concepts of Right and Left were dated and no longer allowed an accurate understanding of the positions of parties and politicians. In March 1981 the figure was 33%; in February 1986, 45%; in March 1988, 48%; in November 1989, 56%; in 2011, 58%.[2] Three years after that, the figure was 73%—with over 60% saying they had no confidence in either the Left or Right governing the country.[3]

This development is obviously remarkable, and for three reasons. First, because it displays a tendency that is becoming gradually stronger: whereas in the 1960s, 90% of Frenchmen positioned themselves on the Left-Right axis without any particular qualms,[4] the concepts of Left and Right appear every year more

---

[1] Alain [Émile-Auguste Chartier (1868–1951) — Trans.], *Eléments d'une doctrine radicale* [*Elements of a Radical Doctrine*] (Paris: Gallimard, 1925).

[2] Sofre poll in *Le Point*, November 27, 1989, 62–65.

[3] Cevipof poll of January 2014.

[4] Cf. Emeric Deutsch, Denis Lindon, and Pierre Weill, *Les Familles politiques aujourd'hui en France* [*Political Groupings in France Today*] (Paris:

discredited. Secondly, because it has been a rapid development and is even showing a tendency to accelerate. Finally, because it involves all political milieus and all sectors of public opinion: in April 1988, a Sofres poll even allowed us to observe that this conviction of the obsoleteness of the concepts of the Left and Right made its greatest gains on the Left since 1981.[5]

All these figures clearly show that the opposition of Left and Right—which has structured the French political landscape for two centuries, which Emmanuel Berl was able to describe in his day as "by far the most vital distinction for most of the French electorate," and which François Sirinelli described not so long ago as "the great, essential French divide"[6]—is in the process of losing a great part of its significance. The concepts of Left and Right "have essentially lost their structure," believes polling specialist Jérôme Sainte-Marie, "and, moreover, no longer serve to structure elections."[7]

*

This is all the more surprising—but perhaps all the more revealing as well—because it was in France that the concepts of Left and Right are generally thought to have been born.

In fact, they are traced back to August 28, 1789, when the Estates General—which had been meeting for a month already and had been transformed into a Constituent Assembly—opened a debate at Versailles concerning the King's right of veto.[8] The

---

Minuit, 1966), 13–14.

[5] Cf. *Le Nouvel Observateur*, April 1, 1988, 42–43.

[6] Jean-François Sirinelli, interview in *Le Magazine littéraire*, April 1993.

[7] Jérôme Sainte-Marie, "Les derniers jours du clivage gauche-droite," ["Last Days of the Left/Right Divide"], website *Figaro Vox*, May 6, 2016, 5. Cf. also Jérôme Sainte-Marie, "Le système électoral et le changement démocratique" ["The Electoral System and Democratic Change"], *Le Débat*, September-October 2016, 33–37; and Vincent Tiber, ed., *Des votes et des voix. De Mitterrande à Hollande* [*Votes and Voices: From Mitterand to Holland*] (Nîmes: Champ social, 2013).

[8] The date August 28, 1789, is the most often cited one, but there is no unanimity about it. Some authors refer to August 11, others to the month of September. In their *Histoire parlementaire de la Révolution française* [*Parliamentary History of the French Revolution*], published in

question was whether in the reformed monarchical regime then being instituted the King could dispose of a right of decision superior to national sovereignty, i.e., a power with priority over that of the people's representatives united as a political body for expressing the law. To manifest their choices, the partisans of the absolute right of veto, soon joined by those of the suspensive veto, took up their places in the hall (which was not semicircular) to the right of President Jean-Joseph Mounier, while their adversaries, partisans of a constitutional regime reserving legislative power for the assembly, took up their position on the left. The Left/Right distinction was born. It gradually spread all over Europe, then across the world, installing itself durably in the Latin countries and more according to circumstance in the Germanic and especially Anglo-Saxon countries.

First of all, we note that the divide was provoked by a debate on a very particular subject, the King's prerogatives, which does not correspond to anything existing today. And we note above all that it is of a purely topographical character. In putting themselves "on the right" or "on the left," the deputies limited themselves to describing a space and nothing more. Being on the right side of the room had not yet become being "Right-wing" any more than being on the left side of the room meant being "Left-wing." At most, the two terms etymologically suggested qualities ("uprightness" [*droiture*]) or faults ("clumsiness" [*gaucherie*]) that were quickly forgotten.[9]

1834, Buchez and Roux say the Right-Left polarization appeared before June 27. Two years later, in any case, a text from *L'Ami des Patriotes* published August 27, 1791, speaks of "Right" and "Left" within the Constituent Assembly.

   [9] The Left suffers from the pejorative view always taken of the left side or the left hand with respect to the right. With "right" is associated rightness, rectitude (cf. the German *richtig*), royalty (Latin *rex*, Sanskrit *rājā*, Gaulish *rix*, Old Irish *rí*, Frankish *rīkī*; **reg-s* is at the origin of he who shows the way to travel with his right hand, *rectus* having at first meant right like the line traced by the King); with "left" is associated clumsiness, a crooked character. In Latin, *dextra* indicates the favorable direction; left on the contrary is "sinister" (*sinistra*). Left, explains Ovid, because *studiosa sinistri: natae ad furta sinistrae* (zealous for evil; the left hand

But this traditional reference to the age of the French Revolution is still misleading, for it was not at that time but much later that the concepts of Left and Right spread through public discourse. They did not form part of it at the time of the revolutions of 1830 or 1848, nor that of the Commune, an age when no socialist described himself as "on the Left" and when one was only familiar with reactionaries, republicans, radicals, "progressive conservatives," and "progressive liberals." During the whole first half of the nineteenth century, it was liberals who formed the heart of the parliamentary "Left." "To speak of the Left in the eighteenth century, or even in the first three quarters of the nineteenth century," declares Jacques Julliard, "is to deal with a subject that did not yet exist, or at least which was not apprehended as such by contemporaries."[10]

It was only in the very last years of the nineteenth century that the dyad Left/Right took on its current meaning and genuinely passed into everyday language, especially at the time of the Dreyfus Affair (1894–1899), which witnessed an alliance between socialism and the progressive "Left" out of concern for a "republican defense" against the monarchist, clerical, or nationalist Right.[11] Passing beyond its purely parliamentary usage, the Left/Right dyad then transformed itself considerably, the "Right" renouncing the idea of monarchical restoration and partly coming under the control of liberals, and the "Left" only

---

born for theft).

[10] Jacques Julliard, *Les Gauches françaises, 1762–2012. Histoire, politique et imaginaire* [*The French Lefts, 1762–2012: History, Politics and Imagination*] (Paris: Flammarion, 2012).

[11] Cf. Marc Crapez, "De quand date le clivage gauche-droite en France?" ["When Did the Left-Right Divide Begin in France?"], *Revue française de science politique*, 1998, no. 1, 42–75 (reprinted in *Krisis*, May 2009, 28–63); Jacques Le Bohec and Christophe Le Digol, eds., *Gauche/droite. Genèse d'un clivage politique* [*Right/Left: Birth of a Political Divide*] (Paris: PUF, 2012); and Marcel Gauchet, "La droite et la gauche" ["The Right and the Left"], in Pierre Nora, ed., *Les Lieux de mémoire*, vol. 3: *Les France. 1: Conflits et partages* [*Places of Memory*, vol. 3: *The Various Frances. 1: Conflicts and Common Ground*] (Paris: Gallimard, 1993), which locates the change around 1900.

constituting itself by discarding whole swathes of the socialist and revolutionary tradition.

The use of the words "Left" and "Right" then spread, especially with the Left Bloc of 1899–1902, which grouped radical "Poincarists"[12] and radical socialists, then the Left Cartel of 1924 in which the Communists did not participate, which formed four years after the split in the French Section of the Workers' International (the SFIO) at the Congress of Tours. The appearance of new formations on the Left then displaced those formations that preceded them to the Right or Center (this is the "sinistrogyrous movement" Albert Thibaudet spoke of in 1932 in *Les idées politiques en France* [*Political Ideas in France*]). Thus, the Radical Party, founded in 1901, ended by finding itself in the center of the political landscape, belying its own name (originally, the "radical Left" was the name of the group that sat next to the radicals), while the liberals were themselves displaced to the Right. André Siegfried would say that a modern Right "is always an old Left." But the Left/Right divide is scarcely mentioned by the first great political scientists, whether Moisei Ostrogorski (1902), Roberto Michels (1911), André Siegfried (1913), or Albert Thibaudet (1927), who do not place it at the center of their analyses at all.

Marc Crapez summarizes the situation as follows:

> The concepts of Left and Right are limited to the language of the nineteenth century's parliamentary topology; they only gradually occupy the ideological and cultural field, becoming polarized at the beginning of the twentieth century. Only then does the idea appear that there can be men of the Right quite different from those of the Left. The divide was probably neither implicit nor latent after 1789. The Third Republic was built in the center, and did not witness two camps confronting one another in a bipolar contest. Despite advance signs, it is the twentieth century that constructed a dichotomy that took possession of the

---

[12] Raymond Poincaré (1860–1934), the President of France from 1913 until 1920. — Trans.

whole of society.[13]

It was from that point that the Left/Right divide was able to become a structural division. It would in fact be a grave error to believe this divide never corresponded to anything. In the past it explained many things, and René Rémond was not wrong to write that "for nearly two hundred years, six or seven generations of men, millions of citizens and voters have believed in it as in an objective datum and behaved all their lives in their voting, and in their commitments, as if Left and Right existed."[14] Right and Left most certainly did exist, but have not always meant the same thing. They have only existed due to circumstances that have greatly changed, their value (and content) coming exclusively from their socio-historical context.

The first observation one can make in this regard is of a historical character: the three great debates that kept the Left/Right divide in existence for two centuries have today been essentially concluded.

The first of these debates concerned institutions. It clearly began with the Revolution and for nearly a century would oppose advocates of the Republic, partisans of constitutional monarchy, and those nostalgic for monarchy by divine right. It was at first a debate concerning the Revolution itself, which ended in the Restoration and, with it, the compromise of 1815, which in a sense marks the birth of modern France. Later, beginning with the July monarchy, there followed a debate on the political regime's definition—republican or monarchic—which ended in 1875 with the establishment of universal suffrage and the definitive installation of the republican regime. From that point on, nearly the whole Right becomes republican, while monarchist movements are gradually driven to the margins of the political spectrum.

The second great debate, beginning in the 1880s, concerns the

---

[13] Crapez, "De quand date le clivage gauche-droite en France?," *Krisis* version, 61.

[14] René Rémond, *Les Droites en France* [*Right-Wing Groups in France*] (Paris: Aubier-Montaigne, 1982), 29.

religious question. It opposed partisans of a "clerical" conception of the social order against advocates of a purely secular vision, naturally picking up where the debate on institutions left
off, and was expressed in polemics of a violence that is often forgotten today. For a time, this opposition would even be fully
identified with the Left/Right divide and serve as a touchstone
for all political life. "In comparison," writes René Rémond, "every other difference seemed secondary. Whoever observed the
commands of the Catholic Church was *ipso facto* classed on the
Right, and the anticlerical man had no need to produce further
proofs of his democratic sentiments than his attachment to the
Republic."[15]

Under the Third Republic, the movement to the Left was also
stimulated by Jules Ferry's school reforms. It was in this climate
that the Affair of the Cards[16] unfolded, followed by the Dreyfus
Affair (which caused anti-Semitism to pass from Left to Right
and instituted the Left/Right divide in intellectual circles). This
dispute would result in the separation of church and state in
1905. It would leave profound marks on French political life
even as it gradually lost its sharpness with, on the one hand, the
rallying of an increasingly large share of the Catholic hierarchy
to republican institutions and, on the other, the appearance of a
secularized theory of the traditional social order (from Auguste
Comte to Hippolyte Taine), a double movement that resulted in
a gradual dissociation of the Church from the Counter-
Revolution. Later, the extent of religious controversy would continue shrinking, soon to survive only in scholarly quarrels. The
"Demo for everybody" protest against homosexual marriage
represents it dying echo.

The last debate is obviously that on the "social question,"
an expression that originally covered all the effects of the first

---

[15] René Rémond, *La politique n'est plus ce qu'elle était* [*Politics Isn't What
It Used to Be*] (Paris: Calmann-Lévy, 1993), 26.

[16] A political scandal of 1904 which erupted when it became known
that the French Minister of War had established a secretive system for
recording evidence of officers' political and religious convictions in order
to prevent the advancement of Catholics and Royalists. — Ed.

Industrial Revolution. Beginning in 1830, when capitalism imposed itself on the economic forms inherited from the past, thus opening the front of a class struggle between bourgeoisie and proletariat, it became sharper with the development of industrial society, the birth of socialism, and the rise of the workers' movement. Interrupted for a time during the "sacred union" of the First World War, it returned in strength in 1917. Beginning in 1920, to be on the Left was no longer only a matter of being republican at the political level (since everyone, or nearly so, was republican), nor even secular (since by that time there were Left-wing Catholics); it was to be a socialist or Communist.

The social question above all posed the problem of the state's role in the regulation of economic activity and the possible redistribution of wealth. Divided between reformists and revolutionaries, the Left was identified with the rejection of the market economy and even of private property, often committed to a planned, centralized economy controlled by the state. Its aim was to assure collective promotion or liberation by means of economic and social institutions realizing a sort of general contractuality through collectivization of the means of production. Moreover, the Left made essentially quantitative and material demands, which amounts to saying that it denounced capitalism's methods (the exploitation of labor and inequalities in the distribution of wealth) without contesting its central objective (ever higher productivity). Finally, it sought to anchor itself in the class of wage earners, of which the working class was at the center, in an attempt to forge a political force to serve as a vehicle for a concrete project of liberation. This statist and productivist project would endure for decades before collapsing in its turn under the combined effects of the implosion of "real socialism" and the exhaustion of the welfare state model, while the working class, itself increasingly reformist, would gradually lose consciousness of itself as a result of contact with consumerism and mass stockholding.

Thus, as René Rémond also writes, "in a brief time, nearly all the issues on which elections turned, making and unmaking majorities, the issues that nourished debates and gave political life meaning and color, stopped raising passions, lost their sparkle, and even disappeared from the scene."[17] Numerous questions that had only recently been extremely divisive disappeared or culminated in a more consensual approach. "In every era, certain oppositions disappear or lose their importance while others that seemed secondary suddenly come to occupy center stage."[18] But at the same time, the dividing line between Left and Right never ceased fluctuating. Moreover, emphasizes Claude Weil:

> None of the great choices, none of the crises that divided French society in the recent course of history (apart, perhaps, from the Popular Front) opposed Left and Right in binary fashion, bloc against bloc. Neither the war over public schooling, nor the Dreyfus Affair, nor the colonial adventure, nor the Occupation, nor the creation of the Fifth Republic, nor May 1968, nor the debate on the death penalty and abortion, nor, more recently, the two referenda on Europe: all, to varying degrees, have divided the two camps, sometimes irremediably.[19]

It was in the twentieth century that the Left/Right divide experienced its golden age. Several factors contributed to this. First, the play of forces within legislatures, which rapidly structured themselves around a confrontation between two coalitions or large opposing parties. Then there was the human mind's spontaneous tendency to reason in binary terms, as if all reality's complexity could be reduced to a Manichaean schema—a natural enough tendency in a culture shaped by Christian and Cartesian dualism (the distinction between the soul and mind, subject and object, etc.), which has lost sight of its own principle of identity and the complementarity of contraries. To this we may add that people of the Right generally have no Left-wing culture, just as people of the Left have no Right-wing culture, so that both

---

[17] Rémond, *La politique n'est plus ce qu'elle était*, 21.

[18] Etienne Schweisguth, *Droite-gauche: un clivage dépassé?* [*Right-Left: An Obsolete Divide?*] (Paris: Documentation française, 1994), 3.

[19] Claude Weil, *Les Droites en France, 1789–2008* [*The Rights in France, 1789–2008*] (Paris: CNRS Editions, 2008).

have a tendency to interpret ideas with which they do not identify as a homogeneous "bloc," something that does not facilitate an understanding of the subject.

Essentialism, which always amounts to a reification, is never far away under such circumstances. Left and Right then become eternal values: realities *per se*. Gradually, the Left/Right opposition comes to designate two philosophies, two conceptions of the world, two psychologies, and finally two human types. In the 1960s and 1970s, André Malraux said ironically that "the Left is no longer on the Left, the Right is no longer on the Right, and the Center is no longer in the middle." But at the same time, under the pretext that "everything is political," every subject gave rise to an interpretation in terms of Left and Right, including matters of artistic taste, dress, or culinary habits. The necktie is on the Right and jeans on the Left; Peugeots are on the Right, Renault on the Left; adolescence is on the Right, childhood on the Left (unless it is the other way around), and all the rest accordingly.

Defining the man of the Right and the man of the Left thus becomes a sort of party game. Jean Plumyène and Raymond Lassierra actually made a brilliant attempt in this direction.[20] Before them, Emmanuel Berl had also gone in for the practice: "The man of the Right prefers things and the man of the Left people"; "Michelet loved France like a person, Maurras loved it like a house"; "The man of the Right easily loses his temper; he thinks he is following necessity when he follows his aggressive tendencies"; "The man of the Left has more faith in words, the man of the Right in one's motive for speaking"; "Brevity is Right-wing, prolixity Left-wing"; "Grammar is Right-wing, linguistics Left-wing." Amusing formulas, but quite arbitrary. Berl, moreover, also acknowledges his doubts as to whether he "can define the man of the Right and the man of the Left, because they tend to behave the same way in a world tending towards uniformity."[21]

---

[20] Jean Plumyène and Raymond Lassierra, *Le Complexe de gauche* [*The Left-Wing Complex*] (Paris: Flammarion, 1967) and *Le Complexe de droite* [*The Right-Wing Complex*] (Paris: Flammarion, 1969).

[21] Emmanuel Berl, *Essais* (Paris: Bernard de Fallois, 2007).

Others have busied themselves projecting the Left/Right divide back upon the ages preceding its emergence: Corneille was on the Right because he described men as they are, Racine on the Left because he described them as they ought to be; Aristotle is on the Right, Plato on the Left; the quarrel of the Ancients and the Moderns prefigures the opposition between Left and Right, and so on. Were the Armagnacs on the Right? The Ghibellines on the Left? What about the Capulets?

From an almost religious perspective, certain people have even maintained the existence of an "eternal Right," if only at the price of grotesque extravagances.[22] For certain traditionalists, the Left/Right divide has more of a metaphysical than a political character.[23] "I lay down as an axiom that the Right has always existed, since it was identical to traditional civilization's political organization. The Left, on the other hand, only appeared in modern times," wrote Jacques Anisson du Perron.[24] Jean Madiran defended precisely the opposite thesis: the Right only appeared in opposition to the Left,[25] so it is nothing more than the anti-Left. Paradoxically, this was also the opinion of the Marxist Con-

---

[22] For Henry de Lesquen, "What makes up the unity of the Right is not agreement on a list of values; it is the rejection of the Left's nihilism. All values are on the Right because this is the normal state of political thought, while the Left is a pathology, a syndrome of decadence. . . . So the Left is homogeneous, and it is the Right that is plural" ("Droite et gauche, un clivage toujours actuel" ["Right and Left: A Still Valid Divide"], online at the website *Club d'Horloge*).

[23] Boris Dewiel, who is in no sense a traditionalist, has approached the question of the metaphysical roots of the Left/Right dyad in an original way: "Athènes vs. Jérusalem. Une source du conflit droite-gauche dans l'histoire des idées" ["Athens vs. Jerusalem: A Source of Right-Left Conflict in the History of Ideas"], *Krisis*, May 2009, 88–110. The author's thesis is that the response to the question "Are the rules discovered or created?" is what distinguishes Left from Right.

[24] Jacques Anisson du Perron, *Journal d'un homme de droite. Réflexions d'un contre-révolutionnaire* [*Diary of a Man of the Right: Reflections of a Counter-Revolutionary*], 1980–1990 (Puisseaux: Pardès, 1993), 159.

[25] Jean Madiran, *La Droite et la gauche* [*The Right and the Left*] (Paris: Nouvelles Editions latines, 1977).

stanzo Preve: "The Left is primary, the Right derivative."[26]

There has never been unanimity concerning the Left/Right divide, however. "At certain times, it seems that the principal trait of the man of the Right is to deny that he is one," said Emmanuel Berl on this subject, agreeing with Alain's opinion cited above. In fact, historically speaking, it is above all on the Right that this divide has been rejected as a Procrustean dichotomy, interpreted as an abusive way of privileging certain concepts at the expense of others just as necessary. Such a mutilation has generally been perceived as being of a sort to split man in two, and especially as a way of artificially fracturing the national community by dividing what should remain indivisible, at the risk of forming the basis for a civil war. The general idea here is that the Right is as necessary as the Left. The Left has been less susceptible to that argument, firstly because it is rightly suspicious of the mystifying character of the appeal to "national unity," and then because it has always had a tendency to consider itself self-sufficient by identifying itself symbolically with every possible good cause, something that has often led it to intolerance and withdrawal into itself.

Everyone knows the famous saying of José Ortega y Gasset: "To be on the Left or on the Right is to choose one of the many ways available to man for being an imbecile; both, in effect, are forms of moral hemiplegia."[27] The same point of view is found in

---

[26] Constanzo Preve, "Une discussion pour l'instant interminable. Considérations préliminaires sur la genèse historique passée, sur la fonction systémique présente et les perspectives futures de la dualité politico-religieuse droite/gauche" ["An Interminable (For Now) Discussion: Preliminary Considerations on the Historical Origins, Present Systemic Function, and Future Prospects for the Politico-Religious Duality Right/Left"], *Krisis*, May 2009, 5.

[27] José Ortega y Gasset, *La Révolte des masses* [*Revolt of the Masses*] followed by an *Eloge des Anglais* [*Panegyric Upon the English*], trans. Louis Parrot and Bernard Dubant (Paris: Livre-Club du Labyrinthe, 1986), 32. Ortega returned to this idea several times, especially in a 1930 article ("Organización de la decencía nacional" ["Organization of National Decency"]) and a 1931 collection (*Rectificación de la República* [*Rectification of the Republic*]), where he describes the terms Right and Left as "sterile slo-

José Antonio Primo de Rivera, founder of the Spanish Falange, when he declared on January 9, 1936 that, "To be on the Right or Left is always to exclude from the soul half of what it ought to feel."[28] Bernard Charbonneau said, "We are Maurassians or Marxists in the same way certain insects preserve an eye in the depths of the abyss."[29] He added:

> Discussion of principles between Right and Left is absurd because their values are complementary. . . . Freedom *per se* or order *per se* can only be a lie disguising tyranny or chaos. Truth is neither on the Right nor Left, nor does it lie in any happy medium; truth contains all three in a tension between their extreme demands. And if one day they must meet, it will not be in repudiation but by pushing themselves to their own logical conclusions.[30]

And in conclusion: "The day has finally come for us to reject both Right and Left in order to reconcile within ourselves the tension between their fundamental aspirations."[31]

The Left/Right divide has also been disputed by political currents claiming to represent a "third way," an ambiguous expression generally understood in the Hegelian sense of an overcoming or synthesis (*Aufhebung*) and a logic of included middle. Between the World Wars, this "third way" idea, far from being peculiar to fascism, was frequently found in the constellation of non-conformists,[32] from Robert Aron to Philippe Lamour, from

---

gans" and "expressions from the past."

[28] José Antonio Primo de Rivera, *Escritos y Discursos. Obras completas (1922–1936)* [*Writings and Speeches: Complete Works (1922–1936)*], vol. 2 (Madrid: Instituto de Estudios políticos, 1976), 895.

[29] Bernard Charbonneau, *L'Etat* [*The State*] (Paris: Economica, 1987), 152.

[30] Charbonneau, *L'Etat*, 150–51.

[31] Charbonneau, *L'Etat*, 158.

[32] A group of French thinkers of the 1930s who sought a communitarian alternative to the political Right and Left of their day. The name is derived from a later study of the men in question by the historian Jean-Louis Loubet del Bayle, *Les non-conformistes des années 30:*

Daniel-Rops and Emmanuel Mounier to Thierry Maulnier and Denis de Rougement, who rejected communism, fascism, and parliamentary liberalism. It is also found after 1945. As for the slogan "neither Right nor Left" — revived in 1995 by Jean-Marie Le Pen, who was unable to make it stick,[33] and to which one preferred the inclusive form ("both Right and Left") — it goes back at least to the end of the nineteenth century.[34]

*

Many people who sincerely consider themselves to be on the Left or Right are happy to give a definition, often quite clear, of what this means, but their definition is rarely accepted by others of the Left or Right. Everyone is of course convinced he knows what the "true Right" or "true Left" is, but these subjective definitions — everyone privileges the notions most important to himself — are merely the reflection of an entirely personal conviction. Debate is still poisoned by the polemical use of some of these labels ("extreme Right," "Leftism," etc.), as well as by certain discursive strategies that aim to reduce what is new to what is familiar, or group in the same category antagonistic concepts or opposed families. For liberals, socialists and fascists belong to the same family ("totalitarian"); for socialists, fascists and liberals belong to the same family ("capitalist"); and for fascists, socialists and liberals belong to the same family ("the heirs of the Enlightenment"). All of this prevents us from getting to the bottom of things.

---

une tentative de renouvellement de la pensée politique française [*The Non-Conformists of the 1930s: An Attempt to Renew French Political Thought*] (Paris: Éditions du Seuil, 1969). — Trans.

[33] Cf. Grégoire Kauffmann, *Le nouveau FN. Les vieux habits du populisme* [*The New National Front: Populism's Old Clothes*] (Paris: Seuil, 2016), 67.

[34] Cf. the brochure published in 1885 under the title *Ni à droite, ni à gauche! En face! Lettre à Henri Rochefort* [*Neither Right nor Left! Face Forward! Letter to Henri Rochefort*]. The slogan would be revived in 1926 by Georges Valois but, contrary to what Zeev Sternhell states (*Ni droite ne gauche. L'idéologie fasciste en France* [*Neither Right nor Left: Fascist Ideology in France*] [Brussels: Complexe, 1987]), there is nothing specifically fascist about it.

If one turns to specialists in political science, the result is scarcely more satisfactory. To demonstrate the pertinence of the Left/Right divide, they usually invoke the historical character of this dichotomy and allege the existence of two fundamentally opposed political cultures to which the dyad Left/Right applies. But their conclusions have never found unanimous acceptance. Political scientists have never arrived at agreement on a criterion or concept that could serve as a common denominator for all forms of the Left or Right. Many propositions have been set forth, of course, practically all of them based on binary oppositions: freedom or equality, conservatism or progressivism, order or justice, immobilism or movement, belief in or rejection of the idea of human nature, the perfectibility or imperfectability of that nature, the primacy of the innate or primacy of the acquired characteristics, a taste for the concrete or a taste for the abstract, nostalgia for the past or confidence in the future, anthropological pessimism or optimism, transcendence and imminence, etc. But whatever criterion is chosen, there are always too many exceptions.

Let us take the pair equality/freedom as an example. In 1994, the famous political scientist Norberto Bobbio published a book that was enormously successful in Italy.[35] In it he maintained, following many others, that equality is the key concept that allows us to distinguish Right and Left: the former will always be hostile to it, the latter always favorable (even if, as Bobbio recognizes, the Left has also created new forms of inequality). Bobbio distinguishes an egalitarian and authoritarian Left; a center-Left both egalitarian and liberal; a liberal and non-egalitarian center-Right; and an authoritarian, non-egalitarian Right. But this thesis does not stand up to careful examination. Not all the political forces habitually classed on the Left can be defined by the demand for greater equality. In both camps we find parties that think that certain inequalities are not unjust (which raises the question of when they become so). Besides, legal equality and

---

[35] Norberto Bobbio, *Destra e sinistra. Ragioni e significati di una distinzione politica* [*Right and Left: The Reasons for and Meaning of a Political Distinction*] (Rome: Donzelli, 1994).

social equality are not the same thing. An old dilemma: Is it better to distribute less wealth in a more equal fashion or accept inequality in order to accumulate greater total wealth? Finally, what should we think of the concept of community, which seems to resolve and overcome the opposition between equality and freedom?[36]

Marx, moreover, explicitly disavowed egalitarianism and never structured his conception of the classless society around any idea of equality. Equality is in his eyes a fundamentally bourgeois idea that allows the justification of labor power's exploitation. Thus, the abolition of inequality is not to be confused with the abolition of domination, the latter being defined as the subordination of one group's interests to those of another.[37] Engels himself writes that "the proletarian demand for equality amounts to a demand for the abolition of classes. Any demand for farther-reaching equality necessarily falls into absurdity."[38] The slogan Marx takes from Louis Blanc — "from each according to his abilities, to each according to his needs!" — is no egalitarian slogan, either. "If people have unequal needs, explains Wood, then we cannot expect that they should have both equal wealth and equal satisfaction of their needs."[39] We may add that in September 2016, an IFOP poll sponsored by L'Humanité revealed that the word invested with the highest value by persons declaring themselves on the Left is "freedom" (with "equality" coming in third).

Another classic dichotomy is that of order (or conservation) and movement (or progress). But no sooner have we stated this than we spot the ambiguity: What is to be conserved? In what

---

[36] Cf. Marcello Veneziani, Sinistra e destra. Risposta a Norberto Bobbio [Left and Right: A Response to Norberto Bobbio] (Florence: Vallecchi, 1995) and Sergio Benvenuto, "Par-delà droite et gauche" ["Beyond Right and Left"], Krisis, May 2009, 74–87.

[37] Cf. Allen Wood, "Marx et l'égalité" ["Marx and Equality"], Krisis, June 2009, 51–73, who believes we should view Marx "as an opponent of the ideal of equality, although he was also an opponent, and not the least important, of all forms of social privilege and oppression" (p. 52).

[38] Friedrich Engels, Anti-Dühring [1878] (Moscow, 1954), 143.

[39] Wood, "Marx et l'égalité," 61.

direction does one want to move? Edmund Burke, in *Reflections on the Revolution in France* (1790), stated that "a state without the means of some change, is without the means of its own conservation." Moisei Ostrogorski also noted that "it is as impossible for a social order to preserve itself without change as to transform itself instantly."[40] "There is," said de Gaulle, "the eternal current of movement toward reforms, toward changes, which is naturally necessary; and then there is also a current of order, rule, and tradition, which is also necessary. It is with all of this that France was made." "Conservatism and progressivism," observes Vincent Coussedière, "are categories that in themselves do not mean anything. Everything depends on what one wants to conserve and toward what one wants to progress."[41]

Jean-Claude Michéa, for his part, has shown that socialism, if often associated in people's minds with the spirit of progressivism, is at its origin completely foreign to it, just as it is foreign to "blank slate" ideology that rejects all the traditions of the past in the name of "sunny tomorrows": "The memory of practices of mutual aid proper to traditional village communities—from which the rising industrial proletariat generally issued—certainly played an important role in constituting the socialist imagination." Better still, he adds, it was undoubtedly because of its association with the idea of progress that it invited people into communion with the scientistic cult of modernity, in which it is possible to see a threat to individual autonomy, which socialism has so often rejected.[42] The Left ended up confusing that

---

[40] Moiséi Ostrogorski, *La Démocratie et les partis politiques* [*Democracy and Political Parties*] [1902] (Paris: Seuil, 1979), 221. Cf. also Pierre-Joseph Proudhon: "Qui dit révolution dit nécessairement *progrès*, dit par là même *conservation*" ["Whoever Says Revolution Necessarily says *Progress*, and Thereby Says *Conservation*"] (*Idées révolutionnaires* [*Revolutionary Ideas*] [1848] [Antony: Tops-Trinquier, 1996], 223).

[41] Vincent Coussedière, interview with Alexandre Devecchio, website *Figaro Vox*, March 18, 2016, 5.

[42] "Jean-Claude Michéa répond à dix questions" ["Jean-Claude Michéa Answers Ten Questions"] in Gilles Labelle, Éric Martin, and Stéphane Vibert, eds., *Les Racines de la liberté. Réflexions a partir de l'anarchisme tory* [*The Roots of Liberty: Reflections Based on Tory Anarchism*], 302–304;

which was innovative (or "modern") with that which was genuinely liberating. It did not see that modernity is rich in all sorts of new forms of alienation.

The ideology of progress is first of all a bourgeois liberal ideology that secularizes the old Biblical idea of a linear conception of history oriented toward the best by restricting it to the secular sphere. Theorized by Turgot, and then by Condorcet (*Esquisse d'un tableau historique des progrès de l'esprit humain* [*Sketch for a Historical Picture of the Progress of the Human Spirit*], 1794), it postulates that humanity as a whole is being directed — thanks especially to scientific progress — toward a moral progress without end. This is the basis of Enlightenment philosophy.[43] Fundamentally oriented toward the future, and having nothing but distrust of what Pasolini called the revolutionary force of the past, it demonizes the concepts of tradition, custom, and rootedness, seeing in them only obsolete superstitions and obstacles to the triumphal forward march of humanity. Aiming to unify the human race, it demands that one repudiate every archaic form of belonging, and that the organic base of all traditional forms of solidarity be systematically destroyed. The new world must necessarily be built upon the ruins of the previous one. As Jacques Julliard correctly noted, this also goes

> Hand in hand with individualism, that form of individualism which asserts itself with the French Revolution. It is associated with the political and moral flourishing of the individual, while the absolutist doctrine of the *Ancien Régime* gives priority to communal values, those found within the family, social bodies, the province, and the state itself. The "revolution of the rights of man" (Marcel Gauchet) is essentially a revolution of individuals: they and they alone bear rights.[44]

---

317. Cf. also Christopher Lasch, *The True and Only Heaven: Progress and Its Critics* (New York: Norton, 1991).

[43] "It is absurd to say that the *philosophes* of the Enlightenment were on the Left," writes Jacques Julliard, "but it is legitimate to hold that the Left is the party of the Enlightenment" (*Les Gauches françaises, 1762–2012*).

[44] Julliard, *Les Gauches françaises.*

In his works, Louis Dumont has also demonstrated that individualism is fundamentally an ideology of the Left. "It is the human individual who is the measure of all things," said Jaurès.

Thus, the concept of change is not fundamentally characteristic of the Left. With the idea of progress, the cult of novelty, especially in the technical sense, affected all political families. Progress has been challenged on the Left (by ecologists and the partisans of degrowth) as it has been on the Right (by positivists and liberals). Today it is rather the liberal Right that wants to "get things moving" in the face of a Left intent on preserving social gains (and which for this reason finds itself charged with being "archaic"). We could say the same about the conventional scheme that puts social justice and generosity on the Left, and authority, tradition, and the defense of the family and private property on the Right. Going back merely to configurations of circumstance, this amounts to plastering concepts over an accidental divide, concepts that cannot themselves be derived from that divide.

There have also been attempts to relate the difference between Left and Right to a question of "temperaments." André Siegfried, e.g., in his celebrated *Tableau politique de la France de l'Ouest sous la IIIe République* [*Political Portrait of Western France Under the Third Republic*] (1913), lists three "principal temperaments," five "principal parties," and five "basic tendencies." The procedure is tempting, since temperaments, i.e., stable psychological dispositions, are a reality. Arising long before the Left/Right divide, and attesting to the diversity of human nature, they even have a biological basis that numerous studies have allowed us to grasp. But what political conclusions can we draw from this? That there are more conservative temperaments and others more drawn to change is obvious, but historical experience has never allowed us to make any of them the prerogative of a single political family. The same goes for the "authoritarian personality" (Theodor W. Adorno), which was said not so long ago to be coextensive with the temperament of men of the Right. Nor do temperaments and characters allow us to predict actions exactly. Besides, it is not temperaments that delineate the field of politics, but ideas.

"There are several ways to be on the Right and as many to be on the Left," remark Michel Marmin and Eric Branca.[45] This is the least one can say. What is there in common, e.g., between the counter-revolutionary Right, the personalist and communitarian Right, the European federalist Right, the liberal Right, the bio-hygienist Right, the libertarian Right, the national-revolutionary Right, the racialist Right, the Christian democratic Right, the monarchist Right, the national liberal Right, the Gaullist Right, the Pétainist Right, the regionalist Right, the Jacobin Right, the nationalist Right, the positivist Right, the aesthetic Right, the anarchist Right, the fascist Right, the Hussard Right, the entrepreneurial Right, the activist Right, the moralistic Right, the republican Right, the anti-Communist Right, the technocratic Right, the organicist Right, the Poujadist Right, the Atlanticist Right, the moderate Right, the romantic Right, the militarist Right, the Catholic Right, the *völkisch* Right, the conspiratorialist Right, the traditionalist Right, the ecological Right, and the esotericist Right? And we could pose the same question regarding the various forms of the Left.

Thus, we observe the impossibility of identifying a common denominator that could describe all forms of the Left or Right. All the more so in that there is no airtight barrier between the ideologies and themes that compose them (all combinations are possible), and a number of these themes, far from being assigned a particular locus, have historically never ceased passing from Right to Left or Left to Right.

"In 1815 nationalism, 'La Marseillaise,' and the tricolor flag were symbols of the extreme Left. In 1900 they had become those of the extreme Right," observed Dominique Venner.[46] Arnauld Imatz confirms this:

Certain themes frequently pass from Left to Right and vice

[45] Michel Marmin and Éric Branca, *Gauche-Droite. Le tour de la question* [*Left-Right: The Whole Question*] (Paris: Chronique, 2016).

[46] Dominique Venner, "L'âge d'or de la droite 1870–1940" ["The Golden Age of the Right 1870–1940"], *Enquete sur l'histoire* [*Examination of History*], no. 6, Spring 1993.

versa. This is the case with imperialism, colonialism, racialism, anti-Semitism, anti-Masonry, anti-Christianism, anti-
parliamentarism, anti-technocracy, federalism, centralism,
anti-statism, anti-capitalism, anti-Americanism, and more
recently, regionalism, ecologism, anti-immigrationism, and
anti-Islamism. All completely evade the opposition, the ob-
sessive Left/Right debate.[47]

For example, historically liberalism is a doctrine of the Left,
which was dominated for the entire nineteenth century by the
English ideology, and which the rise of socialism and then of
Communism displaced toward the Right (which explains the
sense that the word liberal has preserved in the United States).
Racialism, eugenics, and social Darwinism were also born on the
Left at the same time as scientistic materialism. The same goes
for modern nationalism, which is tied to a political conception of
the nation not older than the Revolution, and also the reference
to "our ancestors the Gauls" (which originally sought to mini-
mize the Franks' importance). Colonialism was at first defended
by the Left before being defended by the Right. Contrariwise,
ecologism first appeared on the Right before passing to the Left.
As for the Republican idea, it completely changes meaning depending on whether it is perceived by way of the French Revolution, French-style secularism, or civic republicanism from Ti-
tus Livy to Harrington.

It is no less difficult to situate certain individuals. Napoleon,
Clemenceau, and de Gaulle have in turn been rejected and
claimed by both Left and Right. Likewise, certain unexpected
declarations also confuse things. In 1945, the Communist Jacques
Duclos who shouted, "France for the French!"[48] while ten years
earlier the Falangist José Antonio Primo de Rivera condemned

---

[47] Arnaud Imatz, *Droite/gauche: pour sortir de l'équivoque. Histoire des idées et des valeurs non conformistes du XIXe au XXIe siècle* [*Right/Left: Escaping the Ambiguity. History of the Nonconformist Ideas and Values of the Nineteenth and Twentieth Centuries*] (Paris: Pierre-Guillaume de Roux, 2016), 71.

[48] Jacques Duclos, in *L'Humanité*, November 26, 1945.

nationalism and saluted the "genius" of Karl Marx![49]

Many other examples could of course be cited. As Arnauld Imatz reminds us:

> The historian of ideas knows that according to historical ages, places, and sensibilities the various forms of Right and Left have in turn been universalist or particularist, globalist or patriotic, free-tradist or protectionist, capitalist or anti-capitalist, centralist or federalist, individualist or holist, and organicist, positivist, agnostic, and atheist, or theist and Christian.[50]

There has been a revolutionary Right and a conservative Left, an anti-colonialist Right and a colonialist Left, a communitarian Right and an individualist Left, a materialist or atheistic Right and a Christian Left, a Right that wanted everything to be uniform and a Left that defended differences, a mechanistic Right

---

[49] "We are not nationalists, because nationalism is the individualism of peoples," he said on November 17, 1935 (*Escritos y Discursos*, 811). Echoing this thought, we may cite Jean Mabire: "I am not a Communist because I am a revolutionary" (*L'écrivain, la politique et l'espérance* [*The Writer, Politics and Hope*] [Paris: Saint-Just, 1966], 50). On April 9, 1935, José Antonio Primo de Rivera declared in Madrid:

> From the social point of view, I find myself in agreement (without trying to be) on more than one point of Karl Marx's critique. . . . What did he do? Just this: he sat beside the living reality of an economic form of organization, that of English manufacturing at Manchester, and he deduced from it, implacably, that within this structure certain constants prevailed which would end by destroying it. Karl Marx wrote this in an enormous book . . . but truly just as interesting as it was enormous, a densely written book full of genius.

[50] Arnaud Imatz, "Le clivage droite/gauche en question" ["Questioning the Right/Left Divide"], in *La Nouvelle Revue d'histoire*, July–August 2016, 17. Cf. also "L'antagonisme droite/gauche en question" ["Questioning the Antagonism Between Right and Left"] in Arnaud Imatz, *Droite/gauche: pour sortir de l'équivoque*, 35–115.

and an organicist Left, a conspiratorial Left and a rationalistic Right, an optimistic Right and a pessimistic Left, a philo-Semitic Right and an anti-Semitic Left, a permissive Right and an authoritarian Left, a cosmopolitan Right and a nationalist Left, an anti-racist Right and a racialist Left, a Right involved in the Resistance and a Left involved in Collaboration. Equally, there have been Left- and Right-wing productivists, Left- and Right-wing anti-productivists, Left- and Right-wing statists, Left- and Right-wing anti-statists, Left- and Right-wing centralists, Left- and Right-wing local autonomists, and so on.

Things get still more complicated once we cross national frontiers. From one country to another, the same political families are differently configured, and the same concepts do not necessarily have the same content. In Spain, Carlist traditionalism explicitly rejects Maurassianism and the traditionalism of a de Bonald or Joseph de Maistre. The German concepts corresponding to the *völkisch* or *bündisch* movements scarcely have equivalents in the Latin countries. Spanish anarcho-syndicalism is not the same thing as revolutionary Italian syndicalism, and so on.

In the Germanic and Anglo-Saxon countries, the division occurs between Conservatives and Labour, conservatives and liberals or social-democrats. In the United States, the Left/Right distinction had practically no meaning until after the Civil War. It only appeared at the beginning of the twentieth century as the result of the disintegration of the pre-existing political infrastructure, which essentially rested on communal life and local autonomy. Moreover, on the other side of the Atlantic this distinction only covers an opposition between "two different versions of liberalism: the classical version of laissez-faire inherited from the nineteenth century as against the twentieth-century version based on the welfare state." [51] In Israel, Left and Right only really oppose one another concerning peace with the Palestinians and the annexation of the occupied territories.

---

[51] Paul Piccone, "De la Nouvelle Gauche au populisme postmoderne" ["From the New Left to Postmodern Populism"], *Krisis*, February 2008, 77.

Whereas in Germany, England, the United States, or Canada, conservatives constitute a family unto themselves and the term is widely employed to designate a current of thought benefiting from a strong intellectual tradition (from Hume to Oakeshott by way of Burke and Coleridge, in the case of the English Whigs), the word "conservative" (or "conservatism") is remarkable for its absence from the French political vocabulary, as André Siegfried observed in 1930 in his *Tableau des partis en France*. François Huguenin advances a historical explanation for this.[52] Observing that in Germany and the Anglo-Saxon countries, we find among conservatives both "nationalists" and "liberals," he believes such an alliance was made impossible in France by the Revolution of 1789. The Revolution in fact irremediably opposed those who absolutely rejected the revolutionary ideas (from Joseph de Maistre or Louis de Bonald all the way to Charles Maurras) and those who, on the Right, accepted their essential elements even as they rejected revolutionary practice (from Tocqueville and Benjamin Constant to Raymond Aron and Bertrand de Jouvenel). So the two camps split definitively, thereby making any "conservatism" impossible. All through the nineteenth and twentieth centuries, the liberal Right, won over to the ideology of progress, attached to the primacy of the individual, and traditionally mistrustful of political power, has never ceased opposing a Right that, traditionalist or not, defended the state's prerogatives, the concept of the common good, and an organic and communitarian conception of society.

The question remains, however, whether it is possible to be both liberal and conservative. In 1960, the great liberal theoretician Friedrich Hayek answered in the negative in a text that has remained famous: "Why I Am Not a Conservative."[53] He explained that conservativism is a form of constructivism while liberalism presupposes no social project. At most, as partisans of

---

[52] François Huguenin, *Le Conservatisme impossible. Libéraux et réactionnaires en France depuis 1789* [*Impossible Conservatism: Liberals and Reactionaries in France Since 1789*] (Paris: La Table Ronde, 2006).

[53] Friedrich Hayek, *The Constitution of Liberty* (Chicago: Chicago University Press, 1960).

"spontaneous order" (as opposed to "constructed order"), liberals can admit the well-foundedness of some traditions or "traditional values." Analyzing society beginning from the individual, they can only reject any collective approach to society's problems.[54]

So across space as across time, we observe an extreme diversity of Lefts and Rights. This diversity explains why certain Rights have recognized greater affinity with certain Lefts than with other Rights — or certain Lefts with certain Rights than with other Lefts. It also explains why appeals to a "union of the Rights," indefatigably preached in certain milieus, have never resulted in anything: "If we call Right everything that is not Left, this leads to strange groupings so heterogeneous that they cannot result in any common political action."[55] As for the "union of the Left," it existed only during the Popular Front (1936–1938); within the National Council of the Resistance (1943–1947), when the "common program" was adopted in 1972; and when the Communist Party participated in the government between May 1981 and July 1984 — in other words, for less than 13 years over nearly two centuries.

Since it is not possible to reduce all the forms of the Left and Right to a single criterion, most political scientists have stopped talking of them in the singular, preferring to speak in the plural of Rights and Lefts.[56] At the same time, they have undertaken to class them by means of a certain number of typologies.

One of the best-known classifications is that proposed by René Rémond, who distinguishes the traditional and counter-revolutionary Right — supposedly the "original" Right — from the

---

[54] Cf. Pascal Salin, "Est-il possible d'etre 'libéral-conservateur'?" ["Is it possible to be 'liberal-conservative'?"], *Les Cahiers de l'indépendance*, Summer 2016, 59–65.

[55] Henri Guaino, in *Valeurs actuelles*, September 8, 2016, 20.

[56] Cf. Jean François Sirinelli, ed., *Histoire des droites en France*, 3 vols. [*History of the Rights in France*] (Paris: Gallimard, 1992) and Jacques Julliard, *Les Gauches françaises*. René Rémond, who in 1954 published *La Droite en France*, significantly adopted the plural beginning with the fourth edition: *Les Droites en France* (Paris: Aubier-Montaigne, 1982). In it he describes the Right as "a hybrid being, full of contradictions."

liberal or Orleanist Right, as well as from the Bonapartist or plebiscitary Right represented not only by Bonapartism properly
so-called, but also by fascism and Gaullism:

> Other authors distinguish two Rights: radical and conserva-
> tive, and two Lefts, progressive and revolutionary. Others
> hold that there is only a single (eternal or sublime) tradi-
> tional Right and four Lefts: authoritarian-nationalist, liberal-
> bourgeois, anarcho-libertarian, and socialist-Marxist. Still
> others mark out a single reactionary Right and two Lefts,
> bourgeois and totalitarian. Finally, there are some who think
> there are a dozen tendencies: six Rights and six Lefts.[57]

Marc Crapez for his part distinguishes an egalitarian Left, a fra-
ternitarian Left, a liberal Left, a liberal Right, a conservative
Right, and a reactionary right.[58] In 1999, the journal *Eléments*
even identified 36 "families of the Right," each of which can be
described by certain watchwords, references, theoreticians, writers, films, and so on.[59]

On the Left, Jacques Julliard discerns four principal families:
the liberal Left, the Jacobin Left, the collectivist Left, and the libertarian Left. The liberal Left mainly favors a certain culture of
government. It advocates for the market economy, the separation of powers, the ideology of the rights of man, and the distinction between civil society and the state. It is distinct from Right-
wing liberalism only by its principled attachment to the concept
of equality. The Jacobin Left also favors a "society of individuals" but insists on "republican" values at the same time. It
preaches civic virtue, gives the state a prominent role, and is in-
stinctively hostile to "communitarianism," regionalism, and decentralization. It strongly professes secularism, a single national

---

[57] Arnaud Imatz, *Droite/gauche: pour sortir de l'équivoque*, 23.

[58] Marc Crapez, *La Gauche réactionnaire. Mythes de la plèbe et de la race
dans le sillage des Lumières* [*The Reactionary Left: Myths of the Plebians and
Race in the Wake of the Enlightenment*] (Paris: Berg International, 1997).

[59] Alain de Benoist, Charles Charpentier, Michel Marmin, and Gré-
gory Pons, "Les 36 familles de droite" ["The 36 Families of the Right"],
Éléments, February 1999, 24–32.

form of education, regional *Gleichschaltung*, and the one and in-divisible republic ("unity is the philosophical and political name of centralization," says Julliard). The collectivist Left, which is not historically limited to the Communist Party, is distinguished from the Jacobin Left in that it believes in the power of organiza-tion, rejects the idea of a general reconciliation under the auspi-ces of procedural reason, and remains convinced that the antag-onism between the world of capital and the world of labor is ir-reducible. The libertarian Left, the Left's least familiar form (it has never had legislative representation), goes back at least to Proudhon. It does not reject order but power ("The highest per-fection of society," writes Proudhon, "is found in the union of order and anarchy," proof that in his eyes these terms are not incompatible). Hostile to parties and intellectuals, it puts all its confidence in the ability of producers to organize themselves on the basis of freely negotiated contracts.

None of these typologies is without interest, but none suc-ceeds in "explaining the complexity of possible combinations and alliances within a constellation of elements between which movement is continuous."[60] Their very diversity—and their con-tradictions—show that none is a permanently valid truth. At best, they can help us better understand the disposition of forces at a given moment. At bottom, the categories that flow from them remain problematic, and are inevitably oversimplifications. Jacques Julliard recognizes this in his book on the varieties of the Left when he tries to discern "aggregates" that unite—e.g. collec-tivism, traditionalism, and fascism (those who above all want to avoid a society only formed of rights-bearing individuals); Jaco-binism and Bonapartism (those who make the state the founder and organizer of the social bond); or Left-liberalism, Orleanism, libertarianism, and Christian Democracy (those who share a similar distrust of the state and have confidence in civil society's capacity to resolve its own problems). "There are now Jacobins of the Left and extreme Left, but also of the Right and extreme Right," he observes. This demonstrates well the relative charac-ter of any typology.

---

[60] Arnaud Imatz, *Droite/gauche: pour sortir de l'équivoque*, 32.

So there is no eternal Left or Right, nor any man of the Left or Right constituted from all eternity. Left and Right are labels that do not rigorously correspond to distinct ideas or different strategies of action. They are certainly not insignificant, but they cannot be dissociated from particular *topoi*. If circumstances change, if the relations of *topos* to *topos* are overturned, the representation of the political system as a binary axis becomes unable to account for the situation.

"I deny that there exist 'permanent values of the Right' and 'immortal principles of the Left,'" concludes Arnaud Imatz:

> I am not unaware that numerous politicians and journalists of the Left (and of the Left of the Left) and of the Right (and of the Right of the Right) cling desperately to the old dyad as to a sacred relic, but I think they are mistaken. . . . The constant ideological back-and-forth in the course of the years . . . demonstrates that this obsessive dichotomy does not in any way correspond to any intangible opposition between two kinds of temperament, character, or sensibility; they are not inalterable essences, original and absolutely irreducible data of public life; there is no eternal definition of Right and Left valid for all times and in all places. Right and Left are relative positions; each clarifies and explains the other. They are the result of contingent situations.[61]

In 1955, in *The Opium of the Intellectuals*, Raymond Aron already characterized the concepts of Left and Right as "equivocal." Since then, there has been no lack of observers and authors to observe that this dyad, which has been so widely employed, no longer means anything. Regarding the Left/Right distinction, described by Costanzo Preve as "an artificial prosthesis of political science,"[62] Jean Baudrillard writes: "If one day the political imagination, demand, and will have a chance to recover, it can

---

[61] Arnaud Imatz, "Le clivage droite/gauche en question," 16.

[62] Constanzo Preve, "Une discussion pour l'instant interminable," 2–15.

only be on the basis of the radical abolition of this fossilized distinction that has invalidated and disavowed itself over the course of decades, and that is only held together today by complicity in corruption."[63] "For a long time now," states Cornelius Castoriadis, "the Left/Right divide in France and elsewhere has no longer corresponded to the great problems of our time or to radically opposed political choices."[64] For his part, Régis Debray observes: "When there are no more differences between Left and Right than between the services of a nationalized bank and a private bank, or between the news program of a public network and a commercial network, we can, with no cause for regret, get by without either, and, who knows, perhaps even without realizing it."[65]

We seem to have reached this point, and it gives one the impression of the end of an age. "The political form of modernity is exhausted, because it has run its course," thinks Serge Latouche:

> The Left and Right have essentially achieved what they set out to do. The game of alternation has succeeded extraordinarily well. The enlightened Right and the Left claim the Enlightenment's heritage, but neither claims it entirely. Each has seen part of its program realized. The Left, whose imagination is attached to the Enlightenment's radical side, is in love with progress, science, and technology; from Condorcet to Saint-Simon, we find these same themes. The liberal and enlightened Right, from Montesquieu to Tocqueville, exalts individual freedom and economic competition. The Left demands welfare for all, the right to growth, and the right to enjoy the fruits of one's undertakings. The modern state has realized all of these

---

[63] Jean Baudrillard, *De l'exorcisme en politique ou la conjuration des imbéciles* [*On Exorcism in Politics or the Conspiracy of Fools*] (Paris: Sens et Tonka, 1998), 19–20.

[64] "Castoriadis, un déçu du gauche-droite" ["Castoriadis, Disappointed with the Left-Right"], *Le Monde*, July 12, 1986.

[65] Régis Debray, *Que vive la République* [*That the Republic May Live*] (Paris: Odile Jacob, 1989).

things, albeit not without jolts and crises.[66]

Deep social transformations induced by changes in the capitalist system are most responsible for rendering the Left/Right distinction obsolete. But we also see that all great events cut transversally across all political families. Whether the question is the Gulf War, the intervention of NATO forces in the Balkans, negotiations within the framework of the projected Transatlantic Treaty, the reunification of Germany and its consequences, the attitude to be adopted with regard to Vladimir Putin's Russia, the debate on the construction of Europe and the common currency, controversies with regard to ecology, Islam, secularism, cultural identities, or biotechnologies—all the debates that have taken place in these last years have produced divisions irreducible to the traditional divides. The fracture lines are henceforward transversal: they run through the Left as well as the Right. Henceforth they sketch out new divisions.

Born of modernity, the Left/Right divide is disappearing along with it. Only those who fail to understand that the world has changed, and that obsolete conceptual tools no longer allow us to analyze it, still cling to this divide for reasons of habit, convenience, laziness, or self-interest. In the domain of public opinion, the concepts of Left and Right can still create illusions because they continue to form part of political and parliamentary language, which uses them as mantras in the hope of triggering conditioned reflexes. Then people have recourse to phantasmagorical foils[67] (an anti-fascism without fascism, an anti-Communism without Communism), while those who notice the end of the traditional divide are criticized for "deliberately creating confusion" or are accused of muddying the waters for their own

---

[66] Serge Latouche, "Le MAUSS est-il apolitique?" ["Is MAUSS Apolitical?"], *La Revue du MAUSS*, third trimester 1991, 70–71. [MAUSS is the French acronym of the Anti-utilitarian Movement in the Social Sciences. — Trans.]

[67] "*Repoussoirs*." A *repoussoir* is a pictorial device used especially in Baroque painting that places an object such as a curtain or tree in the foreground extremely close to the picture plane, to create a sense of depth. — Trans.

obscure purposes. In the world of politicians, the theatrical use of the Left/Right opposition in fact aims principally at masking the convergence of camps whose identities have been lost. Arnaud Imatz is not wrong to see in this a "debilitating myth designed to break popular resistance to an oligarchy's crystallization."[68] All this will only go on for just so long.

---

[68] Imatz, *Droite/gauche: pour sortir de l'équivoque*, 13–14.

GOVERNING WITHOUT
THE PEOPLE

Books on the crisis or dysfunction of democracy have been multiplying for some time now.[1] Their authors belong to different political families, but many agree on at least one point that seems to serve as their central theme: the idea that we have already passed into a realm beyond the democratic model that gradually came to prevail during the modern age. The most frequently expressed idea is that we are entering into a "post-democratic" regime that might just as well be defined as the regime of postmodernity. For example, Matthieu Baumier writes, "My thesis is that democracy, if not dead, has undergone a rapid evolution, that it has transformed itself into something other than what we have been familiar with: *post-democracy*."[2]

---

[1] To cite only a few recent titles: Daniel Innerarity, *La Démocratie sans l'État* [*Democracy Without the State*] (Flammarion); Daniel Bougnoux, *La Crise de la représentation* [*The Crisis of Representation*] (La Découverte); Bernard Stiegler, *La Télécratie contre la démocratie* [*Telecracy Against Democracy*] (Flammarion); Raymond Boudon, *Renouveler la démocratie* [*Renewing Democracy*] (Odile Jacob); Robert Kurz, *Critique de la démocratie balistique* [*Critique of Balistic Democracy*] (Mille et une Nuits); Matthieu Baumier, *La Démocratie totalitaire* [*Totalitarian Democracy*] (Presses de la Renaissance); Robert Charvin, *Vers la post-démocratie* [*Toward Post-Democracy*] (Le Temps des cerises); Samuel Pelras, *La Démocratie libérale en procès* [*Liberal Democracy on Trial*] (L'Harmattan), etc. *Cf.* also Jean-Pierre Le Goff, *La Démocratie post-totalitaire* [*Post-Totalitarian Democracy*] (Paris: La Découverte, 2002) and Marcel Gauchet, *Comprendre le malheur français* [*Understanding What Is Wrong with France*] (with Éric Conan and François Azouvi) (Paris: Stock, 2016).

[2] Matthieu Baumier, *La Démocratie totalitaire. Penser la modernité post-démocratique* [*Totalitarian Democracy: Interpreting Post-Democratic Modernity*] (Paris: Presses de la Renaissance, 2007), 11. *Cf.* also Colin Crouch, *Post-Democracy* (Cambridge: Polity Press, 2004); and Guy Hermet, "La gouvernance serait-elle le nom de l'après-démocratie?" ["Is Governance the Name of Post-Democracy?"] in Guy Hermet, Ali Kazancigil, and Jean-François Prudhomme, eds., *La Gouvernance. Un concept et*

The most visible symptoms of this crisis have often been described: the worldwide discrediting of the political class, abstention from voting, protest voting, a growing chasm between those on top and those below, and a feeling of democratic dispossession. Regarding all these points we are in the presence of pronounced tendencies that are getting stronger.

Asked in the autumn of 2005 about their perception of the political class, 71% of Frenchmen admitted to having a "poor opinion" of their leaders, 76% stated they have "no confidence" in them, and 49% judge them "corrupt."[3] According to another more recent poll, 53% of Frenchmen think democracy today is "not working well or not working at all."[4] Finally, according to a third poll, nearly seven Frenchmen in ten say they have confidence "neither in the Right nor in the Left to govern the country."[5] Thus, we are confronted with a massive loss of credibility concerning men first of all, but which also extends to institutions. This loss of confidence is expressed both by rising abstention rates and by disaffection with the large political parties, which are increasingly becoming mere electoral committees. Citizens are losing hope in the capacity of a political class that continues to present objectives as achievable but never achieves them (full employment, for example). People's attitudes commonly oscillate between lack of interest and rejection, abstention and systematic opposition.

In the presidential election of April 2002, less than half of Frenchmen voted in both rounds. Moreover, in the first round 64% of voters chose neither Chirac nor Jospin. Twenty years earlier, in the first round of the presidential election of 1981, the "antisystem" candidates received only 2% of the vote; they reached 34% in 2002. In 2007 and 2012, the figures were scarcely different. The result is that today's "majorities" are the expression of barely

---

ses applications [*Governance: A Concept and its Applications*] (Paris: Karthala, 2005), 17–47.

   [3] CSA-Le Parisien poll, October 6–7, 2005.

   [4] TNT-Sofres poll carried out March 8–9, 2006.

   [5] Barometre politique français (Centre for Political Research at Sciences Po/Ministry of the Interior), published May 17, 2006.

a quarter of the "sovereign people."

Another poll carried out in 2006 shows that six Frenchmen out of ten are no longer able to tell the Left from the Right. This is obviously a consequence of the recentering of party programs, which is itself merely one aspect of the process of uniformization of political discourse involving, really, its neutralization. This recentering has multiple causes, but results above all from an implicit consensus regarding social ends that prevents any general questioning of the system. Thus, writes Robert Katz, "no opposition party attributes social problems to the political system *per se* or the mode of production on which that system is based, but always to their adversaries currently holding the reins of power and their 'bad' policies."[6] Alternatives thereby become impossible (replaced by mere alternation), and a growing number of voters realize that elections are only free insofar as they assure the reproduction under interchangeable labels of the same dominant class. In other words, the political system is programmed in advance so that only those who are certain to change nothing about the system can win. "Pluralist elections," writes Robert Charvin, "are only admissible if the voters do not stray outside the implicitly determined framework; they must assure political continuity by keeping variation within a narrow range."[7] The advertised pluralism is just an illusion.

---

[6] Robert Kurz, *Avis aux naufragés. Chroniques du capitalisme mondialisé en crise* [*Advice to the Shipwrecked: Chronicle of a Globalized Capitalism in Crisis*], trans. Olivier Galtier *et al.* (Paris: Lignes-Manifeste, 2004), 49.

[7] Robert Charvin, *Vers la post-démocratie?* [*Towards Post-Democracy?*] (Pantin: Le Temps des cerises), 45. The obligation incumbent since 1976 upon candidates for the presidential election, even if they are already leaders of parties representing more than 10 or 15% of the electorate, of finding 500 mayors disposed to sponsor their candidacies draws democracy in an oligarchic direction, since it amounts to according a right of veto to local officials. To give just one example: a CSA poll carried out on January 4, 2006, indicated that 26% of Frenchmen wished that Jean-Philippe Allenbach, founding President of the Federalist Party, which adheres to the ideas of Guy Héraud and Alexandre Marc, might take part in the presidential election of 2007. The same poll revealed an intention of voting for him of about 12%. Unable to obtain the 500 sig-

The discrediting of the system never appeared more obviously than during the referendum on the projected European Constitution held on May 29, 2005. Eleven years before "Brexit," the
major government parties, unanimous in support of a "yes"
vote, were incapable of convincing the people of the well-
foundedness of their choice even as their recommendation was
relayed via all the media giants. The "no" vote that finally prevailed was essentially delivered by the "anti-system" political
forces that had decided to react against what seemed to them an
agreement among the elites to impose liberalism on the people.
Paradoxically, this referendum was organized by political leaders who immediately let it be known that the question was only
being posed as a pure formality, since one could only reasonably
and sensibly respond with a "yes." They were therefore very
surprised to observe that the people considered it a real question, and that one could just as well respond with a "no," as the
majority did.[8]

This gap between the voters and their representatives is
matched by an obvious sociological fracture, since it appeared
all the larger where the voters' social situation was difficult or
precarious. "The feeling of experiencing a social rise or decline,"
notes François Miquet-Marty, "henceforth explains the vote better than belonging to this or that social category."[9] The perception of social identity can thus increasingly be derived from the
subjective evaluation of an individual's situation.

In his Nobel Prize acceptance speech delivered in Stockholm
on December 7, 2005, the dramatist Harold Pinter declared: "The

---

natures, Allenbach was unable to run.

[8] The polemics that developed in 2006 concerning the projected
Bolkenstein directive were no less revealing. They originated when
voters realized that a European Commissioner could, on his own authority and without any debate, make decisions involving consequen-
tial social and economic regulations. This confirmed that the European
project, with no democratic legitimacy, was moving in a direction
whose correctness could not be questioned.

[9] François Miquet-Marty, "Les quatre crises de la représentation politique" ["The Four Crises of Political Representation"], *Esprit*, February
2006, 83.

majority of politicians, on the evidence available to us, are interested not in truth but in power and maintenance of that power. To maintain that power it is essential that people remain in ignorance, that they live in ignorance of the truth, even the truth of their own lives." This viewpoint summarizes the most widespread opinion fairly well. Everything indicates that what has disappeared is the relation of confidence between rulers and ruled. Now, where this confidence no longer exists, no consent is possible, for the former is a necessary condition of the latter.

So, as has been confirmed by many observers, we are confronted with a major crisis of representation. This should lead us to ask ourselves about the limits of representative democracy, but also about the relations between democracy and representation.

As Montesquieu reminds us, Antiquity was unfamiliar with any concept of representation.[10] That concept appeared at the very beginning of the Middle Ages, when it was formed within the domain of public law under significant influence from private law (representation of the father by his son, or the son by his father, of the slave by his master, of a monastery by its abbot, etc.). Beginning in the eighteenth century, the idea became a key concept for the functioning of "liberal representative" regimes. Montesquieu again is one of the first to defend the argument, made thousands of times since, according to which the people, although not well suited to making its own decisions, is perfectly capable of choosing its representatives:

There was a great fault in most ancient republics: that the people had the right to take active resolutions, and which demand some execution, something of which they are entirely incapable. The people should only enter into the government to choose its representatives, something well within its capacity. . . . It is important that the people do by

---

[10] "The ancients were unfamiliar with government based upon a body of nobles, and still less with government based on a legislature consisting of representatives of the nation." Montesquieu, *Spirit of the Laws*, XI, 8.

way of a representative all that it cannot do by itself.[11]

Let us note that the argument is not that within collectivities of a certain size, the exercise of democracy is technically difficult or even impossible. Instead, the very aptitude of the people to make decisions is being questioned, without taking the trouble to explain how the people, legally declared incapable of deciding for itself, can suddenly and magically become capable of choosing those who will have the job of deciding in its place.

For other authors, such as Benjamin Constant, the necessity of representation is derived from the division of labor. The thesis is in any case of liberal origin, since it derived from the representation of interests in private law. A great part of the non-liberal Right will rally to this position later on, often by way of elitism, when democracy has entered into people's habits. When democracy is summarily defined as consecrating the "law of number," representative democracy will be perceived as a lesser evil, since it amounts to drastically reducing the number of deciders.

Rousseau defended the converse of Montesquieu's thesis. An advocate of the imperative mandate, he maintained that a people could only lose its sovereignty the moment it was turned over to representatives. The people must not allow its representatives to decide in its place, says Rousseau, for if it "promises simply to obey, it thereby loses its character as a people; from the moment there is a master, there is no more sovereign, and from that time on the political body is destroyed."[12] The observation is not without its logic. But this point of view did not win out. On August 26, 1789, the celebrated Declaration of the Rights of Man and of the Citizen is passed by vote of the "representatives of the French people," and during the whole Revolution, the most respected title will be that of "people's representative."

From that time forth, Western democracies have nearly all been representative, constitutional, parliamentary, and liberal. The part played by the direct exercise of sovereignty is slim to none, the essential part of the political game being entrusted to

---

[11] Montesquieu, *Spirit of the Laws*, XI, 6 and II, 2.

[12] Jean-Jacques Rousseau, *The Social Contract*, Book I, chapter 1.

representatives, and the prerogative of citizens being limited to designating them in the course of elections. The imperative mandate, consisting of giving representatives precise instructions that they must respect on pain of revocation, does not exist here — it has consistently been prohibited in France since the Revolution, especially on the grounds that one elected "by the nation" also represents those who did not vote for him — public opinion only ensuring a very hypothetical control of representatives in view of the accounts that they are willing to render regarding the mandates conferred upon them. From the liberal point of view, the representatives are perfectly justified even in contradicting the will of those who elected them, provided that the formal procedural rules of their election continue to be respected.[13] This is why, according to Bernard Manin, these democracies ought rather to bear the name of "representative governments." (Raymond Aron for his part spoke of "pluralistic constitutional regimes.")

Proudhon accepts representation, but on the express condition that techniques be employed allowing the "organization of democracy," specifically to realize as much as possible an identity of interests between voters and representatives, rulers and ruled, in the absence of which this democracy would only be "mystification" or "tyranny":

> If the great act whose object is to produce national representation consists in uniting, once every three or five years, a bunch of designated citizens and having them name a deputy with a blank-check mandate, and who by virtue of this mandate represents not only those who gave him their vote but even those who voted against him, . . . if this is what is understood by universal suffrage, there is nothing to hope for, and our political system is a mystification and a tyranny.[14]

---

[13] Cf. William L. McBride, "The End of Liberal Democracy as We Have Known It?," *Synthesis Philosophica*, 2005, no. 2, 461–70.

[14] Pierre-Joseph Proudhon, *Oeuvres completes*, vol. 13 (Geneva: Slatkine, 1982), 275–76.

This is why Proudhon rejects the idea of a general mandate granted by the people and wants to replace it with a series of special delegations that seem to him all the more justified given that, in his eyes, the people "is not a homogeneous, compact, undifferentiated entity."[15]

Not only does representation not form an intrinsic part of the concept of democracy, but many authors think that democracies become less democratic as they become more representative. Notably, this is the opinion of Carl Schmitt who, as we know, also defended the thesis of the fundamental incompatibility between liberalism and democracy.

In his *Constitutional Theory*,[16] where he distinguishes three different forms of representation, Schmitt emphasizes that the form corresponding to the liberal conception of the state is directly borrowed from the techniques of private law. The representation of the electorate results from the adoption in the political sphere of the mandate model, allowing the representation (*Vertretung*) of private interests, either individual or collective.[17] To

---

[15] Proudhon, *Oeuvres completes*, vol. 13, 280.

[16] Carl Schmitt, *Théorie de la Constitution*, trans. Lilyane Deroche (Paris: PUF, 1993).

[17] We will note, however, that a mandatary is normally supposed to be accountable to the person who mandates him and can be recalled in the course of his mandate. This is not the case with a parliamentary representative who, not being subject to an imperative mandate, cannot be recalled over the course of his term of office, is not accountable to his voters, and enjoys an absolute immunity for the legal acts he performs in the exercise of his office. It is with a view to this difference between the deputy and the mandatary in the sense of private law that Carré de Malberg was able to say that in the course of elections, citizens do not so much delegate a power to their representatives as confer a status upon them (whence they derive their power). He writes:

The deputy is neither the mandatary nor the delegate nor the representative of his voters. He is elected and not commissioned by them. The same idea has been expressed by saying that what the people give those they elect in an election is not a mandate but their confidence. To characterize elections as an act of confidence is also to note that on the voters' part it is an act of surren-

this liberal conception of representation he opposes the Hobbesian conception (*Repräsentation*) where the people's political unity must be represented personally "as a whole."

So it is important when we speak of the "crisis of representation" to understand that, from the beginning, representation has above all been a means of preventing the people from expressing themselves directly, and that the crisis in question apparently results from the people beginning to perceive this. That is what Jacques Rancière observes when he writes:

> Representation is not a system invented to relieve inconveniences caused by growing populations. It is not an adaptation of democracy to modern times or larger areas. It is a form of oligarchy plain and simple, a representation of minorities entitled to occupy themselves with public affairs. . . . The assumption that assimilates democracy to the representative form of government resulting from elections is very recent in history. In its origin, representation was the exact opposite of democracy. No one was unaware of this at the time of the American and French revolutions. The Founding Fathers and a number of their French imitators saw in it precisely the means whereby an elite could in fact exercise power in the name of the people, power that the elite is obliged to recognize belongs to the people, but that the people cannot exercise without ruining the very principle of government. . . . "Representative democracy" may sound like a pleonasm today, but at first it was an oxymoron.[18]

---

der rather than an act of mastery. (*Contribution à la théorie générale de l'État* [*Contribution to the General Theory of the State*], vol. 2 [Paris: Sirey, 1922], no. 347)

[18] Jacques Rancière, *La Haine de la démocratie* [*Hatred of Democracy*] (Paris: La Fabrique, 2005), 60–61. Cf. also Pierre Rosanvallon, *Le Peuple introuvable. Histoire de la représentation démocratique en France* [*The Elusive People: History of Democratic Representation in France*] (Paris: Gallimard, 1998).

Representation is by its very essence an oligarchic system, for it inevitably results in the formation of a dominant group whose members coopt one another into defending their own interests, first and foremost. The entire "elitist" school of political science (Pareto, Michels, Mosca, Wright Mills), moreover, has demonstrated how the system of representative and parliamentary democracy unavoidably leads the representatives to constitute themselves as an elite or oligarchy that gradually becomes more autonomous from those who are represented. This is one reason why, in a famous text that first appeared in February 1950 and was republished in 2006, Simone Weil advocated the suppression of political parties on the grounds that a party "is an organization constructed to exercise collective pressure over thought," and that "the only goal of every political party is its own growth, and that without any limit."[19]

Distrust of representation, moreover, was one reason for the hostility to universal suffrage shown in the nineteenth century by the revolutionary and libertarian tendencies within the workers' movement. "The Elector: Behold the Enemy!" proclaimed Libertad in 1906 by means of a poster. In April 1848, Proudhon declared that "the surest means of getting a people to lie is the institution of universal suffrage." In his introduction to *Reflections on Violence* (1908), Georges Sorel wrote: "All deputies say that nothing more closely resembles a representative of the bourgeoisie than a representative of the proletariat." In democracy reduced to representation, the people can just as well expropriate itself of its own character as a people by means of suffrage. "Democratic method then consists in the consensual renunciation of democracy as content," remarks Costanzo Preve.[20]

---

[19] Simone Weil, "Note sur la suppression générale des partis politiques" ["Notes on the Universal Suppression of Political Parties"] [1940], *Écrits de Londres* [*London Writings*] (Paris: Climats, 2006), 35.

[20] Costanzo Preve, *Il popolo al potere. Il problema della democrazia nei suoi aspetti storici e filosofici* [*The People in Power: The Problem of Democracy in its Historical and Philosophical Aspects*] (Casalecchio: Arianna, 2006), 203. Cf. also Pierre Rosanvallon, *Le Sacre du citoyen. Histoire du suffrage universel en France* [*The Crowning of the Citizen: History of Universal Suffrage in France*] (Paris: Gallimard, 1992).

Voting in fact is never anything but a technique of aggregating momentary preferences under the sanction of majority rule. And for this reason the establishment of universal suffrage has never resulted in the people's access to political sovereignty, i.e., to the sovereign capacity for decision.

Besides, the "people" has been considerably transformed over the course of the last few decades, especially as regards class membership. The near disappearance of "electoral families" of the sociological or religious type, where one voted regularly in the same way from generation to generation, has had the consequence of making the vote more volatile, the same voters successively giving their support to the most different candidates (or even successively supporting all the parties, still without being satisfied). Today, mere socio-professional belonging is not a determining element for electoral behavior any more than religious conviction.

Social classes have certainly not disappeared (in France, the working class still includes six million persons), but they have been restructured in complex strata and lost a good part of their identity, swept away as they have been since the age of the Fordist compromise that led to the middle classes' inflation, in a vast movement of homogenization of desires or needs in which everyone wants more or less the same thing, but without the same means of getting it.[21] Deprived of their *habitus*, the way of life and even language that used to be specific to them, the popular strata have largely lost consciousness of themselves, which correspondingly restricts their capacity for mobilization. This loss of orientation is heightened today by the threats of downward social mobility weighing on the middle class.[22]

---

[21] While the Fordist compromise undeniably homogenized society by integrating the masses into consumption, it did not realize equality of conditions. Rather, it offered a higher standard of living to the greatest number in order to allow an economy to function that permitted a small number to benefit from a standard of living immeasurably higher and thus to reinforce its grip on society.

[22] Cf. Jean-Noël Chopart and Claude Martin, eds., *Que reste-t-il des classes sociales?* [*What Remains of Social Classes?*] (Rennes: Éditions de l'École nationale de la santé publique, 2004); Jean Lojkine, *L'Adieu à la*

Popular demands have thereby been transformed. Christopher Lasch already remarked that "not only do the new social movements—feminism, gay rights, welfare rights, agitation against racial discrimination—have nothing in common, but their only coherent demand aims at inclusion in the dominant structures rather than at a revolutionary transformation of social relations."[23] In fact, these movements do not aspire at all to a change in society, but on the contrary to ever greater integration into the system already in place. The excluded, one might say, reveal themselves as "included" in their very manner of denouncing exclusion. Demanding rights or recognition from the state, they become at once the state's creditors and debtors.

This abandonment of any revolutionary perspective goes hand-in-hand with a sectoralization and "privatization" of struggles that contrasts with the social movements of the past. We can take the measure of this change by remembering that originally, as Jacques Rancière reminds us,

> the dispute regarding salaries was first of all a dispute seeking to deprivatize the salarial relation, to affirm that it was neither the relation of a master to a domestic servant, nor a mere contract signed on a case-by-case basis between two private individuals, but a public concern relating to a collective, and consequently implying forms of collective action, public discussion, and legislative rule. The "right to

---

classe moyenne [*Farewell to the Middle Class*] (Paris: La Dispute, 2005); Louis Chauvel, *Les Classes moyennes à la dérive* [*The Middle Classes Adrift*] (Paris: Seuil, 2006); Louis Maurin and Patrick Savidan, eds., *L'État des inégalités en France 2007* [*The State of Inequalities in France 2007*] (Paris: Belin, 2006); and Louis Chauvel, *La Spirale du déclassement. Essai sur la société des illusions* [*The Vortex of Downward Mobility: Essay on the Society of Illusions*] (Paris: Seuil, 2016).

[23] Christopher Lasch, *The Revolt of the Elites and the Betrayal of Democracy* (New York: Norton, 1995), 27. Cf. also Serge Denis, *L'Action politique des mouvements sociaux d'aujourd'hui. Le déclin du politique comme procès de politisation?* [*The Political Action of Today's Social Movements: The Decline of Politics as a Process of Politization?*] (Sainte-Foy, Québec: Presses de l'Université Laval, 2006).

work" demanded by the workers' movements in the nine-teenth century first of all meant this: not the demand for assistance from a "welfare state" into which one has sought to assimilate, but the constitution of work as a structure of collective life freed of the mere reign of private interests and imposing limits upon the naturally limitless process of accumulating wealth.[24]

Modernity, born of industrial capitalism, established itself as a movement overturning the society of orders, rent, and status. Today we are watching an overturning of this overturning. The tertiarization of societies and the financialization of capital (and private estates) mean that wealth no longer comes fundamental-ly from materially productive work. The economy has become "immaterial," and wealth is henceforward obtained by stock purchases, dividends, and monetary movements. (In the United States, Bill Gates and Walmart have replaced Ford and General Motors.) At the same time, larger states redistribute 15–20% of their budget in the form of financial income. Under such condi-tions, everyone aspires to recognition of a status. Whereas social conflicts used to be caused by antagonisms of production, today, having departed from the domain of class struggle, they gravi-tate around the defense of acquired positions and the demand for statutory rights. Teachers, nurses, farmers, railway workers, intermittent workers in the performing arts, and Airbus employ-ees no longer demonstrate to "defend workers" (the working class) but only to defend their own interests in order to be guaran-teed employment or better work conditions — i.e., a better status.

These demands are therefore no longer part of a fundamen-tally oppositional attitude toward the dominant order; on the contrary, they reinforce public power by providing it with an ever-growing share of manna for redistribution. As Ahmed Henni writes:

Discourse is no longer based upon identifying workers as producers of value harmed by their condition as wage

---

[24] Jacques Rancière, *La Haine de la démocratie*, 63–64.

earners. It centers upon the idea that work of whatever sort is a status that deserves consideration and respect. . . . No one struggles any longer to get out of this status but to remain in it—not get fired—and to extract statutory rights unrelated to the rules or antagonisms of capitalism, or any aspirations toward the free development of the individual by means of work. . . . Social struggles are no longer essentially circumscribed within the sphere of material production and aimed at a better financial distribution of the wealth produced between bosses and workers. Such struggles do not so much oppose social groups as express the demand of one group for an improvement in its situation—not to the detriment of another group, but in search of greater social recognition involving better financial returns.[25]

The Left, as has already been said, has cut itself off from the people today.[26] As the Communist Party becomes more social-democratic, the Socialist Party has ceased to affirm itself as socialist, limiting itself to wanting to temper the market society by placing greater weight on improving public safety, as the classic concepts regarding capital's technical and organic composition (labor power, accumulation, surplus value) disappear from its discourse and practice. Under the pretext of "realism" and in conformity with the demands of the "modern world," the great majority of socialists adhere to all the canons of managerial orthodoxy, while politics becomes nothing more than a set of practices and institutional games meant to conquer, exercise, and preserve a form of power whose center and peripheries are unstable.

Social democracy, ever since its creation, has proposed an alliance between working parties and certain other social actors

---

[25] Ahmed Henni, "Fin de la modernité? Une mutation capitaliste: le retour des sociétés de statut et de rente" ["End of Modernity? A Capitalist Mutation: The Return of Societies of Status and Rent"], in *Les Temps modernes*, September–October 2006, 200–202.

[26] Cf. "Mais où est passée la gauche?" ["Where Has the Left Gone?"], *Éléments*, no. 99, November 2000, 23–44.

because it thought, on the basis of an analysis of social classes, that such an alliance would allow better mobilization regarding the social question and democratic reforms. Socialists today have abandoned that vision because they, too, have become incapable of articulating individual revolt and social mobilization in relation to any genuine collective project. As Roland Guillon observes, "Everything happens as if the directing thought of the Socialist Party were based on the paradigms of territorial governance or expertise instead of a frontal confrontation with one essential aspect of any social reality connected with capitalism: the tensions between the individual and the collective."[27]

The rise of "social" liberalism has done the rest. Having left the field open to liberals in the economic and social domains, the "caviar Left," i.e., the liberal and Leftist *grande bourgeoisie*, being as morally permissive as it is indifferent to social questions, keeps its distance from popular milieus in which it no longer recognizes itself.[28] "The caviar Left lives geographically far from the poor classes," admits Laurent Joffrin. By a strange process, it also decided to cut itself off from them politically. This occurred by means of a cultural and ideological operation displaying a tragic frivolity: the spiriting away of the people."[29]

Alexander Zinoviev designated this New Class a "suprasociety"; in Russia today, it calls itself the "creative class." Faced with a people it both fears and despises, it constitutes an oligarchic authority concerned mainly with preserving its privileges and reserving access to power for those who come from its own ranks.[30]

---

[27] Roland Guillon, *Les Avatars d'une pensée dirigeante. Le cas du parti socialiste* [*The Avatars of Ruling Thought: The Case of the Socialist Party*] (Paris: L'Harmattan, 2005), 40.

[28] The same phenomenon has occurred in the United States, where for some time we have been witnessing a real transformation of the Democratic Party. Under the influence of political correctness and rampant matriarchy, it now devotes itself to a lifestyle politics that amounts to abandoning the people to the Republicans.

[29] Laurent Joffrin, *Histoire de la gauche caviar* [*History of the Caviar Left*] (Paris: Robert Laffont, 2006).

[30] Guy Harmet writes: "According to this conception, we must re-

This contempt for the people, of course, is nourished by a critique of "populism" assimilated to any and every form of demagogy and mass "irrationalism." Having become a political insult, populism is presented as a sort of permanent "infantile disorder" of democracy with a view both to pejoritizing and discrediting it. Recourse to the term "populism" thus furnishes a theoretical, if not learned, way of justifying dismissal of the people.

In France, the rallying of a large part of the old working class to the National Front (NF) played a decisive role in this respect. In effect, it allowed the Left to repudiate the people on the pretext that it "thinks badly," whereas a loudly broadcast but conventional anti-racism allowed it to mask its own ideological meanderings. Anti-LePenism was thus substituted for anti-capitalism, a valuable alibi allowing them to relegate the social question to the background at the very moment it was reemerging with a strength unseen since the post-war era. That the popular classes vote for the NF makes it possible to hold them responsible for the rise of a party regularly characterized as morally unworthy and politically nefarious. These classes can then be discredited by contagion. As Annie Collovald writes, "Only socially illegitimate voters can identify with the illegitimate ideas of this party."[31] By way of contrast, the affluent *grande bourgeoisie* sees itself

---

main as much as possible among ourselves, among competent, professional people, by removing troublemakers" ("Nous sommes en 1775. Gouvernance et après-démocratie" ["We Are Living in 1775 : Governance and Post-Democracy"], *Catholica*, Summer 2005, 12). *Cf.* also Nathalie Brion and Jean Brousse, *La Bulle. La France divorce de ses élite* [*The Bubble: France Divorces its Elites*] (Paris: La Table Ronde, 2006).

[31] Annie Collovald, "Le populisme: de la valorisation à la stigmatisation du populaire" ["Populism: From Valorization to Stigmatization of the Demotic"], *Hermes*, no. 42, 2005, 156. The author of an essay in which she disputes the label "national populist" given to the National Front, especially by Pierre-André Taguieff (*Le "populisme" du FN: un dangereux contresens* [*The "Populism" of the National Front: Dangerous Nonsense*] (Broissieux: Éditions du Croquant, 2004), Annie Collovald also reminds us that historically speaking, "populism" is a current clearly associated with the Left, and that the "appeal to the people" was originally "a strategy aiming to give authority and dignity to social

issued with a certificate of right-mindedness and moral superiority inherent in its class position. Protected by its standard of living, it is sheltered from the "bad ideas" in which the people take pleasure. At the same time, this allows them to pay no attention to cultural insecurity, social misery, the explosion of inequality, the effects of free trade, stock option scandals, and "golden parachutes."

More than ever, of course, this attitude masks a diffuse fear of the "dangerous classes." To fight populism is to ensure that the elites are not threatened by this people that must be neutralized. Such a procedure, writes Jacques Rancière,

> both masks and reveals the oligarchy's great wish: to govern without any people, i.e., without any division of the people; to govern without politics. . . . It allows them to interpret any movement of struggle against the depoliticization carried out in the name of historical necessity as a manifestation of a backward fraction of the population or of an obsolete ideology.[32]

This use of the term "populism," which resembles that of "an amulet used to conjure away evil spirits," has not escaped the attention of Laurent Joffrin, who observes:

> As soon as an idea does not have the establishment's endorsement, it is tossed aside under the slanderous label "populism." . . . A strange semantic reaction: the word being at once vague and very pejorative, it amounts to saying that any demand of the people is by definition illegitimate and dangerous. Any idea that comes from the people and displeases progressive elites is populist.[33]

---

groups excluded from political representation, and along with them, to secure a hearing for the social and political causes they defended" (*Le "populisme" du FN*, 159).

[32] Jacques Ranciere, *La Haine de la démocratie*, 88.

[33] Laurent Joffrin, *Histoire de la gauche caviar*.

Whence the question posed by Annie Collovald:

> Is not the stigmatization of the popular via the "populism of the National Front" the sign of a new intellectual and political configuration in which today's political elites (and their auxiliaries and advisors) no longer see the popular groups as a cause to be defended, but as a "classless people" that has become a problem to be solved?[34]

We know that, from the liberal point of view, democracy has never been characterized as the regime that allows the broadest popular participation. Such participation is, on the contrary, perceived as having more inconveniences than advantages. Thus, abstention is not viewed unfavorably by liberals who, in the past, always sought to restrict the citizens' political capacity whether by opposing the vote for women or by favoring property qualifications.

Today there are several ways of removing the people from politics. The most classic is of course recourse to the media and the entertainment business, television, and sports and shows, which obviously allow the people to be "diverted" in the Pascalian sense of the term. The media, moreover, never cease sanctifying the existing order by constantly giving us to understand that we live, if not in the best of all possible societies, at any rate in the least bad. Citizens are systematically diverted or conditioned to mask the obvious fact that matters are henceforward being decided without them.[35] Critical thought is thus weakened by removing its *raison d'être*. The increasing homogenization of ways of life—even as "pluralism" and "diversity" are everywhere celebrated—works in the same direction, for it leads the members of society to share the same desires and needs without the difference in their purchasing power altering anything about market demands.

---

[34] Annie Collovald, *Le "populisme" du FN*, 159.

[35] Cf. François Brune, *De l'idéologie, aujourd'hui* [*On Ideology Today*] (Lyon: Parangon, 2005), 141–45; "L'idéal démocratique dévoyé" ["The Democratic Ideal Gone Astray"], *Le Monde diplomatique*, May 1997.

As political life itself is assimilated to a market, and the citizens' votes become purchases, democracy naturally becomes the reign of the consumer "flipping" between party programs as he does between consumer goods or television channels. Individual participation in public life then comes about not by political involvement but through communion with a public opinion formed by the media, a forming that itself bears witness to the disappearance of any social body able to generate its own interpretation of current events. Media ideology is the vehicle of a representation of the world that is as homogeneous as it is politically correct, and that substitutes itself for the social conscience as a "false consciousness" of reality. The citizen-people is transformed

> into a people of passive and irresponsible spectators. The political spectacle masks basic problems, substitutes charm and personality for political programs, and numbs the capacity for reasoning and judgment for the benefit of emotional reactions and irrational feelings of attraction and antipathy. With media politics, the citizens are infantilized. They are no longer engaged in public life; they are alienated, manipulated by gadgets and images.[36]

This is something Silvio Berlusconi understood well. He twice became Prime Minister of his country, and his ideology, perfected within his private company, constantly relied on the

---

[36] Gilles Lipovetsky, *L'Empire de l'éphémère* [*The Empire of Fashion*] (Paris: Gallimard, 1987), 236. Christopher Lasch makes the same observation: "When politicians and administrators have no other aim than to sell their leadership to the public, they deprive themselves of intelligible standards by which to define the goals of specific policies or to evaluate success or failure" (*The Culture of Narcissism*, 78). On this subject cf. also Javier Barraycoa, *Du pouvoir dans la modernité et la postmodernité* [*Power in Modernity and Postmodernity*], trans. Emmanuel Albert (Paris: Hora Decima, 2005), 134–35; and Bernard Stiegler, *La télécratie contre la démocratie. Lettre ouverte aux représentants politiques* [*Telecracy Against Democracy: An Open Letter to Our Political Representatives*] (Paris: Flammarion, 2006).

language of management, i.e., on a collection of beliefs concerning economic efficiency as well as the techniques of a commercial television and spectator sports industry dealing in cheap
dreams. Not only did politics become with him a sort of continuation of seductive advertising by other means, but it was mainly with reference to his practice as a private entrepreneur that he
sought to legitimize himself as the CEO of "Italy incorporated."
"With his entry into politics," writes Pierre Musso, "Berlusconi
simply pushed commercial logic to its conclusion by treating the
citizen-voter as a telespectator-consumer, i.e., by managing his
passage from the shopping cart to the voting booth by way of
the small screen."[37]

Another way of diverting attention consists in rewriting social problems in terms of individual psychology in order to lose
sight of responsibilities or real causes. For the state, losing control of economic or financial activity over which it previously
had authority in effect makes it ever less capable of responding
to social demands. Whence the need to "psychologize" social
problems in individual terms, which allows the system in place
to treat them no longer in a properly political fashion but in a
humanitarian and moral fashion, at once compassionate and
lachrymose. In a society that proclaims its love of the poor with
all the greater strength the more of them it manufactures every

---

[37] Pierre Musso, "Le phénomene Berlusconi: ni populisme ni vidéo-
cratie, mais néo-politique" ["The Berlusconi Phenomenon: Neither Populism Nor Videocracy, but Neo-Politics"], *Hermes*, no. 42, 2005, 177.
He adds that

> The stainless smile and permanent tan of the *Cavaliere* go back to
> the playful creativity promoted by neomanagement. . . . His
> smile also covers grief: that of the "seriousness" of the state and
> its institutions, and social and cultural mediation originating in
> Fordist capitalism. This cult of the smile is one of the signs of tel-
> evisual and managerial training of the ideal body: young,
> sporty, happy, triumphant. . . . Berlusconi's wager is that of af-
> firming that the symbolic body in the age of neopolitics is no
> longer that of the state, but that of the CEO and the television
> host. (p. 178).

day, socialism in practice is gradually replaced by associative charity and the appeal to private generosity, punitive hygienics, and the recipes of self-management. Social struggles are then reduced to claims of victimhood, i.e., trying to collect dividends from the symbolic preeminence of victim status, with the individual who seeks to identify the parties responsible for his fate finally being referred back to himself.

Liberalism pushes naturally toward this subjectivization of social problems. Robert Kurz observes:

> The social system's dominant order was raised by [liberal ideology] to the rank of a law of nature above all critical evaluation, so the responsibility for any negative experience can only fall on individuals in the immediate framework of their lives. Everyone is therefore personally responsible for his own sufferings and misfortunes. . . . The system *per se* can never be guilty.[38]

"In sum," writes Zygmunt Bauman, "individuals are condemned to resolve the system's contradictions at the biographical level."[39]

In his book on democracy, Jacques Rancière does not merely develop the idea that "hatred of democracy" is today the result of liberal elites who seek by all possible means to conjure away the specter of a popular power contesting the existing order of things. He very correctly says that this hatred is nourished by a "compulsion to rid oneself of the people, and with it, of politics itself," and that "under the name of democracy, what is implied and denounced is politics itself."[40] Slavoj Žižek also speaks of "post-politics": "In post-politics, the conflict between global ideological visions incarnated by different parties finds itself replaced by collaboration between enlightened technocrats and

---

[38] Robert Kurz, *Avis aux naufragés*, 47–48.

[39] Zygmunt Bauman, *La Société assiégée* [*Society Under Siege*], trans. Christophe Rosson (Rodez: Le Rouergue-Chambon, 2005), 271. Cf. also Caroline Eliacheff and Daniel Soulez Larivière, *Le Temps des victims* [*The Age of Victims*] (Paris: Albin Michel 2007).

[40] Jacques Ranciere, *La Haine de la démocratie*, 89 and 40.

devotees of liberal multiculturalism; through the process of ne-
gotiating interests, a compromise is reached in the form of a
more or less universal consensus."[41]

This post-democracy is nothing but the program of liberal
capitalism in its postmodern form. It is a social project whose
fundamental *raison d'être* is to legitimate and keep in place the
dominant order by creating conditions as favorable as possible
for social adjustment in accordance with the planetary expansion
of the logic of capital. It is a matter of "reforming" democracy by
depriving it of its content to render it compatible with the evolution of the world, dictated by the mutations of Form-Capital.[42]
Already in the 1970s, the leaders of the Trilateral Commission
asked themselves how they could fight against the "excesses of
democracy," the general idea being that democracy is only
"governable" when the people no longer have any means of
making themselves heard. It is to this task that the theoreticians
of governance and the new liberal world order are devoted to
this very day, the ideal being to govern without the people — and
finally against them.

---

[41] Slavoj Žižek, *Plaidoyer en faveur de l'intolérance* [*A Plea for Intolerance*] (Castelnau-le-Lez: Climats, 2004), 39.

[42] This term defined in Chapter 5 as "capital insofar as it forms
global society, and insofar as it becomes the general form of that society." — Trans.

WHAT IS POPULISM?

Illusion, threat, wrong turn, and *temptation* are some of the words that recur most frequently nowadays in public discourse regarding populism. Having become a genuine foil, accused of awakening bad inclinations within the popular classes, useful to the dominant classes for stigmatizing those who accuse them of having confiscated power for their exclusive use, populism is systematically presented so as to appear fit only for being "cast out of history, as if it were a phenomenon without roots or real causes" (Alexandre Dorna). Whoever speaks of the people thereby exposes himself to the reproach of "populism," which consists essentially in "flattering the people's base instincts" — with the implication that the ruling class has only exceptionally elevated instincts. As Federico Tarragoni says, "Populism is a "magical concept that can assimilate and discredit anything, condemn anything with a mere name."[1]

We had a perfect example of this in June 2016 after the British people's decision to leave the European Union, which enraged and nearly stupefied all the establishment's representatives. Bernard-Henri Lévy saw in Brexit the "victory of the most rancid sovereignism and the most stupid nationalism," Jacques Attali the "dictatorship of populism," and Alain Minc the victory of "uneducated people over the educated." Daniel Cohn-Bendit belched, "Enough of the people!" Everyone immediately asked how the result of the vote could be neutralized while overflowing with criticism of David Cameron, who was blamed for having wanted to ask his compatriots their opinion. The people

---

[1] "La science du populisme au crible de la critique archéologique. Archéologie d'un mépris savant du peuple" ["The Science of Populism Sifted by Archeological Criticism: The Archeology of a Learned Contempt for the People"], *Actuel Marx* [*Marx Today*], 54, 2013, 2, 56–70. Cf. also Federico Tarragoni, "Raison populiste, démocratie et émancipation populaire" ["Populist Reason, Democracy, and Popular Emancipation"] in Hadrien Buclin *et al.*, eds., *Penser l'émancipation* [*Theorizing Emancipation*] (Paris: La Dispute, 2013), 215–34.

must not be consulted; they do not understand anything and will say anything, some observers assured us. We must prevent any repetition of this at all costs, said others.

*

While the motives for "Brexit" were much more complex than was said,[2] everyone came up with his own suggestion. Indignant "that a people could question all development considered irreversible up to that point," which amounts to "denying the very idea of progress" (*sic*), Jacques Attali, who clearly believes that history is written in advance, coldly proposed to quarantine certain matters by removing them from the voting process.[3] The idea (probably mistaken)[4] that a majority of young British were favorable to the European project since they were

---

[2] The rejection of immigration played a major role, but does not by itself explain Leave's success. We must also take into account Great Britain's peculiar character. Whereas in France, opponents of the European Union are generally anti-liberal, in Great Britain the Euroskeptics, libertarians, or disciples of Thatcherite liberalism blame European institutions for being overregulated and insufficiently open to the world. The British intellectual Philipp Blond, the theoretician of Red Toryism, who sees in the vote in favor of Brexit "the greatest rejection of globalization that the Western world has seen in the voting booth," also drew attention to "this paradox: popular classes in search of protection from globalization have followed the libertarians who think that Britain should unilaterally abolish its tariffs! (website *Figaro Vox*, July 1, 2016). "During the referendum campaign," observes the Italian political scientist Marco Tarchi for his part, "those in favor of Brexit used mainly sovereignist arguments that partially coincide with populist ideas and suggestions, but cannot be identified with them completely" ("Pourquoi le populisme hante l'Europe" ["Why Populism is Haunting Europe"], *Causeur*, July–August 2016, 44). Cf. also Jean-Louis Bourlanges, "Un 'Brexit,' deux histoires" ["One 'Brexit,' Two Stories"], *Commentaire*, Autumn 2016, 486–90.

[3] Jacques Attali, "Sanctuariser le progrès" ["Sheltering Progress"], *L'Express*, June 21, 2016.

[4] This is based on a simple opinion poll carried out one week before the vote and has not been confirmed by any investigation of the vote's details. Afterwards it turned out that two-thirds of those 18–25 years old abstained.

more "modern" and therefore "enlightened," while their elders were hostile, served as a pretext for the dubious notion that the vote would lose its value over time. François Fillon even suggested that the young should have a right to two votes while their elders only got one![5]

Criticism was concentrated on referenda, which had long been blamed for allowing the people to formulate the questions being asked. Jean Quatremer accuses referenda of instituting the "dictatorship of the majority" (the dictatorship of minorities no doubt being preferable in his eyes). To remedy the situation, certain observers such as the international lawyer Laurent Cohen-Tanugi advocate quite simply that a ban on referenda be written into European treaties. Others propose that certain subjects be withdrawn from the popular vote on principle, and that certain decisions be treated as beyond challenge, or that a 60% majority be required to overturn them (why not 90%?). Jean-Claude Juncker had already said, "There can be no democratic choice against the European treaties!"

Élisabeth Lévy, who amusingly defined populism as "the name the Left gives to the people whenever the people do something they do not like," writes:

To believe that millions of voters voted without understanding what they were doing and without reflecting on the consequences of their act is, strictly speaking, to take them for fools. . . . In Paris, the narrative that paints the Brexiters as uneducated cattle, narrow-minded xenophobes (and why not inbred while we're at it?) who should have their voting rights taken away, is revealing of

---

[5] Those who used this argument seem not to have considered that in France increasing the weight of the youth vote would automatically increase electoral support for the National Front. "But we must remember that in the twentieth century, if we had always (from a cult of youth) followed the younger generations' ideological preferences," writes Mathieu Bock-Côté, "political liberty would be in a very bad way." "Mépriser le peuple, le censurer, le déconstruire" ["Despising the People, Censuring It, Deconstructing It"], Le Journal de Montréal, June 24, 2016.

the esteem in which a part of the ruling class holds those it claims to govern.[6]

Thus, it comes to be taken for granted either that the people does not know what it wants, or when it expresses its preferences, there is no reason to take this into account. So there is no need to ask it before speaking in its name. And above all it is dangerous to consult it because it never votes as expected. The proletarian whose dignity ("poor but dignified"), bearing, and honesty used to be praised becomes a *petit blanc*, a "hexagonal" and "franchouillard," a mixture of Bitru[7] and *Dupont-Lajoie*,[8] uneducated, malicious, xenophobic, backwards, and desperately Franco-French. The poor, suspected on principle of harboring bad thoughts, must be more closely watched than ever. This negative image of the people reveals a contempt approaching genuine class hatred.[9]

---

[6] "Qui a peur du grand méchant peuple?" ["Who's Afraid of the Big Bad People?"], *Causeur*, July–August 2016, 32. Cf. also Élisabeth Lévy, "Le peuple, voila l'ennemi!"["The People: That Is the Enemy!"], website *Figaro Vox*, July 24, 2016.

[7] The hero of a series of novels by Albert Paraz (1899–1957). — Trans.

[8] The title of a celebrated French "anti-racist" film from 1975. — Trans.

[9] "In just a few years we have gone from defending the 'people's cause' to demophobia, to class contempt, to hatred of what is popular," remarks Arnauld Imatz (*Droite/gauche*, 96). "The populists are blamed for addressing themselves to the people. So what!" writes Vincent Coussedière for his part.

Who else should a politician address himself to in a democracy? They are blamed for using demagogy, proposing unrealistic solutions, in short: of flattering the people. So be it. But then one must make an effort to demonstrate how these solutions are unrealistic, which the adjective 'populist' excuses one from doing. In short, the usage of this term allows us to spare ourselves the effort of a political debate and lets democracy go to rust. (website *Figaro Vox*, March 18, 2016, 3)

Cf. also Serge Halimi, "Le populisme, voila l'ennemi" ["Populism: That Is the Enemy"], *Le Monde diplomatique*, April 1996; and Jacques

This insistent emphasis on the people's "lack of education" is especially revealing. During the presidential election of 2002, with the National Front once again winning most of the working-class vote, the political scientist Pascal Perrineau made this comment: "[The NF voters] are people of modest income, but also of modest knowledge. The higher one's level of culture, the more one is protected against voting for Le Pen." The same argument has been used against the partisans of "Brexit," while in the United States it is also among those with the fewest degrees that Donald Trump achieved his best results. Whereas in the 1950s and 1960s no one reproached Communist voters for any lack of educational certifications, we are now given to understand that a lack of education automatically leaves one receptive to simplistic or harmful ideas. Advanced education has become the guarantee of a tendency to adhere to correct ideas—it is hard to suppress a smile. We could just as well consider that the less educated are also less conditioned by the dominant ideology, and that the most "cultivated" are in reality those most given to social conformism and repeating fashionable mantras. In the popular classes, disbelief is not the result of ignorance but of repeated disappointment. In any case, everyone knows that intelligence and culture have never protected people against false ideas. We might also remember what Marc Bloch said of the elites of 1940: "Badly informed regarding the infinite resources of a people who have remained much healthier than poisoned lessons have inclined them to believe."[10] Great historical disasters have more often had their origin in the failure of elites than in the blindness of the people.

Anti-populism has been constructed in three stages. First, protest parties previously denounced as being of the extreme Right have been characterized as "populist," with "populism" being the "new clothes" of this "new extreme Right." Later, the

---

Rancière, "Non, le peuple n'est pas une masse brutale et ignorante" ["No, the People Are Not a Brutal, Ignorant Mass"], *Libération*, January 3, 2011, 7.

[10] Marc Bloch, *L'Étrange Défaite* [*The Strange Defeat*] (Paris: Franc-Tireur, 1946).

critique has gradually been extended in a learned or pseudo-learned manner in order to delegitimize any political option constructed upon an opposition between the people and the elites, such a construction being condemned in principle as apt to "delude the electorate." This second stage has allowed disrepute to be thrown not only on movements of the "extreme Right," but also on the most varied political formations with very different orientations, all of which are presented as pathological because they supposedly encourage the people to abandon its natural civic mission: namely, the confidence it should have in its representatives. Liberal representative democracy being posited from the start as the norm from which every deviancy is to be measured, any sort of departure from the dominant consensus, any party or movement whose ambition is to articulate the social demands of those who consider themselves excluded from or forgotten by the System in place, finds itself disqualified, usually in a polemical fashion. Finally, in a third stage, by a sort of natural slippage, the stigmatization of populism has mutated into stigmatization of the people.

This stigmatization is nothing new. Contrary to Machiavelli, whose ideal was the free citizen in a free republic, the Enlightenment *philosophes* already had nothing but disdain for the people they were intent on "enlightening" ("Enlightenment can only come from above"). On the Right, hostility toward the people has often gone hand-in-hand with the rejection of democracy, perceived as consecrating the law of quantity. This still pops up here and there, sometimes reaching the point of utter contempt.[11] But in fact, in the nineteenth century the Right was divided regarding the people. With Bonald and Joseph de Maistre, who denounced the "tyranny of popular sovereignty," counter-revolutionary traditionalism radically excluded the people from the calculus of power. For Maurras, the people cannot confer any power because it does not possess any; power can only

---

[11] For Henry de Lesquen, President of Radio Courtoisie, "the repression of the Paris Commune was excellent and salutary. Adolphe Thiers is a model" (Twitter, June 25, 2016). He also speaks of the Communards as "criminal scum!"

come from above. On this point, he opposed the Count of Chambord and La Tour du Pin, both partisans of an "organic democracy." The liberals, without being so radical, did not conceal their revulsion for the "dangerous classes" and sought to neutralize them by means of property qualifications, reserving the right to vote for the wealthiest. Adolphe Thiers, following Voltaire, denounced the "vile masses"! In the best case, they sought to reconcile the social classes by finding a place for the decent common man in the orbit of the enlightened elites. Legitimists, associated with the social Catholics who reproached the old monarchy with having been corrupted by absolutism, often favored a "popular monarchy" and generally took the lead in defending the world of work.

The Bonapartist Right, on the contrary, always privileged the appeal to the people at the same time as anti-parliamentarianism, anti-liberalism, and the plebiscitary tradition. We find this again in Boulangism (1889), which united legitimists, Bonapartists, and republicans in a common movement, and then in Gaullism. Believing the head of state could only derive his legitimacy from the people, de Gaulle instituted the presidential election based on direct universal suffrage. "It is above all with the people itself," said General de Gaulle, "that he who is their mandatary and guide keeps in direct contact."[12] This is also the reason why he always refused to recognize the authority of the European Court of Human Rights (ECHR): "In France, the only supreme court is the French people."

In most Western countries, the liberal conception of democracy has won out. This consists of substituting parliamentary sovereignty for popular sovereignty. Liberal democracy is, moreover, an aggregative form of democracy that sees in the political field merely a conglomeration of interests where individuals and groups are supposed to try to maximize their best interest politically without any concern for the common good. Its partisans are clearly hostile to the imperative mandate, as to all forms of direct democracy.

The people being considered "irrational" while liberalism

---

[12] General de Gaulle, press conference of September 9, 1965.

posits that the individual is above all a rational calculator seeking
to maximize his private best interests,[13] the tendency within liberal milieus is to limit popular participation as much as possible
to the electoral ritual in order to guard to the greatest extent
against that ritual's results. Property qualifications for voting
clearly tend in this direction. In 1925, Walter Lippmann was already rejoicing over the fact that political involvement was not
permanent.[14] Seymour Martin Lipset also encouraged abstention
and even political apathy on the pretext that it was better to
leave concern for public affairs to "those who know." Cornelius
Castoriadis for his part observed that "present-day institutions
turn away, drive off, and dissuade people from participating in
public affairs."[15] Everything is done to substitute the management of things, the sovereignty of financial markets, the authority of "experts," and the government of judges for popular decision-making. Since citizens are no longer able to demand an accounting from their representatives, the system is transformed
into an oligarchy that is responsible only to the private interests
that support it. Democracy, which normally implies the primacy
of politics over economics, becomes a mode of electoral legitimation for the sovereignty of oligarchies, financial markets, and
multinational corporations. From this point of view, the popular
classes must be prevented as much as possible from interfering
in politics. Democracy will never be so lovely as when it rids itself of the *demos*! We are most of the way there now, since the
great majority of those who exercise power today are appointed

---

[13] Nonna Mayer and Pascal Perrineau note on this subject that "the
very concept of political rationality is quite relative. The voter faithful
to the party that seems to him to defend the interests of his social
class or the values of his religion is not less rational than the voter
who switches parties; the one who wavers between parties that belong to the same political family is not more rational than the one
who crosses the Left/Right boundary" (*Les Comportements politiques*
[*Political Behavior*] [Paris: Armand Colin, 1992], 87).

[14] Walter Lippmann, *The Phantom Public: A Sequel to "Public Opinion"* (New York: Harcourt Brace & Co., 1925).

[15] Cornelius Castoriadis, *Une société à la dérive* [*A Society Adrift*]
(Paris: Seuil, 2005).

or coopted, not elected. The people, in the end, are nothing but dead wood.

The idea that society should be governed by "those who know" goes back at least to the "philosopher-king" praised by Plato, by way of contrast with the people whom he represents as immature and incorrigible, a dangerous crowd always ready to let itself be charmed by the first pied piper to come along. This idea is the basis of contemporary expertocracy, the constantly rehashed argument being that the people are "incompetent."

But just what is "competence"? Today it is always pictured as technical expertise and knowledge, whereas competence in politics is something else entirely. In politics competence does not reside in technical knowledge, but in the ability to decide between several possibilities, i.e., in a capacity for decision. Experts are competent about *how* to do things; they have no competence about *what* must be done. Populism is not mistaken when it proposes removing democratic practice from the professionals in cabinet ministries and electoral rituals, for it has long noted the experts' tendency to be mistaken. The people are in fact perfectly competent to distinguish between what is politically good and bad, what satisfies their aspirations and what disappoints them.[16] When they vote it is not to pronounce upon truth but to indicate their preferences and say whether or not they are in accord with those who govern them. You don't have the citizens vote on the truth-value of Darwin's theory or the Council of Trent's decisions, but to find out what they think politically!

But the idea according to which the best government is that

---

[16] "If the citizens are not competent and do not have enough distance from their own passions to pass judgement concerning the most important subjects," writes Emmaneul-Just Duits, "where does their right to decide stop? Do they have enough reason and competence to choose their representatives? Would it not rather be the business of reasonable and 'competent' people to coopt or elect one another into a predetermined college? This reasoning tends to send us back to property qualifications. To avoid populism, we are falling back into oligarchy" ("Après le Brexit, inventer une démocratie éclairée" ["After Brexit: Inventing an Enlightened Democracy"], website *Causeur*, July 22, 2016, 2).

of "experts" does not aim only at dismissing popular sovereignty because of its "incompetence." It also involves dismissing politics as such. It suggests that political problems are, in the final analysis, nothing but "technical" problems for which there can rationally only be one best solution which it is the business of experts to determine. This is the basis of the liberal idea according to which "there is no alternative" (a formula attributed to Margaret Thatcher), which is also one of the principles of "political correctness." One thus creates the impression that politics might be "pacified" and that antagonisms could be called upon to die out under the peaceable effect of a common "technical" culture. This neutralization amounts in fact to depoliticization and, ultimately, to the death of politics. Human aspirations being different and in potential conflict, one can only decide between them in the name of normative criteria that can never be reduced to unity. Political decision-making consists in choosing between possibilities, none of which imposes itself "objectively" upon everyone. In politics, there are always alternatives insofar as political decision-making is always liable to make different choices as a function of circumstances and the criteria it employs.

Expertocracy has spread the idea that many negative phenomena are henceforward unavoidable. In the first place, of course, this means the "laws" presiding over the market economy in modern societies, to which is added the uncontrolled rise of technologies obeying their own internal dynamic. On the model of migratory flows, all these phenomena have been decreed inevitable because we have lost the habit of questioning ends and have become accustomed to the idea that it is no longer possible to impose a decision (which is increasingly the case, in fact). The result is a negation of the very essence of politics and its reduction to the level of a mere administrative technique.

Thibault Isabel also correctly remarks that the denunciation of populism "attests to the contempt with which intellectuals have long regarded currents openly hostile to progressivism."[17]

---

[17] Thibault Isabel, "Christopher Lasch: un populiste contre le progrès" ["Christopher Lasch: A Populist Against Progress"], *Krisis*,

The conviction that one is in agreement with the direction of history, in fact, nourishes the idea that "men of progress" must prevent the retrograde popular classes from putting the brakes on evolution. "Those who know" must impose themselves upon the ignorant, and even prevent them from expressing themselves; the "technicians" and self-proclaimed experts must remove the direction of public affairs from the backward masses. For the experts, "pluralism always results either from a misunderstanding or from a lack of intelligence: on the one hand there are experts who know, on the other individuals who do not. If the latter are rational and well-informed, they will go along with the former's opinion."[18]

*

Like "communitarism," "populism" has today become a garbage-bag term. The proof is that this label has been applied to people as different as Donald Trump, Hugo Chávez, Evo Morales, Nigel Farage, Beppe Grillo, Viktor Orbán, Nicolas Sarkozy, Georges Marchais, Jean-Luc Mélenchon, Bernard Tapie, José Bové, Marine Le Pen, Oskar Freysinger, Pim Fortuyn, Geert Wilders, Boris Johnson, Pablo Iglesias, Christophe Blocher, Jörg Haider, Umberto Bossi, and Silvio Berlusconi, but also to Mao Zedong, Juan Perón, Getúlio Vargas, Fidel Castro, Colonel Gaddafi, Mahmoud Ahmadinejad, and Luiz Inácio "Lula" da Silva. Similarly, the National Front and the Left Front in France are both currently characterized as "populist," as are Syriza in Greece, both the Indignados Movement and Podemos in Spain, both the Tea Party and "Occupy Wall Street" in the United States, both the Five Star Movement and the Northern League in Italy, the Austrian Freedom Party (FPÖ) in Austria, the Swiss People's Party (UDC) in Switzerland, the Freedom Party in the Netherlands, Fidesz in Hungary, the People's Party in Denmark, etc.

Made to fit every occasion, the word "populism" "loses any significance and prevents any lasting diagnosis" (Edgar Morin).

February 2008, 106.

[18] Pierre Rosanvallon, "Repenser la gauche" ["Rethinking the Left"], L'Express, March 25, 1993, 116.

Those who reproach populist parties with being "catch-all" parties are the first to make "populism" into a rubber word (*Gum-
miwort*, as the Germans say), allowing any interpretation, usually pejorative. "The word is everywhere, its definition nowhere,"
said the historian Philippe Roger some time ago. "We have nothing resembling a theory of populism," added the political scientist Jan-Werner Mueller. It is clearly easier to pillory "populism"
than to look closely into the nature of this emerging political alternative.

In reality, if the term "populism" is incontrovertibly complex,
ambiguous, and polysemic—as all who have studied the phenomenon have emphasized—it is no more so than many other
terms currently employed such as "democracy," "republic,"
"community," etc., which have also been given totally contradictory interpretations. "Discussions of democracy, arguments in
its favor or against it, are characterized by intellectual vacuity,"
said Bertrand de Jouvenel, "for people do not know what they
are talking about."[19] It is no different with populism, all the
more so in that the word is relatively new.[20] The vagueness sur-
rounding it is an additional motive for trying to dissipate it. That
populism is not a very clear concept and can assume different
forms must not prevent us from trying to define it.

As a category of political science, populism has already been
the object of a significant number of studies.[21] But the specialists

---

[19] Bertrand de Jouvenel, *Du pouvoir. Histoire naturelle de sa crois-
sance* [*On Power: A Natural History of Its Growth*] (Geneva: Le Cheval
ailé, 1945), 411.

[20] In France, the term "populist" was accepted in the *Larousse men-
suel* in 1906. The word *"populisme"* appears in 1929 in the writings of
André Thérive and Léon Lemonnier to refer to a new literary school
(the first Populist Prize was awarded to Eugène Dabit for *Hôtel du
Nord*). Cf. Gérard Mauger, "'Populisme,' itinéraire d'un mot voya-
geur," *Le Monde diplomatique*, July 2014, 3.

[21] Cf. especially, in chronological order: Ghita Ionescu and Ernest
Gellner, eds., *Populism: Its Meaning and National Characteristics* (London:
Weidenfeld & Nicolson, 1969); Margaret Canovan, *Populism* (London:
Junction Books, 1981); Guy Hermet, *La Trahison de la démocratie. Popu-
listes, républicains et démocrates* [*The Betrayal of Democracy: Populists, Re-*

do not agree among themselves. They are divided into those who see in populism an ideology (or ideological schema), like Ludovico Incisa di Camerana; those who see in it only a style (or

---

publicans, and Democrats] (Paris: Flammarion, 1998; Alexandre Dorna, *Le Populisme* [*Populism*] (Paris: PUF, 1999); Paul Taggart, *Populism* (Buckingham: Open University Press, 2000); Yves Surel and Yves Mény, *Par le peuple et pour le peuple. Le populisme et les démocraties* [*By the People and For the People: Populism and the Forms of Democracy*] (Paris: Fayard, 2001); Guy Hermet, *Les Populismes dans le monde. Une histoire sociologique, XIXe–XXe siècle* [*Forms of Populism in the World: A Sociological History, Nineteenth and Twentieth Century*] (Paris: Fayard, 2001); Roger Dupuy, *La Politique du peuple. Racines, permanences et ambiguités du populisme* [*The Politics of the People: Roots, Permanent Aspects, and Ambiguities of Populism*] (Paris: Albin Michel, 2002); Pierre-André Taguieff, *L'Illusion populiste. De l'archaique au médiatique* [*The Populist Illusion: From the Archaic to the Journalistic*] (Paris: Berg international, 2002) (revised second edition: *L'Illusion populiste. Essai sur les démagogies de l'âge démocratique* [*The Populist Illusion: Essay on the Forms of Demagogy of the Democratic Age*] (Paris: Flammarion, 2007); Marco Tarchi, *Italia populista, dal qualunquismo a Beppe Grillo* [*Populist Italy from Qualunquismo to Beppe Grillo*] (Bologna: Il Mulino, 2003) [*Qualunquismo* (anybodyism) was a brief postwar movement that sought to remove the influence of parties from political life. — Trans.]; Chantal Delsol, *La Nature du populisme ou les figures de l'idiot* [*The Nature of Populism or the Figures of the Idiot*] (Nice: Ovadia, 2008); Daniele Albertazzi and Duncan McDonnell, *Twenty-first Century Populism* (Basingstoke: Palgrave Macmillan, 2008); *Populisme contre populisme*, special issue of the journal *Actuel Marx*, 2008, 2; Dominique Reynié, *Populismes: la pente fatale* [*Populisms: The Fatal Inclination*] (Paris: Plon, 2011); Vincent Coussedière, *Éloge du populisme* [*In Praise of Populism*] (Grenoble: Elya, 2012); Pierre-André Taguieff, *Le Nouveau National-populisme* [*The New National Populism*] (Paris: CNRS Éditions, 2012); Raphaël Liogier, *Ce populisme qui vient* [*This Emerging Populism*] (Paris: Textuel, 2013); Catherine Colliot-Thélène and Florent Guénard, eds., *Peuple et populisme* [*People and Populism*] (Paris: PUF, 2014); Chantal Delsol, *Le Populisme et les demeurés de l'histoire* [*Populism and the Idiots of History*] (Paris: Le Rocher, 2015); Vincent Coussedière, *Le Retour du peuple, an I. Le véritable défi de la République* [*The Return of the People, Year One: The Real Challenge to the Republic*] (Paris: Cerf, 2016); Benjamin Moffitt, *The Global Rise of Populism: Performance, Political Style, and Representation* (Stanford: Stanford University Press, 2016).

mindset) such as Pierre-André Taguieff, who characterizes it as a "political style applicable to different ideological contexts";[22] and those who define it as a new form of political organization. In her pioneering work published in 1981, Margaret Canovan abandons all definition according to ideal type in favor of a typological approach which is in fact more fruitful: protest-populisms, national populism, and so on.

On the other hand, everyone agrees that populism, historically speaking, appeared at the end of the nineteenth century in Russia and the United States with movements that, in both cases, sought to mobilize disfavored groups against the elites of the moment.

Between 1860 and 1880, the *narodniki* (from *narod*, "people") were Russian socialists who wanted to "go to the people," bringing basic literacy to the peasant masses, opening dispensaries and reading rooms, and attempting to set up a kind of socialist agrarian economy. Hostile to Russia's Westernization, considering the peasantry the only revolutionary class, and agrarian structures as the best way of preventing capitalism's expansion, they emphasized the traditional rural "community" (*obshchina*) as a system of mutual aid and solidarity and tried to awaken in the peasants an awareness resulting in a will to fight. The principal representatives of this Russian populism (*narodnishestvo*) were Alexander Herzen (who would go into exile in France, where he notably collaborated with Proudhon), Nikolai Chernyshevsky, and Dmitri Pisarev.[23]

At about the same time, on the other side of the Atlantic, American populism also asserted itself as an essentially rural movement. Created in 1867 by Oliver Hudson Kelley, the Grange Movement sought to enlarge agricultural workers' social rights

---

[22] Pierre-André Taguieff, "Le populisme et la science politique. Du mirage conceptuel aux vrais problèmes" ["Populism and Political Science: From the Conceptual Mirage to the Real Problems"], *Vingtieme siecle*, no. 56, October–December 1997, 4–33.

[23] Cf. especially Franco Venturi, *Les intellectuels, le peuple et la révolution. Histoire du populisme russe au XIXe siècle* [*Intellectuals, the People, and Revolution: History of Russian Populism in the Ninteenth Century*] [1952], trans. Viviana Pâques, 2 vols. (Paris: Gallimard, 1972).

and protect small producers' autonomy by limiting salaried workers and dependence on the state as much as possible, and trying to put an end to speculation and mass industrialization. Confronting the prohibitive fares that privileged access to public land allowed railroad companies to impose, the populists advocated a return to the roots of American democracy ("We, the People"). The People's Party, an agrarian populist party founded in 1891 in Saint Louis, also played an important role. Led primarily by James B. Weaver and Thomas E. Watson, it supported the charismatic figure of William Jennings Bryan in the 1896 presidential election (his opponent, William McKinley, won by only 600,000 votes). Its ideas rested on the Jeffersonian dream of the smallholder's autonomy, which the philosopher Ralph Waldo Emerson summarized with his concept of self-reliance. Thus, American populism expressed an "authentically plebeian" protest (Guy Harmet).[24]

The *narodniki* opposed the rural way of life to capitalism; the American Grangers also denounced the finance capitalism that reigned in the big cities. As for Latin American populism, such as Mexican Cardenism or Argentine Peronism (too often confounded with "*caudillismo*"), it aimed mainly at agrarian reform and politically enfranchising the popular classes (the *descamisados*, the "shirtless"). In all three cases, writes Federico Tarragoni, "populism maintains strong links with a popular base."[25] It belongs to the socialist tradition even while it is hostile to the ideology of progress (which explains the Bolsheviks' hostility to the Russian *narodniki*). From its first appearance in history, whether in Russia or the United States, populism has not let itself be easily classed on the Left or Right. At first, observes historian Michel Winock, "populism did not specifically belong to the extreme

---

[24] Cf. also Lawrence Goodwyn, *Democratic Promise: The Populist Movement in America* (New York: Oxford University Press, 1976); David Da Silva, "La tradition populiste dans la culture des États-Unis" ["The Populist Tradition in the Culture of the United States"], *Krisis*, March 2016, 138–45.

[25] Federico Tarragoni, "La 'menace populiste': l'éternel retour du meme (peuple)?" ["The 'Populist Threat': Eternal Return of the Same (People)?"], *Mouvements*, February 2015.

Right. The word refers to a confidence in the people which one encounters in Robespierre's speeches or Michelet's writings."

The diversity of populist movements has increased further in our day: "Left-wing" populisms, "Right-wing" populisms, liberal populisms, anti-liberal populisms, etc. As regards statism, decentralization, the economy, the functioning of institutions, and the problem of immigration—the populist parties do not necessarily take the same positions, so it would be vain to look for any sort of ideological unity or homogeneity. Vincent Coussedière emphasizes:

> What populist movements have in common is more the political situation of the peoples who cause it to emerge. The situation can be summarized very simply: the European political peoples (and the American people is perhaps less distant from them than commonly believed) find themselves confronted with dramatic demographic, cultural, and economic challenges, and with an obsolete party-political spectrum whose divisions no longer match the reality and depth of the crisis. The unity of populism cannot be grasped unless one moves from the level of what is being offered politically to the situation of the European peoples themselves. It is this situation they have in common and which explains what I call the "populism of the people.[26]

The first mistake to avoid when speaking of populism is therefore to seek in it an ideology or to identify it with a definite doctrine. The diversity of politicians who have been charged with "populism," as well as the term's polysemy, show not only that populism does not constitute an ideology, but that it can be combined with any ideology. The Argentine political scientist Ernesto Laclau is not wrong to say that it is a "neutral" word from this point of view. For this reason, it is just as erroneous to

---

[26] Vincent Coussedière, "Brexit, Trump, Rome: les populistes gouverneront-ils un jour?" ["Brexit, Trump, Rome: Will the Populists Govern Someday?"], website *Figaro Vox*, June 21, 2016, 2.

make it into a new avatar for nationalism or fascism.[27] Populism does not aspire to create a "new man." Contrary to fascism, it accepts the rules of democracy. Populist movements can be sovereignist, but populism is not synonymous with sovereignism (many sovereignists are not populists). They can be identitarian, but populism is not synonymous with identitarianism, either (many identitiarians are not populists). Identitarian populism, finally, is not necessarily the same thing as "national populism," for identity is not always based on the idea of the nation.

Certain groups on the Right or extreme Right have been tempted during these last few years to rename themselves "populist" for reasons of opportunity, if not opportunism. This assimilation of populism and nationalism, too common in the media, is not convincing for at least two reasons. First of all, populism is fundamentally directed against the elites, while the Right has nearly always defended elites — whether by opposing them to the people or (in the most favorable case) in order to say there cannot be any fundamental opposition between the elites and the people. The Right has generally been elitist because it does not believe the people capable of governing itself directly, and that is why its conversion into a "populist" movement poses a fundamental problem (of which it is not always conscious). On the other hand, to affirm itself as "populist," a certain radical Right must forget the total incompatibility of its traditional critique of democracy with a movement that demands more democracy.

It is more tempting to see in populism not an ideology, but a style. For example, Marco Tarchi proposes defining populism "as a specific mental form tied to a vision of social order based on belief in the innate virtues of the people, the people for whom one proclaims primacy as the source of legitimation for political action and government."[28]

There is incontestably a populist style classically characterized

---

[27] Cf. Guy Hermet, "Populisme et nationalisme" ["Populism and Nationalism"], *Vingtieme siecle*, no. 56, October–December 1997, 34–47.

[28] Marco Tarchi, "Qu'est-ce que le populisme?" ["What Is Populism?"], *Krisis*, February 2008, 11.

by the theme of an "appeal to the people" and the will to institute a more direct relation between the people and their rulers;
but these two traits do not exhaust the reality. A certain number
of other elements are generally associated with them: a reference
to the people as a homogeneous social aggregate that is the privileged depositary of permanent positive values; the will to give it
power, to give it a voice, or at least to speak in its name; the idealization of the national community posited as a more or less
"organic" unitary whole; hostility to elites and confiscation of
the power attributed to them; the nostalgic reappropriation of
values inherited from the past; the demand for direct democracy
often based on referenda; a taste for charismatic leaders in the
service of an "incarnate democracy," and so on. This is not
wrong, but these conventional traits are not necessarily found in
all cases.

To say that populism aspires, by means of a "leader," to establish for example an "authoritarian regime" does not always
correspond to reality. Populist movements have often been led
by charismatic leaders (Boulanger, Péron, de Gaulle, Nasser,
etc.), but populism as such, even if it favors a personal incarnation of political decision-making thanks to a "spokesman of the
people" in which it is scarcely distinct from classical democracy,[29] does not automatically involve recourse to a "providential
man." Marco Tarchi notes quite correctly that "the populist
leader must not be confused with the charismatic boss: he must
certainly offer some uncommon qualities, but he must never fall
into the error of presenting himself as different from the ordinary man he addresses; his first talent consists precisely in never
crossing that line."[30]

It would also be a mistake to make populism a matter of mere
"demagogy." For a number of populism's critics, the populist
leader is simply a demagogue. Populism abusively simplifies

---

[29] Jean-Claude Monod thinks, as does Ernesto Laclau, that democ-
racy cannot do without leaders (*Qu'est-ce qu'un chef en démocratie?
Politiques du charisme* [*What Is a Leader in Democracy? The Politics of
Charisma*] [Paris: Seuil, 2012]).

[30] Marco Tarchi, "Qu'est-ce que le populisme?," 18.

problems by "demagogy" and that demagogy supposedly
awakens or crystallizes the people's bad instincts. For example,
Pierre-André Taguieff defines populism as the "form assumed
by demagogy in contemporary societies." This critique is not
always mistaken, especially as there is a great difference between speaking in the people's name and working to give the
people the means of expressing themselves. But this conception
of populism forgets that the elites' demagogy can very well
compete with that of the "tribunes of the people." Similarly, a
democracy that makes extensive use of referenda is said to leave
the door open to demagogy. But why is this any different from
representative democracy? The apocalyptic scenarios sketched
out on the other side of the Channel by the opponents of "Brexit" in the event that option wins out are no less demagogic than
those of its supporters. Marcel Gauchet says more accurately
that "democracy is competition between forms of demagogy."
To reduce populism to demagogy amounts to avoiding the essential, which is the very concept of the people. As Vincent
Coussedière writes, "If political science, and in its wake all critical and media discourse, seeks to reduce populism to a form of
demagogy, it is because they do not dispose of any concept of
the people that would allow them to take the phenomenon's
true measure."

As for the "excess" extravagance with which populists are often reproached, in general it is merely a way of distinguishing
themselves from the coded language which the elites employ to
their own benefit in order to provide the dominant ideology
with the benefits of a consensus that does not in fact exist. Besides, the argument can easily be turned around, as Jean-Claude
Michéa remarks with a certain humor:

> In the world of the official media (whether of Right or
> Left), celebrating the ordinary people's decency or their
> ability to govern themselves directly is regarded very bad-
> ly. At best, this is held to be a "Rousseauist" illusion; at
> worst, *populist* ideas, and "we know only too well where
> *they* lead." But it is curious that these zealous media per-
> sonnel never think to apply their negative anthropology to

the elites themselves. . . . The maxim "they're all rotten"[31]
is supposedly terrible when it is applied to the dominant
class, but quite plausible as soon as it concerns ordinary
people.[32]

Another mistake consists in seeing in populism an intrinsically anti-political phenomenon. Thus, Guy Hermet thinks one of
the keys to the populist mentality resides in distrust of everything which cannot be immediately resolved, which would
make populism an unpolitical and even anti-political form of
politics. Populists, he writes, ignore the need to "give time to
time." They define themselves by "the anti-political temporality
of their supposedly instantaneous response to problems or aspirations which in reality no governmental action is able to resolve
or satisfy in a sudden manner. This relation to political time constitutes the distinctive nucleus of populism as a whole."[33] The
same idea is found in Pierre Rosanvallon, for whom populism is
merely a "simplifying and perverse response," "a perverse twist-
ing of democratic procedures."[34] Najat Vallaud-Belkacem also
assures us that populism, which she characterizes as an "intimate
enemy of the Republic," rests upon the "desire to believe that
things can be changed without effort": "Populism promotes a rapid tempo, an immediacy opposed to the long duration presupposed by any concrete and ambitious politics." In liberal milieus,
reformist patience has always been opposed to revolutionary
haste. Populism wants everything, and it wants it now. But is
this true? "One gets the impression that all political action today

---

[31] "*Tous pourris*," a popular expression referring to the supposed
corruption of the elites as a whole. — Trans.

[32] "Jean-Claude Michéa répond à dix questions" ["Jean-Claude
Michéa Answers Ten Questions"] in Gilles Labelle, Éric Martin, and
Stéphane Vibert, eds., *Les Racines de la liberté* [*The Roots of Liberty*],
322–23.

[33] Guy Hermet, "Le populisme dans l'histoire" ["Populism in History"], *Krisis*, February 2008, 25.

[34] Pierre Rosanvallon, *La contre-démocratie. La politique à l'âge de la
défiance* [*Counter-Democracy: Politics in the Age of Defiance*] (Paris: Seuil,
2006).

is carried out in slow motion," observes Alain Duhamel. How is it that the "slow tempo" from which politicians have benefitted for at least the past 30 years has had so few results?

In reality, when there are no more political divisions, there is no more politics. Now, it is precisely in reaction to the erasure of divisions that populism has arisen. The people see that politics today is buried by economics, morality, procedural law, and expertocracy. The people are calling for a return to politics, because it is only politically that they can exist as a people. A community becomes a political being as soon as it defines itself as such. Thus, it is opposed to the technocratic doctrine of Saint-Simon according to which "the government of men must be replaced by the administration of things." Jacques Sapir explains:

> The cause of this is the depersonalization of political action. This depersonalization leads to a depoliticization of societies, a process that carries the seeds of their disappearance. In today's regimes called parliamentary democracies, power appears no longer to be that of men but of laws. Now, these laws do not "reign"; they are imposed upon individuals in a "technical" fashion as general norms. In such a regime there is no place for controversy, or the struggle for power or political action. There is room only for a polarity between supposedly technical reasoning and moral posturing. This depolitization is felt as an unbearable aggression by a majority of the people, for it aims at depriving it of its ability to decide, i.e., its sovereignty.[35]

It is therefore altogether false to say that populism expresses a disgust or rejection of politics. It only expresses a hostility toward the political class, which is blamed specifically for no longer engaging in politics. Populism does not necessarily aspire to "doing everything right away," but it does aspire to decisions that the dominant class no longer seems capable of making. As

---

[35] Jacques Sapir, "Populismes et politique" ["Populisms and Politics"], website *RussEurope*, June 12, 2016, 4.

Vincent Coussedière writes:

> There is no politics without people, nor people without pol-
> itics. The people are a living reality whose being-together is
> politics. . . . The populist being-together is reacting to the
> empty space where politics should be. It corresponds to
> that stage in the life of democracies where the people un-
> willingly takes up politics because they have despaired of
> the attitude of their rulers, who no longer do.

Far from being "anti-political," populism represents a powerful
protest against the depoliticization of public affairs due to the
recentering of political programs and the rise of the expertocracy.

The same equivocation appears with reference to the relation between populism and democracy. Not democratic enough
for some, populism is too democratic for others. To hear some
tell it, populism takes democracy too seriously! Populism contradicts democracy especially by aspiring to the political body's
unity, whereas democracy institutionalizes divergences. For
Christian Godin, populism is the "principal danger for democracy," the proof that the populists are anti-democratic being that,
in order to fool people, they assume "hyperdemocratic positions." In other words, they say what they do not believe, and
they believe what they do not say. You can easily demonstrate
whatever you want on that assumption.

This type of reasoning abstracts on principle from the people.
Yet populism is inseparable from the people and thus from the
very idea of democracy. The people cannot be removed from
democracy. Democracy is a regime founded on the people's sovereignty, which means that power, in order to be legitimate,
must receive the citizens' approval or consent. The democratic
tradition is based not on the principle of the rule of law, but on
popular equality and sovereignty. In democracy, the people are
(or should be) sovereign, and sovereign first of all on the essential question of social reproduction.[36] But democracy is also, and

---

[36] Sovereignty is no more a "Right-wing" concept than nation.

above all, the only political regime that allows all citizens to participate in public affairs and to decide as much as possible for themselves about matters that concern them. It is wrong to see in democracy nothing but a regime founded on the "law of quantity." Universal suffrage is in reality only a technique allowing preferences to be revealed. "In democracy the key concept is neither quantity, nor suffrage, nor election, nor representation, but the participation of all citizens in public life. . . . The maximum degree of democracy is thus the same as maximum participation."[37] "Democracy is the participation of a people in its own destiny," said Arthur Moeller van den Bruck.

Populism has no quarrel with democracy but with representative democracy's insufficiently democratic character and the oligarchic regression of systems based on representation.[38] What it seeks by appealing to a principle of delegating power is to take democracy out of the hands of electoral professionals who are monopolizing it. It also relies on democracy to criticize elites. "If populism incarnates an ideological corruption of democracy, it also expresses a real demand for participative democracy or active citizenship which the well-tempered functional system of representative democracy is unable to satisfy," recognizes even Pierre-André Targuieff, who also thinks that "what characterizes the present situation is that the revolt against the confiscation of democracy tends to become confused with the project of revivifying national sovereignty and giving it meaning

---

"The extension of domains of sovereignty has been the form taken by the social struggles that have built institutions over the course of time," Jacques Sapir reminds us ("La gauche, le Brexit et la souveraineté" ["The Left, Brexit, and Sovereignty"], website *RussEurope*, July 4, 2016, 6).

[37] Arnaud Imatz, *Droite/gauche: pour sortir de l'équivoque*, 45. The author takes inspiration from our essay: Alain de Benoist, *Démocratie: le problème* [*The Problem of Democracy*] (Paris: Labyrinthe, 1985).

[38] "The principal enemy of the democratic state and of democratic principles of order," says Jacques Sapir, "is the collusive state, that state which is dominated by the oligarcho-technocratic caste toward which we have been headed for some 30 years now" ("La gauche, le Brexit et la souveraineté," 8).

once again."[39] In fact, populism does not accuse democracy of undermining sovereignty, an accusation the extreme Right has often made, but binds these two concepts together. Similarly, when it denounces liberal representative democracy, it is not in the name of any dictatorship or return to monarchy, but by demanding stronger democracy and valorizing all forms of popular or direct democracy.

What is correct, on the other hand, is that populism has above all revealed a crisis or serious malfunction of liberal democracy. Populism only appears when liberal democracy has demonstrated its limits, is no longer able to respond to social demands, and fuels a feeling of democratic dispossession and seems to be a mere masquerade or even a brake on popular aspirations. Paul Piccone observes:

> Populist movements generally appear at particular historical junctures when the democratic process has so degenerated that it calls for a genuine democratic reaction. . . . Populism is generally a reaction against a deficit of democracy, and it is always much more democratic than any system based on representative democracy. . . . In an authentically democratic style, populists demand that each person be considered equally qualified to participate in decisions that affect his life.[40]

"The condition for the emergence of a populist campaign," writes Pierre-André Taguieff, "is a crisis of political legitimacy

---

[39] Pierre-André Taguieff, *L'Illusion populiste*; Pierre-André Taguieff and Jacques Sapir (interview), "Du Brexit à la présidentielle française en passant par l'élection américaine, la vengeance des peuples contre leurs élites sera-t-elle un plat qui se mange froid . . . ou très chaud?" ["From Brexit to the French Presidential Election By Way of the American: Is the People's Revenge Upon the Elites a Dish Best Served Cold . . . or Very Hot?"], website *Atlantico*, June 17, 2016.

[40] Paul Piccone, "De la Nouvelle Gauche au populisme post-moderne" ["From the New Left to Postmodern Populism"], *Krisis*, February 2008, 87–88.

or legitimation affecting the entire system of representation."[41] Populism proclaims the people's sovereignty with all the more force as it observes the breadth of the crisis of legitimacy confronting the ruling class. If you do not perceive the full extent of this crisis, you will never understand anything about populism.

Populism basically wants nothing but to *put the people back* in democracy. This is why Christopher Lasch saw in it "the authentic voice of democracy,"[42] as well as a resurgence of the republicanism of Antiquity and the Renaissance, which wanted virtue (in the ancient sense of *virtus*, manly courage) to be the foundation of citizenship conceived not merely as a legal status but as a principle of collective action. To question populism is thus not merely to question the legitimacy of popular demands, but also the well-foundedness of popular sovereignty, which is the basis of democratic regimes. Secondarily, it gives us the means of analyzing the "deconstruction of the political people" begun nearly a half-century ago.

So it is essential to know what must be understood by "people" in the expression "populism of the people." We know that the word can have three different meanings: the political people (*demos*), the people defined by its history and culture (*ethnos*), the people in the sense of ordinary people, and the popular classes (*plebs*). The key concept is obviously that of *demos*, for it is the only fundamentally political meaning, contrary to *ethnos*, whose roots are pre-political. But *ethnos* is tied to mores, which constitute an essential element of sociability and thus of the people's identity; populism cannot do without taking this into account. A political community, the foundation of citizenship, the *demos*, without being identical to the *ethnos*—any more than the state is identical to the nation[43]—is nevertheless instituted on the basis of something *already there*, wherein it is distinct from both "civic

---

[41] Taguieff, *L'Illusion populiste*.

[42] Christopher Lasch, *The Revolt of the Elites and the Betrayal of Democracy* (New York: Norton, 1995), 106.

[43] The people is not synonymous with the nation. It was the revolutionaries of 1789, beginning with the Abbé Sieyès, who assimilated the two terms, allowing them to substitute national sovereignty for popular sovereignty.

nationalism" and "republican citizenism," which are based on universal abstract principles, especially legal equality, or on the dream of a cosmopolitan citizenship, which does not merely separate citizenship from nationality but also frees itself from both *demos* and *ethnos*.[44] Finally, the people as *plebs* may appear opposed to the *demos* and *ethnos* insofar as, strictly speaking, it represents only a part (generally the most numerous part) of the historical or political people. But this is also what allows it to oppose the elites, in which respect the people as plebs is an essential component of populism.

Populism's great characteristic is in fact to mix these three meanings of "people," to seek to incarnate them simultaneously beyond anything that distinguishes them. If it refers back to a specific social base (the popular classes allied to the middle classes threatened with downward mobility), populism also represents a form of political imagination where the people is above all conceived as assembled. In populism, *demos*, *ethnos* and *plebs* — political people, organic people, and dominated classes (of, if you prefer, the democratic people, the national people and the social people) — are all closely associated.

This is why we cannot follow those who, even as they recognize the populist aspiration's well-foundedness, want to make an ideology of it and busy themselves with separating the "bad" (xenophobic and reactionary) populists from the "good" (progressive and democratic) populists. The former, according to Federico Tarragoni, base themselves on the *ethnos*-nation dyad, the latter on the *plebs-demos* dyad.[45] But this opposition between "social populism" and "national populism" is merely an ideal-typical opposition that rarely corresponds to reality. There is not

---

[44] "In a system of cosmopolitan citizenship," observes Chantal Mouffe, "we have a whole series of rights, but without the power to exercise them. . . . The exercise of citizenship rights, which demands participation in decision-making, becomes impossible insofar as a process of deciding involving the entire planet cannot exist. One can only exercise one's rights within the framework of a *demos*" ("Pour une démocratie radicale et plurielle" ["In Favor of A Radical and Pluralist Democracy"], *Krisis*, February 2008, 120).

[45] Federico Tarragoni, "La 'menace populiste'."

one populism over here exclusively concerned with protecting the people *already there*, and another populism over there attempting to foster the emergence of a new popular subject. Most forms of populism combine these two aspirations. The movement in Greece that resulted in the creation of Syriza, to give only one example, displayed both tendencies.[46]

Nor is it any more accurate to state, as Pierre-André Taguieff does, that populism only conceives of the people in a unanimist manner, "as a single entity without social or class divisons." A great many forms of populism can be interpreted as class phenomena (or as phenomena with a class dimension). This does not prevent those who advocate for such forms from seeing in the people an organic totality threatened with artificial divisions by hostile forces. The people do not like those who dissolve its fraternity!

The people are defined first of all by a common sociability, which Aristotle takes as the basis of *philia politikē*, or political friendship. This must be distinguished from the societal, which is merely the sociability produced by the welfare state's machinery. But neither can this common sociability be reduced to any more or less fantasized "identity." It is the result of an "imitation-custom" which is at once the essence of the social bond and the basis of traditions, and which allows the citizens to test what they have in common. Populism's implied objective is to reinstitute a common world, a (public) common space—that "space-between-men" that Hannah Arendt designated as the site where freedoms meet.

Vincent Coussedière, who describes populism as "the party of conservatives who have no party," thinks populism is the people's opposition to the decomposition of sociability and mores, i.e., to their decomposition as a community. In the face of a globalization perceived as a "machine for killing peoples," in the face of immigration that weighs upon the mores to which they are attached, in the face of a sovereignty paralyzed by post-

---

[46] Cf. Andreas Pantazopoulos, "The National-Populist Illusion as a 'Pathology' of Politics: The Greek Case and Beyond," *TelosScope*, August 11, 2016.

national alliances, he writes, "The peoples want to continue being peoples, i.e., they want to conserve a certain unity of mores, a 'national' form and sovereignty, a free capacity to make decisions on matters important to them."[47] He also says:

> Populism is a stage where the people struggles for their survival while rediscovering the solidarity between their social being and their political being. In wanting to conserve their sociability, the people rediscovers the necessity of politics as a condition and reinforcement of that sociability. The populist moment is the moment where such politics does not exist and where it contributes, on the contrary, to destroying the people's being-together. Populism is the aspiration, not yet realized, to rediscover that form of politics which will allow the people to continue being a people. . . . [It is the] beginning of a people's resistance to their elites because they have realized that they are being led toward the abyss.

For the peoples, it is a matter of preserving themselves as peoples — or even of reinstituting themselves as peoples. What the people want is, as always, to create the conditions for their autonomy, but also to win back what José Ortega y Gasset defined as "the fundamental right of man: the right to continuity" ("Man is never a first man; he can only start living at a certain level of the accumulated past").

It is easy to denounce the "fears" that nourish populism, and even more those who "manipulate" such fears, but one would do better to ask oneself about the causes of these fears and whether they are well-founded. In a society that has in fact become good at generating fears, fears are not necessarily imaginary. Gaël Brustier has written that "'Left-wing populism,' if one takes the trouble to think beyond the term's pejorative connotations, is the great strategic question being put to the radical Left, but also to social democracy (that social democracy which has not rallied to social-liberalism) or to political

---

[47] Vincent Coussediere, website *Figaro Vox*, March 18, 2016, 3.

ecology."[48] This "great strategic question," at a time when various forms of populism have become forces to be reckoned with, has in fact been posed to society as a whole.

---

[48] Gaël Brustier, "Le peuple, c'est par ou?" ["The People: Where Are They?"], website *Temps présent*, July 21, 2016, 4.

JEAN-CLAUDE MICHÉA'S THESES

In January 1905, the regulations of the French Section of the Workers' International, the Socialist Party of the time, still indicated that it was a "class party whose goal was to socialize the means of production and exchange, i.e., to transform capitalist society into a collectivist or Communist society, and that its means to this end was the economic and political organization of the proletariat." Of course, no "socialist" party would dare say this today. Socialists have mutated into social democrats and, increasingly, into social liberals.

That the Left has today become almost entirely reformist, that it has rallied to the market economy and has gradually cut itself off from the workers and the popular classes is certainly not news: the spectacle of political life demonstrates it constantly. This is why, for example, the voice of the Left is so weak amid the great global financial crisis of the moment. It is no more disposed than the Right to take the measures necessary for launching a real war against Form-Capital's planetary grasp. As Serge Halimi observes, "The reformist Left distinguishes itself from the conservatives for the duration of a political campaign by a kind of optical illusion. Then, when it gets the chance, it governs like its adversaries so as not to upset the economic order, to protect the silverware of the nobility in their castles."[1]

The question arises as to why. What are the causes of this development? Can they be fully explained in terms of individual opportunism on the part of former revolutionaries who have become distinguished citizens? Is it a distant consequence of the Fordist system? Or an effect of particular historical circumstances, the collapse of the Soviet Bloc having destroyed the idea of any credible alternative to the market system?

In *Orpheus's Complex*, Jean-Claude Michéa gives a more original and also deeper answer: the Left has cut itself off from the

---

[1] Serge Halimi, "Où est la gauche a l'heure de la tourmente économique?" ["Where I the Left in This Time of Economic Turmoil?"], *Le Monde diplomatique*, November 2011, 14.

people because it adhered very early to the ideology of progress, which diametrically contradicts all popular values.[2]

Aiming at the unification of the human race as well as the advent of a "liquid" universe (Zygmunt Bauman), the theory of progress implies the repudiation of all "archaic" (i.e., previous) forms of belonging, the systematic destruction of the basis of traditional solidarity (as in the famous enclosure reform that forced the exodus of thousands of peasants deprived of their customary rights, converting them into deracinated workers easily exploitable by factories).[3] In the "progressive" view, any positive evaluation of the world as it was before necessarily comes from a "nostalgic" cult of the past:

> All who — ontologically incapable of admitting that times change — display any attachment (or any nostalgia), *in any domain whatsoever*, for what formerly existed thus betray a disturbing "conservatism" or, for the most impious among them, an irremediably "reactionary" nature.[4] The new world must necessarily be raised on the ruins of the previous world. The liquidation of roots forms the basis of the program; it follows that "only the deracinated can attain intellectual and political freedom" (Christopher Lasch).

Such is the image of the world that, in the eighteenth century, accompanied the bourgeoisie's social rise, and with it the spread of mercantile values. It is a modern attitude ordered toward an abstract universalism in which Friedrich Engels rightly saw "the idealized rule of the bourgeoisie." (Sorel, in his own time, also emphasized the profoundly bourgeois character of the ideology

---

[2] Jean-Claude Michéa, *Le Complexe d'Orphée. La gauche, les gens ordinaires et la religion du progrès* [*Orpheus's Complex: The Left, Ordinary People, and the Religion of Progress*] (Paris: Climats-Flammarion, 2011).

[3] Michéa notes here that contemporary "migratory movements are simply the transposition to a planetary scale of that permanent rural exodus without which capitalism would soon cease to function" (*Le Complexe d'Orphée*, 112).

[4] Michéa, *Le Complexe d'Orphée*, 14.

of progress.) It is also an old monotheistic procedure that hurls anathemas at particular realities in the name of a conceptual iconoclasm — an ancient Platonic attitude discrediting the sensible world in the name of pure ideas.[5]

The theory of progress is directly associated with liberal ideology. The liberal project was born in the seventeenth century from a desire to break with civil and religious wars while rejecting absolutism, which was judged incompatible with individual liberty. After the wars of religion, liberals thought civil war could only be avoided by ceasing to appeal to shared moral values. They advocated a state *neutral* on the issue of the "good life." Since society could no longer be founded on virtue, common sense, or the common good, morality had to remain a private affair (the principle of axiological neutrality). The general idea was that one could only found civil society on the principled exclusion of all reference to *common* values — which amounted, in turn, to positing the legitimacy of any desire or whim that was the object of a "private" choice.

The liberal project, as Jean-Claude Michéa explains, resulted in two things:

> On the one hand, the rule of law, officially neutral on the level of moral and "ideological" values, and whose only function is to make sure the freedom of one group not infringe upon that of any other (a liberal constitution has the same metaphysical structure as a roadmap). On the other, the self-regulating market, supposed to allow each person to reach agreement with his fellows on the exclusive basis of the self-interest properly understood of the parties concerned.[6]

---

[5] Michéa emphasizes in passing that when one speaks of the Left's universalism, one must not "forget its Christian roots and especially its Pauline origin." St. Paul, in fact, is the first to posit a disincarnate conception of the universal, where "every particular determination must be thought of as a major obstacle to the arrival of a just order and, consequently, as a politically incorrect configuration that must be eradicated as quickly as possible" (*Le Complexe d'Orphée*, 27).

[6] Jean-Claude Michéa, "Il y a une unité du libéralisme" ["Liberalism

The Left/Right dichotomy is often traced back to the French Revolution. This is to forget that it only truly entered public discourse at the very end of the nineteenth century. On the eve of the Revolution, the principal division did not oppose the "Left" to the "Right" but a landed aristocracy endowed with political power to a mercantile bourgeoisie won over to liberal ideas. No one at that time truly defended the people. Retrospectively, Michéa's book explains the French Revolution's ambiguity: a bourgeois revolution, but carried out in the name of the "third estate" (and above all the "nation"), inspired both by Rousseau's ideas and by the liberalism of the Enlightenment, "progressive" along with Condorcet, but fascinated by Antiquity along with Robespierre or Saint-Just.

In the nineteenth century, liberals would once again take up this fundamentally modern idea that consists in seeing "the uprooting from nature and tradition as the emancipatory act *par excellence* and the only means of access to a 'universal' and 'cosmopolitan' society."[7] Benjamin Constant, to cite just one, was the first to celebrate this disposition of human nature that leads one to "sacrifice the present to the future."

While the Third Republic saw the bourgeoisie gradually, and not without difficulties, assume the heritage of the Revolution of 1789, the socialist movement was organizing itself into associations and parties. Let us recall that the word "socialism" only appeared around 1830, especially in the writings of Pierre Leroux and Robert Owen, just as capitalism was affirming itself as the dominant force. The right to strike was recognized in 1864, the same year the First International was founded. But the first socialists, whose social base was found especially among trade workers, did not present themselves as men "of the Left" at all. Michéa recalls, moreover, that "socialism was originally neither of the Left nor Right,"[8] and that it would never have occurred to

---

Has a Unity"], interview in *Le Spectacle du monde*, October 2011, 22–24.

[7] Jean-Claude Michéa, "Socialisme ou barbarie, il faut choisir. Maintenant!" ["Socialism or Barbarism, We Must Choose—Now!"], interview in *Causeur*, October 2011, 17–18.

[8] Michéa, "Socialisme ou barbarie," 22.

Sorel or Proudhon, Marx or Bakunin to define themselves as men "of the Left." The "Left" at that time meant nothing beyond "radicals."

In fact, the socialist movement presented itself at the beginning as an *independent* force with respect to the conservative bourgeoisie and "ultras," as well as to the "republicans" and other forces of the "Left." It was of course opposed to the caste privileges attached to the *Ancien Régime* — privileges preserved in another form by the liberal bourgeoisie — but it was equally opposed to the individualism of the Enlightenment inherited from British political economy with its defense of mercantile values, which had already been so well criticized by Rousseau. So it did not embrace the "progressive" Left's ideas, and saw that the values of progress exalted by the Left were also those of the liberal bourgeoisie that was oppressing the workers. In reality, it was struggling against the monarchist and clerical Right, against bourgeois capitalism, the exploiter of living labor, and against the progressive "Left" who were heirs of the Enlightenment. So we have a contest between three parties, very different from the Left/Right divide that would win out following the First World War.

Moreover, it was by way of opposition to the Left's reformism and parliamentarianism that Proudhonian socialism and Sorelian revolutionary syndicalism developed the ideal of mutualism, or the autonomy of trade unions and the revolutionary will at work in "direct action" — an ideal that would crystalize in 1906 in the General Confederation of Labor's celebrated Charter of Amiens.

The first socialists were not enemies of the past, either. More exactly, they readily distinguished those aspects of the *Ancien Régime* that embodied the principle of hierarchical dominion, which they rejected, from those that embodied the communitarian principle (Marx's *Gemeinwesen*) and the traditional moral and cultural values that underlay it. "For the first socialists, it was clear that a society in which individuals would have nothing in *common* apart from their rational aptitude for concluding exchanges based on self-interest could not constitute a community worthy of the name."[9] This is why Pierre Leroux, one of the very first socialist theoreticians, affirmed not only that "society is not the result of a contract," but that "far from being independent of all society and tradition, man has his life within tradition and society."

For the people, the past is not merely what enables them to place themselves in a particular historic lineage and continuity, but also what helps them judge the value of proposed innovations. "Tradition," from this point of view, is less a constraint than a protection. In the past, a good number of popular revolts have originated in a clearly advertised will to defend popular customs and traditions against the Church, the bourgeoisie, or princes. The reason is that the customs, traditions, and particular forms of local life allow the emergence of a *common* world and constitute the framework within which "the elementary structures of reciprocity can be established and thus also the anthropological conditions of different ethical and political processes that may allow the extension of their fundamental principle to other human groups, or even to humanity as a whole."[10]

This view of the past in no way contradicts internationalism or the sense of the universal. The first socialists were perfectly aware that it is "always from a particular cultural tradition that it appears possible to attain truly universal values,"[11] and that "in practice, the universal can never be constructed on the ruins of particular rootedness."[12] To borrow the words of the Portuguese writer Miguel Torga, they thought that "the universal was the local without walls." "Since only he who is emotionally attached to his community of origin — its geography, history, culture, ways of living — is really able to understand those who feel a similar sentiment toward their own community," writes Michéa again, "we can conclude that the true national sentiment (of

---

[9] Jean-Claude Michéa, "Orwell, la gauche, l'anti-totalitarisme et la *common decency*" ["Orwell, the Left, Anti-Totalitarianism, and Common Decency"], interview with Élisabeth Lévy, *Le Magazine littéraire*, December 2009.

[10] Michéa, "Socialisme ou barbarie," 18.

[11] Michéa, interview with Élisabeth Lévy.

[12] Michéa, *Le Complexe d'Orphée*, 134.

which love of the language is an essential component) not only does not contradict, but on the contrary tends generally to favor the development of the internationalist spirit that has always been one of the socialist project's principal drivers." [13]

Just as patriotism must not be confused with ("Right-wing") nationalism, internationalism must not be confused with ("Left-wing") cosmopolitanism. The abandonment or forgetfulness of one's own culture makes one unable to understand the attachment of others to theirs. The final result of abstract universalism is not the reign of the universal good but the establishment of a "hypnotic, glacial, and uniform universe" whose subject is that narcissistic, pre-Oedipean, immature, and capricious being: the contemporary consumer.

In France, it was at the time of the Dreyfus Affair (1894) that the historic alliance was formed between socialism (influenced first by German Social Democracy, then by Marxism) and the progressive "Left." Born of a concern for "republican defense" against the monarchic, clerical, or nationalist Right, a compromise emerged that would first give birth to those called "progressive republicans." Then a confusion arose between what is *liberating* and what is *modern*, the two wrongly being treated as synonymous.

It was at this moment, writes Michéa, that the socialist movement was

> gradually led to substitute for its initial struggle of the workers against bourgeois capitalist domination a different struggle that would soon oppose—in the name of "progress" and "modernity"—a people "of the Left" to a people "of the Right" (and from this new point of view it would be self-evident that a worker of the "Left" was always much closer to a banker or International Monetary Fund director of the Left than to a worker, peasant, or employee who gave his vote to the Right). [14]

---

[13] Michéa, "Socialisme ou barbarie," 18.
[14] Michéa, "Socialisme ou barbarie," 22–23.

This initial compromise had two aspects:

> One the one hand, it led to anchoring liberalism—the principal engine of the Enlightenment's philosophy—in the camp of the "forces of progress." . . . On the other, it contributed to make the original socialist critique illegible in advance, since that critique was born precisely of a revolt against the inhumanity of liberal industrialization and the injustice of its abstract law.[15]

It was then—and only then—that the cause of the people began to be synonymous with that of progress, under the banner of a Left that wanted above all to be the "party of the future" (as against the past) and the herald of "sunny tomorrows," i.e., of modernity on the march. It was only then that it became necessary, when one wished to place oneself "on the Left," to proclaim a "principled contempt for everything that still wore the disgraceful mark of 'yesterday' (the dark world of the fields, traditions, 'prejudices,' 'withdrawal into oneself,' or 'irrational' attachment to beings and places)."[16] It was only then that the socialist (followed by the Communist) movement made the "progressive" ideal of endless productivity its own—this industrial and hyper-urban project that completed the uprooting of the popular classes, rendering them even more vulnerable to the grip of Form-Capital (which also explains why this ideal was better received by already rootless workers than by peasants).

Henceforth, to defend socialism one had to believe in the promise of humanity's forward march toward a radically new world governed only by the universal laws of reason. To be "on the Left," one had to class oneself among those who on principle refused to look back, as Orpheus was commanded (whence the title of Michéa's book: descending to the realm of the dead in the hope of finding Eurydice and bringing her back to the world of the living, Orpheus was forbidden by Hades to look back on pain of losing his beloved forever; of course, he violated this

---

[15] Michéa, interview with Élisabeth Lévy.
[16] Michéa, *Le Complexe d'Orphée*, 12–13.

prohibition at the last moment). Michéa opposes, with both firmness and talent, this wrong turn, which he rightly sees as deceptive.

Cut off from its roots, the workers' movement was at the same time deprived of the conditions and means of its *autonomy*. As George Orwell saw, the religion of progress effectively deprives man of his autonomy at the very moment it claims to guarantee his liberation from the past. By way of historical necessity, heteronomy with regard to the future replaces heteronomy with regard to the past. "As soon as an individual (or collective) has lost the means of his autonomy," emphasizes Michéa, "he can only continue his existence by having recourse to artificial prostheses. And it is precisely this artificial (or 'alienated') life that consumption, fashion, and spectacle are supposed to offer by way of illusory compensation to all those whose lives have thus been mutilated."[17]

With the Left considering itself "innovative," capitalism is at once denounced as "conservative." This was another fateful wrong turn, for Form-Capital is anything but conservative! Marx had already clearly shown capitalism's intrinsically progressive character, which he credited with having suppressed feudalism and drowned all the old values in the "icy water of egoistical calculation." To this fundamental trait we may add another, proper to the modern forms of this same capitalism. Michéa explains:

> An integral market economy can only function in the long run if most people have internalized a culture of fashion, consumption, and unlimited growth, a culture necessarily founded on the perpetual celebration of youth, individual caprice, and immediate gratification. . . . So it is indeed cultural liberalism (and not moral rigorism or religious austerity) that constitutes consumer capitalism's most effective psychological and moral complement.[18]

---

[17] Michéa, "Socialisme ou barbarie," 21.
[18] Michéa, "Il y a une unité du libéralisme," 24.

By becoming "Left-wing," socialism made the principles of cultural liberalism its own. The "permissive" Left thus became the natural soil for the growth of Form-Captial.

For decades, two totally different things would find themselves associated in a permanent state of ambiguity under the label "Left-wing": the just protest of the working class against the capitalist bourgeoisie and the bourgeois liberal belief in a theory of progress which held that "before" could only be worse and "tomorrow" could only better. In fact, the socialist movement deviated from its initial inspiration the moment it became "progressive," i.e., adhered to the theory (or religion) of progress — i.e., to the metaphysics of limitlessness — which is the heart of Enlightenment philosophy, and thus of liberal philosophy. Since the theory of progress is intrinsically tied to liberalism, the "Left," by becoming "progressive," condemned itself to rejoining the liberal camp one day or another. The worm was in the apple. Cultural liberalism had already foreshadowed the shift to economic liberalism.

The final rampart to give way was the Communist Party, which gradually ceased playing the role that had made for its success in the past: providing "the working class and other popular categories with a political language that allowed them to live their lives with a certain pride and to give meaning to the world before their eyes."[19]

We note that what Michéa said of the Left could also of course be said of the Right by means of a converse proof: the Left rallied to economic liberalism because it was already devoted to the idea of progress and "social" liberalism, while the Right rallied to a liberalism of mores because it had first adopted economic liberalism. In fact, it is just as illusory to believe one can be lastingly liberal at the economic level without ending up being liberal at the political or "societal" level as well (as a majority of the Left used to believe). In other words, there is a deep unity to liberalism: it forms a whole.

To the Left's stupidity, which thinks it possible to fight capitalism in the name of progress, corresponds the Right's imbecility,

---

[19] Michéa, "Il y a une unité du libéralisme," 25.

which thinks it possible to defend both "traditional values" and a market economy that never stops destroying such values: "Integral economic liberalism (officially defended by the Right) carries within itself a permanent revolution in mores (officially defended by the Left), just as the latter demands in its turn the total liberation of the market."[20] This is what explains today's convergence of the Left and Right in the ideology of the rights of man, the cult of infinite growth, the veneration of mercantile exchange, and the unrestrained desire for profits. This at least has the merit of clarifying things.

The Left quickly persuaded itself that the globalization of capital represented an inevitable development and an unavoidable future, politics becoming *ipso facto* nothing more than a means of adapting oneself to economic and financial globalization. The great divorce of the people and the Left has been the most resounding consequence of this.

The Club Jean-Moulin opened the way in the 1960s. The Rocardian "second Left" of the 1970s and the Saint-Simon Foundation in the 1980s widened the breach through which the Left began to bet on "civil society" and rally to the market economy. At the same time cultural liberalism triumphed, a triumph that found expression in a shift in the political debate toward social issues and new social groups in the process of becoming autonomous (women, immigrants, homosexuals, etc.). Finally, money became completely hegemonic in the domain of values. "The winner was Alain Minc," remarked Jacques Julliard. "He understood that by taking up the second Left's ideas, one could cut a very nice deal with the neocapitalism then being established."[21]

There thus emerged a Left "whose dogmata were anti-racism, hatred of limits, contempt for the people, and obligatory praise for uprootedness."[22] This is how the imagination of the "modern

---

[20] Michéa, *Le Complexe d'Orphée*, 216.

[21] Jacques Julliard, "A gauche, le retard des idées sur les faits" ["On the Left, Ideas Have Not Caught Up with Facts"], interview in *Esprit*, March–April 2011, 56.

[22] Olivier François, "Michéa et les bons esprits" ["Michéa and the Good Spirits"], *Causeur*, October 2011, 24.

Left" — symbolized in France by *Le Monde*, *Libération*, *Les In-rockuptibles*, and other publications of the ideologically dominant "circle of reason" — came to be confused with that of the masters of the Central European Bank and the IMF. And this is also why, "behind the once-liberating conviction that progress cannot be stopped, it has become increasingly difficult to understand anything but the idea, now dominant, that capitalism and globalization cannot be stopped."[23] Henceforth the Left celebrated growth, i.e., the production of merchandise *ad infinitum*, in the same terms as liberals. Where some speak of "deterritorialization" (in the style of Deleuze-Guatteri or Antonio Negri), others speak of "delocalization." Concerning immigration, the reserve army of capitalism, the "modern" Left uses the same language as Laurence Parisot ("mixture" and "nomadism" set up as norms). Under the influence of those who "destroyed socialism by converting it into the individualism of universal rights and integral liberalism" (Hervé Juvin), the enemy is no longer the capitalist who exploits men's living labor, but the "reactionary" with his mistaken regret over the loss of past eras.

Michéa continues:

> Thus it is normal that the "citizen" Left (which has broken with any popular and socialist feeling) appears today as the privileged political place where all civilizational and legal transformations required by the global market are carried out. It is no longer anything but the pilot fish of a capitalism without borders or, if you prefer, the militant cultural avant-garde of the liberal Right.[24]

The Left's "values" are no longer socialist but "progressive": support for illegal immigrants, the opening or abolition of borders, the defense of homosexual marriage, the celebration of "contemporary art," the decriminalization of certain drugs, etc. — all options with which the working class is in total disagreement, or in which it is completely uninterested. For the

---

[23] Michéa, *Le Complexe d'Orphée*, 22.
[24] Michéa, "Il y a une unité du libéralism," 25.

"modern" Left, which has achieved an alliance between government employees, the upper bourgeoisie, immigrants, and "bobos," it is

> a single thing to reject the dark heritage of the past (which can only, as a matter of principle, call forth an attitude of "repentance"), to fight all symptoms of the "identitarian" sickness (i.e., in other words, all signs of a collective life rooted in a particular culture), and to celebrate endlessly the transgression of all moral and cultural limits inherited from past generations (the final reign of the liberal-Paulist universal coinciding by definition with absolute indifferentiation and *unlimitedness*).[25]

What one does not speak of anymore is capitalism or the class struggle, to say nothing of revolution, that obsolete notion. Even the Communist Party has practically suppressed the word "socialism" from its vocabulary. Having lost its ideological identity, it is no longer able to influence the social-democratic current on which it depends electorally.[26]

The aim is no longer the struggle against capitalism but the fight against all forms of identitarian concern, regularly described as the resurgence of a reactionary and backward mentality. Jean-Claude Michéa observes:

> This explains why the "migrant" has gradually become the central redemptive figure in all ideological constructions of the new liberal Left in place of the archaic proletarian, constantly suspected of not being sufficiently indifferent to his community of origin, or, *a fortiori*, the peasant whose defining bond with the earth destines him to become the most despised and mocked figure of capitalist culture.[27]

---

[25] Michéa, *Le Complexe d'Orphée*, 28–29.

[26] Cf. Anicet Le Pors, "Communisme: mais ou est donc passé le socialisme?" ["Communism: But Where has Socialism Gone?"], *LeMonde.fr*, February 17, 2011.

[27] Michéa, *Le Complexe d'Orphée*, 142.

The Left is therefore looking for a "substitute people." The Terra Nova foundation, established in 2008 by friends of Dominique Strauss-Kahn, became famous by publishing a report in May 2011 suggesting that the Socialist Party reestablish its electoral base on an alliance between the affluent classes and suburban "minorities," abandoning the workers and low-level employees to their "Right-wing values" (criticism of immigration, economic and social protectionism, the promotion of strong norms and moral values, the struggle against welfare, etc.). The report's language is very clear:

> Contrary to the Left's historical electorate, brought together by socioeconomic issues, this France of the future is united above all by its progressive cultural values. . . . Between the two losers of globalization—the ghettoized immigrants and the threatened low-level employees—the Terra Nova-style Left is banking on the first group to the detriment of the second.[28]

So it is not surprising that the people are turning away from a Left more interested in celebrities and riffraff than in working people, which supports globalization even when it is mainly the globalization of capital, which is more interested in citizens' initiatives than in structural transformations, in a maternal society of "care" more than in social justice, in associative life more than political life, in media spectacle more than the people's sovereignty, in social consensus more than class struggle—and which,

---

[28] Guillaume Desanges, "Terra Nova ou la nouvelle idéologie socialiste" ["Terra Nova, or the New Socialist Ideology"], *Valeurs actuelles*, October 13, 2011. In his essay *La Gauche et la préférence immigrée* [*The Left and Immigrant Preference*] (Paris: Plon, 2011), Hervé Algarrondo, journalist at the *Nouvel Observateur*, writes: "The legalization of all the undocumented is not merely an anti-republican slogan insofar as it flouts the state's prerogatives. It is also, and even more, an anti-worker slogan insofar as this is naturally the social category most affected by the arrival of new immigrants." Cf. also the book by Gaël Brustier and Jean-Philippe Huelin, *Recherche le peuple désespérément* [*Desperately Seeking the People*] (Paris: François Bourin, 2009).

aligned with the liberal model, no longer conceives a general interest distinct from a mere aggregate of individual interests. The people no longer recognize themselves in a Left that has replaced anti-capitalism with a simulated "anti-fascism," socialism with "bobo" individualism, and internationalism with cosmopolitanism or enthusiasm for illegal immigration. This Left has nothing but contempt for authentically popular values, indulges in the absurdity of celebrating both "mixture" and "diversity,"[29] and exhausts itself in campaigns for social responsibility and struggles "against all forms of discrimination" (with the notable exception of class discrimination) for the exclusive benefit of the banks, the *Lumpenproletariat*, and a whole series of marginal groups.

Nor is it surprising that the people, disappointed as they are, often turn to movements described contemptuously as "populist." To quote Michéa again:

The gap between the accusatory representation of society now imposed by official sociology (viz., a minority of excluded persons relegated to "ethnic ghettos," suffering all imaginable persecution, and surrounded by a "residential" France supposedly belonging to the middle class) and the dark reality experienced by the popular classes, in the majority and yet forgotten, has become altogether surreal. The result is that those suffering all the harm of globalization do not find in the politically correct language of the modern Left any means of expressing their lived experience.[30] . . . By undermining every possibility of legitimating any moral judgment (and consequently refusing to understand the *popular usage* of concepts of merit and individual responsibility), the progressive Left inexorably condemns itself to handing over to its enemies on the Right whole segments of these popular classes that are only demanding

---

[29] Cf. Pierre-André Taguieff, "Diversité et métissage: un mariage forcé" ["Diversity and Mixture: A Shotgun Marriage"], *Le Débat*, March–April 2010, 38–44.

[30] Jean-Claude Michéa, "Il y a une unité du libéralisme," 25.

in their way to live honestly in a decent society. . . . In reality, it was the Left itself that chose, toward the end of the 1970s, to abandon the most modest and exploited social classes to their fate by wanting to be "realistic" and "modern," i.e., by renouncing in advance any radical critique of historic development that for 30 years now has been burying humanity beneath an "immense accumulation of merchandise" (Marx) and transforming nature into a desert of concrete and steel.[31]

Georges Sorel said that "the sublime is dead within the bourgeoisie, and so it is condemned no longer to have any morality." Michéa also speaks of morality. In his case, however, it is not a question of the "sublime," but merely of the common decency so often celebrated by Orwell.

"Everything is moral which is a source of solidarity," said Émile Durkheim, "everything that forces man to reckon with others, to regulate his movements according to something besides the impulses of his own egoism." "This explains," adds Michéa, "why the revolt of the first socialists against a world based on mere egoistical calculation was so often brought about by a moral experience."[32] One thinks of the "virtue" celebrated by Jaurès, and of the "social morality" of which Benoît Malon spoke. "Common decency," which is far removed from any form of moral order or puritanism, is in fact one of the main traits of "ordinary people." It is among the people that one finds it most widespread. It involves generosity, the sense of honor, and solidarity. It is at work in the triple obligation to give, to receive, and to give back which Marcel Mauss made the basis of the logic of gift and counter-gift. It was on this basis that the protest against social injustice was expressed in the past, for it is common decency that allows one to perceive the immorality of a world exclusively founded on rational self-interest and the permanent transgression of all limits. It is also common decency that is protesting today with all its strength

---

[31] Michéa, *Le Complexe d'Orphée*, 245, 252.
[32] Michéa, "Il y a une unité du libéralisme," 25.

against that "modern" Left in which it no longer recognizes itself. "From this point of view," writes Michéa, "the socialist project (or, if one prefers another term used by Orwell, that of a decent society) appears to be a continuation of popular morality by other means."[33]

So we see that Michéa is not criticizing the Left from a Right-wing point of view, but in the name of the founding values of socialism and the workers' movement. All his work is an effort to rediscover the spirit of that original socialism and lay the foundations for its renewal in the world of today. By taking up the defense of "ordinary people," what he is rejecting above all is the discrediting of the values of rootedness and organic structures that in the past were often the only protection the poorest and most exploited had.

This is not an isolated point of view. Jean-Claude Michéa's reasoning fits rather well into a vast galaxy where one finds first of all the great Orwell, to whom Michéa has devoted a book, *Orwell, anarchiste tory* [*Orwell: Tory Anarchist*],[34] as well as Christopher Lasch, theoretician of a socialist and communitarian "populism," another great adversary of the ideology of progress.[35] We also find, to cite only a few names, the young Marx who criticized the "rights of man"; the first French socialists; William Morris, Charles Péguy, and Chesterton; Antonio Gramsci and his emphasis on popular cultures; the Pasolini of the *Écrits corsaires* (the one who said, "That which motivates us to go back is as human and necessary as that which drives us to go forward"); Clouscard and his critique of libertarian-liberals, Jean Baudrillard and his denunciation of the "divine Left"; the movies of Ken Loach and Robert Guédiguian; the songs of Brassens; and the novels of René Fallet and Léo Malet, not forgetting Jacques Ellul and Bernard Charbonneau, Walter Benjamin and Günther Anders, Cornelius Castoriadis, André Gorz, Guy Debord,

---

[33] Michéa, *Le Complexe d'Orphée*, 87–88.

[34] Jean-Claude Michéa, *Orwell, anarchiste tory* [*Orwell: Tory Anarchist*] (Castelnau-le-Lez: Climats, 1995).

[35] Christopher Lasch, *The True and Only Heaven: Progress and Its Critics* (New York: Norton, 1991).

Jaime Semprun, Serge Latouche,[36] and many others.

Michéa compares liberalism to a Möbius strip, which presents a "Left" and "Right" side, but without any break of continuity. This means that between the "Right-wing" bourgeois and the "Left-wing" bourgeois, both heirs of the Enlightenment's liberal philosophy, there will always be more objective affinities than between both the bourgeois and the anti-bourgeois. Conversely, there is an equally natural complementarity between those who defend the people from the exploitative bourgeois, whether they still place themselves on the Left or come from the Right. This is what the author of *The Orpheus Complex* means when he writes, "It does not much matter, really, from what historical tradition one has drawn his particular reasons for respecting the principles of common decency and indignation at their permanent violation by the capitalist system."[37] In an age when the Left means more than ever to rally the "forces of progress," Michéa does not hesitate to add that it is "the pathetic inability to assume the anti-capitalist critique's conservative dimension which explains, to a large degree, the profound ideological disarray (not to say intellectual coma) into which *the whole of the modern Left* has been plunged today.[38]

*

No doubt we should have expected this. The views developed by Jean-Claude Michéa were not slow to earn him many critiques, mostly directed at two of his books, *Orpheus's Complex* and *Mysteries of the Left*.[39] Rushing into a breach opened by the

---

[36] Jean-Claude Michéa, who is one of MAUSS's interlocutors, has also expressed sympathy for the theory of degrowth (Serge Latouche), denouncing the logic of "ever more" which is at the heart of the process of unlimited accumulation that is global capitalism. On Jaime Semprun and the publishing house Éditions de l'Encyclopédie des Nuisances, cf. Olivier François and Aurélie Mouillard, "Jaime Semprun avait indiqué la voie" ["Jaime Semprun Has Shown the Way"], *Eléments*, January–March 2011, 61.

[37] Michéa, "Socialisme ou barbarie," 23.

[38] Michéa, *Le Complexe d'Orphée*, 76–77.

[39] *Le Complexe d'Orphée; Les Mystères de la gauche. De l'idéal des Lumières au triomphe du capitalisme absolu* [*The Mysteries of the Left: From the*

sociologist Luc Boltanski,[40] Serge Halimi began hostilities in the pages of *Le Monde diplomatique*, which he has edited since 2008, followed by the economist Frédéric Lordon in *La Revue des livres*, and finally by Philippe Corcuff, a militant anarcho-third-worldist who has passed through the Socialist Party, the Greens, and Alain Krivine's and Olivier Besancenot's New Anti-Capitalist Party.[41] They were immediately copied by a number of bloggers.

The most striking thing about this barrage, as observed by the target himself, is that it has not come from the bobo Left that Michéa has regularly attacked in his books, but by authors much more resolutely engaged "on the Left" from whom we had learned to expect better (Boltanski and Lordon's critiques of capitalism, to cite only them, have often been suggestive). One possible explanation: the influence of a Pierre Bourdieu's coagulated thought on these "state-appointed insurrectional sociologists" (Aude Lancelin). The "bourdivine" Left does not like to be questioned, as Jean Baudrillard had already observed.

It is worth lingering over this polemic, not to defend Michéa, who has been quite capable of defending himself—especially in a text published online on August 2, 2013, by Médiapart in the form of an open letter to Philippe Corcuff, in which he responds to his other critics as well—but because despite the caricatures

---

Ideal of the Enlightenment to the Triumph of Absolute Capitalism] (Paris: Climats-Flammarion, 2013). Cf. also *Impasse Adam Smith. Brèves remarques sur l'impossibilité de dépasser le capitalisme sur sa gauche* [*The Adam Smith Impasse: Brief Remarks on the Impossibility of Overcoming Capitalism from the Left*] (Castelnau-le-Lez: Climats, 2002; Paris: Flammarion, 2006).

[40] Luc Boltanski, "Michéa, c'est tout bête" ["Michéa, It's So Stupid"], *Le Monde*, October 6, 2011.

[41] Serge Halimi, "Le laisser-faire est-il libertaire?" ["Is Laissez-Faire Libertarian?"], *Le Monde diplomatique*, June 2013; Frédéric Lordon, "Impasse Michéa" ["The Michéa Impasse"], *La Revue des livres*, July–August 2013, 2–13; and Philippe Corcuff, "Intellectuels critiques et éthique de la responsabilité en période trouble" ["Critical Intellectuals and the Ethics of Responsibility in a Troubled Time"], website *Médiapart*, July 25, 2013.

and bad faith arguments, he raises important fundamental questions. This is a trait characteristic of most debates on Left-wing ideas (one would unfortunately have difficulty finding the equivalent on the Right, where the debate concerning ideas generally amounts to an accumulation of slogans and associated insults).

But what exactly is Michéa being criticized for? For having broken ranks with the Left, as one might think when reading the Frédéric Lordon's horrified exclamation: "Now he is breaking with the Left"? This would obviously be absurd, since what Michéa is fundamentally reproaching the Left with is having broken with socialism.[42] Michéa has not chosen to break with "the Left" in order to rally to "the Right"! Besides, one would have to be singularly foolish to imagine that criticizing the Left means *ipso facto* to rally to the Right or defend its positions (it was with reasoning of this sort that those who denounced the fraud of a "free world" dominated by the Americans during the Cold War were denounced as "objective allies" of the Soviet Union). Michéa is a socialist and partisan of a classless society, as well as a radical democrat of libertarian sensibility and an advocate of degrowth whose emancipatory project has nothing to do with any sort of restorationism. Affirming explicitly that we must "think with the Enlightenment against the Enlightenment,"[43] according to the excellent formula we owe to Theodor Adorno, he appeals to the young Marx, Marcel Mauss, Guy Debord, George Orwell, and Christopher Lasch, not to Bonald or Joseph de Maistre, and still less to Maurras!

In his response to the "new guard dogs" who have attacked him, Michéa himself says that he "must have tapped into quite a hornet's nest to have elicited such hostility." That must indeed be what happened, since he put his finger on the essential. By saying what? Quite simply, that if the Left has betrayed

---

[42] Jean-Claude Michéa, "Pourquoi j'ai rompu avec la gauche" ["Why I Broke With the Left"], *Marianne*, March 12, 2013.

[43] Jean-Claude Michéa, "Pas de société socialiste sans valeurs morales communes" ["No Socialist Society Without Common Values"], interview in *L'Humanité*, March 15, 2013.

the people by rallying to the market society, it is because it has broken with the inspiration of the original socialists, something only possible because the cultural and social liberalism to which it appeals takes its inspiration from the same sources as the economic liberalism (what the Italians call "liberalism" *simpliciter*) it pretends to fight against. This is all that was necessary for the mechanism of suspicion to be triggered. Like many others before him, Michéa has been pronounced "unclear." He has confused issues, deconstructed ready-made ideas, and upset labels. This is what he cannot be forgiven for.

But let us have a closer look.

The chasm now separating the Left from the people has been the object of numerous studies these past few years (especially on the part of Vincent Coussedière, Pierre Sansot, Laurent Bouvet, Gaël Brustier, Christophe Guilley, etc.). "This people whose revolutionary instinct used to be praised is now caricatured by the dominant Left as a reactionary and racist ox condemned for its narrow conservatism and attachment to old moral principles, which make it resistant to the new spirit of capitalism." [44] In spite of appearances, the same goes for Jean-Luc Mélenchon, for whom the people "more closely resembles a somewhat vague group of victims and the oppressed rather than the Marxist revolutionary proletariat or the laboring masses the Communist Party once claimed to defend," [45] as witness his irenical conception of the problems of integration. [46]

---

[44] Olivier François and Jacques de Guillebon, "Le peuple et la gauche: un malentendu?" ["The People and the Left: A Misunderstanding?"], *La Nef*, January 2013, 23.

[45] François and Guillebon, "Le peuple et la gauche: un malentendu?," 24.

[46] The same irenicism appears in Fédéric Lordon, who subscribes to the immigrationism promoted by business interests even as he proposes to legalize all illegal migrants, thinking that will prevent them from being used as the reserve army of capital. He does not see that such legalization will instantly create a leak through which a new crowd of illegal immigrants will arrive. We would thus be caught in a never-ending spiral, whereas even Lordon, not really contradicting himself, declares it "obvious that the abandonment of any regulation of popula-

The Left has dismissed the people at the same time as it has abandoned its will to social change and submitted to liberal logic, which has led it to appropriate the idea that there is basically no alternative to capitalism's unlimited expansion and the establishment of a market society. This double shift should be analyzed dialectically, for each orientation is both the cause and effect of the other. It has been Michéa's merit and originality to give an explanation that cannot be reduced to questions of circumstance or a mere rise in "reformism." We must rather see in it the final result (and logical consequence) of an internal contradiction of the Left resulting from its dual inspiration: on the one hand, the defense of the popular classes inherited from the workers' movement, on the other, that of "progressivism," i.e., the ideology of progress inherited from the Enlightenment to which liberals also appeal.

Workers' socialism was born out of an opposition to modernity which generalized the exploitation of salaried work, the destruction of traditional structures, and the atomization of society, whereas the philosophy of the Enlightenment was at the leading edge of that very modernity, affirming itself from the start as the militant "party of change" in favor of a progress posited as intrinsically "liberating."[47] The alliance between workers' socialism and the progressive Left was formed, as we have seen, at the time of the Dreyfus Affair, when it was necessary to make a

---

tion flows is an indefensible aberration" ("Ce que l'extrême droite ne nous prendra pas" ["The Extreme Right Will Never Take This From Us"], *Le Monde diplomatique*, July 8, 2013, 4).

[47] It is well-known that the excellent Jacques Julliard — who defines himself as "a Christian, and therefore an individualist" — disputes this point with Michéa on the grounds that, according to Julliard, the Left has always presented itself as an alliance between the progressive bourgeoisie and the popular classes insofar as it claimed to draw its political philosophy from the French Revolution. This would amount to forgetting that the Left has never been monolithic and that the philosophy of the Enlightenment was only one source of inspiration among others. This difference of views has been the occasion for a passionate dialogue: Jacques Julliard and Jean-Claude Michéa, *La Gauche et le peuple* (Paris: Flammarion, 2014).

common front against a clerical and reactionary Right devoted to the "alliance of Throne and Altar." This Right has very nearly disappeared today, since it has been buried beneath the liberal Right, whose ideological presuppositions are the same as those of the Left. When Jacques Julliard writes, "On the Left, moral liberalism and economic regimentation; on the Right, moral regimentation and economic liberalism. It is on this sort of cultural Yalta Agreement that the Left-Right opposition still operates," he is being anachronistic. It has been a long time since "the Right" renounced every impulse toward "moral regimentation," and since the Left rallied to a free-trade economy of liberal inspiration.

The circumstances that gave rise to the alliance between socialists and the progressive Left having disappeared, the equivocation inherent in that alliance has appeared once again in the light of day and allows us to understand the causes of the profound and general state of crisis in which the Left now finds itself. The alliance between socialists and progressives has today exhausted all its positive virtues, as Michéa says. Deprived of its old enemy, the reactionary Right, the Left has launched a desperate gambit to compete with the liberal Right on the grounds of modernity and modernization (involving the eradication of the "world of yesterday"). This explains its rallying to a society governed by the dyad of the market economy and the ideology of the rights of man, i.e., by the idea that we can succeed in "living together" by the simple mechanism of competing private interests and abstract procedural law. For the class struggle and the denunciation of social inequalities there has been substituted a "struggle against all forms of discrimination" that aims above all, with impeccable progressive logic, to do away with "archaisms" in the name of "foreverybodyism."[48] Hence Michéa's lapidary observation: "Socialism is by definition incompatible with capitalist exploitation; the Left, alas, is not."[49] Under these conditions, socialism can no longer (without definitively ceasing to be

---

[48] An allusion to "marriage for everybody," the slogan under which homosexual marriage was promoted in France. — Trans.

[49] Michéa, "Pourquoi j'ai rompu avec la gauche."

itself) base itself on a philosophical heritage common to the "Left" and on a liberalism that today remains its principal enemy, insofar as the primacy of "rational" (calculating) individualism antagonizes above all everything that is collective and common.

As soon as "the Left and Right agree in considering the capitalist economy the unsurpassable horizon of our time," it is obvious that the Left/Right divide no longer has any meaning and, correlatively, that the question of class alliances is posed in a new way. This is why Michéa does not hesitate to say, following Pier Paolo Pasolini, Cornelius Castoriadis, Christopher Lasch, and many others, that the Left/Right dichotomy has today become obsolete and fraudulent. Marx, he reminds us, never refers to the opposition of Left and Right but rather to the class struggle. We may add that he did not even oppose equality to inequality, but called for us to pass from the "realm of necessity" to that of "freedom." Henceforth, the only division that matters opposes not Left and Right, but the partisans (wherever they come from) and the adversaries (wherever they come from) of globalized capitalism as a system of total control and dehumanization—a divide that we ourselves have recently described as the opposition between "center" and "periphery." Such a partitioning involves a joint critique of the Left and Right's elites whose convergent interests, above and beyond any partisan divisions, are based on class solidarity. It took courage to say this. That is what Michéa did, and for that he cannot be forgiven.

Michéa likes to recall, citing Marcel Mauss, that capitalism is not simply an economic system but a "total social fact." We have employed the expression "Form-Capital" in the same spirit: capital insofar as it informs global society and becomes the general form of that society. Now, Michéa shows that the partisans of "permanent moral and cultural transgression" are acting in the interest of the predators of global finance insofar as capitalism can only extend its grasp by dislocating not merely the structures of traditional communitarian life but the social bond, shared values, specific ways of life, popular cultures, and so on. Capitalism cannot transform the planet into a vast market—which is its goal—unless that planet has been atomized beforehand, and unless it has renounced any form of symbolic imagination incompatible with feverish devotion to the *novum*, the logic of unlimited profit and accumulation. As he emphasizes: "Without the new paths opened by cultural liberalism, the market cannot continually take over all human activities, including the most intimate."[50]

Serge Halimi says that to consider economic and cultural liberalism "bound together" is an "error." Of course, he does not offer the least bit of proof in support of this contention. We note, moreover, that his article is not directed exclusively against Michéa but also against Geoffrey de Lagasnerie, the author of a book in which he argues exactly the same thesis as Michéa . . . except that he celebrates the very thing Michéa condemns unreservedly, since this unconditional adept of a "Left-wing" modernity goes so far as to appeal to the ultra-capitalist thinkers of the University of Chicago such as Gary Becker, assuring us that he finds in their "pluralism" (?) the best rampart against the Left's "authoritarian impulses"![51] Lagasnerie's program is interesting in that he defines the "central problem" he has chosen to confront as follows: "How to thwart the nostalgic or reactionary impulse necessarily found at the heart of any critical project" (note the "necessarily"!). To this question we may oppose another, well stated by Michéa: "How can we liberate individuals and peoples without thereby destroying the social bond itself, and thus humanity?"

Jean-Claude Michéa's critics are therefore blaming him for confronting "the Left" with its own contradictions, and demonstrating that a choice will henceforth have to be made between defending "progressivism" and defending the popular classes, not only because those two themes are ideologically, politically, and sociologically incompatible, but also because the historical circumstances that led the two tendencies to form an alliance

---

[50] Michéa, "Pas de société socialiste sans valeurs morales communes."

[51] Geoffroy de Lagasnerie, *La dernière leçon de Michel Foucault. Sur le néolibéralisme, la théorie et la politique* [*Michel Foucault's Last Lesson: On Neo-Liberalism, Theory and Politics*] (Paris: Fayard, 2012).

have today disappeared. Their reaction can thus be interpreted as a desperate effort to evade this analysis and "save" the ideology of progress.

The method to which they have recourse consists in saying that the popular classes are not perfect and that the ideology of progress is not completely without merit. Significantly, their criticism concentrates on the notion of "common decency" that Michéa takes from George Orwell—but of which an equivalent could easily be found in Victor Hugo, Jack London, Jules Vallès, Elisée Reclus, Sorel, Proudhon, and many others.

They criticize as idealistic or essentialist the idea that the popular classes are spontaneously inclined to mutual aid, generosity, reciprocity, and collective solidarity, and are more given to the form of gratitude that makes one capable of accepting a gift as something other than what is due or a right, and also more given to judge on the basis of shared values that there are "things one simply does not do." They denounce the very notion of "common decency" as a myth, pure and simple. Corcuff make it a "timeless characteristic of human nature" (*sic*). Lordon sees in it the "manifestation of an imaginary people's eternal essence." "Common decency," he adds, is not for Michéa an anthropological or sociological observation, but an "act of faith." Frédéric Lordon as well, wanting to bring out the "repugnant consequences" of "traditional values" whose inheritance Michéa is accused of wanting to assume, laboriously reminds us that ordinary people sometimes attack racial minorities, go about looking for gay men to beat up, and, of course, vote for Hitler. In short, ordinary people are like everyone: capable of anything— as Spinoza already noted. What a revelation!

This critique of "common decency" is extraordinarily impoverished. One would need to be very naïve to think Michéa does not know that many traditional customs have proven as absurd as they are repugnant. ("There have been societies where having a priest tear out a child's heart was a regular part of 'what is done'!") It is also very naïve—or in very bad faith— to think he does not know that the people can be mistaken; that they can be abused, manipulated, and bewildered; that they can display intolerance, cowardice, or bigotry; that they can beat up immigrants and homosexuals; that they are "always in favor of material progress" (Julliard); that they often dream of becoming bourgeois in their turn, and so on. Michéa, as far as we know, has never pretended that the people were naturally good, naturally infallible, or that they received their virtues from an essence that fell from the sky.

Contrary to what his critics say, Michéa has never been vague about "common decency." He has even given some dozen definitions of what he means. In *Doublethink*,[52] he emphasizes that the virtues covered by this expression are rooted in what Mauss calls the logic of the gift. He has even gone so far as to describe "common decency" as the "modern reappropriation of the spirit of the gift." But this is precisely the sore spot: for the logic of the gift, organized around the triple obligation to give, receive, and give back, is proper to traditional societies as opposed to modern societies, which are only familiar with the logic of commercial exchange.

Concerning "common decency," Michéa simply makes the empirical observation that it is obviously more common among the people whose way of life has long encouraged this type of ordinary virtue than among the bourgeoisie or the elites, who are more often victims of money's dissolving power ("I observe more common decency in the simple and popular circles than among the affluent"). He does not say that these virtues fall from the sky or can be explained by the proletariat's genetics.

Lordon reproaches Michéa with failing to see "that the people owe only to exterior social conditions (and not to its 'essence' *qua* people) its failure to fall into indecency" — in other words, that the people only have moderate desires because they have been "deprived of the means for intemperance," so much so that "common decency merely makes a virtue of necessity." We recognize Bourdieu's influence in this insistence on emphasizing social determinism's importance regarding individual desires and behavior. Michéa wrote explicitly in *Orpheus's Complex* that

---

[52] Jean-Claude Michéa, *La Double Pensée, retour sur la question libérale* [*Doublethink: Return to the Liberal Question*] (Paris: Champs-Flammarion, 2008).

"the popular classes are still relatively protected from liberal egoism, not so much by their supposed 'nature' as by the maintenance of a certain type of social fabric capable of keeping the most invasive forms of possessive individualism at bay from day to day." Ordinary decency, which confers a greater capacity for intellectual and moral resistance, is historically rooted in practices of mutual aid and systems of solidarity that have played an essential role in the lives of villages or popular neighborhoods, while the higher classes' way of life contributed instead to inhibiting these qualities, whether we are speaking of the capitalist system's principled amorality (in which honesty does not pay) or the mere fact of living amid wealth, which leads people to lose their sense of life's realities.[53]

It would be an equally serious error to interpret "common decency" as a new form of moralism. Jean-Claude Michéa himself emphasizes that it is "light years away from *moralizing* and puritanical constructions."[54] "Common decency" is not part of the moral order but of common sense, indeed of what Marx called "common reason." The conviction that "there are things one does not do" obviously does not prevent drunkenness, lying, or adultery, and even less the freedom to relax and amuse oneself, but represents the popular form of an ancient ethic of honor for which certain mental attitudes and forms of behavior are simply dishonorable, i.e., socially shameful. Michéa emphasizes:

---

[53] "Jean-Claude Michéa répond à dix questions" ["Jean-Claude Michéa Answers Ten Questions"], *Les Racines de la liberté*, 324–26. Cf. also Bruce Bégout, *De la décence ordinaire. Court essai sur une idée fondamentale de la pensée politique de George Orwell* [*On Ordinary Decency: A Short Essay on a Fundamental Idea of George Orwell's Political Thinking*] (Paris: Allia, 2008); Rémi de Villeneuve, "Du sens commun au sens interdit. Genèse de l'abrutissement technoscientifique" [*From Common Sense to Fobidden Sense: The Genesis of Technoscientific Mindlessness*], *Les Racines de la liberté*, 127–52; and Pierre Prades, "Christopher Lasch et 'la Common Decency'. Un héritage puritain" ["Christopher Lasch and 'Common Decency': A Puritan Inheritence"], *Les Racines de la liberté*, 209–38.

[54] "Jean-Claude Michéa répond à dix questions," 310.

It is not that the man from the working-class neighborhood is an ideal being by nature, in Rousseau's sense of the term. He is a complex being, capable of the worst as well as the best. But in popular neighborhoods there remain structures of common life founded on the anthropology of the gift which, even if they are under serious attack from modern society, still make possible symbolic relations of exchange between neighbors.

Ordinary men, wrote Christopher Lasch, "have a more developed sense of limits than the higher classes. They understand, unlike the latter, that there are limits to man's control of social development, of nature and the body, of the tragic elements of life and human history."[55] Similarly, they are conscious that loyalty and solidarity are only effective if anchored in a social fabric of physical proximity. The capacity for loyalty, adds Lasch,

> needs to attach itself to specific people and places, not to an abstract ideal of universal rights. We love particular men and women, not humanity in general. The dream of universal brotherhood, because it rests on the sentimental fiction that men and women are all the same, cannot survive the discovery that they differ.[56]

"The humblest strata of the middle and lower classes, populism's natural constituency," writes Arnaud Imatz, "can sometimes display a narrowness of mind capable of engendering xenophobia, racism, chauvinism, and anti-intellectualism, but it remains no less true that the rootedness, solidarity, organicism, and moral realism that they defend are the best guarantees of respect and the survival of democracy."[57]

It is in fact the critique of common decency that we must question. What does this critique mean? What does it reveal if not a mistrust of or even contempt for the people? The critique

---

[55] Lasch, *The True and Only Heaven.*
[56] Lasch, *The True and Only Heaven*, 36.
[57] Imatz, *Droite/gauche*, 232.

of the people as naturally irrational is not new, since it goes back at least to Plato. Irrational, badly informed, manipulable, often uneducated, full of base instincts — their situation is aggravated in our time because they think there are too many foreigners in France, or are mostly favorable to self-defense and the death penalty; the people must be kept away from questions that require expertise ("those who know"), and ultimately can only be allowed a minimal role in political decision-making. In this view, the *demos* is no different from the *plethos*, the dangerous crowd.

Serge Halimi proclaims that our "possible salvation" will not come from "resurrecting last century's proletariat" — a proletariat to which he may prefer late modernity's atomized masses. "Michéa's people," he writes, are Jean Gabin in *La Belle Equipe*: muscular, French, head of the family [*sic*]." This is a stupid remark, but it leads us to recall that Julien Duvivier's *La Belle Equipe* (1936) was greeted in its time as the movie most inspired by the Popular Front — and that this admirable movie was certainly not a reactionary work. But the allusion is revealing: Halimi thereby shows how foreign the Popular Front's spirit is to him — and above all how the very idea of a Popular Front today would repulse him. Frédéric Lordon, who admits he is unable to understand what could concretely be meant by the invitation to conduct himself "decently" in daily life, does not hesitate to write that the people is among the "most tangled of sociological concepts" and that "celebrating the people" could be a form of "social racism"![58] He adds that "one does not see very well" just who these "ordinary people" evoked by Michéa are. He should read somewhat less Spinoza and look around himself a bit more. In any case, the negative descriptions of the people made by Michéa's critics can only receive approbation from liberals who have always mistrusted the "little people." It forms part of the standard demonization of

---

[58] This does not prevent him from recalling that democracy rests on popular sovereignty: "Democracy, popular sovereignty: the same idea, viz., that of a community's mastery of its own destiny" ("Ce que l'extrême droite ne nous prendra pas," 2).

populism flourishing today in all circles.[59]

Lordon also reproaches Michéa with "breaking with his time" — in other words and in plain English, criticizing modernity and the very idea of progress. But with what does he credit modernity? Exactly the same thing as the liberals: having legitimated the right of secession (the right of "clearing off," to quote his own term) from excessively constraining social structures; and permitting "divorce" — in short, rendering the individual able to satisfy his "desirous impulses" independently: "To leave, to quit: this is what individualistic modernity allows." You would think you were reading Benjamin Constant! But how does he not see that in defending the possibility of "clearing off," he is first of all defending the secession of elites which is characteristic of a new transnational class that wishes both to free itself of borders as well as of all the rules to which it wants everyone else to submit?

Michéa's crime is thus to have recalled the popular classes' attachment to values that the idea of progress regards as so many limitations upon the abstract autonomy of a subject cut off from primal belonging. Michéa annoys people because he recognizes, and even emphasizes, the "conservative" reflexes of a working class whose values are most often traditional and communitarian. Such values, diametrically opposed to the market society's individualism and humanity's transformation into atomized monads, obviously refer back to the *Ancien Régime* (which explains why they concur on certain points, even if obviously not all, with the critique of liberalism made by counter-revolutionary thought). With remarkable bad faith, Michéa's adversaries conclude that in the final analysis, his work demonstrates an unacknowledged desire to go back to the *Ancien Régime*. Their bad faith consists in forgetting the fundamental

---

[59] Cf. Frédéric Santos, "Le populisme: une réponse aux mensonges des élites?" ["Populism: A Response to Elite Lies?"], website *Ragemag*, April 11, 2013. The author recalls populism's historical past, which he defines minimally as "a form of thought opposing, within a single society, the people as a whole to the elites (those holding political or media power) in an extremely simplified form of class struggle."

distinction Michéa draws between the *Ancien Régime*'s values, which are all traditional values (i.e., permanent values) and its hierarchies, which he expressly rejects, as (obviously) did the first socialists.

This inability to distinguish between the *Ancien Régime*'s hierarchic and inegalitarian structures and the largely egalitarian sociality of its base — i.e., the forms of solidarity and popular traditions basic to the social bond which then prevailed among the people (often serving as a beneficial form of compensation for the dominant hierarchy) — appears with perfect clarity in Lordon's accusation that Michéa is dreaming of a "return to familial and village communities." This remark is certainly not without merit at a time when everyone is celebrating the merits of localism and local distribution channels — but it is very revealing of the author's preferences, apparently directed toward megalopolises where mass solitude reigns, but where everyone can "clear off" (to go where?). Above all, it shows that for Lordon, traditional society can only be analyzed as constraint, superstition, or a damper, without any positive aspects. The very idea of symbolic debt is only imagined as a constraint, taking no account of mutual aid and friendship's liberating aspects. This hatred of roots, this refusal to admit that the universal is only reached by way of a concrete singularity, is an unmistakable sign.

Then come the criticisms at the level of electoral politics, in other words, the most pathetic criticisms. In the eyes of his detractors, explains Aude Lancelin, Michéa has become "the seductive intellectual Trojan Horse of an authoritarian [*sic*] 100% French socialism whose definitive and only real political expression today is Le Penism."[60] Philippe Corcuff accuses Michéa of contributing to "disarming the Left" [*sic*] through his writings.[61]

---

[60] Aude Lancelin, "Tempête sur Michéa" ["Storm Over Michéa"], *Marianne*, August 31, 2013, 74–76.

[61] "Michéa today, he writes, is a libertarian socialist endowed with certain conservative leanings. He is of mixed origin, but his philosophy, fascinated by essences, has difficulty thinking about mixture" [*sic*]. We may easily grant Corcuff that he has much less difficulty thinking about mixture than Michéa, but what can we conclude from this at the level of ideas?

The same tone is heard from Luc Boltanski, who does not hesitate to describe Michéa's ideas as capable of leading to a "conservative revolution." Fancy that! In short, it would be dangerous to appeal to new divisions "at a time when Marine Le Pen is bombarding the 'UMPS' alliance"[62] (Aude Lancelin)!

Rather than pose a question as hollow as "Into whose hands is Michéa playing?," these low-level critics would do better to ask why Marine Le Pen is monopolizing a "bombardment" that any critical Left worthy of the name would have begun well before her. But of course, this would oblige them to ask how to win back the popular classes that have shifted to the Right because the Left abandoned them. Rather than examining their consciences as to why the people do not recognize themselves in the Left anymore (the answer would be, because the Left has rallied to the dominant ideology), these critics prefer to accuse the man who has put his finger on their overwhelming responsibility for this development—at the risk of letting it be understood that, all in all, they prefer globalized capitalism to "100% French socialism."

The accusation of "playing into the National Front's hands" by blurring the Left/Right opposition, a contemporary variant of Sartre's watchword ("not to rob Billancourt of hope" by telling the truth about the Soviet camps), obviously represents the bottom rung of thought. It amounts to saying that the truth should be disguised according to circumstance and that thought is just a question of tactics. To this repulsive idea that an intellectual should not say what he thinks but what he imagines he ought to say as a function of the most recent poll numbers, Michéa gave the best possible answer: "If there is one thing of which I am absolutely certain—in light of all the twentieth century's revolutionary experience—it is that, as Gramsci wrote, *only truth is revolutionary.* And that one must always be ready to speak it as it is, *whatever the context and whatever the consequences.*"

---

[62] This was an alliance between France's main establishment parties, the center-Right UMP (which was dissolved in 2015) and the center-Left Socialist Party (the PS). Compare the American expression "Republicrats." —Trans.

Indeed, only the truth is revolutionary! How can one be taken seriously if one is not convinced of this?

Does all this mean that Jean-Claude Michéa's thought cannot be criticized? Of course not. But the criticism must be intelligent and honest. In 2008, for example, Anselm Jappe published a "critical examination" of *The Empire of the Lesser Evil*, another of Michéa's books, which was far better and more constructively argued that the critiques of Lordon, Corcuff, and Co.[63]

Jappe approves of Michéa's having described "the Left" as a form of liberalism ("this bitter observation is, in fact, essential for understanding the history of capitalism") and of his having reminded us that capitalism is absolutely not conservative in its essence. He adds that, "Michéa's great strength is insistence on the necessity of a *moral* reform if we are to escape the morass of market society." He criticizes Michéa, on the other hand (relying on the critique of value developed notably by Robert Kurz, an author to whom we were among the first in France to draw attention), for not sufficiently taking into account the "centrality of the critique of political economy for understanding capitalist society." On this point he is not mistaken. Emphasizing that "the materialist explanation of history is not logically identical to belief in progress, concerning which Marx began to have doubts in his old age," Jappe writes:

> One of the strong points of the critique of value is to have broken radically with the base/superstructure dichotomy, not in the name of any supposed "plurality" of factors, but relying on the Marxist critique of fetishism. Commodity fetishism is not a form of false consciousness, a fraud, but a total form of social existence upstream from any separation of material reproduction and mental factors, because it determines the very forms of thought and action.

---

[63] Anselm Jappe, "Examen critique de l'ouvrage de Michéa" ["Critical Examination of Michéa's Work"], *Revue du MAUSS permanente* [e-journal], September 17, 2008. Jean-Claude Michéa, *L'Empire du moindre mal. Essai sur la civilisation libérale* [*The Empire of the Lesser Evil: Essay on Liberal Civilization*] (Castelnau-le-Lez: Climats, 2007).

One can only agree with this remark, which also allows us to understand Form-Capital's irresistible tendency to limitlessness, i.e., the pure dynamism of capital accumulation. Moreover, Michéa has not failed to take this into account.

The situation is quite different with Michéa's more recent detractors. In reproaching him for revealing "the Left's" internal contradictions, for his "extolling of the people," for showing signs of "Manicheism," "essentialism," and other minor sins, for showing that social liberalism is merely the "cultural" face of the market system, and above all for not positively evaluating the "social advances" that they for their part have no intention of renouncing, the critics give proof that they are unable to take the necessary critique of liberalism to its logical conclusion.

The truth is that one part of the extreme Left refuses to abandon the ideology of progress, just as it refuses to abandon globalization on the pretext that another version of it can be given. They want to save precisely what is most destructive in modernity: social liberalism. In this regard, it is revealing that Philippe Corcuff blames Michéa for, "Giving his readers conservative footholds by struggling primarily against individualism, political liberalism (and the cultural liberalism that is its continuation)." We can obviously conclude that for Corcuff it is the contrary that must be done. For example, he justifies "enjoyment without restraint" by having recourse to the same arguments as liberals for defending the "market without restraint" — like the sinister José Manuel Barroso, former President of the European Commission who is today employed by Goldman Sachs, denouncing the criticism of free trade as a "xenophobic and reactionary" fantasy!

These folks have forgotten the young Marx's devastating criticism of the ideology of the rights of man. They want a world without borders without asking themselves if such a world would still be human. They do not acknowledge the idea, hammered at by Michéa, that "the logic of liberal individualism, by constantly sapping all still-extant forms of popular solidarity, necessarily destroys the whole set of moral conditions that make an anti-capitalist revolt possible." They have forgotten that a revolution is not simply a radical change involving a clean sweep of everything that came before, but that etymologically (*revolvere*) it involves turning back to find a foothold the better to launch oneself forward. In so doing they themselves are providing, though they don't know it, a striking confirmation of Michéa's theses by showing to what extent a "Left-wing" party has been corrupted by liberal thought. This is the proof that a transversal cut is now running through all political camps.

LIBERALISM & MORALITY

In the eighteenth century, in order to put a definitive end to the wars of religion, liberalism attempted to "pacify" society politically and ideologically. As Jean-Claude Michéa has correctly explained:

> The idea then gradually become established that the only way to prevent the return of ideological civil wars was to rely upon an axiologically neutral state, i.e., a state that gets rid of any appeal to moral, religious, or philosophical values, and which therefore speaks only the language of "expertise."[1]

In other words, the state must no longer claim to decide between the different systems of values to which individuals choose to appeal. It must no longer decide upon what Aristotle called the "good life." It must no longer say some ways of living are better than others, nor attempt to propose, realize, or incarnate any particular philosophical or spiritual ideal. This attitude involves a strict separation between the public sphere, "neutralized" in this manner, and the private sphere where values continue to be lived out and shared, but only on condition of not seeking to spill over into the public sphere.

So the solution adopted by liberal modernity to conjure away the specter of civil and religious wars is not the model of Hobbes (who proposes to install the Leviathan, the absolute state, to prevent the "war of all against all"), but a "neutrality" that naturally results in modelling the government of men upon the administration of things. Alain Caillé observes: "The aim then becomes to define neutral, objective procedures—of which the market and law are the principal incarnations—that allow the

---

[1] *Cf.* Sylvain Dzimira's review of the meeting organized by MAUSS on February 16, 2008, with Jean-Claude Michéa, to mark the publication of his book *L'Empire du moindre mal* [*The Empire of the Lesser Evil*] (www.journaldumauss.net/spip.php?article308).

society to function on its own, independently of men's good or bad motives."[2] Since the decisions of the public authorities must be as "objective" as possible, the model for objectivity is sought in science and more especially in technical expertise. Supposedly the only court of appeal is to speak a "language with no subject." Thus begins the era of the "experts" for whom all social problems are, in the final analysis, mere technical problems. They are supposed to be resolvable through technical solutions as well. From such a point of view, it is always possible to uncover one solution that is "objectively" better than the others. Consequently, politics is no longer a matter of choosing between various possible orientations. Ideological discussions are useless, since in the end there is only one rationally possible solution, only one solution worthy of the name.

On the liberal view, the neutral state is the state that rises above society, in which the most different opinions coexist, in order to allow men to live "freely." The church had already distinguished between spiritual and temporal power; liberal modernity both separates powers and separates the state from civil society. The liberal attitude toward the state is ambivalent, however. On the one hand, the grasp of this "mortal God" (*deus mortalis*) must always be limited so that it does not threaten the privileges of civil society, conceived as the place for the natural exercise of freedom. But on the other, we expect the state to allow that same civil society to remain sheltered from the political and religious confrontations of the past.

Michéa shows here the congruence of economic and political liberalism. The former must contribute to ideological "pacification" by means of "peaceful trade" — not simply because commerce, posited as a new form of human bond, is supposed by its intrinsic nature to escape the fatal violence of politics by substituting for conflict a contractual model based on a negotiation advantageous for all parties — but also because the priority attributed to the economy allows one to glimpse the possibility of

---

[2] Alain Caillé, "L'homme est-il un animal sympathique? Le contr'Hobbes" ["Is Man an Animal Capable of Sympathy? Against Hobbes"], *La Revue du MAUSS*, no. 31, January–June 2008, 27.

delegating the management of societies to the impersonal mechanisms of the "self-regulating" market. Political liberalism, based
on the "rule of law," is organized around the idea that individuals are entirely free to lead the life they want under the protection (and authority) of an axiologically neutral law charged only
with acting so that the exercise of one person's freedom does not
infringe upon the freedom of others (without it ever being explained why, if the individual is to be truly free, he should respect this injunction not to harm others, which quite obviously
limits his freedom).[3] "If liberalism must be understood as the
most radical form of the modern political project," writes Michéa, "this is first of all because it proposes nothing less than *fully privatizing* the timeless sources of discord that morality, religion, and philosophy necessarily represent."[4]

In such a system, everything that belongs to morality or values thus finds itself limited to the private sphere. Moral questions are *privatized* and the public sphere "ethically purified."
From the point of view of "pluralism," beliefs receive the status
of mere opinions, one being as good as another in principle, the
important point being that economic and commercial society can
function "freely," without arbitrary judgments disturbing the
free play of "natural" market mechanisms. "This means," writes
Michéa, "that if the liberal state intends to renounce on principle
any definition of what the good life consists in, it is the market
(and through it the images of growth and consumption) that will
de facto take charge of defining the concrete manner in which
men must live."

To this view Michéa opposes the idea that societies cannot
live without a minimum of shared values, i.e., without agreeing

---

[3] The reason for such silence is probably that respect for this principle implies a certain sense of reciprocity, a term that liberalism excludes because of its "social" overtones. "How do I establish that the
exercise of a particular liberty *does not harm that of others*," asks Jean-
Claude Michéa, "if I must forbid myself recourse to any value judgment in deciding?" ("De quoi le libéralisme est-il le nom?" ["What Is
Liberalism Called?"]. *La Revue de MAUSS*, no. 31, January–June 2008,
307).

[4] Jean-Claude Michéa, "De quoi le libéralisme est-il le nom?," 305.

on a minimal definition of what the "good life" is—obviously, without this minimal definition being supposed to result in a "metaphysical ideology of the Good," any more than it should legitimate a warlike attitude always susceptible to leading to authoritarian (if not totalitarian) aberrations. Whence the importance he accords to Orwell's concept of "common decency," which covers qualities to which common sense has always adhered, above all in the popular classes: honesty, solidarity, generosity, loyalty, the spirit of giving, the sense of gratitude, the sense of honor, a taste for reciprocity and mutual assistance, and so on.

The liberal state's postulation of neutrality is not really tenable. On the one hand, as Carl Schmitt has shown, the resolute choice of "neutrality" is itself never neutral, and the liberals' will to eliminate morality from the public sphere itself results from an obvious moral (and moralizing) choice. On the other, even liberal milieus hold that some things are better than others, including of course on the moral level. No liberal, however concerned about "neutrality" he may be, can think a non-liberal proposition is as good as a liberal one. In real life, liberals affirm their principles and values as strongly as anti-liberals. So liberalism cannot escape the "moral temptation." Hostile to traditions, it is itself part of a tradition. It has its own peculiar social character.

Let us take the example of freedom, which liberalism makes such a fuss about. The essential point for a liberal is freedom of individual choice, without any value or substantial reference point to guide it. But if everything is as good as everything else, what would be the use of this very free choice? Is it not rather because some things are worth more than other things that freedom can acquire a meaning? Freedom cannot be practiced in a normative desert, but only beginning from some meaningful axiological horizon. In other words, there is no free choice without values to guide it. We cannot in real life do without a shared normative horizon.

The adhesion of liberals to the ideology of progress is no less significant. In this ideology, the future is automatically assumed to be the bearer of something better, with man himself supposed to improve insofar as the conditions of his existence improve, since he is posited as indefinitely perfectible and endlessly plastic. So one cannot "neutrally" hold that the past was just as good as the future. At the same time, let us note that this "moral" amelioration, presented as the result of an objective historical necessity, justifies not having to ask ourselves moral questions about its concrete consequences, i.e., about all the problems to which modernization can give rise.

Finally, liberalism is also the vehicle of an ideology of the rights of man. These rights are, as we know, subjective and inalienable; every man is supposed to hold them because of his own nature (and even, usually, because of an ancient state of nature that preceded his life in society). Now, there is no doubt that the ideology of the rights of man, apart from its legal underpinning, is a profoundly moral ideology. At the same time, however, since the morality of which it is the vehicle implies the priority of the just over the good (we will return to this subject), it can also give itself the appearance of a certain "neutrality" insofar as these rights are imagined and constructed independently of any particular conception of the good.[5] It is for this reason that the rights of man were not originally conceived as contradicting the liberal belief in the state's necessary neutrality. "Justice" is posed here as reconcilable with moral neutrality, and even as demanding such neutrality. But it is no less true that beginning with the rights of man, the "neutral" liberal state will favor the invasion of the public domain by the ought-to-be. To make the whole of society conform to the principles of rights-of-man ideology would be to render it more "just." Thus, moral obligation no longer concerns so much individual behavior as the way society must transform itself to become "better." At the same time, in daily life the incessant multiplication of demands derived from the rights of man, the continual slippage from "rights of" to "rights to," and the bidding war occasioned by this slippage will gradually result in what Philippe Muray has called the "Empire

---

[5] "[P]olitical liberalism," Rawls writes, "looks for an idea of rational advantage within a political conception that is independent of any particular comprehensive doctrine" (*Political Liberalism* [New York: Columbia University Press, 1993], 180).

of the Good."

But the ideology of the rights of man will also allow the West to posit itself as incarnating the Good *vis-à-vis* the rest of the world. Being applicable to all men, the rights of man, a purely Western creation, have been posited from the beginning as valid in all times and places. It is in their name, by draping itself in its pretention to be the only culture capable of enunciating a "universal" discourse, that the West will teach the cultures of the entire world by suggesting they renounce customs and ways of life of which the West disapproves. Such a procedure amounts to an endlessly renewed struggle against otherness. Convinced they are the bearers of the only conceivable universal values, the West wants to extend them to the entire planet, which leads it to delegitimize as perverse or archaic any singularity opposed to it, "including that singularity which is death itself" (Baudrillard). It means to institute the reign of Sameness at a planetary level in the hope of making ambivalence disappear, the negative principle, what Georges Bataille called the "accursed share." Fundamentally, the West wants to negotiate otherness away, and becomes enraged at being unable to manage this.[6]

Ritual invocation of the rights of man thus presents the obvious advantage of allowing one, from the right motive, to violate the sacrosanct principle of non-discrimination. When it comes to denouncing "backward" traditional cultures, the "superstitions of another era," and other practices that "progress" is tasked with erasing, it is permitted to designate for universal condemnation a certain number of "rascals" (or "rogue states").

Challenging on this point Samuel Huntington's theses concerning the confrontation between Islam and the West, Jean Baudrillard writes:

---

[6] An attitude which allows it to disguise, while regularly reproducing, its own criminal behavior and acts of "bravado." Tzvetan Todorov writes, "A precept for the next century might run: begin by fighting not evil (in others) in the name of the good (which we possess), but the assurance of those who claim always to know where the good and the evil are to be found; not the devil, first of all, but the Manicheans" (*Le Débat*, November–December 1999).

It is not a clash of civilizations, but an almost anthropological confrontation between an undifferentiated universal
culture and everything in any domain that retains something of an irreducible otherness. For the world power,
which is just as fundamentalist as religious orthodoxy, all
different and singular forms are heresies. As such, they are
destined either to be reintegrated (willingly or forcibly) into the world order, or to disappear. The mission of the
West (or rather of the ex-West, since it has not had any
values of its own for a long time now) is to force the various cultures to submit to the fierce law of equivalence by
every possible means. A culture that has lost its values can
only avenge itself on those of others. . . . The aim is to suppress the refractory domain and to colonize and domesti-
cate all untamed spaces, whether in geographical space or
in the mental world.[7]

Although it also proclaims itself "neutral" with regard to the
various religious "denominations," American neoconservatism,
heir to the puritan tradition, puts politics in a relation of direct
dependency on morality, especially by representing relations of
force and international conflict as a kind of "struggle of Good

---

[7] Jean Baudrillard, *Power Inferno* (Paris: Galilée, 2002). Alain
Brossat notes:

The name of the Universal can, if necessary, be remarkably
plastic: to ridicule Arabs and Muslims, and associate them with
terrorists, obscurantists, and enemies of republican institutions
and democracy by a game of rough associations is a practice
generally covered in France today by one of the names of the
Universal — in this case, freedom of opinion and expression. . . .
Conversely, to mock rabbis, attack so-called communitarian institutions, or violently denounce the policies of the state of Israel are all practices that would leave those who risked them
vulnerable to the blows of another decree of the Universal. (*Le
Sacre de la démocratie. Tableau Clinique d'une pandémie* [*The Coro-
nation of Democracy: Clinical Portrait of a Pandemic*] [Paris: Ana-
bet, 2007], 93–94).

against Evil." The United States, in this view, is always on the side of Good: it is even "God's nation," whose Manifest Destiny is to export its model of society to the utmost limits of the planet. Evil consists of any obstacles to the Americanization of the world, which at the same time are survivals of a "premodern" consciousness that the Enlightenment thought it had abolished by proclaiming the principle of reason's omnipotence.

But let us return to the fundamental distinction between morality founded on the primacy of the good and morality founded on the primacy of the just.[8]

The debate over the priority of the just and the good partly overlaps with the classic opposition between deontic morality of the Kantian type and teleological or virtue-based morality of the Aristotelean type. Aristotelean ethics is a virtue ethics founded on the priority of the good. It is an "attractional" ethics that makes morality rest upon aiming at some good inseparable from a *telos*, i.e., a specific finality. Modern societies, on the contrary, are the product of a moral revolution consisting in according the just priority over the good.[9] Each morality obviously makes use of both terms, but placed in the opposite order. If the just is fundamental, the good will be defined as that desired by the individual insofar as his acts and desires are in conformity with the demands of moral obligation. The good will be the object of a just desire. If the good is fundamental, the just will be what one does to arrive at this good. The former say: the good is what is just; the latter respond: the just is what is good.

Kant was one of the first to reverse the order of priority, breaking with the teleology of the Aristotelian search for the good to content himself with the deontology of respect for the just. The transcendental subject is for him a necessary presupposition of freedom, for only a subject conceived as independent of and anterior to the determinations of the sensible world can escape heteronomy. "All action is just," writes Kant in his

---

[8] This distinction, at the descriptive and typological level, goes back at least to Henry Sidgwick (*The Methods of Ethics*, 1874).

[9] Cf. especially Michel Forsé and Maxime Parodi, *La Priorité du juste* [*The Priority of Justice*] (Paris: PUF, 2004).

Metaphysics of Morals, "which can, or whose maxim can, allow the coexistence of each person's freedom of will with the freedom of all according to a universal law."[10] He infers from this that justice demands society be governed by principles not involving any particular conception of the good, nor passing judgment on any particular substantial good. Kant lays as his foundation a moral law unconditionally binding upon individuals, whatever their desires, wishes, or interests. This moral law defines the good, and not the other way around. Thus, a deontic morality succeeds to a morality of *arete*, i.e., a virtue ethics (the ethic of honor, for example). The political domain thus finds itself dissociated from moral communities, and public norms are no longer necessarily the prolongation of private individuals' values. The moral validity of an argument no longer necessarily coincides with its political legitimacy. This corresponds to the wishes of a Benjamin Constant: "Let us ask authority to remain within its limits, limiting itself to being just, while we concern ourselves with being happy."

Major contemporary liberal authors such as John Rawls, Ronald Dworkin, Bruce Ackerman, or Charles Larmore are heirs of Kant (even if they sometimes attempt, as Rawls does, to rid his doctrine of its metaphysical basis). Rawls maintains that a theory of justice must correspond to the concern rational individuals have for the satisfaction of their interests without ever imposing upon them a particular conception of the world. "Justice," he writes, "is the first virtue of social institutions, as truth is of systems of thought."[11]

In the epistemological sense, the priority of the just means that "the principles of justice that specify our rights do not depend for their justification on any particular conception of the good life,"[12] i.e., that the just must be formulated independently

---

[10] Immanuel Kant, *Oeuvres philosophiques*, vol. 3 (Paris: Gallimard, 1986), 479.

[11] John Rawls, *A Theory of Justice* (Cambridge, Mass.: Harvard University Press, 1971), 3.

[12] Michael Sandel, *Liberalism and the Limits of Justice* (Cambridge: Cambridge University Press, 1990).

of any conception of the good. In a liberal regime, the good is thus defined in a purely formal, and not substantial, sense. Thus, for John Rawls a person's good is determined by the rational life project he would choose on the basis of a rational deliberation concerning a maximal class of projects (the principles of justice being the principles that would be the objects of an agreement between rational persons placed in an original situation of equality). Finally, for liberals the individual is always anterior to the ends he assigns himself. There is always a "priority of the self over its ends," states Rawls. "What is important first of all to the unencumbered self, what intrinsically defines its personality," remarks Michael Sandel, "is not the ends it chooses but its capacity to choose them."

Michael Sandel has defined the liberal ideal very well:

> Its central thesis can be put like this: a just society does not try to promote any particular project, but gives its citizens the opportunity to pursue their own projects insofar as these are compatible with equal freedom for all; consequently, this society must be guided by principles which do not presuppose any idea of the good. The fundamental justification for these regulatory principles is not that they maximize the general well-being, cultivate virtue, or promote the good in any other way, but rather that they are conformable to the concept of justice, a moral category to which is attributed a priority and independence with regard to the good.[13]

Thus, by way of the distinction between the just and the good we find once again the postulate of "neutrality," but associated this time with a preconceived view of morality. The classic justification of this point of view is that if the state were not neutral, and if it affirmed a particular conception of the good in the face of the society's "pluralism" — which continues to grow today — its partisanship would amount to a lack of impartiality (because

---

[13] Michael Sandel, "The Procedural Republic and the Unencumbered Self," *Political Theory*, February 1984.

the values of only one part of the citizens would be promoted or favored), and thus a limitation on individual rights. Now, for liberals the state must furnish everyone the conditions allowing him to live out the conception of the good life to which he adheres in the private sphere without privileging any one such conception (a principle matching that of secularism in France). The role of public power is neither to contribute to make the citizens virtuous, nor to promote particular ends, but only to guarantee fundamental freedoms. In this view, what makes a society just "is not the *telos*, the goal or end it pursues, but precisely its refusal to choose in advance among competing goals or ends."[14] The political system must abstain from taking a position in the conflict of value systems or conceptions of the world, which must remain restricted to the private sphere.

The priority attributed to the just over the good in liberal doctrine therefore rests ultimately upon three foundations. First, the idea that the individual is the only source of moral value, which excludes any conception attributing to any collectivity aspirations not reducible to those of its members. Then, the idea that the state should remain neutral for the reasons indicated. And finally, the idea that political judgment should be based exclusively on formal and procedural norms. Whence the definition of the liberal state as a "Procedural Republic," itself resting on the principle of the neutrality of public action and the primacy of the subjective rights of an individual freely choosing his ends without in any way being led to do so by what is upstream from him, e.g., his heritage or belonging.

The unrealistic character of this last postulate leaps out at us: no more than there can be extra-societal (or presocial) freedom do there exist subjective rights inherent in human nature. Given that justice is defined as an equitable relation, there is no possible justice except in society. Man, on the other hand, cannot choose all his forms of belonging, since a number of them are established before he is born. So it is an illusion to imagine that his forms of belonging do not help to determine his choices: identity can be constituted in opposition to them, but not

---

[14] Sandel, "The Procedural Republic and the Unencumbered Self."

without reference to them.

Communitarian theorists (Charles Taylor, Michael Sandel, and Alasdair MacIntyre) have had no difficulty showing that the priority of the just over the good rests on an imaginary anthropology: the subject of Kantian morality, like that of Rawls' theory of justice, is an abstract subject with no affiliations, and thus "neutral" as well, whereas in real life there only exist men embedded in concrete structures of belonging. While liberals proclaim that the self is always anterior to its ends, communitarians, taking their inspiration from Aristotle or Hegel, show that man discovers his ends more than he chooses them, and that the way he determines them is indissociable from recognition of the forms of belonging and attachments to others that constitute him. They thus emphasize the constitutive character of bonds and social relations for the identity of agents. Since no one is able to stand outside his culture and history, even when he means to contradict and reject them, an "unencumbered" self, free of all belonging, is merely an abstraction. Once emptied of all the concrete characteristics of concrete men, it is not the "essential" that is left over (a "supra-empirical" man); nothing is left over. The result is that it is quite simply impossible to posit an abstract justice independent of any determinate conception of the good, still less anterior or prior to it.

So liberalism's relationship with morality is not simple. On the one hand, the liberal state claims to be "neutral" in the domain of values. On the other, the ties it maintains with the ideology of the rights of man, an eminently moral doctrine, seem to forbid liberalism from respecting this ideal. But this observation should be qualified by taking into consideration the difference between moralities that deduce the good from the just and those that deduce the just from the good—the first being able to boast of a certain neutrality, even if basically illusory (insofar as a position on the relation between the just and the good is anything but neutral).

To complicate things a bit more, we must still examine another set of problems that modernity has not been able to avoid: that of the existence of evil. The presence of evil in the world has always been a problem for theodicy. How can we explain the presence of evil in a world created by an infinitely good and all-powerful God? The classic Christian response is that man is responsible for the appearance of evil, since it results from the bad use he made of his free will at the time of original sin. The gnostic response brought into play the existence of an evil God, a competitor of the good God. In the modern age, this set of problems shifted. The alternative is no longer whether man or God is responsible for the appearance of evil, but whether man or society is responsible. This new question is, of course, only possible from a point of view, itself typically modern, wherein man (put back into an imaginary "state of nature," for example) can be analyzed separately from society. Thus evil does not come from man, whom certain writers go so far as to call "naturally good," but from society. The Enlightenment concludes from this that, not being an intrinsic property of human nature, evil can (and must) be eliminated. For this it is enough to change society (or move to another). We run into the ought-to-be once again.

Let us recall that human society is conceived by the moderns as a mere aggregation of individuals, elementary atoms who have chosen to leave a pre-political and pre-social state of nature and associate with each other with a view to maximizing their interests. This image is itself founded on an anthropological model: that of a fundamentally egoistical individual constantly trying to calculate his material best interest rationally. This egoism is not viewed negatively. On the contrary, according to liberal authors from Adam Smith to Bernard Mandeville ("private vices, public virtues"), everyone's egoism supposedly contributes to the social optimum and the happiness of all, thanks to the action of the market's "invisible hand."

Thus, along with modernity appeared the idea that evil cannot merely be channeled or suppressed but definitively eliminated by way of a particular social order that merely has to be constructed. This idea supposes, as we have just said, that evil is exterior to man and does not come from him, but results rather from the effects of power, authority, and unjustified domination. From that moment, justice consists in creating the conditions in which injustice can no longer appear. At the same time, the idea came to prevail that man is all the more human insofar as he frees himself from all naturalness, which opens the way to radical historicism: the human species will be what we want it to be.

The concept of evil, which in the modern era has often aroused a certain unease, has over the past 30 years tended to reenter public language. But it has done so in an odd way. On the one hand, our contemporaries continue to think it possible to eradicate evil by means of appropriate measures. On the other, adhering to a conception of the good derived from what they believe to be just, they no longer hesitate to denounce what they call "absolute Evil." This absolute Evil is not the counterpart of an absolute Good, to which no one thinks of appealing (for positing the existence of an absolute Good would run counter to the "neutrality" inherent in the liberal conception of justice). It is rather an absolute Evil posited as the radical contradiction of the dominant ideology. It is incarnated today in a number of repulsive figures that constantly get brought up: the terrorist, the holocaust denier, the pedophile, the Nazi, the racist, the serial killer, etc. The images we give of these are rarely derived from psychological or political analysis, but rather from a hysterical or demonological approach that makes any in-depth analysis impossible.

From a strategic point of view, assimilating anything to absolute evil pays quite well: any suspicion one raises in this domain earns one complete disqualification. On the basis of an arbitrary chain of equivalences (which give rise to just as many inquisitions into bad intentions), one can thus slap a badge of public disgrace on the presumed bearers of bad ideas. Insofar as they incarnate absolute Evil, these figures have the great advantage that they can be used to suspend judgment. In the fight against them, in fact, everything is permitted. To fight terrorism, it is only natural to restrict civil liberties. To face down "pedophile networks," it is only natural to put all Internet users under surveillance. To get the better of the "Evil Empire," it is legitimate to kidnap, torture, bomb, and atomize entire populations. Absolute Evil ends up being defined as radical otherness, "unspeakable" horror, and irreconcilable heterogeneity. Evil is simultaneously denied in principle (we will eventually end up making it disappear) and recognized in a form that forbids any relativization. This is an absolute evil corresponding not to any absolute good, but to a set of values in respect of which it plays the role of a foil.

The will to "eradicate evil" often crystalizes around the idea that it is possible to make conflict disappear and outlaw war. This idea can be formulated in the manner of pacifists (we will abolish war by making "warmongers" disappear), but also in the manner of liberals who, here as well, allege the pacifying power of commerce and the market's "invisible hand," which is supposed to transform all of society into a peaceful, self-regulating structure. On this last point of view, the underlying postulates are, first, that individual interests are spontaneously consistent with collective interests (which are merely the sum of the former) provided that one gives free play to the mechanisms of the market, and second that there is no conflict to which a "reasonable solution" cannot be found, for opposed points of view, assimilated to conflicting interests, are always reconcilable insofar as communication between the parties is possible. They mean by this that all conflict is negotiable, without realizing that there are things which by their very nature cannot be negotiated (values are not interests).

Such a procedure is not merely destined for failure; it usually results in the opposite of the result sought. The rejection of conflict finally results in generalized competition, in that same war of all against all that the liberal project was supposed to neutralize (but in which Engels, already in 1845, saw the very essence of liberal society). The dream of universal peace leads to a totally unrestrained "just" war that spontaneously takes the most extreme forms, since it is a matter of triumphing in the name of humanity over an enemy thereby placed outside humanity. The wars of religion that one wanted to leave behind gave way to ideological wars obeying the same logic. The hope for perpetual peace results in perpetual war.

Wanting to make conflict disappear in order to work toward the dawn of an age of universal justice and harmony, and desiring to make the ontological, constitutive dimension of conflict disappear, is in fact once more to deny (or want to suppress) otherness. Since conflict is born of the contradictory plurality of human aspirations, difference gets presented as intrinsically productive of war. But one forgets that the denial of differences is no less so. The more men resemble one another, the more they desire to distinguish themselves, and therefore they do not stop fighting, with mimetic rivalry representing just one form of this confrontation. "Far from being pacified," observe Michel Benasayag and Angélique del Rey, "contemporary societies that deny or repress conflict are pregnant with extreme and unlimited violence — latent or actual."[15]

Beyond the desire for the extinction of conflict, we observe in contemporary Western societies a tendency to deny the power of the negative, which, as we have already said, is only acknowledged and recognized in extreme and pathological forms ("absolute evil"). The general idea is that one can eliminate the negative, keeping only the positive side of human existence: cooperation without conflict, reason without passion.

Evil is in fact defined in a privative manner. At bottom, what our contemporaries denounce as evil is what follows from the *tragic* character of human existence. They want to eliminate the tragic dimension of existence because it is fundamentally ambivalent and thus "opaque." To this opacity they oppose an ideal of social "transparency." This aspiration to "transparency" is a classic demand of rationalism. It pushes the "disenchantment of the world" to its utmost consequences: the eradication of its mystery and ambivalence. Every organic social bond, every "prerational" social relation, all spontaneous vitality that cannot be controlled, everything that is not reducible to calculable self-interest is considered a form of "opacity" that must be made to disappear. This is the "transparency" of Orwell's *Nineteen Eighty-Four*: Big Brother is watching you; Big Brother knows everything. (Obviously, this does not prevent the preservation of a few juicy opaque zones: money-laundering operations, payoffs, bribes, and tax havens.) The ideal of transparency is totalitarian in the proper sense.

---

[15] Michel Benasayag and Angélique del Rey, *Éloge du conflit* [*In Praise of Conflict*] (Paris: La Découverte, 2007), 81. "The suppression of conflict can produce barbarism," we read on page 10.

As Jean Baudrillard emphasizes:

All the discourses of Good are ravaged by ambivalence. This is particularly visible in the relation to stupidity, which is the murkiest, but also the most direct and massive, expression of this ventriloquacity of Evil. Philippe Muray has magnificently described this beatification, this grotesque pacification of the real world, this festive reduction in perpetuity of the whole of modernity to a party. Now, it is precisely here, in this extension of the domain of Farce, that Ventriloquous Evil advances on all sides, establishing the hegemony of stupidity — which is the equivalent of hegemony plain and simple. . . . As soon as Good rules and claims to embody truth, it is Evil that comes through. . . . [16]

We believe naïvely that the progress of the Good, its rising power in all domains, corresponds to a defeat of Evil. No one seems to have understood that Good and Evil increase in power at the same time, and according to the same movement. . . . Good does not reduce Evil, nor *viceversa*: they are irreducible to one another, and yet their relation is inextricable. . . . Absolute evil is born of an excess of Good, an unchecked proliferation of Good, of technological development, infinite progress, a totalitarian morality, a radical and unopposed will to do good. At that point, Good turns into its opposite: absolute Evil.

Faced with the conflicts that inevitably reappear in society, Jean-Claude Michéa observes that:

Liberal justice has no other solution (since it is obviously impossible to satisfy two contradictory demands simultaneously) than to base its final decision on the power relations acting upon society *at a given moment*, i.e., concretely,

---

[16] Jean Baudrillard, *Carnaval et cannibale. Suivi de: Le Mal ventriloque* [*Carneval and Cannibal, followed by: Ventriloquous Evil*] (Paris: L'Herne, 2008), 65–66.

on the existing relations of force between different interest groups that speak in society's name, and whose relative weight is commonly a function of how much of the communications media they have been able to occupy.[17]

Hence the role of lobbies, competing with one another to impose their own views as a function of their interests.

Michéa continues:

> It is, however, clear that such an *atomization of society by liberal law* (and the reappearance of the old war of all against all that it involves) can only finally end by rendering all common life impossible. A human society only exists, in fact, insofar as it succeeds in permanently reproducing a *bond*, which presupposes that it can rely on a minimum of *common language* between all who compose it. Now, if that common language must, conformably with the demands of liberal dogma, be axiologically neutral (since any "ideological" reference would reintroduce the conditions of civil war), there remains only one coherent way of resolving the problem. It consists in basing society's anthropological cohesion on the only attribute liberals have always held to be common to all men: *their "natural" disposition to act according to their self-interest properly understood*. So the philosophical task of organizing the peaceful coexistence of individuals must quite logically finally devolve upon self-interested exchange (the famous "give and take" that is the basis of the rationality of all commercial relations); everything else is supposed to oppose such coexistence. . . . In the end, that is the main reason the economy has become the *religion* of modern societies.[18]

Here, liberal "neutrality" reaches its ultimate limit. The good, in modern society, is the reign of money.

---

[17] Michéa, "De quoi le libéralisme est-il le nom?," 308–309.
[18] Michéa, "De quoi le libéralisme est-il le nom?," 309.

MONEY & THE RIGHT

"To be on the Right is to be afraid for what exists," said Jules Romains. A nice definition. We find it again in many authors. In 1931, Amédée d'Yvignac wrote that "The Right is that group of politicians who think the *permanent* is the substance of things, and not change."[1] More recently, Alain-Gérard Slama observed: "The traditional Right has always been characterized by a distrust of man's power over the world and a fundamental respect with regard to the order of things."[2] Let us pass over the ambiguities connected with this tendency to affirm a fact without wanting to qualify it: traditionally, the Right has always been, if not the camp of conservatism, at least that of *conservation*.

The liberal bourgeoisie whose reign was consecrated by the capitalist system has, however, played a very different role in history. The pages in which Karl Marx emphasizes its revolutionary and destructive character are well known, but one never tires of quoting them:

> The bourgeoisie, wherever it has got the upper hand, has put an end to all feudal, patriarchal, idyllic relations. It has pitilessly torn asunder the motley feudal ties that bound man to his "natural superiors," and has left remaining no other nexus between man and man than naked self-interest, than callous "cash payment." It has drowned the most heavenly ecstasies of religious fervor, of chivalrous enthusiasm, of philistine sentimentalism in the icy water of egotistical calculation. It has resolved personal worth into exchange value, and in place of the numberless, indefeasible chartered freedoms, has set up that single, unconscionable freedom—Free Trade. . . . *The bourgeoisie cannot*

---

[1] In Emmanuel Beau de Loménie, ed., *Qu'appellez-vous droite et gauche?* [*What Do You Call Right and Left?*] (Paris: Librairie du Dauphin, 1931), 96.

[2] Alain-Gérard Slama, "Considérations sur la droite" ["Considerations On the Right"], *Contrepoint*, January–March 1978, 57.

exist without constantly revolutionizing the instruments of pro-
duction, and thereby the relations of production, and with them
the whole relations of society. . . . Constant revolutionizing of
production, uninterrupted disturbance of all social conditions, everlasting uncertainty and agitation distinguish the
bourgeois epoch from all earlier ones. . . . All that is solid
melts into air, all that is holy is profaned.[3]

The key sentence is in italics. The bourgeoisie cannot exist
without permanently *revolutionizing* society, for the capitalist
system itself can only develop under the effect of a tendency to
the unlimited, which demands a constant series of innovations
to the detriment of the old order. The essence of capitalism is the
suppression of all limits.

Jean-Claude Michéa has likewise shown that the capitalist
system can only permanently "revolutionize" the social world
insofar as it demands the systematic destruction of any common
language beyond the mere logic of self-interest and contract. He
writes: "If the logic of consumer capitalism is to sell anything to
anybody it cannot do without eliminating one by one all cultural
and moral obstacles (all the 'taboos,' in liberal and media new-
speak) that might resist the commercialization of goods or services."[4]

So we can pose the following apparently naïve question:
How has the Right, naturally attached to conservation, been able
so consistently to support a capitalist system so destructive of
what it intends to conserve? How has it been able to believe that
this system was intrinsically "conservative," "patriarchal," or
"reactionary," thus making a mistake symmetrical to that of a
Left which used to fight it for exactly the same reasons?

A first possible explanation, which has become classic, is
that the Right takes the side of the "haves." This has not always
been the case, but clearly there is some truth to it. Ever since

---

[3] Karl Marx, *Manifesto of the Communist Party,* 1848, Chapter 1.

[4] Jean-Claude Michéa, *Le Complexe d'Orphée. La gauche, les gens ordinaires et la religion du progrès* [*Orpheus's Complex: The Left, Ordinary People, and the Religion of Progress*] (Paris: Climats-Flammarion, 2011).

the old aristocracy was devoured by the bourgeois class, the Right has supported capitalism insofar as it has identified with the bourgeoisie. Hence that remark by Beau de Loménie: "If capitalist society is still holding together, it does not owe this to businessmen who, beneath their realistic appearances, reveal themselves to those who look closely as the most chimerical of dreamers; it owes it to the patient and stubborn defenders of that old reactionary ideology that, in the eyes of the crowd, serves as a windscreen for the contrivances of the cleverest."[5]

The Right, which knows society is prior to exchange, rejects the idea found in most liberal authors according to which it is from the market or self-interest that human societies are created in a contractual manner. Moreover, it likes to profess that principles are more important than interests. But it also knows how to transform its own interests into principles, as its conception of property shows. Undoubtedly, when it defended property in the nineteenth century, it was not in the manner of Locke or Adam Smith. It did not say that property is a "natural right" given to man with his nature, nor an institution that by itself realizes human freedom. When it speaks of property, it is thinking of patrimony, especially land, often associated with a family, far more than of capital, which must be mobile to make greater profit. Nonetheless, in a second phase it ends up seeing in property an abstract asset that can give rise to market exchanges.

In his book on the French forms of the political Right, René Rémond distinguishes three principal varieties: the Orléanist or liberal Right, the legitimist or counter-revolutionary Right, and the "Bonapartist" or plebiscitary Right. It is easy to see that over the course of time, the first has won out over the other two.

The term "Orléanism" refers to the Duke of Orleans, the son of Philippe-Egalité, the regicide member of the revolutionary convention, who himself became King in 1830 under the name Louis-Philippe. The golden age of Orléanism runs from that date until 1848, a period in which the liberal Right held uninterrupted power to the detriment of both the legitimist Right and the republican Left. Greeted in its time by Jules Michelet as the

---

[5] Beau de Loménie, *Qu'appellez-vous droite et gauche?*, 164.

"liberal resource of France," Orléanism is a not very democratic parliamentary regime largely dominated by the great landholders and industrialists, whose electoral base was limited by property qualifications. It consecrates the power of the bourgeoisie, especially the grand bourgeoisie. "Orléanism," emphasizes René Rémond, "is nothing but the regime and political thought corresponding to the reign of the bourgeoisie: a regime of interests by definition, with thought subordinated to the justification of those interests."[6]

We will not rehearse the list of traits characteristic of Orléanism. The point to remember is that it marks the moment politics began to give way to a "managerial" conception of the state, where the principle of honor faded before the logic of money. The liberalism proclaimed by the men of the July Monarchy was still at the beginning of this process, however. In an age when the principal industrial enterprises were still family-run, when capitalism was itself above all "national," and when the bourgeoisie was above all represented by the "notables," land remained the principal form of wealth (rent on land provides most capital), which allowed the aristocracy to rally to the system. Liberalism then went hand-in-hand with paeans to the bourgeois virtues (Guizot: "Make yourselves rich by work and savings"), as with a certain form of rationalism that values the spirit of compromise and the "happy medium," along with social conservatism.

Another possible explanation is that, historically, the Right has not been especially fond of the common man. Above all, it does not like the idea that power can be exercised by the people, which it considers lacking in "competence" (an argument that will later nourish expertocracy). Basically, this is its main criticism of democracy: making the legitimacy of power reside in popular sovereignty (the "government of the crowd" as opposed to that of "elites"). Whence its frequent mistrust of the people.

In the nineteenth century, the Right was divided between

---

[6] René Rémond, *La droite en France, de la premiere Restauration à la Ve République* [*The Right in France from the First Restoration to the Fifth Republic*] (Paris: Aubier, 1963), 82.

those whom the social question left largely indifferent and those who realized its importance, but limited themselves to seeking how they might aid the poor in order to achieve the "extinction of pauperism."

In August 1832, Saint-Marc Girardin explained in the *Journal des débats*: "The barbarians who threaten society are not in the Caucasus or on the Tartar steppes; they are in the suburbs of our manufacturing cities!" On the bourgeois Right at this time, the denunciation of the "dangerous classes" became a commonplace, and a number of economic proposals aimed at preventing social upheavals. The social question was thus reduced to the "social danger." The factory was a place of production, but also became a place of surveillance. Strikes were perceived as "attempts at social disturbance that cannot be tolerated" (Adolph Thiers). Jean-Baptiste Say and Frédéric Bastiat defended free trade and devoted themselves to the radical critique of all state intervention. Others, such as Charles Dunoyer or Alfred Deseilligny, did so by calling for "moderation," if not resignation, and relied on employment contracts, religion, and charity to mitigate inequalities. Everyone was in agreement that salaries must not be raised, whether because this would diminish the profits of ownership, or because it would only increase the workers' tendency to "laziness," in a rush to spend their money at the café. The poor, as everybody knows, make poor use of their income, only spending it to satisfy their vices: alcoholism, criminality, attempts at insurrection . . . .

At this same time, however, socialism was beginning its rise—and certain developments made themselves felt on the Right as well, especially in Catholic milieus. Arnaud Imatz reminds us:

> Beginning in 1834, Villeveuve-Bargemont, a former prefect under Louis XVIII, attacked the harm done by unbridled capitalism and proposed cures in a *Treatise of Christian Political Economy*. In 1840, another legitimist, Dr. Villermé, carried out the first significant study of the terrible working and living conditions of workers in large-scale industry. Numerous authors such as Msgr. Ketteler, Frédéric Le

Play, Albert de Mun, Armand de Melun, and René de La Tour du Pin took over from these precursors.[7]

Bonald, for his part, forcefully denounced the domination of civil society by the market. Let us also recall the *Open Letter to the Workers* published in 1865 by the Count of Chambord: "To individualism oppose association; to unbridled competition oppose the counterweight of common defense; to industrial privilege oppose the voluntary and regulated constitution of free corporations."

After the Commune of 1871, two great parties opposed one another in France: the republicans and the conservative monarchists, but the rift between the center-Right and center-Left passed through the liberal family. Capitalism was the object of criticism from the Right, but such criticism, often drifting into anti-Semitism (Édouard Drumont), targeted "speculation," the "big-shots," the "200 families," and so on. The socialist workers' movement was not insensible to these problems.

The first Catholic Workers' Circles, created in 1871, marked the beginning of social Catholicism. Bills proposed in the Chamber of Deputies by La Tour du Pin, theorist of a "Christian social order" based on a corporatism nearly amounting to a return to the *Ancien Régime*, were fairly dramatic, for he proposed "the elaboration of international workers' legislation, assistance to elderly and sick persons, limits on work by children and women, shortening of the work day, the establishment of pension funds and workers' insurance funds, protection for workers injured on the job, the establishment of a minimum wage, an obligatory day off every week, the settling of social conflicts by arbitration boards, sanctions against employers who dismiss workers for trade union membership, the struggle against unhealthy living quarters, education for prisoners, judicial assistance, etc."[8] While criticizing "class hatred," La Tour du Pin also

---

[7] Arnaud Imatz, *Par-delà droite et gauche. Permanence et évolution des idéaux et des valeurs non conformistes* [*Beyond Right and Left: Permanence and Development of Non-Conformist Ideas and Values*] (Paris: Godefroy de Bouillon, 1996), 105.

[8] Imatz, *Par-delà droite et gauche*, 106.

denounced economic liberalism. This got him accused of "social-ism" by the liberals, especially Charles Périn, an economist close to Msgr. Freppel and the Angers School, which published a book directed against the Catholic Workers' Circles, *Christian Social-ism*, in 1879.[9] Georges Valois saw in them merely an "authoritar-ian corporatism full of archaic traits."

The "Bonapartist" current, for its part, made much of the "ap-peal to the people." On a basis of anti-parliamentarism, plebiscita-ry rhetoric was often directed at the working class. This had al-ready been seen with the revolts by the Lyons silk workers (1831–1834), whose background was the alliance between Bonapartism and textile workers. It would become even more obvious with Boulangisme in 1888–1889 (two-thirds of the Boulangist deputies came from the Left at that time), then with Pierre Biétry's "Yel-low" movement in its beginnings, before 1902. In 1894–1895, workers' socialists such as Camille Pelletan, Eugène Fournière, and Clovis Hugues collaborated on Maurice Barrère's *La Cocarde*.

The original Action Française, born in 1898 in a milieu still imbued with Boulangism, and of which it has been rather accu-rately said that its nationalism was based on "a patriotism much closer to the spirit of 1793 than to that of the old France,"[10] dis-played a certain anti-capitalism. "If the proletariat is resisting, if that resistance has taken the form of a violent offensive, they are not the ones who began the fight," observed Charles Maurras; "Capitalist oppression and exploitation came first." Léon Daudet for his part expressed his sympathy for a General Confederation of Labor which, under the influence of revolutionary syndical-ism, rejected "electoral humbug" (Émile Janvion), while the Maurrassian Jean Rivain, in an article entitled "The Future of Syndicalism," wrote: "The capitalist who has money has the power, and for the worker who is obliged to sell his services to earn his bread, it is freedom that oppresses him and rules that

---

[9] In December 1891, Paul Laforgues, Karl Marx's son-in-law, greet-ed a speech by the Catholic deputy Albert de Mun as "one of the best socialist speeches which has been delivered here."

[10] Paul Sérant, *Ou va la droite?* [*Where Is the Right Going?*] (Paris: Plon, 1958), 24.

liberate him."[11] We also remember Maurras' positions taken in 1908 following the events of Villeneuve-Draveil[12] and the Prou-dhon Circle's ephemeral experiment. But this promising movement did not survive the First World War. From the beginning of the 1920s, Action Française was increasingly held prisoner by a reactionary and self-righteous public that led it to condemn unconditionally all the Popular Front's social reforms.

Between the wars, doctrinaire liberalism appeared discredited for a time by the rise of planning and fascist temptations. But the Right-wing leagues fell into the orbit of conservative and petty-bourgeois nationalism. A large part of the Right, out of hostility towards the Left, rejected any idea of social justice, just as part of the Left, out of hostility towards the Right, rejected the political idea of the nation, although born of the Revolution. "Supporting labor union demands amounts to playing Moscow's game," said some people. "To fight in the name of the nation is to play the extreme Right's game," said others: crass stupidity on both sides. To find any critique of capitalism one must turn to the non-conformists of the 1930s, nearly all of whom appealed to Proudhon and Péguy.[13]

The Right in France long remained an essentially sociological phenomenon, expressing class interests but not basing itself on any intellectual capital peculiar to itself. Its anti-intellectualism and relative indifference to economic questions have often been mentioned.[14] Albert Thibaudet said of Orléanism that "it did not

---

[11] Cited by Hervé Bizien, "La vraie droite française contre le capitalisme" ["The True French Right versus Capitalism"], *Le Choc du mois*, September 2007, 23.

[12] A strike in the suburbs of Paris during May through July 1908 in which six workers were killed. — Trans.

[13] Cf. especially the texts published by Jean-Pierre Maxence and Thierry Molnier in *l'Insurgé* beginning in 1937. Cf. also Jean de Fabregues, "Capital et capitalisme," *Réaction*, March 1932. In June 1936, Pierre Gaxotte writes: "The working class is part of the nation, the poverty of workers is that of the fatherland" (quoted by Eugen Weber, *L'Action française*, trans. Michel Chrestien [Paris: Stock, 1985], 416).

[14] On the inability of the Right to formulate an alternative economic theory, cf. Pierre Rosanvallon, *Misère de l'économie* [*Poverty of the Econo-*

represent any idea; it was only against ideas." An undoubtedly exaggerated statement when one recalls Guizot glorifying the July Monarchy, Benjamin Constant theorizing the "Liberty of the Moderns" by opposing it to that of "the Ancients," Victor Cousin, and so on. But there is still an element of truth in the remark. The Right is mistrustful of doctrines, in which it claims to see merely "intellectual constructions" or "utopias," but it is all ears for those who claim to speak in the name of "facts," beginning with economists and financiers. Then it rallies, naturally or by default, to economic liberalism, which it makes into a pillar of support for a wavering pragmatism. "Marxism teaches historical materialism," said Emmanuel Berl, "but in fact I have always found faith in historical materialism much stronger among men of the Right than those of the Left."

The few times the Right has developed an economic and social doctrine, it has always been with a declared intention of putting an end to the class struggle. Corporatism, "popular capitalism" (or "capitalism for all"), the capital-labor alliance, or any other doctrine of this sort aims to demonstrate that, in a society conceived in a healthy manner, the interests of the propertied classes and those of the working class can be naturally harmonized. The idea that a good economy is one which assures the harmony of class interests is also found among liberals (Bastiat, *Economic Harmonies*, 1849), paired with a theory of the spontaneous harmonization of individual interests and the general interest. But this will to "reconcile" the boss with the worker, and capital with labor, often by way of a mystical idea of national unity, will also be found in fascism. The great idea is always to "harmonize" existing interests instead of opposing them. The aim is "social peace," by attempting to convince the workers and bosses that their true interests are the same. It is an idea that would scandalize Georges Sorel.

This idea seemed to be justified in the Fordist era, which saw the formation of a large middle class when the holders of capital understood that raising salaries allowed a rise in purchasing power, and thus the flow of merchandise. At once the class

---

my] (Paris: Seuil, 1983) ("Une droite sans idées," 134–38).

struggle seemed to dissipate, which facilitated the acceptance of the capitalist system on the Right as well as the Left. The anti-liberal current within the Right has never ceased to diminish since that time, with the market system finding defenders even in the ranks of the radical Right.

After the Revolution of 1917, anti-Communism also played a very negative role. There were of course good reasons to criticize the Soviet system. Its true nature also had to be revealed, viz. that of a totalitarianism associated with a form of state capitalism. At the time of the Popular Front, this anti-Communism made any social legislation suspect in the eyes of a great part of the Right.

Paul Sérant writes:

The exclusive nationalism practiced by the Right led the world of the Right to misunderstand the economic and social upheavals of the modern world. "Economics depends on politics," said Maurras; but many men of the Right used this statement as a pretext for refusing to examine the problems of the common good except in terms of national politics. We see this clearly in 1936, at the moment of the Popular Front's triumph. Most on the Right were indignant at the alliance between radicals and Communists, and they referred to the Soviet danger—but did not understand that it was dangerous to appear to tie the defense of the nation from Communism to the cause of conservatism. Young writers—and more generally the young elements of the Right who were able to see this danger and who, appealing at once to Proudhon, Sorel, and the young Maurras, affirmed the need to go beyond the old positions of Left and Right, and to struggle as vigorously against liberal capitalism as against Marxism—only won over a rather small audience within the Right. For most men of the Right, the strikers of 1936 were no doubt fine Frenchmen, but Frenchmen who had fallen victims of Moscow's agitators, and who had to be set straight. . . . The drama of 1936 lies in this: the French Left and Right divided as they had never been before—with the nation proclaimed on one side and social justice on the other—in a tumult that prefigured civil war.[15]

After 1945, in the context of the Cold War, anti-Sovietism led the Right to assume solidarity with a "free world" dominated by American imperialism, which it loudly supported in its predatory political, commercial, and military undertakings (recall the displays of fidelity with the very corrupt regime of South Vietnam). This made it into the forward point of a "defense of the West" that in the end was never more than the defense of international capital. The obsession with "Communist subversion" and "Moscow's hand" also led to the condemnation not only of decolonization (Mossadegh's Iran, Lumumba's Congo, and Salvador Allende's Chile, not forgetting Fidel Castro, who at the beginning was merely a revolutionary Cuban nationalist), but all attempts by oppressed peoples to rid themselves of capitalist domination.

With the goal of not "playing the Kremlin's game," the Right validated every system of exploitation set up by bourgeois *compradores*, every act of pillage by oligarchies enriched by commercial traffic. It supported the most odious dictatorships as soon as they opposed the "subversives" who demanded agrarian reform, the sharing of land, and a bit more social justice. The only result was to throw all these popular revolts against social injustice into Moscow's arms; they only became "Communist" because they were left no other hope.

And this is how we came to be in the situation described by Alasdair MacIntyre as follows: "The contemporary debates within modern political systems are almost exclusively between conservative liberals, liberal liberals, and radical liberals. There is little place in such political systems for the criticism of the system itself, that is, for putting liberalism in question."

After the Second World War, liberal ideas never stopped gaining ground on the Right, less in their doctrinal form than by the effects of a gradual contagion. Georges Pompidou's liberalism already represented a stage in this process. In the 1980s, the

---

[15] Paul Sérant, *Ou va la droite?*, 62–63.

apostles of deregulation, Margaret Thatcher and Ronald Reagan, became idols of the Right, while the social-democratic Left rallied unhesitatingly to the market society. A few years later, the "new economists" (Jacques Garello, Henri Lepage, Alain Laurent, etc.) tried to popularize the ideas of the libertarians (Murray Rothbard, David Friedman) and Friedrich Hayek, according to whom "the concept of social justice is strictly empty and without meaning." This was also the era when the Club de l'Horloge held a colloquium on "liberalism in the service of the people" (Nice, October 20–22, 1989)! We had to wait for the crisis of 2008 to witness a certain questioning of this perspective. But by that time, we had long since entered the era of "winners" and "easy money," with all social life operating in dependence on the market.

The critiques contained in the church's social doctrine had themselves long remained a dead letter. At the Vatican, these critiques went back to Leo XIII's encyclical *Rerum Novarum* (1891) and its condemnation of an "unbridled competition" resulting in the

> concentration of industry and commerce in a few hands, imposing an almost servile yoke on an infinite multitude of proletarians. . . . The rich and the bosses [must not] treat the worker as a slave; it is just for them to respect human dignity in him, heightened by the dignity of a Christian. . . . What is shameful and inhuman is to use man as a cheap instrument of gain, not to value anything but the strength of his arms.

Rerum Novarum amounted to an encouragement of that social Christianity, made famous notably by Albert de Mun and La Tour du Pin, which we have already spoken about and which would give birth at the beginning of the twentieth century to a whole galaxy of organizations and journals (*Action Populaire*[16] was founded in 1903, the first *Semaine social* was held the following year in Lyon). But the Papacy quickly intervened, notably with the encyclicals *Graves de communi* (1901) and *Singuli quadam*

---

[16] A Jesuit association. — Trans.

(1912), to turn social Catholics from political action and remind them of the priority of moral action. The movement, marked off on the Left by the condemnation of Marc Sangnier's *Sillon* movement in 1910 and on the Right by that of *Action Française* in 1926, never transcended a purely reformist perspective.

None of these proposals, however judicious they may have been, were accompanied by any fundamental analysis of the nature of capitalism. At the end of the nineteenth century, the social doctrine of the church inspired primarily the sermons of lady patronesses. Rather than appealing to the law or political decision-making, they appealed to the moral conscience or even "natural law"; they cited examples of "good bosses" who concerned themselves with the fate of their workers; they spoke of "just wages," recommended "good works," paternalism, and the spirit of charity that was supposed to correct the misdeeds of the "invisible hand." At best, they were preoccupied with improving the fate of proletarians, but they did not really ask themselves about the deeper causes of the proletariat's emergence. They wanted to "help the poor," but while preserving the system that produced poverty. Remaining in a moral key — it was a matter of morally exhorting both the bosses and the working class — one did not ask oneself about the dominant system of production, nor about what fundamentally moved it. As for poverty, it was considered inevitable. "The dyad paternalism-pauperism satisfied Christian and police demands as well as liberal or reactionary aspirations," writes Anthony Rowley.[17] This is what explains how the church continued to play the role of a "holy gendarmerie" for so long, which cooled things off and disarmed the spirit of revolt by preaching resignation and acceptance of the social disaster.

The proof of this is that, despite the principles of the church's social doctrine, capitalism never ceased finding defenders in the Catholic world. In 1989, Pierre de Calan, an eminent member of the National Council of French Employers, published a series of

---

[17] Anthony Rowley, "L'économie et le marché" ["The Economy and the Market"], in Jean-François Sirinelli, ed., *Histoire des droites en France*, vol. 3: *Sensibilités* (Paris: Gallimard, 1992), 407.

articles on "liberal Catholic capitalism" in the *Revue des deux mondes*. More recently, the critical reactions to Pope Francis's publication of the "ecological" encyclical *Laudato si* have been revealing.

In an article entitled "There Is No Infallibility in Economics," published on July 24, 2015 on the website of the *Institut de recherches économiques et fiscales*, the Christian Jean-Philippe Delsol assures us that the Pope "goes too far," is lacking in "prudence," is stepping outside his area of competence ("Is it his vocation to pass judgment on privatization?"), has fallen into the error of "constructivism," etc. Delsol says of course that "it is not by sharing that one enriches the poor," and takes up the old refrain according to which the market is "the best tool and the best approach the world has ever invented to favor its own development" — the assumption that one must at all costs "favor development" never being examined, of course. After this, Pope Francis is kindly advised to return to the care of souls and the virtue of charity.

The congenial review *Limite*, on the other hand, founded in September 2015, gathers a certain number of Catholic authors, young for the most part, who do not hesitate to pronounce themselves in favor of degrowth or "integral ecology" and to condemn liberal capitalism in light of the writings of Jacques Ellul, Chesterton, Ivan Illich, Orwell, Michéa, and many others. This orientation has been described as a "daydream" by Gaël Brustier, who thinks "the conservative camp should, by its social composition, remain more closely bound to economic liberalism from an ideological point of view and to the (moderate or extreme) Right from an electoral point of view rather than be tempted by the integral ecology of Gaultier Bès or the 'Christian anarchism' of the veterans of *Immédiatement*."[18] Obviously, it remains to be seen whether *Limite* addresses itself only to the "conservative camp" . . .

Equally revealing is the very interesting study carried out between October 2014 and October 2015 by the Catholic journal *La Nef* in collaboration with the Socio-Political Observatory of the

---

[18] Gaël Brustier, website *Slate*, September 11, 2015.

Diocese of Fréjus-Toulon on the theme of "Liberation from Liberalism?" The responses, quite varied, show to what extent the Catholic world remains divided regarding liberal ideology and capitalism.

The first problem was well-put by Falk van Gaver: "Isn't liberal conservatism, a kind of continuation of Orléanism crossed with Bonapartism, a contradiction in terms?" But van Gaver is very nearly the only contributor, along with Philippe Conte, Frédéric Dufoing, and to some extent Bernard Dumont, to condemn liberal ideology consistently. While rejecting philosophical or "societal" liberalism, a number of other persons who were asked continue to look lovingly upon economic liberalism. Thus, Chantal Delsol declares that "the peculiar character of Western culture is that it occasions a gradual retreat of holism, because it believes that each of us is a person" (!). She adds: "It goes without saying that I do not consider liberalism a structure of sin."[19] Pierre de Lauzun assures us that the church has always recognized "the market as natural." François Huguenin thinks "political freedom is a fortunate attainment of liberal thought in the modern era." Pascal Salin assures us that "liberal values are Christian values, or at least entirely compatible with them," for "liberalism and Christianity share a common base from the perspective of universal values," while Bernard Antony confesses his desire to defend liberalism "at least in the economic realm," etc.[20]

In the best case, the dominant opinion on the Right is that one might possibly make accusations against "unbridled" capitalism, its "excesses" or "perversions" — but not the logic of capital itself. This lazy line of argument rests on commonplace observations constantly repeated: the market economy is "more efficient" at creating wealth and producing ever more merchandise; it is the best way of favoring "development," allowing the gradual enrichment of all social classes (the poor certainly still exist,

---

[19] "Structure of sin" is a concept that originated in Latin American "liberation theology." —Trans.

[20] Cf. Falk van Gaver and Christophe Geffroy, eds., *Faut-il se libérer du libéralisme?* [*Should we Free Ourselves from Liberalism?*] (Paris: Pierre-Guillaume de Roux, 2016).

but their relative standard of living is rising), and so on. No one asks about the price to be paid for this "efficiency" of the system, nor about the impact of commodity fetishism on social relations, nor about the primacy accorded commercial values, nor about the anthropological model of the *Homo oeconomicus*, nor about the well-foundedness of the logic of surplus accumulation, nor about the possibility of infinite material growth, etc.

Undoubtedly, as long as capitalism "marched in step with the nation," its expansion could be presented as an addition to national greatness. This no longer applies in a time when the world economy is attempting to suppress all local singularities that present an obstacle to its own movement. Henceforth, liberal capitalism cannot have any "national strategy": the arrival of the globalized economy leads it to assign to the state as its principal task support for ongoing globalization by means of appropriate politico-economic legislation, along with new and matching internal controls to disarm any form of social opposition.

The money-Right does not really have any principled convictions but only principled interests. "This is one reason why it shows itself so masterful at what might be called the relativism of ideologies. All theoretical representations can be useful to it, provided they do not contradict its system of interests." [21]

The recurrent idea is that "one must distinguish between liberalism and liberalism," and not confound "good" productive capital with "bad" financial capital either. Philosophical liberalism might deserve condemnation, and "social" liberalism as well, but political liberalism might under certain conditions be perfectly acceptable ("We are not going to deprive ourselves of liberty!"). As for economic liberalism, there are grounds for condemning only certain "excesses." Such is the position of all those who adhere to one form or another of "national liberalism": liberalism can be "national," and one must only separate the wheat from the chaff, and so on. Éric Zemmour has been among the first to denounce the "swindle" of that branch of the Right that "venerates the market while rejecting its effects: consumption,

---

[21] Sami Nair, "Le socialisme n'est plus ce qu'il était" ["Socialism Isn't What It Used To Be"], *L'Événement européen*, no. 1, 1988, 101–102.

globalization, immigration, moral degradation."[22]

Now, if there is one thing Jean-Claude Michéa (to name only him) has demonstrated, it is the *deep unity* of liberalism and the natural complementarity of liberalism's different forms which, on the Left as well as the Right, people persist in distinguishing in order to oppose them to one another. All are based on the same anthropology, whose principal trait is to legitimate the egoistic impulse considered as a "natural impulse," i.e., the individual desire to maximize one's material and private interest. Obviously, the same goes for capitalism, which is not a mere form of economic organization that could be improved (or "moralized") to make it tolerable, but a "total social fact," generative of a real system of (de)civilization.

Like a certain form of the Left that long saw in capitalism only a means for exploiting the working class and never ceased cherishing the idea that capitalism would cease to be bad the moment the workers succeeded in assuming control of it, a certain form of the Right remains unable to reflect on the very essence of capitalism, on the logic of the unlimited, on commodity fetishism, on the theory of value, on the concept of the market, on the nature of money, etc.

Bernard Charbonneau was thus able to write: "That is how love of country, justifying the protection of economic interests by the state, became its caricature: chauvinism. And leadership by the best justifies the arbitrary will of the richest, making it impossible for us to distinguish between a living aristocracy and a so-called elite indicated by money alone."[23] By behaving in this manner, the Right condemned itself. Charbonneau continues:

For the values to which the Right appeals are precisely those that condemn it: what are the criticisms the Left makes of the Right in comparison with those the Right could make of itself! It champions property, and for the benefit of an individual, capitalism dispossesses millions,

---

[22] Éric Zemmour, *Valeurs actuelles* [*Current Values*], May 30, 2008.
[23] Bernard Charbonneau, *L'État* [*The State*] (Paris: Economica, 1987), 153.

carrying out the first mass expropriations of modern times. It champions the nation, and for the greatness of an individual, nationalism nourishes a will to power that tends to destroy all nations. It celebrates decision and character, and for the arbitrary will of an individual, whether monarch or boss, it transforms all the others into serfs. Defending freedom, everywhere the Right tends to encourage monopoly. . . . Against Marxist materialism, [it] poses as a champion of the authority of the spirit, but it serves a social class whose economic activity is its *raison d'être* . . . .[24]

Correctly considering that society is prior to individuals, the Right has come to adhere to a system one the postulates of which is that a society can function by associating individuals bound only by legal contracts and commercial exchange. It might praise the "common good," but it adheres to an ideology that only wants to recognize independent individuals, i.e., an atomized society. Sometimes it claims to be opposed to modernity, but it continues to support the *most modernizing* system that has ever existed. Wanting to be spiritual, it finds nothing to criticize in the materialist logic of interest and profit. Defending political sovereignty, it supports a system that involves submitting politics to economics and considering borders non-existent, since nothing should hinder the free circulation of men, merchandise, and capital. Occasionally it criticizes commodification but never commodities. It fails to see that genuine socialism rests on the central notions of mutual aid and community, which scarcely differ from the organic bonds of traditional society, and ends by falling into their opposite: individualism. It does not realize that the new industrial order being put in place is based on the Enlightenment's abstract universalism. It remains silent on the generalized alienation of the contemporary world, which makes man a stranger to himself.

Decidedly, nothing can be expected from a Right like this.

---

[24] Charbonneau, *L'État*, 153.

Ernesto Laclau & Left-Wing Populism

Pablo Iglesias, the leader of Podemos, a populist movement that became (with 20.6% of the vote) the third-largest political force in Spain following the elections of December 2015, said shortly thereafter that one could "define Podemos by saying that we have done everything the Left said must not be done." He was alluding, of course, to the "progressive" and governmental Left, for there is at least one theoretician of the Left to whom he did indeed turn for inspiration: Ernesto Laclau.

The writings currently available on populism can be divided into two categories according to whether they take a historico-geographic approach (studies of Russian populism, American populism, Latin American populism, European neo-populism, etc.) or a theoretico-epistemological approach.[1] The second category covers various political or economic theories of populism, along with structuralist theories or those limited to seeing in populism a style rather than an ideology. Ernesto Laclau's "post-structuralist" theory, often called a theory of discursive analysis, belongs to this latter category.

Opposing the contemptuous devaluing of populism that reigns today in the political class, Laclau forcefully champions it. "Democracy today is inconceivable," he states, "without a certain dose of populism."

Born on October 5, 1935, in Buenos Aires, where he studied philosophy, Ernesto Laclau was first associated with Left-wing Peronism. While occupying his first teaching post at the University of Tucuman when still quite young, he became one of the leaders of the Socialist Party of the National Left founded by Jorge Abelardo Ramos (1921–1994), Argentina's future ambassador to Mexico. The author of a monumental history of Latin

---

[1] Cf. Mario E. Poblete, "How to Assess Populist Discourse through Three Current Approaches," *Journal of Political Ideologies*, June 2015, 201–18.

America, Ramos was aware that, contrary to what had happened in Europe, the South American continent never experienced any alliance between liberalism and democracy in the nineteenth century, which explains why populist movements there rarely adopted liberal positions. This is why he proposed using nationalism to heighten the contradictions in which his country was involved. At the beginning of the 1980s, Laclau told *El País*: "Through Peronism I came to understand Gramsci."

Laclau moved to England in 1969, where he was invited by the historian Eric Hobsbawm, and there he founded the "Essex School," named for the town where he taught after 1972. A professor of political theory from 1986, he developed his theories of discursive analysis in his courses, training hundreds of students from all over the world who were looking for a renewal of radical thought. In the 2000s he would support the Argentine governments of Néstor Kirchner and his wife, Cristina. He died in Seville on April 13, 2014.

Laclau is recognized all over the world today as one of the most important political philosophers of the late twentieth and early twenty-first centuries. Even in France, where he remains less well-known and got only a weak reception from institutional philosophy, a large colloquium was devoted to him in 2015 in Paris ("Hegemony, Populism, Emancipation: Perspectives on the Philosophy of Ernesto Laclau, 1935–2014"). Since the end of the 1980s, his views have contributed to renewing the Left's strategic thought, especially in the countries of Southern Europe and Latin America, where his thought is still highly influential. In Spain, the rise of the Podemos movement, which has often appealed to his ideas, has attracted attention to him but also earned him some criticism.[2] He is the principal theoretician of what is generally

---

[2] Some think his analysis of the capitalist system remains somewhat superficial, or accuse him of situating it within a rather reformist perspective (he does emphasize, in fact, the "processual character of every radical transformation"). Cf. Razmig Keucheyan and Renaud Lambert, "Ernest Laclau, inspirateur de Podemos" ["Ernesto Laclau, Inspiration of Podemos"], *Le Monde diplomatique*, September 2015, 3, who reproach Podemos with favoring a "confusion of classes by privileging the con-

called, for want of a better name, "Left-wing populism."

In 1985, in collaboration with his companion the excellent Belgian political scientist Chantal Mouffe, Laclau published a book called *Hegemony and Socialist Strategy: Towards a Radical Democratic Politics*. In it he lays out the basic principles of his doctrine, beginning with what separates him from Marxist orthodoxy. A post-Marxist, he rejects all forms of economic determinism, for this prevents any account of labor processes not reducible to economics. The emergence of new social movements, he emphasizes, show that Marxist categories do not permit a full analysis of contemporary Western societies: present-day fragmentation or diversification forbids us from reducing social struggles to a simple confrontation between the bourgeoisie and proletariat (even if this scheme continues to have a certain validity in various countries of the Third World), all the more so insofar as the repression exercised by power today rests less on *domination*, always external to the one subjected to it, than on *normalization*, whose success rests upon the internalization of the norms imposed. Laclau concludes from this that political identities do not result merely from the position of agents within relations of production, nor can they be analyzed according to purely sociological data. So what do they depend on? His

---

struction of the referent 'people' rather than other referents more accurate from a sociological point of view." Laclau's theses have also been vigorously contested by the Trotskyists of the New Anticapitalist Party. Cf. Emmanuel Barot, "D'Ernesto Laclau à Iglesias: théorie et pratique du (néo)populisme" ["From Ernesto Laclaus to Iglesias: The Theory and Practice of Neo-Populism"], website of the New Anticapitalist Party, November 14, 2015, which accuses him of a "Rightist, gradualist, and electoralist instrumentalization of Gramsci" (!). In Spain, Carlos Fernández Lira has expressed the wish that Podemos would undertake to "make populism republican again" by appealing "more to Kant and less to Laclau" ("La carta que nos queda: republicanizar el populismo" ["The Map That Remains to Us: Republicizing Populism"], website of the newspaper *El Diario*, April 16, 2015)! Cf. Hedwig Marzolf, "Le kantisme de Podemos ou les équivoques du sens commun" ["Podemos's Kantianism, or the Ambiguities of Common Sense"], *Esprit*, September 2016, 91–104.

answer: on social constructs shaped by "discourse."

For Laclau, the social realm should first of all be considered a discursive realm, not only in the strictly linguistic sense, but in the performative sense of a bond between words and actions allowing the establishment of "signifying totalities," as in Wittgenstein's language games:

> The heir of Saussurian structuralism, Laclau borrows from him the idea that there are no positive terms in language, but only differences: a thing is only what it is within relations that distinguish it from another. He extends this linguistic theory to the analysis of social facts in order to privilege a political approach to games and to the articulation of differences.[3]

The social implies articulation, and "identitarian construction is a part of the grammar inherent in a language game."

Since all societies rest upon an unavoidable tension between difference (particularities) and equivalence (community, the common good), social identity is constituted at the meeting point between equivalence and difference. Equivalence allows one to go beyond the opposition between universal and particular. The universal is one of those "empty signifiers" we are destined always to miss, but which are no less indispensable for determining the horizon toward which all action is inevitably directed. "Empty signifiers" are general thematics open to a pluralism of interpretations and to the conflictual game of hegemonic constructs. Social and political identities are the product of the "empty signifiers" they have endowed with meaning. This means the plural, indeed fragmented, character of contemporary societies must be accepted as long as we inscribe that plurality within a logic of equivalences allowing the construction of a public sphere.

The leading idea here is that political identities, which are always collective, are never given *a priori* but rather constructed

---

[3] Evelyne Grossman, "Vous avez dit 'populisme'?" ["Did You Say 'Populism'?"], website *La vie des idées*, May 19, 2008, 2.

from discursive practices, thus allowing for the appearance of a collective will. For Laclau, any social practice has a meaning and constitutes a discourse that expresses that meaning's political potential, which resides in its capacity for a break, i.e., its capacity for distinguishing itself from the dominant system not merely as difference, but as contradiction.[4]

Politics, finally, cannot be understood without taking its autonomous character into account, starting with two key concepts: *antagonism* and *hegemony*.

Contrary to those who regularly announce the end of politics, whether following a "final" revolution or by aligning the government of men with the management of things, Laclau affirms the autonomy and primacy of politics, which leads him of course to reject liberalism with its methodological individualism and its pretention to axiological neutrality, but also the communicational logic of a Habermas, or Michael Hardt's and Antonio Negri's theory of "multitudes."

The idea that antagonisms are inherent to social domains so that they appear as the very condition for the structuration of society has been developed particularly by Chantal Mouffe, who works at the University of Westminster and is one of the most celebrated representatives of "Schmittianism of the Left." Her thought does in fact owe a great deal to Carl Schmitt.[5] She

---

[4] Ernesto Laclau, "Ruptura populista y discurso" ["The Populist Break and Discourse"], in Julio Labastida Martin del Campo, ed., *Hegemonía y alternativas políticas* [*Hegemony and Political Alternatives*] (Coyoacán, Mexico: Siglo XXI, 1985), 39–44.

[5] *Cf.* Chantal Mouffe, "Penser la démocratie moderne avec, et contre, Carl Schmitt" ["Theorizing Modern Democracy With (and Against) Carl Schmitt"], *Revue française de science politique*, Paris, XLII, 1, February 1992, 83–96; "Carl Schmitt, une politique du droit" ["Carl Schmitt, a Politics of Law"], *Esprit*, December 1993, 182–89; "Deliberative Democracy or Agonistic Pluralism?," *Social Research*, Autumn 1999; "The Limits of Liberal Pluralism: Towards an Agonistic Multipolar World Order," in András Sajó, ed., *Militant Democracy* (Utrecht: Eleven International, 2004); and "The Stakes of the Political According to Carl Schmitt," in Patrizia C. McBride, Richard W. McCormick, and Monika Zagar, eds., *Legacies of Modernism: Art and Politics in Northern Europe,*

writes: "It is because there exists a form of negativity that cannot be overcome dialectically that one can never arrive at full objectivity, and that antagonism is an ever-present possibility." Recognizing radical negativity implies renouncing the deadly dream of a homogeneous social space, for such a space will never exist: there is no form of politics that will disarm all antagonisms. This amounts to saying that the conflictual dimension must be institutionalized.

Conflict being inherent to politics, the latter is essentially undetermined. Thus, Laclau rejects the idea of an ultimate foundation of political action, along with the "essentialist" idea of a perfectly reconciled society, transparent to itself, where antagonisms have disappeared (which amounts to saying there is no conceivable society beyond division and power). He proposes understanding politics, and thus also democracy, "starting from its conflictuality-in-principle, and thus from its existential instability. . . . Politics does not, then, function as a representation of a pre-existing natural or social reality, but as the constitution of that reality by the articulation of different actors within movements with hegemonic pretentions."[6] Politics is the basic tool of a collective existential refounding. It is thanks to politics that the emancipatory act can become an act of instituting, i.e., a founding act.

Politics can therefore never in the last resort amount to

1890–1950 (Basingstoke: Palgrave Macmillan, 2007), 203–12. Chantal Mouffe has also edited the volume *The Challenge of Carl Schmitt* (London: Verso, 1999). Cf. also her two books translated into French: *La Politique et ses enjeux. Pour une démocratie plurielle* [*Politics and Its Stakes: For a Pluralist Democracy*] (Paris: La Découverte/MAUSS, 1994); and *Agonistique: Penser politiquement le monde*, trans. Denyse Beaulieu (Paris: Beaux-Arts de Paris, 2014). In English: *Agonistics: Thinking the World Politically* (London: Verso, 2013).

6 Audric Vitiello, "L'itinéraire de la démocratie radicale d'Ernesto Laclau" ["The Itinerary of Ernesto Laclau's Radical Democracy"], *Raisons politiques*, 2009, 3, 208; text reprinted on the website *Journal du MAUSS*, June 17, 2014. Cf. also Jean-Claude Monod, "La force du populisme: une analyse philosophique. A propos d'Ernesto Laclau" ["The Strength of Populism: A Philosophical Analysis with Reference to Ernesto Laclau"], *Esprit*, January 2009, 42–52.

technical problems that expert managers would have to resolve, but calls for *decisions* between incompatible alternatives — something that liberal thought has never been able to understand because of its irresistible tendency to conceive of objectivity as inherent in things themselves. Politics implies conflict, and conflict implies pluralism, which in its turn implies a sovereign political decision necessary for putting an end to indecision. Democracy, as Chantal Mouffe says, "presupposes recognition of the agonistic dimension of politics, and this is why we can only protect and consolidate it by clearly admitting that politics always consists in domesticating hostility" without trying to make it disappear. Domesticating hostility means creating an "agonistic" form in which opponents are not enemies, nor mere "competitors," but adversaries.

Laclau writes: "Stating that social division and antagonism cannot be eradicated amounts to affirming that all social objectivity is the result of a phenomenon of establishing frontiers. It is in this (always contingent) displacement of frontiers that the hegemonic operation consists."

There is never, in fact, just a single antagonism within the social field, but a plurality of antagonisms corresponding to dispersed social demands that must be unified with a view to the "hegemonic creation of a unity." To establish a frontier is to distribute the social elements within chains of equivalence distributed on either side of that frontier. Political action is then defined as a struggle for hegemony through the conquest of "empty signifiers" that articulate the various social demands.

The concept of hegemony obviously comes from Gramsci, to whom Laclau explicitly appeals, but to whom he also gives a new interpretation. He takes from Gramsci the idea that the cultural domain occupies a decisive position in the construction of common meaning, but no longer believes in the central role of the working class in the struggle for "cultural hegemony." While Gramsci limits himself to contemplating the creation of a "popular bloc" associating the proletariat with certain institutional elements prepared to commit themselves to a struggle to construct a counter-hegemony in the face of bourgeois hegemony, he redefines hegemony as "that operation by which a particularity takes on a universal signification incommensurable with itself," which makes it a fundamental category of political analysis. Hegemonic aims are thus synonymous with "logics of equivalence" that seek to produce a regularity beyond differences, i.e., beyond social heterogeneity.

"What is the logic governing the constitution of social and political identities?" Laclau answers that it is the logic of hegemony. Every social order is of a "hegemonic" nature, every common world is the result of a hegemonic construction, and all sense of collective existence depends on a struggle for hegemony. Hegemonic practice is consequently defined as what allows different social demands to be articulated so as to create and fix the meaning of political institutions. Such is precisely the task of populism.

It is in fact by the constitution of a new hegemony that the people become capable of incarnating the whole of social aspirations and demands, thus instituting itself as a "name" representing the whole of society. Laclau writes: "Naming is the key moment in the constitution of a 'people.'" There is hegemony when "the affirmations of a certain group, at a certain time, are totalized to cover the whole of society," and when a "we" capable of articulating demands of heterogeneous social groups around a single name asserts itself. Hegemony is the moment when a social or symbolic particularity takes on a "universal" and political dimension, when a particular force assumes the representation of a totality because it has succeeded better than others in endowing "empty signifiers" with meanings that mobilize the imagination and transform it into a will. "The more populist interventions genuinely play the role of empty signifiers—the more they succeed in unifying the community in an equivalent manner—the more they will become the object of a radical endowment with meaning," he writes. It is the constitution of a new socio-historic hegemony that opens the door of power to the people in their dual symbolic and political dimension.

The error of orthodox Marxism, locked in an "economistic paradigm," is not to have recognized the primacy and autonomy of politics, which explains why it has never been able to conceive hegemony other than as an authoritarian conforming to a predefined norm. Ernesto Laclau for his part is betting on populism to "radicalize democracy." It is a matter of doing what in their times Lech Walesa succeeded in doing in Poland or Salvador Allende in Chile: raising up a people and incarnating their will to change to the point of attaining power democratically.

"Radical democracy" is a democracy that has no root other than itself, viz., the political practice that erects democratic principles into a "new matrix of the social imagination" and "fundamental nodal point in the construction of politics." This democratic practice, which must not forget to take into account the "dynamic of the passions," also serves "to reveal that social relations are always the result of forms of institutionalization that confer upon them their form and meaning."

Laclau observes the historical decline of emancipatory discourse's central categories, which has opened the way to the planetary rise of liberalism: "As soon as institutions that channeled social demands—and especially trade unions—lose their articulating role, the social field presents itself in the form of the dispersion of actors and demands." How can we take this dispersion into account? Precisely by means of populism.

In one of his first books, Laclau suggested that populism, insofar as it is rooted in an anti-elite sentiment, articulates popular traditions and class positions, without the former being able to do without the latter.[7] Later on, he qualified and refined his analysis. Populism is in fact no more reducible to any particular social base—the "popular classes"—than it is an irrational phenomenon reducible to demagogy and the manipulation of base instincts. It is rather a revelation of what the construction of social identity demands. It is a political logic that aims at constituting or reconstituting the people as a historical actor beginning from a plurality of antagonistic situations. "Populism is not an ideology," says Laclau. "It is a form of political construction that appeals to those below against those in power while passing over all established channels."

Populism appears when power is no longer able to respond

---

[7] Cf. Ernesto Laclau, *Politics and Ideology in Marxist Theory: Capitalism, Fascism, Populism* (London: Verso, 1977).

to social demands coming from the base. These demands can then establish "relations of equivalence" between themselves that will allow their unification and, consequently, the creations of collective wills allowing the affirmation of a legitimacy opposed to the legality handed down "from above." The central "discursive" moment is that of unification. When the different social demands opposed to the order in place have become part of a whole, a hegemonic aim becomes possible. This is exactly what happened on the eve of the French Revolution, when the Third Estate proclaimed itself (on the basis of the *cahiers de doléances*) the true depository of national legitimacy. The same goes for populism: a partial element aspires to be regarded as the only legitimate totality. "This relation by which a certain particularity assumes representation of a universality that is perfectly incommensurable with it," write Ernesto Laclau and Chantal Mouffe, "is what we call a hegemonic relation."

So it is indeed a matter of "constituting or reconstituting the people" in the face of a minority represented by the dominant elite called oligarchy, New Class, Caste (*la Casta*), *poderes fácticos*, etc. Creating a "people," for Ernesto Laclau, is the very condition for a revitalization of politics. You create a people by the effort to unite into a single hegemonic aim the various social demands expressed within it. Populism presupposes the constitution of a people as a political and socio-historic subject from a plurality of antagonistic situations. So the people is above all an eminently political concept, a *demos* called upon to construct itself as such so as to itself produce political effects. As *demos*, the people can never be reduced to anything already given, such as a mere *ethnos*, any more than it can be reduced to a simple social base or a particular ideological orientation. It is above all a political construction. Now, if populism is a logic constitutive of the people as a historical subject, "politics [becomes] synonymous with populism . . . since the construction of the people is the political act *par excellence*." It is in this sense that "populist reason" is equivalent to political reason, and that its contemptuous rejection is a "rejection of politics altogether."

We mentioned above the influence of Ernesto Lacau on

Podemos.[8] The heirs of the Puerta del Sol occupation in Madrid on May 15, 2011, which demanded "real democracy now" ("*¡democracia real ya!*"), Podemos has uncontestably tried to incarnate a corresponding "populist moment," no longer via the rising of the proletariat against the bourgeoisie or a "horizontal" confrontation between Right and Left, but via a "vertical" revolt of the middle class and the popular class united against the power of "la Caste." In other words: "those below" against "those above." The principal theoretician of the movement, Iñigo Errejón, has himself said that to speak about the "country" and "sovereignty" is another way of helping the people to emancipate themselves. A figure close to him, Juan Carlos Monadero, speaks of "drawing a bright line that shows who is below and who above." The essential trait of this populism is *transversality*.

As Jean-Claude Michéa thinks:

> Podemos is today the only European radical movement with a mass base to have clearly understood that if you want to rally the great majority of the popular classes around a program for the gradual deconstruction of the capitalist system, you absolutely must begin by questioning the old system of rifts based upon "blind confidence in the idea of progress" (Juan Carlos Monadero), whose increasingly paralyzing philosophical presuppositions have for the past 30 years offered the European Left an ideal

---

[8] Cf. the book of interviews with Iñigo Errejón published by Chantal Mouffe: *Construir pueblo. Hegemonía y radicalización de la democracia* [*Constructing the People: Hegemony and the Radicalization of Democracy*] (Barcelona: Icaria, 2015). Cf. also Juan Branco, "Podemos: l'indignation au pouvoir" ["Podemos: Indignation in Power"], *Esprit*, December 2014; Christophe Barret, *Podemos, pour une autre Europe* [*Podemos: For a Different Europe*] (Paris: Cerf, 2015); Héloise Nez, *Podemos. De l'indignation aux élections* [*Podemos: From Indignation to Elections*] (Paris: Les Petits Matins, 2015); Asis Timermans, *¿Podemos?* (Madrid: Ultima Linea, 2015); and Ludovic Lamant, "La boîte à idées des intellos de Podemos" ["The Idea Box of Podemos's Intellectuals"], website *Médiapart*, December 16, 2015.

means of disguising its total reconciliation with capitalism under the much more seductive exterior of a permanent "citizens'" struggle against all "reactionary" and "nostalgic" (or even "red-brown"!) ideas.[9]

It remains to be seen, of course, what will become of Podemos (or Syriza in Greece) in the face of the double danger of collaboration with established parties and, conversely, the adoption of a "strategy of desertion" of the anti-institutional sort, amounting to belief that a "real" democracy can exist without putting new forms of political institutions in place.[10]

As Freud perceived, the social bond is also a libidinal bond. This is why populism is today perceived as a danger for the "normality" of the New Class, whose critique of populism merely recycles the old critique of the "crowds" or the "dangerous classes." The recent emergence of a "populism of the Right" can be explained by the desertion of the field of social division by signifiers of the Left; therefore, signifiers of the Right have captured the protest vote for their own benefit. Gaël Brustier was not mistaken to ask whether in France the "stalemate over Laclau's work is not one of the causes of the radical Left's present standstill."[11]

WORKS OF ERNESTO LACLAU:

Politics and Ideology in Marxist Theory (London: Verso, 1977).

Hegemony and Socialist Strategy (with Chantal Mouffe) (London: Verso, 1985).

New Reflections on the Revolution of our Time (London: Verso, 1990).

---

[9] Jean-Claude Michéa, interview on the website *Le Comptoir*, February 26, 2016.

[10] Cf. Manuel Cervera-Marzal, "Podemos a-t-il dépassé le clivage droite-gauche?" ["Has Podemos Overcome the Left/Right Divide?"], *Libération*, December 17, 2015.

[11] Gaël Brustier, "Gauche radicale: la clé, c'est Laclau" ["Radical Left: Laclau Is the Key"], online text, *Slate*, March 15, 2015, 4.

The Making of Political Identities, ed. (London: Verso, 1994).

Emancipation(s) (London: Verso, 1996).

Contingency, Hegemony, Universality (with Judith Butler and Slavoj Žižek) (London: Verso, 2000).

On Populist Reason (London: Verso, 2005).

The Rhetorical Foundations of Society (London: Verso, 2014).

"CONSERVATIVES OF THE LEFT" & THE CRITIQUE OF VALUE

The ecologist Fabrice Nicolino, a member of *Charlie Hebdo*'s editorial board who was seriously wounded in the Kouachi brothers' attack in January 2015, declared:

> I am nostalgic for a time when people had a place, when men and women were strongly bound together. I am nostalgic for a time when rural civilization was not the garbage it is today, a monstrosity that stuffs people with pesticides. What made it disappear is something absolutely ugly and degrading, a bizarre mass of techniques and technology that has made people's concrete lives impossible. . . . I understand by the word "peasant" something wonderful: that a man has attached himself to a piece of land, and that he respects it.[1]

In January of 2013, Thierry Jaccaud, the Editor-in-Chief of *L'Ecologiste*, denounced "marriage for everybody": "To suppress the concepts of father and mother would be . . . to do violence to the bonds between people and between the generations." Drawing an analogy with genetically modified organisms (GMOs), he thinks this proposed law "would be a stunning denial of nature, the distressing result of our industrial society that destroys nature not only in reality, but also in our minds." The following year, José Bové, a disciple of Jacques Ellul and Bernard Charbonneau, also declared his opposition to all forms of surrogate pregnancy and medically-assisted procreation on the same principle by which he condemns the manipulation of vegetable life in the form of GMOs.

---

[1] "Contre les terroristes industriels" ["Against the Industrial Terrorists"], *Limite*, January 2016, 9. Cf. also his book *Lettre à un paysan sur le vaste merdier qu'est devenue l'agriculture* [*Letter to a Peasant on the Vast Dungheap That Agriculture Has Become*] (Paris: Les Échappés, 2015).

At the beginning of February 2016, a Congress for the Universal Abolition of Surrogate Motherhood was held in Paris. It was presided over by the feminist Silviane Agacinski, the wife of Lionel Jospin, whose hostility to "gender theory" is well-known.

In each of these instances, the positions taken triggered controversies. That figures classed "on the Left" were able to take "conservative" positions in certain areas, especially "cultural" or "social" areas, seemed incomprehensible or scandalous. The explanation most often advanced by the dominant discourse sees in this a consequence of society "shifting to the Right." Jean-Claude Michéa, Michel Onfray, Christophe Guilluy, and many others have been accused of a "reactionary deviation." This lazy interpretation completely misses what is going on, however. If certain thinkers on the Left and the extreme Left today advertise "conservative" positions, particularly in the domain of morality and culture, this is because they have taken their commitments seriously and reflected more deeply, notably through a deeper analysis of capitalism. This "conservatism of the Left," in other words, is not the result of a reactionary turn, but the logical consequence of a rigorous critical analysis of Capital's nature and functioning.

The expression "conservatism of the Left" appeared recently in Canada following a conference organized at the University of Ottawa in 2010 concerning the thought of George Orwell, a conference whose proceedings were published in part four years later.[2] Situating themselves in the tradition of George Orwell and Jean-Claude Michéa, its two principal organizers, Éric Martin and Maxime Ouellet, both professors in Montreal, proposed to grant the idea of *Tory anarchism*[3] "the philosophical place it deserves," and to seek an "articulation of progress that preserves-the transcendental conditions of the possibility of free-

---

[2] Gilles Labelle, Éric Martin, and Stéphane Vibert, eds., *Les Racines de la liberté. Réflexions à partir de l'anarchisme tory* [*The Roots of Liberty: Tory Anarchist Reflections*] (Montréal: Groupe Nota Bene, 2014).

[3] Cf. Jean-Claude Michéa, *Orwell, anarchiste tory* [*Orwell: Tory Anarchist*] (Castelnau-le-Lez: Climats, 1995), where George Orwell's "Tory anarchism" is defined as a kind of sensibility reversing all the founding principles of liberal anthropology.

dom," rejecting both the reactionary spirit and unbridled progressivism.

From a liberal point of view, freedom amounts to the possibility of making rational choices with a view to one's best interest. This is a purely individual liberty that results from the exercise of a right of which man is supposedly the "owner" by his very nature. It follows that it is independent of any particular condition: man is supposed to construct himself freely from nothing. Now, one cannot seriously think of freedom while skipping over its roots — i.e., the concrete social conditions that allow it to be exercised. What are these social and institutional conditions of emancipation? The answer is that freedom, like autonomy, must be conceived in terms of attachment and bonds, not in terms of uprootedness, of responsibility toward others rather than the transgression of everything that attaches members of a society to a common political and socio-historical base. "Genuine freedom can only exist if it takes root in a political community that precedes and constitutes it," say Éric Martin and Maxime Ouellet.[4] This dialectical relation between freedom and what is in common is clearly essential.

Martin and Ouellet embraced this label of "conservatives of the Left"[5] for a time, i.e., critical conservatives. Maxime Ouellet

---

[4] Éric Martin and Maxime Ouellet, "La crise du capitalisme est aussi la crise de l'anticapitalisme" ["The Crisis of Capitalism Is Also the Crisis of Anticapitalism"] in Éric Martin and Maxime Ouellet, eds., *La Tyrannie de la valeur. Débats pour le renouvellement de la théorie critique* [*The Tyranny of Value: Debates For the Renewal of Critical Theory*] (Montreal: Écosociété, 2014), 50.

[5] The expression was used by Éric Martin in "Politique, idéologie et classes sociales: l'angle mort de la gauche" ["Politics, Ideology and Social Classes: The Left's Blind Spot"], *Nouveaux Cahiers du socialisme*, 2009, 1. We find it in Günther Anders: "Today it is no longer enough to transform the world; above all we must preserve it. Then we can transform it, even a great deal and in a revolutionary fashion. But above all we must be conservatives in the authentic sense, a sense that would not be accepted by anyone proclaiming himself conservative" (*Et si je suis désespéré, que voulez-vous que j'y fasse?* [*If I Am Without Hope, What Do You Expect Me To Do?*], trans. Christophe David [Paris: Allia, 2001]).

also spoke of "liberating anti-modernism" in the fashion of Robert Kurz, just as Michel Freitag used to speak of "ontological conservatism" — before abandoning it so as not to be assimilated to "beyond-the-pale reactionaries" — which did not, however, protect either man from criticism.[6] Besides Jean-Claude Michéa and George Orwell, both appealed to Günther Anders as well, who no longer aims at changing the world but at "preserving it as it is" (joining Albert Camus, according to whom today's task was less to remake the word than to keep it from falling apart), as well as to Michel Freitag,[7] Hannah Arendt, Simone Weil, Jacques Ellul, the historian of the workers' movement Edward P. Thompson, and above all critical value theory, as attested by the

---

Philippe Van Parijs more recently declared: "In response to the attempts to dismantle social policies . . . to be on the Left does not mean to be progressive, but conservative" ("La gauche doit-elle être socialiste?" ["Must the Left Be Socialist?"], *Krisis*, June 2009, 100).

[6] Cf. Félix L. Deslauriers, "Libérer du conformisme une tradition en passe d'être violée par lui. Walter Benjamin et les 'conservateurs de gauche'" ["Freeing a Tradition From a Conformism Now Doing It Violence: Walter Benjamin and the 'Conservatives of the Left'"] (in *Critique*, website *Raisons sociales*, December 2, 2015, a text that provoked a response from Éric Martin and Maxime Ouellet, *Critique*, December 4, 2015). Cf. also Jean-Pierre Couture, "Comptoir d'Amérique: les 'nouveaux réactionnaires' et le nationalisme conservateur au Québec" ["American Trading Post: The New Reactionaries and National Conservatism in Quebec"], in Pascal Durand and Sarah Sindaco, eds., *Le Discours « néo-réactionnaire ». Transgressions conservatrices* ["Neoreactionary" Discourse: Conservative Transgressions] (Paris: CNRS Éditions, 2015), 111–24.

[7] The Quebec sociologist and philosopher Michel Freitag (1935–2009), who was also a critic of the liberal idea of an isolated individual, rational and entirely free in his choices, extensively analyzed the practices of impersonal domination called forth by discourse calling for the liberation of the individual and the reification of his rights. Hostile to positivism as well as utilitarianism, he also established himself as an important theoretician of symbolism, social mediation, and "dialectical sociology" (*Dialectique et société*, 2 vols. [Lausanne: L'Âge d'Homme, 1986]).

important 2014 collective work on the "tyranny of value."[8]

Represented mainly by Robert Kurz, who died in 2012,[9] Anselme Jappe,[10] and, to a certain extent, Moishe Postone,[11] critical value theory (*Wertkritik*) proposes a quite original rereading of Marx that breaks with decades of classical or orthodox Marxism by basing itself on the critique of political economy begun in the *1844 Manuscripts* and continued in the *Grundrisse* (1857–1858), then in the first chapter of *Das Kapital* (the reading of which Louis Althusser warned against because it was too Hegelian!).[12]

---

[8] Martin and Ouellet, eds., *La Tyrannie de la valeur*. Let us recall that Carl Schmitt also wrote a book (of very different inspiration) entitled *Die Tyrannei der Werte* [*The Tyranny of Values*, 1960].

[9] Robert Kurz, *Read Marx* (2000); *Vies et mort du capitalism* [*Lives and Death of Capitalism*, a collection of short texts written 2007–2010], trans. Olivier Galtier, Wolfgang Kukulies, and Luc Mercier (Fécamp: Nouvelles éditions Lignes, 2011).

[10] Anselm Jappe, *Les Aventures de la marchandise. Pour une nouvelle critique de la valeur* [*The Adventures of Commodities: For a New Critique of Value*], trans. Joël Gayraud (Paris: Denoël, 2003); *Crédit à mort. La décomposition du capitalisme et ses critiques* [*Credit Unto Death: The Decomposition of Capitalism and its Critiques*] (Fécamp: Nouvelles éditions Lignes, 2011).

[11] Moishe Postone, *Marx est-il devenu muet? Face à la mondialisation*, [*Has Marx Fallen Silent? Facing Globalization*], trans. Olivier Galtier (La Tour d'Aigues: Éditions de L'Aube, 2003); *Temps, travail et domination sociale. Une réinterprétation de la théorie critique* [*Time, Labor, and Social Domination: A Reinterpretation of Critical Theory*], trans. Olivier Galtier (Paris: Mille et une Nuits, 2009).

[12] She also borrows from authors such as Michel Henry (*Marx*, 2 vols. [Paris: Gallimard, 1976]), Maximilien Rubel (*Marx critique du marxisme* [*Marx as a Critic of Marxism*] [Paris: Payot, 2000]), Jean-Marie Vincent (*Un autre Marx* [*A Different Marx*] [Lausanne: Page 2, 2001]), Edward P. Thompson ("Time, Work-Discipline and Industrial Capitalism," *Past & Present*, vol. 38, no. 1, 1967, 56–97), Günther Anders (*Die Antiquiertheit des Menschen* [*The Obsolescence of Man*] [Munich: C. H. Beck, 1956]), Jean Vioulac (*L'Époque de la technique. Marx, Heidegger et l'accomplissement de la métaphysique* [*The Age of Technique: Marx, Heidegger and the Fulfillment of Metaphysics*] [Paris: PUF, 2009]), as well as the writings of precursors such as Isaak Roubine (*Essays on Marx's Theory of Value* [1928] [Montreal: Black Rose Books, 1990]), and Henryk

Éric Martin and Maxime Ouellet remark that, to illuminate the devastating effects the logic of capital has had on the social bond, Marx "bases himself throughout his works on the criticism of modernity formulated by certain romantic authors, without however believing it possible or desirable to return to pre-modern forms of sociality." It is in this sense that he recognizes, as Adorno and Horkheimer would after him, that there necessarily exists a "conservative moment" within every critical theory. "Marx bases himself on pre-modern forms of sociality," add Martin and Ouellet, "not because he is conservative but because he is a dialectician. He knows that the alternative to alienated labor, which separates the producer from the conditions of his existence, runs by way of a critical recovery of the traditional commune."[13] "The Marxian philosophy," further writes Maxime Ouellet, "rests on a critique of abstract universalism constitutive of modern thought and of the negation of concrete individual particularities that follows from it."[14]

Freed of its historicism and positivism, but also of its Ricardian references, Marx's entire *oeuvre* is a philosophy of freedom that tries to analyze the modern forms of alienation that make man a stranger to himself. Aware that man is a "political animal" — i.e., a social being who exists within a community (*Gemeinwesen*), and who needs common institutions in order to live with his peers — Marx searches for the means that would permit him to recover his being, so to speak.

But at this point the critical theory of value makes an essential distinction between what Robert Kurz has called the "exoteric Marx" and the "esoteric Marx." For the "exoteric" Marx, the contradiction between productive forces and the means of produc-

---

Grossman (*The Law of Accumulation and Breakdown of the Capitalist System* [1929] [London: Pluto, 1992]).

[13] Éric Martin and Maxime Ouellet, interview with Emmanuel Casajus, website *Le Comptoir*, June 22, 2016.

[14] Maxime Ouellet, "Les 'anneaux du serpent' du libéralisme culturel: pour en finir avec la 'bonne conscience'. Un détour par 'La question juive' de Karl Marx" ["The 'Ouroboros' of Cultural Liberalism: An End to Good Conscience. By Way of Marx's 'On the Jewish Question'"], website *Palim Psao*.

tion that the bourgeoisie has appropriated represents the principal contradiction of capitalist society (even though it is never a mere conflict *within* the capitalist system). It is this contradiction (the class struggle) — backed by the categories of "base" and "superstructure," but which prevents us from understanding the essence of labor — that has been retained by vulgar Marxism, as well as by Soviet "Marxism-Leninism." The "esoteric" Marx, a philosopher and sociologist, goes well beyond this in the sense that he considers capitalism as a "total social fact" (Marcel Mauss) and seeks to make its essence apparent by a rigorous critique of political economy's foundations — whence his theory of value.

Beginning from the distinction between use value and exchange value, which is already found in Aristotle (in his critique of chrematistics, which demands that production always remain subject to an ideal of the "good life"), Marx shows that it is because of the process of the abstraction of labor that commodities can have a value. Labor is not so much a standard of measure, as Ricardo believed (along with all the theoreticians of "labor-value" who followed him), as what establishes value and constitutes (*qua* abstract labor) the field of homogenization of the products of human labor transformed into commodities. Abstract labor (by contrast with concrete or "living" labor, a simple social activity of transforming nature to satisfy one's needs) is this abstraction of human activity that allows the products of human labor to be made commensurable and exchanged; it constitutes the form of social mediation specific to capitalism. Value, which is not to be confused with wealth, is the quantity of abstract labor as the unique source of the valorization of capital. This means that, as a social relation, capitalism rests on the absorption of concrete labor by abstract labor, of use value by exchange value. The law of value is precisely that universal norm regulating social practices that rests upon abstraction from the specific particularities proper to each individual's vital activity, i.e., the devaluing of the human world.

In the sense attributed to them today, work and value, commodity and market, and even the economy are not eternal categories but relatively recent historical inventions. Capitalism consists in an unlimitedness where the only goal of the surplus accumulation of capital is to allow the reproduction of the system (according to the famous formula A-M-A'). Capitalism produces for the sake of production, the origin and end of production always being money. Whereas life always comes prior to conceptual rationalization,[15] capitalism rests on a form of abstract and impersonal domination—a "tyranny without a tyrant," as Hannah Arendt said—constituted by the fetishized mediation of value that participates in the social order's material reproduction by reifying the lives of individuals. Value, says Marx, is transformed into an "automated subject."

Martin and Ouellet write:

> Domination is not reducible to the power exercised by one class over another but is tied to the organization of modern society around labor insofar as it is the central form of social mediation. . . . Capitalism then appears as a social power become alien, a heteronomy that renders every man a stranger to himself, alienated under the empire of an abstract master: only capital is free, and all are subsumed by the power of value.[16]

The critique of value is thus a critique of social mediations alienated by commodity fetishism, which is not a product of fantasy or "false consciousness" but a social relation expressed in the form of a relation between things, in which things appear to have intrinsic qualities that are actually the product of a social relation. In that sense it is inseparable from the reification of social relations. The "esoteric" Marx does not put the emphasis on class struggle but carries out a critique of labor as source of value, as the fuel necessary for the reproduction of capital. Contrary to what vulgar Marxism has persisted in believing, it is not class domination but the fetishist relation to value that is at the heart

---

[15] "Individuals are dominated by abstractions," observes Karl Marx in the *Grundrisse*, "whereas formerly they depended on one another" (*Manuscrits de 1857–1858*, translation by Jean-Pierre Lefebvre, vol. 1 [Paris: Éditions Sociales, 1980], 101).

[16] Martin and Ouellet, "La crise du capitalisme est aussi la crise de l'anticapitalisme," 25–26.

of the capitalist system.

This approach allows us to understand how capitalism, considered in its essence, has nothing conservative about it.[17] It never did except at its puritan beginnings, when it had to distinguish itself from the ostentatious forms of dissipation characteristic of feudal lords—and that was merely a way of stigmatizing disinterestedness and gratuitousness. Arnaud Imatz remarks:

> Many authors on the Left, and also on the Right, have difficulty admitting that capitalism presupposes perpetual upheaval of the conditions of human existence. By identifying traditional values with the capitalist system, whereas the former are precisely that system's most implacable enemy, these authors . . . systematically led their troops— workers and employers—to struggle not against their real adversaries, the dominant oligarchy, but against their enemies' enemies.[18]

Everyone is familiar with Marx's famous words about the "icy waters of egoistical calculation" into which the rise of the bourgeois class has plunged society. Capitalism cannot be conservative simply because the reign of the market, characterized by economic exchange acquiring autonomy with respect to the other aspects of social life, implies the dismantling of everything that might possibly present an obstacle to its mad course. Capitalism must liquidate the old social and cultural structures upon which pre-capitalist societies rest, and which might hinder the expansion of markets. It must eradicate the common values deposited over the course of centuries to the benefit of a single abstract norm: regulating social life by economic value. It needs money, land, and labor to be transformed entirely into commodities, into resources to which it is possible to apply the law of

---

[17] "To say Margaret Thatcher was conservative when she destroyed England is absurd," observes Olivier Ray very correctly (debate with Natasha Polony in *Limite*, January 2016, 21).

[18] Arnaud Imatz, "Le clivage droite/gauche en question" ["Questioning the Left/Right Divide"], *La Nouvelle Revue d'histoire*, July–August 2016, 15.

supply and demand — which happens when money has accumulated sufficiently to turn into capital. And for this, it needs men to be transformed into "free subjects" in the Cartesian sense of the term, i.e., liberated as much as possible from social relations.

The generalization of salaried employment itself implies the commensurability of the products of labor, which can only appear when individuals have been "liberated" from any form of traditional relations. Karl Marx writes:

> For money to be transformed into capital, the possessor of money must find the worker free on the market of commodities — free in the double sense that, on the one hand, he disposes as a free person of his labor-power as of a commodity belonging to him, and on the other, that he . . . is completely disencumbered, free in respect of all the things necessary for his labor-power to be realized.[19]

Capital requires bosses and workers to be equally "free" to negotiate the conditions and price of labor, proletarians "who only live if they find work, and only find it if their work increases capital."[20] This is why it drives uprootedness.

Some liberals recognize this themselves. The main thing that characterizes liberalism "is the recognition of property rights and individual liberty. True liberalism . . . therefore rejects any total vision . . . of the life of men in society," writes Pascal Salin, who also rejects any idea of a general or national interest separate from that of isolated individuals. "It is for this reason," he adds coolly, "that globalization, if it effectively contributes to the destruction of nation-states, will be a benefit to humanity."[21]

Éric Martin and Maxime Ouellet observe:

> Value can only be set up as a regulatory norm for the whole of social practice in a society founded on an image of abstract equality. The new capitalist community insti-

---

[19] Karl Marx, *Capital*, vol. 1, 1867.
[20] Marx and Engels, *Manifesto of the Communist Party*, 1848.
[21] Pascal Salin, *Libéralisme* (Paris: Odile Jacob, 2000), 10–12, 490.

tutes as its counterpart a form of subjectivity, that of the cosmopolitan "possessor of commodities" unattached to any concrete community apart from that of money.[22]

This is also what Marx says in the *Grundrisse*: "Money being itself the community, it cannot tolerate any others in its presence. When money is not itself the community, it must dissolve community."[23] Value only imposes itself when ancient symbolic mediations constitutive of traditional society have been destroyed.

Thus, the world of Form-Capital can only be a world of fluid, unaffiliated individuals torn from nature, made potentially nomadic, and moved only by the search for their individual best interest. A world made of monads with no territory, no attachments, no identity or permanent place of residence, transformed into labor-power (objects). A world in which fluidity, flexibility, and precariousness become general norms, where everything must be available as merchandise to be consumed as a function of each person's desires (these being posited as equally legitimate); in short, a world where money imposes itself both as "exchange value become autonomous" (Marx) and as a universal equivalent that renders all things commensurable by converting every quality into a quantity, as a general value and a phenomenal form of commodity fetishism.

It is obvious that under these conditions, any non-hostile glance at the past can only amount to irrational "nostalgia" or "reaction." It is in this respect that the ideology of progress contributes to the rationalization of the world by Form-Capital. It is based in fact on a principled disparagement of the past, seen as a mere mixture of constraints and archaic superstitions. As Alain Finkielkraut writes, "The age of diversity celebrated the republican values of equality, liberty, and fraternity the better to reject what came before it, even that which was republican, as obsolete, and to cast the obsolete back into the darkness of evil."[24]

---

[22] Martin and Ouellet, "La crise du capitalisme est aussi la crise de l'anticapitalisme," 31, 43.

[23] Karl Marx, *Grundrisse 1*, chapter on Money, 1858.

[24] Alain Finkielkraut, *Causeur*, February 2016, 75.

Anyone who looks back is excommunicated. Faced with those who want to "establish a sanctuary for progress" (Jacques Attali's formulation), one becomes "conservative" as soon as one leaves the camp of "progress." Such was the case with Walter Benjamin who, adhering to a Communism that had "annihilated in itself the idea of progress,"[25] saw in the revolution to come not the natural end result of humanity's forward progress, but rather a halt called to a catastrophic development, i.e., a conservative act (in the sense of the Schmittian *katechon*) putting a stop to a mad rush.

At best, the philosophy of the Enlightenment regards social bonds merely as a means for the individual to attain his particular aims. Its strength comes from its having appeared as a vehicle of emancipation (something that some thinkers, such as Georges Sorel, contested from the beginning, having understood that this ideology's only goal was to legitimate the rise of the bourgeois class). But what it emancipated the workers from, along with accentuating the disenchantment of the world inaugurated by Christian desacralization, was living environments, landmarks, and the social bonds that protected them — in order to submit them to new forms of alienation and transform them into interchangeable individuals subject to all the conditioning of merchandise.

Historically, this process has gone hand-in-hand with the homogenization of time (reduced to an abstract, measurable quantity) and space (transformed into a market). For the ideology of progress, time is no longer qualitative and qualified, but a measurable and calculable time without quality, since it is reduced to a space or a quantity ("time is money"), a time that is only an addition of abstract units allowing continual progress within a perpetual present. Individuals thus find themselves expropriated of historical time in order to be confined to the moment.[26]

---

[25] Walter Benjamin, "Paris, Capital of the Nineteenth Century" [1935], in *Reflections: Essays, Aphorisms, Autobiographical Writings*, ed. Peter Demetz, trans. Edmund Jephcott (New York: Harcourt Brace Jovanovich, 1983).

[26] Cf. Franck Fischbach, "Ce que la valeur fait au temps et a

The Revolution of 1789 was itself above all a liberal and bourgeois revolution—even "ultra-liberal," as the very liberal Gaspard Koenig affirms, not failing to celebrate this. He writes: "The French Revolution was at its origin 'ultra-liberal,' aiming to establish the rule of law and the market as tools of individual emancipation."[27] Hence the Allarde Law (March 1791), which suppressed guilds and forbade strikes and trade unions, followed by the Chapelier Law (June 1791), which outlawed workers' fraternal organizations, as well as any gatherings of workers or peasants. "Everyone today senses the need to establish social unity on the destruction of orders and of all large corporations," wrote the Abbé Sieyès in *What Is the Third Estate?* Gaspard Koening comments:

> The terms are laid down. It is in the name of free competition that the fight against the *Ancien Régime* will be led. . . . By creating undifferentiated citizens, . . . [the new freedom] makes general competition possible, where orders created frontiers and particularities. . . . Particular interest is essential, for it constitutes the motor of the market and of progress. . . . It is by separating individuals from one another that the rule of law can be born.[28]

At the end of the nineteenth century, at a time when France was still largely rural and workers balked at the working methods of industry, workers' socialism was often quite reserved toward the ideology of progress. Thibault Isabel emphasizes:

> Far from unilaterally defining themselves as progressives

---

l'histoire" ["What Value Does to Time and History"], in Martin and Ouellet, eds., *La Tyrannie de la valeur*, 145–58. By the same author: *La Privation de monde. Temps, espace et capital* [*The Privation of the World: Time, Space and Capital*] (Paris: J. Vrin, 2011). Cf. also Henri Lefebvre, *La Production de l'espace* [*The Production of Space*] (Paris: Anthropos, 2000).

[27] Gaspard Koenig, "14 juillet: une révolution française 'ultralibérale'" ["July 14: An "Ultraliberal" French Revolution"], website *Contrepoints*, July 14, 2016.

[28] Koenig, "14 juillet."

struggling against obscurantism, the [first] socialists saw themselves as forces of resistance to the modernization of society. . . . The enemy, for the early militants, was the rapid and brutal transformation of society that cast the little people into the street and changed the living conditions of the common people for the benefit of the wealthy.[29] . . .

In the age of Proudhon, socialists laid into technocracy and the cult of experts, the rise of finance, the disappearance of the world of peasants and shopkeepers for the benefit of industry, downward pressure on salaries; they set store by land, militant heroism, sacrifice in the service of the group, and often religion as well.[30]

As Jean-Claude Michéa has often recalled in his books, they contested — rightly — the hierarchies of the *Ancient Régime*, but were in no way disposed to abandon the solidarity, forms of mutual aid, and social bonds that allowed people to face up to those hierarchies within traditional societies.

Many of them were also patriots, for their internationalism was not the same thing as cosmopolitanism. As Alain Peyrefitte has written (following many others), "It is the proletarians who feel the most intransigent nationalism, and the bourgeois who are the most tempted by cosmopolitanism."[31] The Commune's patriotism hardly needs to be recalled, since it was born of the refusal of the people of Paris to see the capital handed over to the Prussians. At that time, many socialists considered themselves the only real patriots (Eugène Fournière, a disciple of Jules Guesde and then of Benoît Malon, denounced the nationalists of the Right as "fake patriots"). "The poor defend the country, the rich sell it" (Péguy). Marx himself said that the class struggle is

---

[29] Thibault Isabel, "Socialisme?," *Krisis*, no. 42, December 2015, 5 & 9.

[30] Thibault Isabel, "Le socialisme comme alternative à la gauche libérale" ["Socialism as Alternative to the Liberal Left"], in *Rébellion*, no. 73, December 2015–January 2016, 29.

[31] Alain Peyrefitte, *De la Chine* [*On China*] (Paris: Omnibus, 1996), 294.

international in its content, but national in its form. "The opposition between nation and internationalism," writes Denis Collin, "is perfectly absurd, at least for anyone who has gone through Marx's school."[32]

The socialist movement has unfortunately too often clung to the mere class struggle, incorrectly believing it would permit a departure from capitalism. But the theory of class struggle (the "exoteric Marx") limits itself to criticizing the unequal distribution of wealth without questioning its substance or taking any interest in the intrinsic nature of the economy and labor. Disputing what is the most just way of distributing surplus value is one way among others of legitimating the principle of surplus value. Substituting the state for the market as the place where value is distributed in no way changes the deeper nature of capitalism, which explains why Soviet "Marxism-Leninism" merely ended up instituting a state capitalism (or, as Jean-Claude Michéa says, a "state imitation of capitalism"). Besides, experience shows that the proletariat has no intrinsic tendency to its own abolition, and so is not revolutionary *per se*. If the dominated classes become dominant classes, the means of production merely change hands, without themselves being changed. The struggle of the working class, most often based on purely quantitative demands, has not opened up any post-capitalist horizons, but merely transformed the proletariat into a petty bourgeois subject.

---

[32] Denis Collin, "Marx, le communisme et la République" ["Marx, Communism, and the Republic"], *Krisis*, no. 42, December 2015, 55. For his part, Costanzo Preve observes that "where revolutions inspired by Marx have triumphed, even temporarily, the national question — and more precisely the question of liberation, independence, and national sovereignty — has been absolutely decisive" ("Communautarisme et communisme. Une réflexion historique et philosophique sur deux termes" ["Communitarianism and Communism: An Historical and Philosophical Reflection on Two Terms"], *Krisis*, June 2009, 30). Cf. also K. Steven Vincent, "Nationalisme et patriotisme dans la pensée socialiste française du XIXe siècle" ["Nationalism and Patriotism in the French Socialist Thought of the Nineteenth Century"], *Krisis*, June 2009, 42–50.

Beginning in 1918, the social democratic forms of the Left have progressively mutated into partners of capitalism, limiting themselves to demanding salary increases or better working conditions, which opens the door to *de facto* collaboration in the perfecting of social compromises. The rise of Fordism accentuated this reformist orientation in which one no longer sought to overturn the system in place, but to obtain a better position within it; the consequence was the creation of a vast middle class living in ever closer symbiosis with the demands of Capital as long as Capital favors consumption and agrees to rising purchasing power.

The various forms of Communism, for their part, took the capitalism they claimed to combat for their model without even realizing it, attempting to outdo it in productivity. In the Soviet Union this resulted in the institution of an economic system that was, as we have said, merely a state capitalism. The goal was no longer to arrange capitalism in a fashion more favorable (quantitatively) to the workers, as in social democracy or reformist socialism, but to create another capitalism piloted by the state and supposed to be more productive than the original. "Socialism in all its various forms, social-democratic as well as Communist," writes Denis Collin, "functioned as a mechanism for integrating the working class into capitalism."[33] Jacques Julliard also speaks of "the internalization of capitalist logic by the workers." The idea thus became established that capitalism, imperfect or open to criticism as it may be, is in the last analysis the only possible system, and that it is impossible to escape it. Hence what Costanzo Preve has called a "collective social impotence without historical precedent."[34]

The 1970s saw a new turn marked by the oil crisis and the end of the "Thirty Glorious Years," the decoupling of the dollar from gold, the beginning of the third industrial revolution (that

---

[33] Collin, "Marx, le communisme et la République," 49. Cf. also, by the same author, *Le Cauchemar de Marx* [*Marx's Nightmare*] (Paris: Max Milo, 2009).

[34] Costanzo Preve, "Un socialisme pour le XXIe siecle" ["A Socialism for the Twenty-First Century], *Krisis*, no. 42, December 2015, 24–25.

of computing), the rise of a financial capitalism based on speculation, public over-indebtedness, and private credit ("fictional
capital"), and, in Europe, the beginnings of immigration as
demographic replacement.

Michel Clouscard in France and Pier Paolo Pasolini in Italy
were among the few to understand early on not only that it was
simply logical for many of the "'68ers" to come to understand
that the capitalist system offered them the best chance of "enjoyment without hindrance," but also that Form-Capital knew
very well how to make use of May 1968 to liquidate whatever
still existed of old organic and traditional societies. Where many
saw nothing more than students having it out with riot police, it
would have been more accurate to see the sons of the bourgeoisie going up against the sons of the proletariat!

During the 1980s, the Left, already in disarray following the
collapse of the twentieth century's ideological "grand narratives," began to break away from the people, as we have already
described. Overtly rallying to the market model, it abandoned
all idea of collective liberation and transformation of society by
any means other than the attribution of individual rights. They
might still criticize economic liberalism, but only to demand a
"social" liberalism resting on the same anthropological foundations.

Thus we arrive at the current situation, where Form-Capital
has succeeded in completely "liberalizing" the culture, along
with family and sexual mores, to the great pleasure of a Left that
has replaced the desire for revolution with the revolution of desire — beginning with the desire for money.[35] "The new Left has
continued to promote the transgression of mores originating in
the disciplinary society, and has thus contributed to the legitimation of neoliberal capitalism," observes Maxime Ouellet.[36] In
fact, the Left has rejoined liberalism insofar as it now adheres to

---

[35] A desire falsely presented as entirely natural, whereas "man does
not desire 'by nature' ever more money, but quite simply to live according to his habits and earn as much money as is necessary for that"
(Max Weber, *The Protestant Ethic and the Spirit of Capitalism*).

[36] Ouellet, "Les 'anneaux du serpent' du libéralisme culturel."

a conception of liberty that amounts to individual desire, the language of rights, and the dissolution of social bonds. It only sets value upon abstract and uprooted freedom in tandem with individualism and "borderlessness," which implies the suppression of everything that might limit it by making it depend upon a precise socio-historical context, all of which correspond perfectly with the capitalist system's logic.

By making the fluidity of identities (especially those not recognized in the Fordist compromise, whether women, ethnic minorities, or "alternative" lifestyles) the precondition for emancipation; by replacing social struggles with identitarian struggles for recognition; by preaching uprootedness, the deconstruction of traditional customs and ways of life; and by defending a model of the "open society" that legitimates the advent of a unified world of rights-bearing individuals soluble in the market, the modern and postmodern Left has gone to meet Form-Capital insofar as "the values associated with the ideology of the network—fluidity, flexibility, the absence of durable relations—are precisely those recommended in today's configuration of capitalism."[37]

The "conservatives of the Left" are thus well-justified in maintaining that the Left's anti-traditionalism prevents the formulation of a serious critique of capitalism's destructive dynamic insofar as that dynamic above all destroys the traditional structures of life. By preaching the transgression of all limits, the endless demand for private rights, and the "struggle against all forms of discrimination," social and cultural progressivism, as promoted especially by feminist and anti-racist lobbies, and beyond them by the spirit of the age, is playing into the hands of globalized capitalism.

This was already observed by Christopher Lasch in the United States when he wrote that the Left "long ago lost any vivid interest in underdogs" and that it is "unable to explain the persistence of religion, pro-family attitudes, and an ethic of personal accountability except as an expression of 'false consciousness'":

---

[37] Martin and Maxime Ouellet, "La crise du capitalisme est aussi la crise de l'anticapitalisme," 35.

By defining the individual as a rational calculator of his own advantage, liberal ideology made it impossible to conceive any form of association not based on the calculation of mutual advantage; that is, on a contract. . . . Orwellian sloganeering about "alternative lifestyles" and the "new diversity of family types" serves to disguise marital breakup as an exhilarating new form of freedom, just as some sloganeering about "women's liberation" disguises the economic necessity that forces women into the labor market. . . . People still cherish the stability of long-term marital and intergenerational commitments . . . but find little support for them in a capitalist economy or in the prevailing ideology of individual rights.[38]

The Left thus finds itself at an impasse. Having renounced its inspiration and its original project, and fantasizing now about an aggregation of "emancipated singularities" within a purely abstract universalism, it has obfuscated the question of social justice in favor of struggles for "recognition," "diversity," and "multiple identities," as if fundamental inequalities did not result first of all from liberalism and capitalism, and as if the "struggle against all forms of discrimination" could serve as a substitute for anti-capitalism.[39] No longer having either the will or the intellectual means of analyzing the essence of social relations, it has hitched its wagon to the powers of the market.

As for the Left that opposes these "cultural" deviations and this postmodern nominalism, it remains too often at the level of a vulgar Marxism, in fact a sort of "alternate capitalism" that privileges the class struggle or the Keynesian model while totally denying the question of identity[40] — a procedure not very dif-

---

[38] Christopher Lasch, "Why the Left Has No Future," *Tikkun*, vol. 1, no. 2, 1986, 92–97.

[39] Cf. Walter Benn Michaels, *The Trouble with Diversity* (New York: Metropolitan, 2006). Cf. also Razmig Keucheyan, *Hémisphere gauche. Une cartographie des nouvelles pensées critiques* [*Left Hemisphere: A Cartography of the New Critical Forms of Thought*] (Montreal: Lux, 2010).

[40] Cf. e.g., Roger Martelli, *L'identité, c'est la guerre* [*Identity Is War*] (Paris: Les Liens qui libèrent, 2016).

ferent in the end from appealing to a (re)territorialized "good capitalism" ("tricolor capitalism"), or to the "real economy" against the "casino economy."

Opposing the logic of unlimitedness inherent in Capital (constant profit is only possible in a regime of accumulation that never slows down) implies restoring a sense of *limits*—which joins up with ecological aspirations and the theory of degrowth. This also implies rejection of the currently dominant model of globalization. "Internationalism has today been converted into cosmopolitan individualism," remark Éric Martin and Maxime Ouellet, "while socialism means the possibility for everyone to belong to a political community of meaning beyond the universal and uprooted abstraction of commercial value."[41] Opposition to globalization derives its legitimacy from this. By favoring the expansion of the commercial form to cover all social relations from one end of the planet to the other, and by instituting Capital as the only historical subject and exchange-value as the universal norm to regulate social practices, globalization *ipso facto* generalizes the destruction of socio-historical, cultural, institutional, and symbolic forms of common existence.[42] As soon as globalization identifies itself with an abstract universal that denies humanity, humanity must negate that negation to affirm itself as freedom.

In this context, the "conservative" rehabilitation of popular pre-capitalist values and traditions is perfectly legitimate, provided it occurs without idealization or nostalgia. It is not a matter of preaching a *return* to the past, which would be impossible (moreover, no one would agree to living in the conditions peasants lived in under the *Ancien Régime*); it is rather a matter of *appealing* to the past, which involves taking a critical, selective—or more precisely, dialectical—view of this past, identifying that in it which is always "actual" (*wirklich*), as Hegel would say, in

---

[41] Martin amd Ouellet, interview with Emmanuel Casajus.

[42] Cf. Michel Freitag, *L'Impasse de la globalisation. Une histoire sociologique et philosophique du capitalisme* [*The Impass of Globalization: A Sociological and Philosophical History of Capitalism*] (Montreal: Écosociété, 2008), interviews with Patrick Ernst.

order to put traditional virtues in step with an emancipatory project. Karel Kosik was not wrong to speak of a "dialectic of the concrete."[43]

As Anne Frémaux writes:

Modernism takes a wrong turn as soon as it plans to make all reference to the past disappear as a sign of a conservatism and immobilism dismissed in advance as "antimodern." There could be no progressive project (turned toward the future) without conservation: conservation of ecological processes in the face of policies of destruction and private appropriation, conservation of existing goods in the face of their systematic destruction by an established system of squandering, conservation of a humanist conception of culture and education in the face of attacks by neoliberalism, conservation of solidary activities and social bonds in the face of the capitalist decomposition of human relations. . . . The spirit of "tradition" in question here does not mean the return to a way of life hierarchized according to natural categories that are very difficult to defend. It is rather a matter of a rehabilitation of the practices that in the past simply honored common sense before the colonization of our actions by the spirit of abstraction, bureaucracy, productivism, and the spirit of competition. . . . This is why we can maintain that conservatism is the only coherent radical position of our age, or even that conservation is today a resolutely revolutionary act.[44]

George Orwell thought that society must not be built from

---

[43] Karel Kosik, *La Dialectique du concret* [*The Dialectic of the Concrete*] (Paris: Éditions de la Passion, 1988).

[44] Anne Frémaux, "La décroissance et l'idée de progrès: entre progressisme et conservatisme critiques," website *Journal du MAUSS*, November 3, 2014. By the same author: *La nécessité d'une écologie radicale* [*The Need for a Radical Ecology*] (Paris: Sang de la Terre, 2011). Cf. also Jean-Paul Besset, *Comment ne plus etre progressiste sans devenir réactionnaire* [*How to Stop Being a Progressive Without Becoming a Reactionary*] (Paris: Fayard, 2005).

the top, but on a democratic base, beginning from a certain common anthropological ground, a certain common sense, and a common sensibility cemented by the common decency of the popular classes. Communism, in the best sense of the term, itself supposes that the common good is posited as the most valuable good, and that society think of itself as a self-governing community. To struggle against the grasp of capital demands something common, collective—local solidarities, organic bonds, and sovereignties reconquered in the face of the world of economic reproduction. The role of politics itself is to *produce the common*. But "for there to be something in common, there must be cultural proximity, and not merely proximity institutionally or in principle" (Laurent Bouvet). The common does not exclude disagreement (without which there would be no political life), but it appeals to shared values. One cannot both promote a life in common and encourage that which weakens it by spreading distrust, reciprocal hostility, or the uncoupling of social bonds. The bond is that which attaches, but also that which connects. There are connections that hinder and imprison, but there are also those that liberate. We must rediscover the "bonds that liberate."

As Éric Martin and Maxime Ouellet say:

> The challenge of this age is to reconcile the search for emancipation with the maintenance of conditions for the existence of nature, as well as for a decent life and society. It is remarkable that to seek to consider both the dimensions of progress and the preservation of a common world is considered reactionary. . . . Individualism has made so much progress that the word "common," contrary to Marx's age, no longer inspires hopes of freedom, but rather distrust, because it would necessarily threaten the pluralism of the monadic "systems of values" that all of us have become.[45]

Confronting the rationalization of the world by value, and the planetary deployment of Form-Capital, forms of discourse that

---

[45] Martin and Ouellet, interview with Emmanuel Casajus.

limit themselves to demanding a more egalitarian distribution of wealth are just as ineffective as the theories of John Rawls (whose theory of justice is merely a social-democratic reformulation of the neoliberal theory of social choices), Hardt and Negri (recourse to the "multitudes" with no institutional mediation), Gilles Deleuze (the emancipation of "productive singularities"), or Michel Foucault.

Liberating oneself from capitalism does not mean replacing the bourgeoisie with the proletariat in a simple class struggle, allowing the latter to appropriate the means of production, or limiting oneself to denouncing "obscene wealth" or the practices of commercial bankers or wicked "speculators," if not "anonymous and vagabond fortune" symbolized by a scapegoat ("the Rothschilds"). It means liberation from the practices constitutive of the fetishistic forms of subjectivity induced by the mediation of money. It does not mean liberating labor, but liberating oneself from labor as a form of organized social relation. It does not mean seeking "growth for everybody," but breaking once and for all with the ideology of growth. "Emancipating society from capitalism means leaving the ontology of labor and value that drives individuals to a war of all against all and subjects them to the depersonalized domination of self-interested calculation."[46] The "conservatives of the Left" can help with this task.

---

[46] Ouellet, "Les 'anneaux du serpent' du libéralisme culturel."

The Ambiguity of "Communitarianism"

Communities, whether ancient or recent, and whether of a historical, ethnocultural, linguistic, religious, sexual, or other nature, are natural dimensions of belonging. They accompany and underlie chosen forms of identity. No individual can exist without belonging, if only to distance himself from it. The self is always situated, in other words, incorporated into a story—which can never be reduced to a *status quo*, still less to a past.

Community is a social form prior to society, just as it is prior to man considered in isolation. It is present before the birth of the state, before any institution. It unites neighbors and similars within families collected into tribes before being collected into cities. Language itself is a communal fact—which implies a community of speakers able to understand one another. In the same way, the *we*, the "our-ness," proceeds any *I*. Community is prior to putting things in common and to common experience. Francis Cousin writes:

> Man is a community-being not by virtue of exterior and posterior contingencies, but by virtue of an intimate and prerequisite dialectic of historical necessity. The human is *genetically* the being of my conscious community. In other words, as soon as man emerges, the community of the "us" and the reality of the "I" appear indissolubly unified in a single synthetic totality.[1]

From political philosophy's point of view, the concept of community goes back at least to Aristotle: man, whom he

---

[1] Francis Cousin, *L'etre contre l'avoir. Pour une critique radicale du faux omniprésent . . .* [*Being Against Having: Toward a Radical Critique of Omnipresent Falsity*] (Aube: Le Retour aux sources, 2012), 82. On "community of habitus" or dispositions, cf. also Olivier Ducharme, *Michel Henry et le problème de la communauté* [*Michel Henry and the Problem of Community*] (Paris: L'Harmattan, 2013).

describes as a "political animal," could just as well be described as a "communal animal." Traditionally, the adversaries of liberal individualism have always adhered to a conception of social reality tending in the direction of *community* rather than that of *society*. The community/society dichotomy has been studied by numerous authors, starting with Ferdinand Tönnies, who in his famous work of 1887 presents community and society as "two fundamental categories of pure sociology" and interprets human history as a gradual replacement of the communal model by the societal model.[2] Heralding the work of Louis Dumont on holism and individualism, Tönnies demonstrates that the *individual* is not an immediate datum found in every form of social organization, but a concept tied to a particular social form, that of *Gesellschaft* (society), opposed in all points to *Gemeinschaft* (community).

Community defines an organic form of sociality; society defines a mechanical type of relation based upon the individual's preponderance. *Gemeinschaft* constitutes a whole whose scope exceeds that of its parts. Solidarity and mutual aid develop there from the concept of the common good, which is not a good equally distributed among all, but a good the enjoyment of which is situated upstream from any division. In the *Gesellschaft* model, on the contrary, the idea of which is already contained in germ in the theory of the social contract, men live together without really being in solidarity and united. Society is there defined as a mere sum of individuals. It was this conception to which the Abbé Sieyès appealed at the time of the French Revolution when he declared:

> One will never understand the social mechanism if one does not make up one's mind to analyze society as an ordinary machine, considering each of its parts separately, and then joining them mentally, one after the other, in order to grasp the chord and hear the overall harmony

---

[2] Ferdinand Tönnies, *Communauté et société* [*Community and Society; Gemeinschaft und Gesellschaft*], trans. S. Mesure and N. Bond (Paris: PUF, 2010).

which must result from it.[3]

Rather than resulting from the consensual effect of an "organic will" (*Wesenwille*), the modern age's social bond proceeds from the "rational will" (*Kürwille*): the members of society decide to live together not because they share the same values, but because they find it in their mutual interest. Concretely, "social" relations go back to a legal contract or commercial exchange.

Tönnies writes of society:

Here, each person is for himself and in a state of hostility towards others. The various fields of activity and power are strongly determined in relation to one another so that each forbids all contact and mixture to the others. . . . No one will do anything for others unless it is in exchange for a similar service or a consideration he considers equal to what he has given. . . . Only the possibility of profit can lead him to give up a good he possesses. . . . Whereas in community men remain bound to one another in spite of all separation, in society they are separated in spite of all which binds them.

He adds: "The big city and society in general represent the corruption and death of the people."

Tönnies' theses have been criticized for their "romanticism," but it must be understood that the concepts he opposes point by point are ideal types in Max Weber's sense. There is no "pure community" nor any "pure society." All collectivities possess communal and "societal" traits, but in different proportions. What must be remembered about the concept of community is that its character is more organic than society, such organicism not being understood in a strictly biological sense but in a metaphorical one: within a body, the organs are not identical, but they are both different and complementary.[4]

---

[3] Emmanuel-Joseph Sieyès, *Qu'est-ce que le Tiers État?* [*What Is the Third Estate?*] (Paris: Société de l'histoire de la Révolution française, 1888), 65.

[4] "The organic has an institutive sense insofar as it rests on a struc-

As an organic phenomenon, community involves the application of a principle of finality at all levels — the common good — which cannot be reduced to efficient causality, and also the principle of subsidiarity as defined in the sixteenth century by Johannes Althusius. Contrary to state sovereignty as understood by Jean Bodin (*La République*, 1576), who calls for the dissociation of political society from civil society, as well as for the elimination of intermediate bodies, Althusius defines the *Res Publica* as a stacking of "simple and private communities" (families, colleges, and corporations) and "mixed and public communities" (cities and provinces) crowned by a "superior political community," with each level being left as free as possible to decide matters of concern to it. Described as "symbiotic," politics is then nothing more than the art of getting men to live in community, with sovereignty (*majestas*) being distributed to all levels of the social body.[5]

This is why the communitarian model is so compatible with integral federalism, which allows considerable space for intermediary bodies and the principle of subsidiarity. The concept of "intermediate body" does not merely refer to the corporations of the *Ancien Régime*, of course, whose suppression by the Revolution left individuals alone to face the state even as it justified the prohibition of workers' coalitions and unions. As Pierre

---

turing vision of the social body. In that case, it serves to characterize a society whose members are bound to one another in a living fashion, as are the organs in the human body, in order to cooperate with a view to the common good, that of the entire body," writes Marie-Pauline Deswarte in a work whose only fault is to excessively idealize the *Ancien Régime* (*La République organique en France. Un patrimoine constitutionnel à restaurer* [*The Organic Republic in France: A Constitutional Patrimony In Need of Restoration*] [Versailles: Via Romana, 2014], 15–16). Cf. also, by the same author, "Retrouver la dynamique organique de la France" ["Rediscovering the Organic Dynamic of France"], *Valeurs actuelles*, January 8, 2015, 79.

[5] Cf. Alain de Benoist, "Johannes Althusius, 1557–1638," *Krisis*, no. 22, March 1999, 2–34. Cf. also Jean-Sylvestre Mongrenier, "Johannes Althusius et l'Europe subsidiaire" ["Johannes Althusius and the Europe of Subsidiarity"], website *Fenêtre sur l'Europe*, June 2, 2009.

Dardot and Christian Laval write: "No federation is possible between communes, people, or productive activities except on the
basis of cooperation. In other words, the federative principle
rightly understood implies a negation of the bases of capitalism."[6]

Federalism itself derives from the model of empire, which
was historically the great form of political organization in competition with the nation state. The characteristic of empire,
whose oldest theoreticians were Marsilius of Padua, Dante, and
Nicolas of Cusa, is to aim above all at the articulation of differences. Sovereignty is divided; ethnic, cultural, religious, and customary particularities are legally recognized insofar as they do
not contradict the common law; the application of the principle
of subsidiarity is the rule. Since nationality is not synonymous
with citizenship, the political people (*demos*) is not the same as
the ethnic people (*ethnos*), but neither is an obstacle to the other.
We notice today that "republicans" reduce nationality to citizenship, while those who hold to an ethnic conception of the nation
reduce citizenship to nationality—both sides agreeing in wanting to fuse the two concepts.

Historically, Enlightenment philosophy began by attacking
organic communities, whose ways of life were denounced as
marked by irrational "superstitions" and "prejudices," in order
to substitute for them a society of individuals. The central idea
was that the individual exists not on the basis of his belongings,
but independently of them—an abstract vision of an unencumbered self prior to its ends, which also constitutes the ideological
basis of the rights of man. Born by a secular vision of the ideology of Sameness, this is how the modern theory formed that defines humanity as deracination or uprooting from all tradition.

Liberalism considers men interchangeable because it only conceives of them in a generic, abstract manner as beings extracted
from all community and detached from all belonging, this break
being in its eyes the first condition of their "emancipation."

---

[6] Pierre Dardot and Christian Laval, *Commun. Essai sur la révolution
du XXIe siècle* [*Common: Essay on the Revolution of the Twenty-First Century*] (Paris: La Découverte, 2014), 461.

Similarly, it only concerns itself with a "freedom of choice," not the empirical consequences of these choices (even a bad choice is always justified if it has been freely taken). For liberals, the concept of the common good has no meaning, because there is no being capable of benefitting from it. In a society composed entirely of individuals, there is no "good" that can be common to those individuals. The "social good," in other words, can only be understood as a mere aggregate of individual goods, the result of individual choices.[7] It was in this sense that Margaret Thatcher was able to say, "There is no such thing as society."[8]

In a more general sense, all modernity has been constructed on a theory based on individuals who can only be called "free and equal in right" because they have been considered as unbound from, or cut off from, all communal belonging. Enlightenment philosophy continues to repeat this when it opposes reason to tradition, civilization to nature, and universalism to particular cultures, while assuring us that freedom and the capacity of the individual depend on his uprootedness from all familial, cultural, or religious roots. Recently, this was precisely the program of Vincent Peillon, the Minister of National Education, when he declared that the school's role is to "uproot the student from all determinisms: familial, ethnic, social, intellectual."

Marx, on the other hand, is in agreement with Aristotle in

---

[7] The very libertarian Ayn Rand thus writes: "The tribe (or the public or society) is only a number of individual men. Nothing can be good for the tribe as such" (*Capitalism: The Unknown Ideal* [New York: New American Library, 1967], 20).

[8] When there was a referendum on Scottish independence in September 2014, Géraldine Vaughan, Lecturer in British history and civilization at the University of Rouen, explained the demands of the partisans of independence in terms of their hostility to liberal individualism:

Thatcherite ideology came up against Scottish values deeply anchored in the idea of community. The exaltation of individualism was not understood or accepted. Thatcher's neo-liberal policy pulverized the welfare state and that was experienced as an attack on the communitarian idea. An ideological and moral abyss was dug with the Scots at that time.

laying down that man is first of all a political, social, and communal animal (*zōon politikon*). He thus agrees with the opinion of all those opposed to the liberal conception according to which man is merely an isolated atom bound to others only by the play of his interests. As François Flahaut writes, "The social interdependence of individuals is not utilitarian; it is ontological."[9] Legal and commercial relations are an insufficient basis for a good society.

Within this framework, broadly sketched here, must be situated the appearance and development of the communitarian current in Anglo-Saxon countries beginning in the early 1980s. Its principal representatives are Alasdair MacIntyre, Charles Taylor, and Michael Sandel. The aim of this school of thought was to enunciate a new theory closely combining moral and political philosophy, partly elaborated with reference to the United States' particular situation, marked as it is by a real inflation of the "politics of rights," and partly as a reaction to liberal political theory reformulated in recent decades by authors such as Ronald Dworkin, Bruce Ackerman, and especially John Rawls.[10]

It is by building upon the work of Tönnies mainly, but also through a salutary return to Aristotle's thought, that the communitarian school has set about demonstrating the fictive character of liberal anthropology, founded on a theory of subjective

---

[9] François Flahaut, *Pourquoi limiter l'expansion du capitalisme?* [*Why Limit the Expansion of Capitalism?*] (Paris: Descartes & Cie, 2003), 92.

[10] The English word "communitarianism" was first used in 1841 by John Goodwyn Barmby, founder of the Universal Communitarian Association. We note that the communitarian movement has greatly evolved since its origins. Some of its representatives, such as Michael Sandel, have abandoned the label. Others have partly modified their positions under the influence of liberal criticism. For a recent statement, cf. Amitai Etzioni, "Communitarianism Revisited," *Journal of Political Ideologies*, October 2014, 241–60. Cf. also Shlomo Avineri and Avner de-Shalit, eds., *Communitarianism and Individualism* (Oxford: Oxford University Press, 1992); Elizabeth Frazier, *The Problem of Communitarian Politics* (Oxford: Oxford University Press, 1999); and Paul van Setters, *Communitarianism in Law and Society* (Lanham: Rowman & Littlefield, 2006).

rights (the "rights of man") and the idea of an individual always prior to his ends, i.e., rationally declaring his choices outside any socio-historical context and defining himself as a consumer of utilities with unlimited needs.

The communitarians' principal criticism of liberal individualism is precisely that it causes the disappearance of communities, which are a fundamental and irreplaceable element of human existence. Liberalism devalues political life by considering political association a mere instrumental good, not seeing that citizens' participation in the political community is an intrinsic good constitutive of the "good life." Because of this, it is unable to give a satisfactory account of a certain number of obligations and commitments, such as those which do not result from a voluntary choice or contractual obligation: e.g., family obligations, the need to serve one's country, or to give the common interest precedence over personal interest. It propagates an erroneous conception of the self by refusing to admit that it is always "embedded" within a socio-historical context and, at least in part, constituted by values and commitments that are neither objects of choice nor revocable at will. It results in an inflation of the politics of rights which has little to do with right itself, along with a new type of institutional system: the "procedural republic." Finally, because of its legal formalism, it fails to grasp the central role played by language, culture, mores, and shared practices and values as the bases of a real "politics of recognition" of collective identities and rights.

For communitarians, a pre-social idea of the self is quite simply unimaginable: the individual always finds society *already there* — and it is this society which orders his preferences, constitutes his manner of being in the world, and shapes his aims. The basic idea is that the self is *discovered* more than it is *chosen*, for by definition one cannot choose what is already given. Consequently, self-understanding amounts to gradually discovering what our nature and identity consist in. It follows from this that one's socio-historical way of life is inseparable from identity, just as belonging to a community is inseparable from self-knowledge. Belonging is part of individual identity. This means not only that it is from a given way of life that individuals can make choices (including choices opposed to that way of life), but also that it is this way of life which constitutes as values or non-values the things which individuals may have to pass judgment upon.

An authentic community is thus not a mere collection or sum of individuals. Its members have common ends as members, bound up with shared values or experiences, and not merely more or less congruent private interests. These ends are proper to the community as such, and not particular aims that happen to be the same for all or most of its members. In a mere association, individuals regard their interests as independent and potentially divergent from each other. Relations existing between these interests thus do not constitute an intrinsic good, but only a means of obtaining the particular goods sought by each. The community, on the contrary, constitutes an intrinsic good for all who are part of it.

Liberal ideology generally interprets the decline of communal reality as closely bound up with modernity's emergence: the more the modern world imposes itself, the more communal bonds are supposed to relax in favor of more voluntary and contractual forms of association, and more individualistic and rational forms of behavior. From this point of view, communities appear as a residual phenomenon that institutional bureaucracies and global markets are called upon to eradicate or dissolve. In the end, this is the prospect of an emerging unified world — after the image of that celestial city that St. Augustine said would "attract citizens of all nations and assemble around itself a composite society of people of all languages without concerning itself with the diversity of their mores, laws, and institutions."[11]

But this is not what has happened. As Christopher Lasch writes, "Uprootedness destroys everything except the need for roots." The dissolution of ancient communities was accelerated by the birth of the nation state, an eminently *societal* phenomenon — society as the loss or disintegration of communal intimacy — which has not incorrectly been connected with the emergence of the individual as a value. Significantly, the crisis of the nation

---

[11] St. Augustine, *The City of God*, book XIX, ch. 17.

state model today goes hand-in-hand with the reappearance of political forms going beyond this model, both upwards (the formation of continental blocs called upon to play a key role in a multipolar world) and downwards (localist demands, the multi-plication of "communities" and "tribes," and a renaissance of regional and transnational forms of rootedness).

Establishing itself as one of the possible forms for transcend-ing modernity, community *ipso facto* loses the archaic status long ascribed to it by sociology. It appears less as a stage of history that modern times have abolished than as a permanent form of human association that gains or loses importance according to the age. It also takes on new forms. In our day, communities no longer merely associate persons on the basis of common origin. In a world where currents and networks are multiplying, they appear in very diverse forms. But it is always communities that allow the individual no longer to find himself facing the state alone.

The Maffesolian theory of postmodern "tribes" is well-known. Postmodernity, according to Michel Maffesoli, marks the end of the age of pure individualism and expresses a "Dio-nysian" renaissance of the need for neighborly proximity and communal forms of belonging, both sensible and emotional; such communities can also be chosen, "elective and plural," which are not thereby less active, even if they rarely last a long time. For Maffesoli, "the anti-communitarian incantation only ends by deepening still further the break between the people and the elites. . . . Beyond the narcissism or egoism proper to a postulated individualism, it is an *us*—that of the community, that of common vibrations—which is surreptitiously tending to spread."[12]

More clearly rejecting Tönnies' approach, Costanzo Preve thinks that society as a whole must be transformed into a com-munity. He writes:

Capitalist society, especially when it is globalized, is in no

---

[12] Michel Maffesoli and Hélène Strohl, *Les Nouveaux Bien-pensants* [*The New Right-Thinkers*] (Paris: Éditions du Moment, 2013), 13.

way a community. . . . A community in fact is a particular
or universal human society that defines itself less by the
physical proximity of its members than by a custom (*ethos*)
or, if you prefer, mores (*Sitten*), i.e., a social ethic that pre-
vails over the blind movements of the economy ruled by
nihilism and relativism.[13]

Costanzo Preve appeals at once to Aristotle, Rousseau, Fichte,
Hegel, and Marx in affirming that in Marx's writings, the class
struggle is itself merely a tactical means of reaching the strategic
goal of community (*Gemeinwesen*) where man can recover his
generic nature (*Gattungswesen*).[14] Preve is also at pains to distinguish communities that allow men to construct themselves from
those that enclose them within obsolete hierarchies. Denis Collin
is of the same opinion when he says that "communities which
enclose individuals in obedience to patriarchal or despotic hierarchies" must be distinguished from "the community of free
men."[15]

Recalling the "absolutely central philosophical role that the
first socialists accorded to the concepts of mutual assistance and
community," Jean-Claude Michéa similarly preaches:

Criticism of the republican mythology of the "Universal"
of which the state is supposedly the agent, at least if by
"universal" one understands the abstract universal conceived as separate from and opposed to the particular. In
sum, the idea that communities should renounce everything that particularizes them to enter into the great uniform family of the nation or the human race. As a good
Hegelian, I think that, on the contrary, the concrete universal is always a result—provisional by definition—and

---

[13] Costanzo Preve, *Éloge du communautarisme* [*In Praise of Communitarianism*], trans. Yves Branca, preface by Michel Maffesoli (Paris:
Krisis, 2012), 213.

[14] Preve, *Éloge du communautarisme*, 32.

[15] Denis Collin, "La forme achevée de la République est la République sociale" ["The Perfected Form of the Republic Is the Social
Republic"], website *Le Comptoir*, November 3, 2014, 4.

that it integrates particularity as an essential moment, i.e., not as a "lesser evil," but as a condition *sine qua non* of its real efficacy.[16]

This is the eternal dialectic of the one and the many, the universal and the particular.

Stéphane Vibert, Professor at the University of Ottawa, remarks:

> The Left's diversitarian progressive ideology is a perfect match for the individualist liberalism demanded by the Right, since both deny the historical and substantial framework that gives concrete meaning to the rights and duties of each citizen. To think that society is based on a contract between rational, free, and moral individuals, or that it is constructed from automatic regulation by means of the market, are two versions of the same liberal myth. This double fiction produces an *ersatz* political community incapable of grasping its history and cultural underpinnings. . . . Neo-republicans should be aware that a political community is not based entirely on rules of coexistence, but also and above all on a historical tradition understood as a permanent reinterpretation of what binds us.[17]

*

In most Western countries, all discussion of immigration today immediately results in a debate about "multiculturalism." In England, the United States, and Germany, to cite only three countries, if one is against immigration, one is also against multiculturalism[18] — and the converse is also true. It is generally

---

[16] Jean-Claude Michéa, "On ne peut être politiquement orthodoxe" ["One Cannot Be Politically Orthodox"], interview published on the website of the journal *Ballast*.

[17] Stéphane Vibert, "L'égalité dans la différence est un slogan creux" ["Equality-in-Difference Is an Empty slogan"], *Causeur*, October 2013, 48.

[18] For a combined critique of multiculturalism and immigration, cf. especially Frank Salter, *Welfare, Ethnicity, and Altruism* (London: Frank

in the name of multiculturalism that immigration is justified. When one is abroad, it is difficult to make people understand that the same symmetry is not found in France: opponents of immigration are certainly also hostile to multiculturalism here, but those who promote immigration as an "opportunity" or a "necessity" are not automatically partisans of multiculturalism. On the contrary, most often they vigorously denounce it under the name of "communitarianism." In France, even if the term remains relatively current, multiculturalism, which is only championed by rather marginal groups (The Representative Council of Black Associations, Indigènes de la République, etc.), is not at the center of debate. Thus, Olivier Roy recently noted the "end of multiculturalist discourse in France."[19] The explanation is found in that French peculiarity: the "republican" ideology founded on "secularism."[20]

The word "communitarianism" is new, since it did not appear in dictionaries until 1997. But today it is on everyone's lips, even though no one advocates it. The communitarian is always someone else! So we are dealing with a polemical category intended above all to denigrate. As Pierre-André Taguieff has noted, the term "communitarianism" immediately became a pejorative, "used (especially in the French language since the 1980s) to designate with a critical intent any form of ethnocentrism or sociocentrism, any group self-centeredness involving self-valorization and a tendency to remain closed off."[21]

Cass, 2004) and *On Genetic Interests: Family, Ethnicity, and Humanity in an Age of Mass Migration* (New Brunswick: Transaction Publishers, New Brunswick 2007).

[19] Olivier Roy, "C'est la fin du discours multiculturaliste en France" ["This Is the End of Multiculturalist Discourse in France"], *Le Monde*, May 30, 2014.

[20] The term *laïcité* itself remains untranslatable in many languages. The English word "secularism" represents only a very approximate equivalent.

[21] Pierre-André Taguieff, "Vous avez dit communautarisme?" ["Did You Say Communitarianism?"], *Le Figaro*, July 17, 2003. Cf. by the same author, *La République enlisée. Pluralisme, communautarisme et citoyenneté* [*The Republic Bogged Down: Pluralism, Communitarianism and Citizenship*]

"Communitarianism" is said to have its origin in an overly intense or exclusive attachment to a "community," whatever its nature (regional, religious, cultural, ethnic, sexual, etc.). It manifests itself by a tendency to "identitarian withdrawal" which can go as far as a desire to secede from the broader society, and by a series of demands amounting to a claim to privileges, thus creating a climate of conflict whose costs accrue to national unity. Socially inexplicable, and politically and morally unacceptable, communitarianism is said to be synonymous with a harmful particularism, sectarian hatred, or even civil war. But we also observe that, in a paradoxical way, the will to "proselytism" is supposed to fall under "communitarianism" as much as an exaggerated taste for keeping to one's group. Regularly associated with the specter of "religious fundamentalism," religious or xenophobic "radicalization," jihadism, and so on, "communitarianism" is in fact perceived as a sort of tribal separatism that generates conflicts ("Lebanonization"). The old accusations of "dual loyalty" and the intent to form a "state within the state" are part of the critique of "communitarianism." Communities are presented as carceral structures that lock people in, and not as liberating bonds. Their recognition would thus be synonymous with "the assignment of identity" and "communitarian confinement." In this connection, any reference to any ethnocultural difference or a "country of origin" is perceived as striking proof of a "lack of integration."

This real or imagined "communitarianism" is rejected in the name of a "republican model" that flatters itself with giving "civil bonds" priority over "communitarian attachments" in the name of civic universalism (although at the risk of falling into a communitarianism of the state). To "communitarianism" is sometimes opposed "national unity," or sometimes "secularism," "republican values," "republican universalism," the "national republican"

(Paris: Éditions des Syrtes, 2005). Cf. also Laurent Lévy, *le Spectre du communautarisme* [*The Specter of Communitarianism*] (Paris: Amsterdam, 2005); and Fabrice Dhume-Sonzogni, *Liberté, égalité, communauté. L'État français contre le communautarisme* [*Liberty, Equality, Fraternity: The French State Contra Communitarianism*] (Paris: Homnispheres, 2007).

spirit, etc. The general idea is that "communities" are incompatible with a "Republic, one and indivisible."[22]

This rejection is shared by all political milieus of the Right
and Left in a revealing way, from the most extreme to the most
moderate. Marine Le Pen appropriates the famous saying of the
Count of Clermont-Tonnerre: "Everything for individuals, nothing for communities." The program of the National Front explicitly declares: "Assimilation, especially via the school system,
must become the rule once again and communitarianism must
be banished. France will inscribe in its constitution: 'The Republic recognizes no community.'" "Nothing is more subversive of
republican order than communitarianism," affirms Union for a
Popular Movement (UMP) deputy Jean-Claude Guibal. "A
strong France is a France that says no to communitarianism,"
adds Nicolas Sarkozy, also denouncing "the intermediate bodies
that come between the state and the people." The "republican"
Left is not left out: communitarianism — that is the enemy!

"Communitarianism" thus shares with "populism" the privilege of having become a semantic whipping-boy. Everyone considers it his duty to denounce it as a dangerous threat. In public
discourse it only exists as a figure for what must be rejected, i.e.,
as a vehicle for delegitimation. But few take the trouble to define
exactly what the term means. This vagueness favors unanimity,
and in politics, unanimity is often suspect. Let us try to see
things more clearly.

To start, let us note a few paradoxes. It is remarkable that the
anti-communitarian rhetoric of certain Right-wing milieus directly borrows its linguistic elements from Enlightenment discourse directed not so long ago against traditional societies. At
that time, it was only a question of abandoning "archaic beliefs," "medieval habits," the principles "of another age," the
"subjection of women," the preference for honor over dignity,
etc. These same arguments used in the past to discredit both
the Catholic religion and the values of the *Ancien Régime* are

---

[22] Cf. Dominique Schnapper, "La République face aux communau-
tarismes" ["The Republic Faced With Communitarianisms"], *Études*,
February 2004, 177–88.

employed spontaneously by certain identitarians—sometime critics of modernity and defenders, if not of Catholicism, at least of the *Ancien Régime*—when it comes time to denounce "communitarianism."

Thus, a certain form of the Right blames immigrants for remaining faithful to traditional values. They reproach them with a way of life based on separatism and endogamy while they themselves are glad to criticize miscegenation. They denounce "identitarian withdrawal" while championing an identitarian conception of life. Sometimes they even reproach immigrants with "rejecting the Western way of life," instead of telling themselves that those who "do not love France" might hate it less and be less tempted to leave it by throwing themselves into terrorist or criminal enterprises if we had not ourselves given the example of such a rejection of this Western way of life based on materialism, spiritual emptiness, the collapse of the social bond, the disappearance of reference points, the primacy of money, the prostitution of commerce, and the obsession with sheeplike consumption.

An equally schizophrenic discourse is found on the Left when it celebrates diversity and miscegenation (two concepts supposed to be "enriching," whereas the latter inevitably impoverishes the former), or cultural diversity and globalization as a process of generalized hybridization, appealing at once to the normative ideal of pluralism and that of "mixism," wanting equal representation for all the ethnic groups whose existence it denies elsewhere, or to note the "multi-ethnic" character of contemporary societies while reacting ever more harshly against any display of otherness.

But the denunciation of "communitarianism," combining a critique of ethnic minorities and a critique of the communitarian anti-individualist principle, is not merely the direct heir of a philosophy that was the primary matrix of liberal ideology. It is also entirely natural among advocates of a French "republicanism" that is the heir to a kind of nation-building in which the formation of the civic nation has led to a nationalization of the social bond, itself tied to centralization, cultural assimilation, and the homogenization of a territory.

The Revolution of 1789 openly aimed at "uniformizing" France in order to replace the vestiges of a shameful past with the superior devices of reason: the creation of *départements*, the declared will to "destroy the provincial spirit," and the "wiping out of regional dialects." The people of France were to become a single people made up of indistinguishable individuals freed from all forms of rootedness: "The people is the totality of French citizens," proclaims Article 7 of the Constitution of June 24, 1793. From the French Revolution, organized according to the fanaticism of the One, "national republicans" have inherited the idea that the nation is an indivisible whole that must be directed from a powerful center equally remote from all of its parts. Nationality and citizenship having become synonymous, there must be a perfect coincidence between political and national unity—which implies the suppression of everything that forms an obstacle between the state and the individual, beginning with intermediary bodies, "communities," regional cultures, and so on. "Republicanism" in this sense is another word for Jacobinism, rooted in the tendency already present in the *Ancien Régime* to centralize a power whose sovereignty is also considered (at least since Jean Bodin) as one and indivisible.

This way of thinking about political life excludes divided (or distributed) sovereignty and the principle of subsidiarity (or of sufficient competence). Making "neutrality" the principal trait of the public domain (i.e., forbidding itself to decide about what Aristotle called the "good life"), it excludes public recognition of specific identities, particular languages and customs, shared ways of life and values proper only to some of the citizens. These differences, discredited by a single and overarching court of appeal, are at best restricted to the private sphere, i.e., asked to remain discreet, or even to make themselves invisible. The "republican" denunciation of "communitarianism" reduces civic belonging to adhesion to abstract principles. It is the equivalent of the "constitutional patriotism" preached by Jürgen Habermas on the basis of his theory of "communicative rationality." Under cover of denouncing self-centered groups, national ethnocentrism is what gets affirmed.

In such a context, the integration of immigrants is necessarily synonymous with assimilation. The Republic does not want to recognize subsidiary forms of belonging, and this implies the negation, banishment, or delegitimizing of communities; it only recognizes individuals and integrates them by assimilating them. This is why it refuses to "differentiate" (make a distinction) between citizens according to ethnic, cultural, or religious criteria. Article 2 of the Constitution of 1958 thus forbids any discrimination—even "positive"—based on origins, race, or religion. The individual is supposed to pay for his assimilation by forgetting his roots. At the same time, democratic equality is understood in the sense of sameness, with society associating citizens who can only be considered politically *equal* because they are anthropologically *alike*.[23]

Today's offensive against "communitarianism" is tied, as everyone knows, to problems arising from the rapid and poorly managed arrival of a mass of immigrants of an origin and culture very different from those of the host country. The same goes for the polemics concerning "secularism," a principle reaffirmed with all the more force inasmuch as people think they can thus conjure away the risks associated with the presence of different traditions, cultures, and ways of life on the same territory. The Republic thinks it can and must restrict itself to the same neutrality in the ethnocultural domain as in the religious domain. We see in this that the republican principle, anti-liberal insofar as it places the state above the individual, fully rejoins liberalism in affirming that the state must refrain from deciding in favor of a particular conception of the "good life," leaving to the citizens the right to choose that which suits them best on the condition that it only express itself within the context of private life.

The problem is that this much-vaunted model of assimilation no longer works, generally speaking (for there are always individual exceptions), first of all because the state is no longer productive of sociality today (social relations being formed outside it), and also because today's immigration, by its character as well as its scope, is no longer compatible with this model.

---

[23] Cf. Pierre Rosanvallon, *La Société des égaux* [*The Society of Equals*] (Paris: Seuil, 2011).

Assimilation, which presupposes a gradual harmonization of behavior, is only possible if a certain number of conditions are fulfilled: immigration must be of relatively moderate volume or else extended over a long time; the immigrants' culture must not be very different from that of the host country; institutional mechanisms allowing individuals to be assimilated must be alive and in a functioning state; the native population must not react in an excessively negative fashion to the arrival and presence of the newcomers; the immigrants themselves must show a genuine will to integrate, and so on. None of these conditions are being fulfilled today. Thus, assimilation cannot function, especially for the reasons set out by the demographer Michèle Tribalat.[24]

Recalling that assimilation is a process "which results from the good will of the newcomers and the involvement of the social body with the approval of its elites,"[25] Michèle Tribalat thinks that assimilation has become impossible because of the widening separation between native and immigrant populations. To justify her opinion, she relies especially on the return in force of the religious identitarian marker among immigrants' descendants — the differential in fertility varying as a function of religious affiliation — and on the fact that, contrary to what was expected, religious endogamy remains the rule for them. She also observes that by way of reaction, the French popular classes, the first victims of the social pathologies tied to immigration, "are seceding and, whenever they can, live where they are able to protect their way of life."

Communities can be denied all one likes, but they are as plain as the nose on one's face.

*

Communitarianism in the proper sense merely means that "the individual does not exist independently of his belonging,

---

[24] Michèle Tribalat, *Les yeux grands fermés* [*Eyes Wide Shut*] (Paris: Denoël, 2010) and *Assimilation: la fin du modèle français* [*Assimilation: The End of the French Model*] (Paris: Éditions du Toucan, 2013).

[25] Michèle Tribalat, interview in *Causeur*, January 2014, 65.

whether cultural, ethnic, religious, or social."[26] This idea is met with again in multiculturalism, which is above all interested in the way differences between groups are to be treated by the public power. Its basic postulate is that minorities' cultural identity must not be left unaccounted for or denied in the name of integration or citizenship. Far from necessarily imprisoning the individual, cultural belonging may also be an instrument of emancipation; keeping apart also allows one to escape heteronymous ascriptions of identity. Beginning from that common basis, the representatives of multiculturalism divide into different schools or tendencies. Some of them, for example, think multiculturalism involves a decoupling of nation and citizenship, thus contradicting the concept of national identity (on which they agree with those on the opposite side who defend national unity against multiculturalism), while others think that policies of recognizing cultural specificities reinforce national unity rather than destroying it.[27]

The term "multiculturalism" emerged in the 1960s and 1970s, mainly in Anglo-Saxon countries, where it enjoyed immediate success.[28] It subsequently occasioned vast ideological debates of which the larger public has usually remained uninformed.[29] A

---

[26] Catherine Halpern, "Communautarisme, une notion univoque" ["Communitarianism, An Unequivocal Concept"], *Sciences humaines*, April 2004.

[27] Cf. Tariq Modood, "Multiculturalisme civique et identité nationale" ["Civic Multiculturalism and National Identity"], in Sophie Guérard de Latour, ed., *Le multiculturalisme a-t-il un avenir?* [*Does Multiculturalism Have a Future?*] (Paris: Hermann, 2013), 243–76. Cf. also Bhikhu Parekh, *Rethinking Multiculturalism: Cultural Diversity and Political Theory* (Basingstoke: Macmillan, 2000).

[28] Cf. Nathan Glazer, *We Are All Multiculturalists Now* (Cambridge, Mass.: Harvard University Press, 1998).

[29] Nevertheless, cf. Lukas Sosoe, ed., *Diversité humaine. Démocratie, multiculturalisme et citoyenneté* [*Human Diversity: Democracy, Multiculturalism and Citizenship*] (Paris: L'Harmattan, 2003); Charles Taylor, *Multiculturalisme. Différence et démocratie*, trans. Denis Armand-Canal (Paris: Flammarion, 2009); Patrick Savidan, *Le Multiculturalisme* (Paris: PUF, 2009); Francesco Fistetti, *Théorie du multiculturalisme. Un parcours en philosophie et sciences sociales* [*Theory of Multiculturalism: A Map of the*

very common mistake is, for example, to think that critiques of multiculturalism come exclusively from immigration adversaries of all stripes, who see in it only a form of "globalism" participating in the subversive deconstruction of national imaginations.

Multiculturalism is in reality a rather complex ideology. At first glance, it gives the impression of being a byproduct of liberalism. Multiculturalists in fact often treat cultural differences in terms of individual preference. They conceive the autonomy of cultures on the model of individual autonomy, the rights of peoples on the model of the rights of man, cultural pluralism on that of values-pluralism, the diversity of cultures on that of the diversity of conceptions of the "good life," etc. The principal spokesman of liberal multiculturalism, Will Kymlicka, is thus at pains to reconcile liberalism and multiculturalism, and to reduce the gap between abstract universalism and practical inscription in a specific national culture.[30]

But it is interesting to observe that multiculturalism, even as it borrows a number of its traits from liberal doctrine, has nonetheless often been attacked by liberal authors simply because it argues on the basis of the concept of "culture," and thus of cultural difference. By analyzing society on the basis of groups or communities and not on that of individuals and the theory of individual rights, by holding that cultural groups are endowed with an authentic form of identity which it is legitimate to defend and protect, multiculturalism falls into the error of "culturalism"; viz., into cultural relativism or "essentialism," thus once again calling into question the foundations of universalism.

Basically, the liberal adversaries of multiculturalism reproach

---

Philosophical and Sociological Territory], trans. Philippe Chanial and Marilisa Preziosi (Paris: La Découverte, 2009); Sophie Guérard de Latour, *Vers la république des différences* [*Toward A Republic of Differences*] (Toulouse: Presses universitaires du Mirail, 2009); and Sophie Guérard de Latour, ed., *Le multiculturalisme a-t-il un avenir?*

[30] Cf. Will Kymlicka, *Liberalism, Community, and Culture* (Oxford: Clarendon Press, 1989); *La Citoyenneté multiculturelle. Une théorie libérale du droit des minorités* [*Multicultural Citizenship: A Liberal theory of Minority Rights*], trans. Patrick Savidan (Paris: La Découverte, 2001).

it with reasoning in terms of belonging, i.e., not envisaging the individual as entirely free in his choices, and with according excessive importance to communities and cultural or ethnic groups. They also accuse it of violating the liberal principle according to which the public powers must adopt a position of neutrality regarding ethnic origin or religion: to preach that cultural minorities, defined above all in terms of ethnicity, be taken into account politically amounts to ignoring the liberal principles of distinguishing between public and private identity and the public sphere's necessary neutrality. Another criticism consists in reproaching multiculturalism's advocates with neglecting the right of individuals to emancipate themselves from the constraints proper to their respective groups' cultural traditions. In the name of tolerance, multiculturalism thus provides comfort to groups whose beliefs or practices contradict liberal principles. Article 4 of UNESCO's Universal Declaration stipulates that "no one may invoke cultural diversity to infringe the rights of man." Such critiques have been developed notably by Derek L. Philips, Susan Moller Okin, Anne Phillips, Anthony Kwame Appiah, Nancy Fraser, Stephen Holmes, and many others.[31]

Some authors have recently gone so far as to maintain that the philosopher Johann Gottfried von Herder (1744–1803), described as a resolute adversary of Enlightenment cosmopolitanism, is the great ancestor both of multiculturalism and of Rightwing populism—and even that, as a "culturalist," he cannot be

---

[31] Derek L. Phillips, *Looking Backward: A Critical Appraisal of Communitarian Thought* (Princeton: Princeton University Press, 1993); Susan Moller Okin, *Is Multiculturalism Bad for Women?* (Princeton: Princeton University Press, 1999); Brian Barry, *Culture and Equality: An Egalitarian Critique of Multiculturalism* (Cambridge: Harvard University Press, 2001); Anthony Kwame Appiah, *The Ethics of Identity* (Princeton: Princeton University Press, 2004); Patrick West, *The Poverty of Multiculturalism* (London: Civitas, 2005); Anne Phillips, *Multiculturalism Without Culture* (Princeton: Princeton University Press, 2007); and Jens-Martin Eriksen and Frederik Stjernfelt, *Les Pièges de la culture. Les contradictions démocratiques du multiculturalisme* [*The Traps of Culture: The Democratic Contradictions of Multiculturalism*], trans. Peer Bundgaard (Geneva: MētisPresses, 2012).

considered "Left wing."[32] In short, for a certain liberal Left multiculturalism is nothing but a Trojan Horse for identitiarian theories hostile to individual rights . . .

The response of multiculturalism's partisans to liberal critiques usually consists in asserting that:

> The idea of citizenship must rest upon "policies of difference," on "policies of recognition," or that it must become "multicultural." This response does not proceed from any communitarian logic seeking to give group rights priority over individual rights. . . . On the contrary, it occurs in the context of a critical reflection on the limits of a universalism "blind to differences" which denounces the shortcomings of a false abstraction without renouncing the principles of liberty and equality.[33]

Concerning the intolerance of certain ethnocultural groups, multiculturalists most often declare themselves in favor of "exit rights" in case of membership in illiberal groups. But the question nonetheless remains valid. How can a multicultural state devoted to the liberal principle of "neutrality" remain neutral when faced with conceptions of the "good life" that illiberal minorities intend to perpetuate? Multiculturalists' answers to this question vary according to whether they give priority to the tolerance of illiberal practices associated with guaranteeing "exit rights" (William Galston) or to individual autonomy (George Crowder).[34]

Let us return to the fundamental aspect of the problem. It cannot be denied that societies are easier to manage the more

---

[32] Cf. Göran Adamson, Aje Carlbom, and Pernilla Ouis, "Johann Herder, Early Nineteenth-Century Counter-Enlightenment, and the Common Roots of Multiculturalism and Right-Wing Populism," *Telos*, no. 169, Winter 2014, 28–38.

[33] Guérard de Latour, ed., *Le multiculturalisme a-t-il un avenir?*, 9–10.

[34] Cf. William Galston, *Liberal Pluralism: The Implications of Value Pluralism for Liberal Theory and Practice* (Cambridge: Cambridge University Press, 2002) and George Crowder, *Liberalism and Value Pluralism* (London: Continuum, 2002).

homogeneous they are, since this homogeneity favors the diffusion of shared values. Nor can it be denied that people feel most at ease in such societies, since they have the feeling that the human landscape around them is made in their own image, which reassures them by confirming them in what they are—whereas the contrary case gives them the impression of becoming "strangers in their own land." It is also generally admitted that the more homogeneous a society is, the more its members are inclined to have confidence in one another, which favors altruistic and cooperative behavior.[35] But such societies are now the exception rather than the rule, at least in the Western world.

We live in a country which has become multi-ethnic within a few decades. This reality requires us to reflect anew on the concept of pluralism, which can be understood in a very different way depending on whether one is referring to liberal pluralism, democratic pluralism, communitarian pluralism, pluralism of values, or pluralism of opinions.

Politics has been defined, among other ways, as the art of the possible. "Ideal" politics organized exclusively around abstract principles or pious wishes is by definition an anti-politics. The leading trait of politics is realism. From this point of view, the denunciation of "communitarianism" suggests voluntary blindness each time one wants to delegitimize communities by using this term. People want to pretend that communities do not exist—or they decide not to see them—whereas they most certainly do exist. The denunciation of "ethnic statistics" by the frightened maidens of official anti-racism suggests the same willful blindness, as does the idea that the best way to combat racism is to deny the existence of races. There are realities to which one must close one's eyes.

There is of course an intolerable form of "communitarianism": that which amounts to a rejection of the law common to all, a will to secede from society, the "communitarianism" that consists in putting the host culture and the culture of origin on

---

[35] Cf. Robert D. Putnam, "*E Pluribus Unum*: Diversity and Community in the Twenty-First Century," *Scandinavian Political Studies*, June 2007, 137–74.

an equal footing as if the former had to adapt to the latter, or as if all identities were valuable except that of the natives (rejection of others is denounced as intolerable even as self-rejection is hinted at); the "communitarianism" which only retains those traits of a cultural identity that can be exaggerated in order to oppose the host culture, or which consigns all members of a group to a sort of house arrest by turning such groups into lobbies that want to make their own interests prevail, or have their demands triumph to the detriment of society as a whole. Such a "communitarianism" must, of course, be fought tirelessly.

The law which applies to all is itself indissociable from the existence of a "dominant culture" (*Leitkultur*) in every country — the result of a shared history, a culture which can certainly evolve, as it always has, but which still constitutes a central referent that cannot be ignored and whose suppression cannot be demanded. Michèle Tribalat writes: "Assimilation does not necessarily suppose that the autochthonous culture's belief is superior to that which the immigrants bring with them. It is merely the culture of the country in which they have chosen to live, and it is thereby the legitimate cultural point of reference."[36] Similarly, we can only agree with Vincent Descombes when he says that "if we believe the existence of a political body is legitimate, then we posit the reality of the nation in the modern sense, viz., a political community of citizens. In that case, communitarian or religious identities can only be subordinate."[37]

But the baby must not be thrown out with the bathwater. "Communities" of all sorts are today trying to affirm themselves and get themselves recognized in public life, i.e., to leave the private sphere within which republican formalism is trying to

---

[36] Michèle Tribalat, "Chercheur en terrain miné" ["Searcher in a Minefield"], *Le Débat*, March–April 2014, 48. On the concept of *Leitkultur*, cf. Bassam Tibi, *Europa ohne Identität. Die Krise der multikulturellen Gesellschaft* [*Europe Without Identity: The Crisis of Multicultural Society*] (Berlin: Siedler, 1998), 2nd ed.; and *Europa ohne Identität? Leitkultur oder Wertebeliebigkeit* [*Europe Without Identity? Dominant Culture or Arbitrary Values*] (Berlin: Siedler, 2002).

[37] Vincent Descombes, *Les Embarras de l'identité* [*The Confusions of Identity*] (Paris: Gallimard, 2013).

confine them.

The question is: Isn't "communitarianism" in its worst aspects the consequence of the public authorities' refusal to recognize the existence of communities? Does "communitarianism" amount to a phenomenon of "identitarian withdrawal" or to a cultural crisis? The refusal to recognize differences can only lead them to affirm themselves in a violent or even pathological fashion. Today, the emergence of radical Islamic currents going as far as terrorism is being explained in terms of "communitarianism." Might it not instead be a refusal to take these communities into account that has contributed the most to this development? People assure us that the wearing of the *hijab* logically entails that of the *burqa*. What if it is rather the forbidding of the Islamic scarf which favors the appearance of the *burqa* by way of reaction? And in whichever direction causality may be operating, does anyone really think the problem of "communitarianism" can be resolved by establishing clothing police?

Does integration imply the abandonment of all identitarian elements the immigrant has inherited from his family or country of origin? Does a refusal to cut oneself off from that part of collective memory really prevent him from finding a place in the host country? Is respect for the rules of coexistence necessarily correlated with the forgetting of roots (as suggested by those who take pride in not having forgotten their own)? The least one can say is that the answer is not self-evident. One might ask instead whether such a demand is not intrinsically tied to the French Jacobin model of a Republic "one and indivisible."[38]

Regarding immigrants, Fares Gillon writes:

Here are people who have been uprooted from their land (or who uprooted themselves), who abandoned their culture, forgot their language, and now have nothing to transmit to their children. These children, perfect experimental guinea pigs for freedom by way of uprootedness, . . . are the first post-human subjects: without roots, and

---

[38] Cf. Hugues Lagrange, *Le Déni des cultures* [*The Denial of Cultures*] (Paris: Seuil, 2010).

soon, after passing through the republican school system, without knowledge or attachment to their new country. Cut off from their origins without being given the chance to take root in a civilization now sabotaging itself, they incarnate most perfectly the neo-human with no attachments, no reference points, of which the ideologues of postmodernity dream. So it is not as strangers to France that the uprooted people of the suburbs pose a problem, but as perfect products of the new France, the France that rejects itself.[39]

Does taking account of certain cultural specificities form an obstacle to integration, or does it facilitate integration? One might well think that faithfulness to certain cultural traditions is necessary for the development of individual autonomy, and that it is by way of public institutions and the law common to all, not by assimilation and cultural conformism, that "integration" can best be brought about.

The only criterion in this matter must be public order, which implies recognition of a common law. A law that applies to everyone is necessary for the co-existence of all who live in the same country. This is a point on which one cannot compromise. It is in the very nature of what is diverse to demand a principle of unity, without which one gets caught up in an endless spiral of demands for "rights" and privileges that amounts to the "tyranny of minorities" feared by Tocqueville. But the law common to all must also be able to take particularities into account, examine demands tied to customary traditions, and permit those which do no harm to public order, and take the necessary measures to allow them to exist. A country does not find its coherence in the destruction of more particular forms of cohesion. The social nature of man can only be conceived beginning from communities that form the stuff of society. Only in this way can diversity, perhaps, be civilized.

---

[39] Fares Gillon, "Le choc des non-civilisations" ["The Clash of Non-Civilizations"], website *Philitt: Revue de philosophie et de littérature*, November 20, 2014.

Daoud Boughezala is not wrong to write on this subject:

I believe with Charles Taylor and Will Kymlicka that the cultural group can be an instrument of emancipation for the individual — on the express condition that a single law apply to all citizens. Reasonable accommodations are only worthwhile if they are genuinely reasonable. . . . That grown female students should wear the veil at university does not bother me. The *burqa*, however, is unreasonable because it is depersonalizing, and thus should remain forbidden in public.[40]

The right to be different is, in any case, merely a right, i.e., a freedom and not an obligation. To recognize difference is to grant those who wish to live according to a form of belonging they consider important the possibility of doing so, not to lock them up in it or forbid them to deviate from it. Moreover, difference is not an absolute. By definition, it can only be relative: one only differs in relation to what is different. The same goes for identity: a group can no more have an identity by itself than an individual. All identity is constructed within a relation. The same goes for cultures: each of them constitutes a world of meaning, but these worlds can communicate. They are not quasi-species, but unavoidable modalities of the expression of human nature. Let us take care here not to confuse the universal with universalism.

It is in this context that we can (retrospectively) pose the question of the "Islamic scarf" (*hijab*, not *burqa*), which has already released floods of ink and called forth the wildest commentary[41] since its outlawing in educational establishments

---

[40] Daoud Boughezala, "Le choc des multiculturalismes" ["The Clash of Multiculturalisms"], *Causeur*, October 2013, 55. In *Situation de la France* [*France's Situation*] (Paris: Desclée de Brouwer, 2015), Pierre Manent maintains a similar point of view.

[41] Referring to the recent murder of a child of French origin carried out by the Islamic State (Daesh), Yves de Kerdel writes that "there is no difference, *mutatis mutandis*, between this 12-year-old boy who left his school in Toulouse to carry out cold-blooded executions and the young

through application of the principle of secularism by the law of March 15, 2004. Does wearing this scarf really undermine public order (more than the wimple, turban, or beret)? If it is legitimate to forbid it to teachers, who are obligated to neutrality by virtue of their status, is it also legitimate to forbid it to female students? To mothers? The 2004 law was passed in the name of the struggle against "communitarianism," at the risk of excluding from public school girls who, far from demanding a particular kind of instruction in a particular sort of school, were on the contrary intending to remain in public school. People have justified this law by reasoning that the wearing of the veil constitutes a violation of the girls' autonomy, moreover going against "republican values." This supposedly justifies the state's paternalistic[42] intervention, although the women in question saw the forbidding of the Islamic scarf as a violation of freedom of religion and/or their dignity. In an age that attaches such importance to freedom of choice, does a young Muslim girl have the right to choose to have an abortion but not to wear the veil? We are confronted here with a typical example of a conflict of values.

As Charles Taylor notes:

It is very difficult to distinguish the share of identity or custom and the share of active faith in the wearing of the headscarf, but the state has chosen to code it as a religious act, and even a pointedly religious act. . . . In 2004, the Stasi Commission[43] chose to say that the subjective value attributed by the individual to the sign he is wearing is less

---

[Muslim] girls who demand the right to wear the veil at university" ("L'insupportable trahison des clercs" ["The Intolerable Betrayal of the Intellectuals"], *Valeurs actuelles*, March 19, 2015, 6)!

[42] Paternalism consists in limiting an individual's freedom for his own good and against his desires or wishes, whether by preventing him from doing what he wants or by forcing him to do what he does not want.

[43] A governmental commission set up by President Jacques Chirac in 2003 to hold consultations and advise on the proper application of the principle of secularism. It was named after its Chairman, Bernard Stasi. — Trans.

important than the objective interpretation the state gives of it. Now, that interpretation remains questionable. First of all, the wearing of the *hijab* has been identified as a sign of feminine oppression—independently of the subjective value the woman wearing the veil attributes to her behavior. . . . Next, the wearing of the veil is supposedly less a sign of piety than a declaration of hostility to the French Republic and its secular foundations. Moreover, the term "pointedly" must, in my opinion, be understood in this way: something is "pointed" which appears in the public space as a message of defiance of republican values. . . . So it amounts less to a "pointed" sign than to an "injurious" one from the Republic's point of view. . . . Personally, I reject this objective interpretation. In a state under the rule of law, a person should have the right to determine the meaning of his own acts.[44]

The recognition of differences obviously does not imply angelism. It is clear that such recognition will not lead to the disappearance of conflicts. But it is the same with difference or identity as with freedom: the bad use one makes of it discredits that use, not the principle itself. In this respect one may disagree with Elisabeth Badinter who, to justify the "right to indifference," assures us that "every time we give differences priority over similarities, we dip our toes into a process of confrontation." Similarity is in reality no less fruitful of conflict than difference: think of the "mimetic rivalry" so well analyzed by René Girard.

Michel Masson writes:

The communitarian mentality is of a different nature than the communitarian spirit. Forms of communitarianism

---

[44] Charles Taylor, "Vivre dans le pluralisme" ["Living in Pluralism"], *Ésprit*, October 2014, 24. Cf. also Cécile Laborde, *Critical Republicanism: The Hijab Controversy and Political Theory* (Oxford: Oxford University Press, 2008) and "Républicanisme critique et multiculturalisme libéral" ["Critical Republicanism and Liberal Multiculturalism"], in Guérard de Latour, ed., *Le multiculturalisme a-t-il un avenir?*, 227–42.

reproduce, on the level of peoples, the characteristics of individualism on the level of communities. . . . On the contrary, the communitarian spirit produces and perpetuates the spaces necessary for the free exercise of various human activities. Communities are the locus of social bonds. . . . Under these conditions, one understands the interest the sorcerer's apprentices have in dragging both communities and communitarianism through the mud of history in the same cart. For if they succeed in doing so, nothing will be able to interpose itself between the people and political power, which can then reign without obstacle or division.[45]

---

[45] Michel Masson, "Communautarisme et communautés" ["Communitarianism and Communities"], *L'Écritoire*, March 2015, 2–6. In *Individu et communauté, une crise sans issue* [*Individual and Community: An Irresolvable Crisis*] (Paris: Edifa-Mame, 2007), Thibaud Collin supports the view that, in the final analysis, "communitarianism is an individualist phenomenon."

"MULTITUDES" AGAINST THE PEOPLE
(ON THE THESES OF MICHAEL HARDT
& ANTONIO NEGRI)

Michael Hardt and Antonio Negri published a book entitled *Empire* (*E.*) in the United States in April 2000,[1] followed four years later by another essay, *Multitude* (*M.*).[2] Soon translated across the entire world, these two big works (nearly a thousand pages total) quickly began—and continue—to exercise great influence on certain segments of the anti-globalist movement. Upon publication, the *New York Times* said of *Empire* that it constituted the "*Communist Manifesto* of the twenty-first century" and described it as the "great theoretical synthesis of the new millennium." In Germany, *Die Zeit* saw in it a "grand analysis of society." Benjamin Stille predicted it would become an "international bestseller."[3] David Sherman spoke of the "most influential neo-Marxist work that has appeared since the monumental political events of the end of the 1980s."[4]

Not everyone agreed with these hyperbolic comments, however. *Empire* also aroused strong opposition, even on the part of those who recognized it as an important work of political philosophy, and there was no lack of criticism, from Slavoj Žižek to Robert Kurz, and from Anselm Jappe to Danilo Zolo. Passionate discussions have resulted. In France, a journal was created to

---

[1] Michael Hardt and Antonio Negri, *Empire* (Cambridge, Mass.: Harvard University Press, 2000). In French: *Empire*, trans Denis-Armand Canal (Paris: Exils, 2000).

[2] Michael Hardt and Antonio Negri, *Multitude: War and Democracy in the Age of Empire* (New York: Penguin, 2004). In French: *Multitude*, trans. by Nicolas Guilhot (Paris: La Découverte, 2004).

[3] Benjamin Stille, "Apocalypse Soon," *The New York Review of Books*, November 7, 2002.

[4] David Sherman, "The Ontological Need: Positing Subjectivity and Resistance in Hardt and Negri's *Empire*," *Telos*, no. 128, Summer 2004, 143.

transmit Hardt and Negri's theses—the journal *Multitudes*[5]—while all over the world publication of the two books has launched, then nourished, an intense discussion that continues today.[6] We propose to take stock of these debates here and to evaluate the theories presented by Hardt and Negri.

Michael Hardt is an American from Seattle, Associate Professor of Literature at Duke University, and the author of a doctoral thesis on Deleuze and Negri. Antonio Negri is a much better-known figure. Born in 1933 in Padua, son of one of the founders

---

[5] In March 2000, *Multitudes* succeeded Jean-Marie Vincent's former journal *Futur antérieur*, whose orientation was very different. The editor of *Multitudes*, Yann Moulier-Boutang, a son of the royalist philosopher Pierre Boutang, is Professor of Economics at the Paris Institute of Political Studies (Sciences-Po) and the University of Compiègne. Longtime member of the economic commission of the Green Party, he belongs to the orientation committee of *Cosmopolitiques* and has also collaborated with such journals as *Chimères, Vacarme, Alice,* etc.

[6] Besides the texts cited in this article, cf. especially "Sovereignty, Multitudes, Absolute Democracy: A Discussion between Michael Hardt and Thomas Dumm about Hardt and Negri's *Empire*," *Theory and Event*, 2000, 3; Paolo Virno, *Grammaire de la multitude* [*Grammar of the Multitude*], trans. Véronique Dassas (Cahors: Éditions de l'Éclat, 2002); Gopal Balakrishnan, ed., *Debating Empire* (London: Verso, 2003); Ugo D. Rossi, "Le contre-Empire qui vient ou le discours du grand compétiteur. Essai de décryptage de l'ouvrage de Michael Hardt et Toni Negri" ["The Coming Counter-Empire or the Discourse of the Great Competitor: Attempt to Decipher the Work of Michael Hardt and Toni Negri"], *Cahiers pour l'analyse concrete*, nos. 49–50, 2003, pp. 11–38 ; *Negrisme et Tute bianche: une contre-révolution de gauche* [*Negrism and White Overalls: A Counter-Revolution of the Left*] (Nancy: Mutines Séditions, 2004); Nicholas Tampio, ed., *Can the Multitude Save the Left?*, special issue of *Theory and Event*, 2005, 2; Atilio A. Boron, *Empire and Imperialism: A Critical Reading of Michael Hardt and Antonio Negri* (London: Zed Books, 2005); Ugo D. Rossi, *Anti-Negri. Le contre-Empire qui vient ou le discours du grand compétiteur* [*Anti-Negri: The Coming Counter-Empire or the Discourse of the Great Competitor*] (Uzès: Inclinaison, 2007); and Louis Pinto, "La pensée post- de Toni Negri" ["Toni Negri's Post-Thinking"], in Bertrand Geay and Laurent Willemey, eds., *Pour une gauche de gauche* [*For a Left-Wing Left*] (Bellecombe-en-Bauges: Éditions du Croquant, 2008).

of the Italian Communist Party in Liverno, he was active when he was very young in Catholic Action (*Azione catolica*). From the end of the 1950s, he participated in the elaboration of the "workerist" current of the Italian extreme Left in the pages of *Quaderni rossi*. In 1955, he spent time on an Israeli Kibbutz. In 1969, he was one of the founders of *Potere operaio*, then of the group *Autonomia operaio* beginning in 1973. At the same time, he has had a career as Professor of the Philosophy of Law at the University of Padua. There he defended armed struggle and exalted the figure of the "criminal worker." During the *anni di piombo*,[7] suspected of being the "brains" of the Red Brigades, he was arrested in April 1979 in the course of a vast dragnet operation and found himself imprisoned on accusations of armed insurrection against the state, forcible confinement, and being an accomplice to murder in the Aldo Moro affair, none of which was ever accompanied by any sort of proof.[8] It was in prison, where he was placed under strict surveillance, that he wrote his first book on the metaphysics of Spinoza, of whom he proposed a "Marxist" rereading in light of French post-structuralism, in particular of Gilles Deleuze.[9] Elected a deputy of the Radical Party in June 1983, the year his trial began, he left prison in the month of July thanks to the parliamentary immunity he had just acquired. When the Italian deputies decided to lift that immunity, he went into exile in Paris in September, where he joined the Collège International de Philosophie. Close to Gilles Deleuze and Félix Guattari, who introduced him to French intellectual circles, he taught at the University of Paris-VIII and at the École normale supérieure. Returning to Italy in July 1997, he was again imprisoned to complete his sentence. Paroled in 1999, he was

---

[7] The "years of lead," a period of violence in Italy between the extreme Left and Right between the 1960s and 1980s. — Trans.

[8] Antonio Negri today states that he has "never approved violence as a practice" (interview in *Philosophie Magazine*, June–July 2006, 57).

[9] *L'Anomalie sauvage. Puissance et pouvoir chez Spinoza* [*The Savage Anomaly: The Power of Spinoza's Metaphysics and Politics*] (Paris: Amsterdam, 2007). Negri has published his academic works under his full name, Antonio Negri, reserving the name Toni Negri for his more militant essays.

finally freed in 2003. Today he divides his time between Venice and Paris, along with his companion, the philosopher Judith Revel. His play *Swarm* was produced in June 2005 at the Théâtre de la Colline.[10]

Empire incontestably represents one of the most ambitious, but also most ambiguous, attempts to reformulate an entirely new analysis and strategy for the anti-capitalist Left. A number of observers, as we have seen, have recognized its importance, as well as emphasizing its imaginative power and the wealth of its philosophical references.[11] The work is in fact based on an impressive theoretical arsenal, which seems to make it difficult to refute. Antonio Negri "knows how to combine the rarely associated forms of prestige of both the revolutionary and the metaphysician," says Philippe Raynaud, who also speaks of a "rather intoxicating music."[12]

What are the book's main theses?

Postmodernity, according to Hardt and Negri, has brought about the disappearance of the Westphalian system of sovereign nation-states. In the age of globalization, the classic states that were the great political actors of the modern age have become exhausted. The world is no longer governed by state systems, but by a single power structure of a sort never seen before. This global structure, with no outside and totally deterritorialized,

---

[10] His ideas have recently been spread in Italy by small activist groups such as *Tute bianche* ("white overalls"), which was created in 1996 in the context of the coalition of alternative social networks, *Ya Basta*. The *Tute Bianche*, observed in Zapatista costumes during the demonstrations against the G8 Summit meeting in Genoa in July 2001, and whose spokesman at that time was Luca Casarini, shortly thereafter gave way to the *Disobbedienti*. On Antonio Negri's political itinerary, cf. also Claudio Albertani, "Toni Negri et la déconcertante trajectoire de l'opéraisme italien" ["Toni Negri and the Disconcerting Career of Italian Workerism"], *A Contretemps*, September 2003, 3–18.

[11] Cf., e.g., Gopal Balakrishnan, "Hardt and Negri's *Empire*," *New Left Review*, September–October 2000.

[12] Philippe Raynaud, *L'Extrême gauche plurielle. Entre démocratie radicale et révolution* [*The Pluralistic Extreme Left: Between Radical Democracy and Revolution*] (Paris: Perrin, 2010), 147, 170.

has cosmopolitan universalism for its political and normative substance. Its form of action, neither statist nor national, is "biopolitical" power. It is this structure to which Hardt and Negri give the name "Empire."

The Empire can be defined as a planetary structure of hierarchies and currents based on a logic of volatile totality that transcends all the old divides between state and society, war and peace, constraint and freedom, center and periphery. Its emergence amounts to a total break with the political forms of classical modernity. "Contrary to imperialism, the Empire does not establish a territorial center of power and is not based on borders or fixed barriers. It is a decentralized and deterritorialized apparatus of government that gradually integrates the space of the entire world within its perpetually expanding open frontiers" (E. 17).

With Westphalian states out of the picture, "governance" is exercised beyond and above governments. However, the decline of nation states has not actually caused sovereignty to disappear. The Empire holds a new form of sovereignty exercised by supra- and transnational organisms "united under a single logic of government" (E. 16). Within the Empire, a totality with no exterior and no outside, "Capital and sovereignty become totally confounded" (M. 380). The Empire is the political form of capitalist globalization. The "politics" of the Empire is no longer based on the state's fictitious unity, the general will, or popular sovereignty, for global "governance" itself tends to become "fractal," i.e., "to integrate conflicts not by imposing a coherent social apparatus, but by controlling differences" (E. 411). No longer building itself upon the centrifugal forces of nation states, imperial normativity—the New World Order—has been established on the ruins of state sovereignty. The Empire is without spatial limits ("no territorial frontier limits its reign") or temporal limits (it presents itself as "an order that genuinely suspends the course of history, and thereby fixes the present state of affairs for eternity"). Abolishing space and time, the Empire "presents its power not as a transitory moment in the flow of history, but as a regime without natural frontiers, and thus in this sense outside history or at the end of history" (E. 19). Bereft of center, it only exists by constantly extending the limits of its grasp. The Empire is "smooth," a non-place.

Hardt and Negri also note that the expansion of this new dominant system is no longer carried out in the name of any right of conquest, but above all in the name of peace — in the name of the right of "humanitarian" intervention and interference. At the same time, the return of "just war" (*bellum justum*) makes of war an "intrinsically self-justifying activity" (*E.* 36), the enemy being at once banalized (reduced to the object of a police action legitimized by universal values) and absolutized (he becomes a figure of Evil threatening the world's moral order). "Imperial justice," a series of techniques based on a permanent state of emergency and the use of an international police power, is confounded with a right of justified interference in the name of superior ethical principles. The Empire's expansionist tendency is thereby radically distinct from that of the old imperialism, which consisted essentially in the expansion of the nation-state. The space of the old imperialism necessarily had an external geographical boundary; the Empire abolishes the distinction between exterior and interior. Instead of being "exclusive," the Empire is fundamentally *inclusive* insofar as it presents itself as the primer for a universal republic.

The two authors go on to affirm, forcefully, that neither the United States nor any other country constitutes the Empire's center. Far from being its heart or motor, the United States merely holds one piece among others of the Empire's apparatus: "Contrary to what the last advocates of nationalism maintain, the Empire is not American."[13] Going still further, Hardt and Negri state that the United States is in no way itself an imperialist power: "The United States is not the center of an imperialist project; and in fact, no state can be today. Imperialism is over. No nation henceforth will be a world power as the nations of Europe used to be" (*E.* 18).

With the Empire, capitalism causes economic and political

---

[13] Toni Negri, "L'‘Empire,' stade suprême de l'impérialisme" ["The ‘Empire': Supreme Stage of Imperialism"], *Le Monde diplomatique*, January 2001, 3.

power to fuse into a single order as it pushes the coincidence between morality and law to an extreme point. It thereby constitutes the very model of "biopower," in the sense that it tends to rule not only human interactions but also human nature (his knowledge and affects). "Biopower" must be understood here in the manner of Michel Foucault,[14] a power issuing from state administrations, non-governmental organizations, multinational corporations, transnational institutions, and agents of "governance," which henceforth tend to manage the most intimate aspects of daily life and the private sphere, i.e., this power itself tends to produce the totality of social relations and forms of life. Biopower results from the interpenetration of the economic, the political, the social, and the cultural. By producing cultural goods, forms of existence, and affects, biopolitical power ends by transforming consciences (subjectivities) and bodies—in short: life itself.

The emergence of biopower marks the passage from the old (modern) disciplinary society to the (postmodern) society of surveillance and control, whose main characteristic is the increased interiorization of constraint:

> While disciplinary society puts the population to work and assures itself of obedience thanks to a ramified network of institutional apparatuses that produce and rule customs and practices (the school, the workshop, the prison, the asylum), the society of control is familiar with mechanisms of mastery that are ever more democratic and immanent throughout the social realm: power is exercised from now on thanks to machines that directly organize brains (communication systems, information networks) and bodies (employment benefits and supervised activities) in the direction of an autonomous state of alienation.[15]

---

[14] Cf. Michel Foucault, "Naissance de la biopolitique" ["Birth of Biopolitics"], in *Dits et écrits* [*Said and Written*], *III: 1976–1979* (Paris: Gallimard, 1994), 818–25; and *Défense de la société* [*Defense of Society*] (Paris: Seuil-Gallimard, 1997).

[15] Céline Spector, "La multitude ou le peuple? Réflexions sur une

The Empire's constitution, as described by Hardt and Negri, "is formed neither on the basis of a contractual mechanism nor by the intermediary of a federative source. The source of imperial normativity is born of a new machine at once industrial, commercial and communicational — of a globalized biopolitics within which economic production and political constitution, far from forming a hierarchy or determining each other in the final instance, tend increasingly to coincide."[16]

Up to this point, Hardt and Negri offer a fairly good description of the transfer of sovereignty happening today from states toward supra- or transnational organisms, the deterritorialization of the dominant forces, and the rise of a global form of "governance" exercised at the expense of governments. Taking polysemy into account, however, one might debate the aptness of the word "empire" to describe this new reality. In any case, the informal concept of empire, as opposed to the formal empire that extends itself by successive territorial conquests, is not as new as the two authors suggest. It has been used in the past to describe many non-military attempts at domination (acculturation, corruption of local elites, etc.), including in Antiquity, and is found in the modern age in so-called dependency theories (Immanuel Wallenstein), and even in neo-Marxist theories of monopolistic capitalism (Paul Baran, Paul Sweezy).[17]

The thesis according to which the Empire has in some sense neither Capital nor "emperors" is even more questionable. Hardt and Negri are not wrong to say that the New World Order has no absolutely identifiable center (which is normal, for it is present everywhere). But it does not follow that certain countries do not benefit from it more than others, that they are not its motors or vehicles more than others, nor that there do not exist elites corresponding to it. In reality, there most certainly

---

politique de la multiplicité" ["The Multitude or the People? Reflections on a Politics of Multiplicity"], *Critique*, November 2003, 885.

[16] Spector, "La multitude ou le peuple?," 882.

[17] On the different present-day uses of the concept of empire, cf. Danilo Zolo, "Contemporary Uses of the Notion of Empire," *Jura Gentium*, 2007, 1.

does exist a transnational elite — the global New Class — which, however decentralized and globalized it may be, nonetheless represents the heart of this new power: a deterritorialized transnational elite to accompany a deterritorialized transnational economy. That this elite is informal rather than institutionalized does not make its existence any less real. This elite controls international markets, while the political elites in the proper sense constitute the part of the transnational elite that controls the New World Order's politico-military dimension. In being unable to identify this new global elite, Hardt and Negri differ from the theoreticians of the New Class (Paul Piccone, Christopher Lasch, etc.) who, most often referring to Theodor Adorno and his theory of "artificial negativity," see in the emergence of this New Class the key step in the advent of a "totally administered society." Moreover, as we shall see, while the theorists of the New Class propose to go back to what remains of the traditions and customs of pre-modern organic societies, Hardt and Negri undisguisedly celebrate the process of capitalist modernity by affirming that it is opening up new paths of action.

Moreover, both authors remain totally indifferent to the diffusion of specifically Western, and more especially Anglo-Saxon, values and criteria of well-being across the entire world under the disguise of "cosmopolitanism." Their statement that the United States is not an imperial power, and therefore that anti-imperialism now only amounts to a reactive "sovereignist" nostalgia, makes them forget the role played by Washington in the most recent wars. More generally, it prevents them from seeing that hegemonic phenomena are still present today via *soft power*, and that current American politics means to be active on a world scale more than ever. Atilio A. Boron, for whom *Empire* "contains very serious diagnostic and interpretive errors," goes so far as to say that "another victim of the Iraq War is Hardt and Negri's theoretical construction."[18] He adds:

Imperialism is neither an accessory fact nor a policy conducted by a few states, but a new stage in the develop-

[18] Boron, *Empire and Imperialism.*

ment of capitalism. This stage is marked, today more than yesterday, by the concentration of capital, the crushing dominance of monopolies, the growing role of finance capitalism, the exportation of capital, and the division of the world into several "spheres of influence."[19]

"In fact," write Jérôme Maucourant and Bruno Tinel, "it does not seem to us as established, unless one wishes to skip over reality, that the American state and nation have dissolved into an imperial form of government on a world scale."[20] Indeed, the reality of American imperialism cannot be contested. Hardt and Negri's mistake is to think the rise of the Empire has put an end to it, whereas the two coexist. The truth is that globalization certainly includes the United States, which is not its only motor (although its principal vehicle), but nevertheless American military, political, and "ideological" hegemony continues to make their effects known. Reducing the real to certain new tendencies—of which they declare rather hastily that they have abolished all that preceded them—Hardt and Negri do not see that the contemporary world remains a place where different and contradictory logics intertwine.

Danilo Zolo, for his part, maintains that it is still perfectly legitimate to speak of a "global empire" to describe the American political system in a geopolitical, systemic, normative, and ideological sense. He adds that for Hardt and Negri, "Empire" tends to become a pure mental category, which poses obvious problems for those who mean to combat it. On the one hand, if everything is imperial, to the point that nothing remains that isn't, then we can just as well say that nothing is imperial (the use of the term amounts to an arbitrary convention); on the other hand, the question obviously arises: "If we exclude the politico-

---

[19] Boron, *Empire and Imperialism*.

[20] Jérôme Maucourant and Bruno Tinel, "Avènement du néocapitalisme: d'une internationalisation à une transnationalisation des économies?" ["Advent of Neocapitalism: From an Internationalization to a Transnationalization of Economies?"], text uploaded on March 28, 2003. They add: "More generally, the whole problem is that Hardt and Negri mistake what they wish for what is" (ibid.).

military apparatus of the great Western powers, in particular that of the United States, who is carrying out imperial functions?"[21] In other words, who or what must we oppose?

But it is when judgement must be passed on the "Empire" that the real debate begins. Hardt and Negri announce this at the outset, in fact; for them, the Empire is not something bad. Quite the contrary. By putting an end to the system of nation-states and substituting for it a cosmopolitan perspective, it has done something rather positive. Hardt and Negri congratulate themselves on the Empire's cosmopolitanism. They adhere to it fully. What they want is merely to extend this cosmopolitanism by taking advantage of the circumstances that have allowed its imposition in order to give it a more "just" form: the "imperial" constitution must be preserved, but placed in the service of non-capitalist ends. In other words, it is a matter of controlling or regulating the Empire, "perfecting" it, but in no case of destroying it (E., 416). The construction of the Empire in this sense represents a "step forward." The Empire is *progress*, "better than what preceded it" (E., 434).

Obviously, the same goes for globalization, which is good because it has created "new circuits of cooperation and collaboration that cut across nations and continents, thus giving rise to an unlimited number of encounters and interactions" (M., 7), and because it "tends to blur the borders separating political, economic, social, and cultural forms of power and production" (M., 380).[22] In the same spirit, Hardt and Negri state that the current

---

[21] Danilo Zolo, *La Justice des vainqueurs. De Nuremberg à Bagdad* [*Victor's Justice: From Nuremburg to Bagdad*] (Paris: Jacqueline Chambon, 2009), 153. Cf. also the debate between Antonio Negri and Danilo Zolo published as "L'Impero e la moltitudine. Un dialogo sul nuovo ordine della globalizzazione" ["The Empire and the Multitudes: A Dialogue on the New Order of Globalization"], *Reset*, 73, 2002, 8–19 (reprinted in *Jura Gentium*, 2005, 1, then in Antonio Negri, *Guide. Cinque lezioni su Impero e dintorni* [*Guide: Five Lessons on Empire and Its Surroundings*] (Milan: Raffaello Cortina, 2003], 11–33). The complete version of this interview has only been published in English, in *Radical Philosophy*, no. 120, 2003, 23–37.

[22] This is why in 2005 Negri publicly supported a "yes" vote on the

decline in international law is rather a good thing (*M.*, 47). We therefore need not less, but more globalization: "Instead of resisting the much-decried globalization, we should accelerate the process so as to build new democratic structures meant to benefit the exploited forces as soon as possible."[23] This way of proceeding is based on taking into account capitalism's ambiguity. On the one hand, it has generalized human exploitation; on the other, it is — by the same title as many currents that oppose it — the vehicle of an intrinsic cosmopolitanism that can only be applauded. Thus, the Enlightenment philosophy that engendered liberalism is good *per se*. It must merely be purged of its dross.

But Hardt and Negri go still farther. Not only is the Empire not something bad, since its inspiration is fundamentally good, but — divine surprise! — it offers superior possibilities of "creation and liberation." Why? Because, says Antonio Negri, "the legal order of the global market does not simply mark a new form of supreme power that it tends to organize: it also registers powers of life and insubordination, of production and class struggle that are new."[24] The key idea here is that the Empire itself generates the conditions leading to its own transcendence insofar as by its very functioning it ends up creating the historical agent that will succeed it, viz., the "multitude," a key concept we will say more about below: "Globalization, insofar as it carries out a real deterritorialization of old structures of exploitation and control, is really a condition of the multitude's liberation" (*E.*, 82). In other words, the authors say explicitly, the Empire is good *in itself* but not *for itself*.

Rosa Luxemburg explained that capitalism's expansion, always going out from a central area in order to gradually absorb the margins, has regularly occurred at the expense of an external world. Today there is no such world, for capitalism has extended

---

referendum on the proposed European Constitutional Treaty which in his view represented a step forward in the weakening of existing forms of sovereignty ("Cette merde d'État-nation" ["This Damned Nation State"], *Libération*, May 13, 2005), which earned him a lot of criticism. Yann Moulier-Boutang took the same position.

[23] Spector, "La multitude ou le peuple?," 883.

[24] Negri, "L'"Empire,' stade suprême de l'impérialisme," 3.

its grasp over the entire planet — or very nearly. This means, for Hardt and Negri, that the Empire can only be challenged from within. This is not wrong, but what is peculiar to Hardt and Negri is drawing the much more debatable conclusion that an internal struggle cannot take the form of frontal opposition. This is why they condemn any form of radical contestation of globalism, whether it occurs in the name of localism, ecologism, the old class struggle, popular cultures, Third-Worldism, communitarian thought, classical Marxism, etc. Against localism, for example, Hardt and Negri state that "the strategy of local defense is harmful, because it obscures and even denies the real alternative solutions and the possibilities for liberation that exist within the Empire" (E., 75). Anti-imperialism is similarly declared "reactionary," for in fact it can only end by reinforcing the power of nation-states (or creating new ones). Finally, it is equally useless to try to reconstruct the old welfare state, as certain Left-wing parties attempt in order to confront the challenges of globalization.

To try to justify their way of proceeding, Hardt and Negri take shelter behind Karl Marx. "We say," they write, "that the Empire is better in the same way Marx affirmed that capitalism was better than the forms of society and modes of production that preceded it" (E., 73). It was in fact the rise of capitalism that put an end to feudalism. Just as it would be a serious error to oppose capitalism in the name of the order that it succeeded, it would be every bit as serious an error to oppose the Empire in the name of the political sovereignty of states. "So *non-global* philosophy must be rejected, as well as any form of naturalistic ecologism and localism, as primitive and anti-dialectical positions, i.e., as essentially 'reactionary.'"[25] But Hardt and Negri forget that Marx, although he did congratulate himself upon the elimination of the feudal system by the bourgeoisie, nevertheless proposed to establish an anti-systemic force radically opposed to the system in place, namely capitalism, while the strategy preached by Hardt and Negri has absolutely nothing anti-systemic; quite the contrary. Marx, in other words, did not refer-

---

[25] Zolo, *La Justice des vainqueurs*, 153.

ence the role capitalism had played in the past to say we must compromise with it or expect any liberation from its development. He rather proposed to confront it head on,[26] while Hardt and Negri assure us that we must above all not try to destroy the Empire. The comparison therefore quickly breaks down.

In fact, Antonio Negri limits himself to recycling old Italian "workerist" theories from the 1970s according to which the development of capitalism can fundamentally be explained as a reaction to workers' struggles, i.e., to the inventions and development of the world of work, since only the movements of the proletariat produce history. Technological innovations, for example, are not the result of competition on the global markets between companies, but a response to the "organized threat" of the proletariat—which is obviously entirely false. In the 1970s, "workerism" defended the idea that the workers are the only artisans of the revolution, since they are the only ones who, starting from the factory, can drive Capital to develop in a liberatory direction. Totally rejecting parties and unions, along with all forms of struggle exterior to the factory, "workerism" thus claimed to "put back into motion a positive mechanism of capitalist development." Since only the working class was creative, the grip of Capital became a mere reactive crystallization of confiscated proletarian energy. As late as 1977, Negri was able to write that "only the construction of capitalism [*sic*] can give us truly revolutionary conditions." As Anselm Jappe has well observed, for Hardt and Negri, in the last analysis, "capitalist development is nothing but a parasitic and repressive redirection of what the proletarian spontaneously creates in his desire for freedom,"[27] which amounts to saying that the limit of capitalism

---

[26] One might also say that Marx simply thought capitalism was better in the sense that it was worse—the worst social system can objectively be called "better" in the sense that it better clarifies the battle lines and arouses more resolute opposition.

[27] "Les habits neufs du marxisme traditionnel" ["Traditional Marxism's New Clothes"], in Anselm Jappe and Robert Kurz, *Les Habits neufs de l'Empire. Remarques sur Negri, Hardt et Rufin* [*The Empire's New Clothers: Remarks on Negri, Hardt, and Rufin*] (Paris: Lignes-Léo Scheer, 2003), 37. Cf. also Anselm Jappe, *Les Aventures de la marchandise. Pour*

does not lie in its internal contradictions, but only in the subjectivity of the exploited.

It was by adopting this scheme that denies any possibility of capitalism's autonomous development that the two authors could present the Empire as the result of social struggles, whereas Marx perfectly demonstrated that one of capitalism's great characteristics is to organize the production of its own demands. In their books, Hardt and Negri maintain that the emergence of the Empire is itself already a positive response to a social critique prior to the power of globalization's political domination. In this sense, the Empire represents a "victory of the proletariat" (*sic*) marking the birth of a new possibility for dissent. "The constitution of the Empire," they write, "is not the cause, but the consequence of the emergence of the power of the multitude" (*E.*, 394), which means that the Empire is merely Capital's reaction to the transformations of labor imposed by the multitude, and to the new social relations that follow from this. Globalization must all the more be accepted in that it is itself the result of concessions that Capital has been forced to make to the forces of subjectivity, thereby constituting a possible source of a different globalization.

*

"The Empire is constructing a biopolitical order because production has become biopolitical," states Antonio Negri.[28] That means that the emergence of the Empire as a paradigm of biopower is indissociable from the appearance of a new form of production, viz. "immaterial" labor, which is defined by Hardt and Negri as "labor that produces a non-material good such as a service, a cultural product, knowledge, or communication" (*E.*, 355). This category, perceived straightaway as "biopolitical," covers service activities, research, innovation, education, computer science, advertising, marketing, communication, cultural industries, and so on. Characterized especially by the penetration of cognitive labor into the sphere of production, immaterial labor,

---

une nouvelle critique de la valeur [*The Adventures of Commodities: Toward a New Critique of Value*] (Paris: Denoël, 2003), 274.

[28] Negri, "L''Empire,' stade suprême de l'impérialisme," 3.

which also includes "the production and manipulation of affect" (*E.*, 358), henceforth represents the dominant form of social labor by contrast with industrial labor, now in decline:

> The secondary sector tends to disappear, in capitalist countries, to the benefit of services. Insofar as labor becomes cognitive, intellectual, it can no longer be quantified. . . . Formerly, capitalist exploitation concerned the brute labor of workers, and the place where that exploitation occurred was the factory. Today it is intellectual aptitudes and affective needs that are exploited.[29]

Of course, Hardt and Negri know quite well that the dominant model of work in the world today is still of the Taylorist sort, so that on the world scale classical exploitation remains hegemonic. They also know that about half the planet's population is still working in agriculture. But they think they must emphasize the tendency that seems to them most pregnant of the future: "An overall analysis is only good insofar as it is illuminated by the tendency that governs its evolution." Immaterial labor is in the process of dethroning industrial labor in the same way industrial labor was in the process of replacing agriculture in the nineteenth century, i.e., it is the tendency that forces even other forms of labor to adopt its characteristics. In this context, one might compare the transition from (exclusive) material property to (reproducible and shared) immaterial property to the transition from immovable property to movable, or the transition from exploitation by rent to exploitation by profit. This is why Hardt and Negri constantly insist on the "ontological" centrality of immaterial labor:

> The object of exploitation and domination tends no longer to be especially productive activities, but the universal capacity to produce, i.e., abstract social activity and its total power. This abstract labor is an activity without a locus. . . . It is the social diffusion of living labor, both not belonging

---

[29] Negri, interview in *Philosophie Magazine*, 59.

to anyone and creative; it is the desire and the effort of the multitude of adaptable and mobile workers, and at the same time, it is the intellectual energy, and linguistic and communicative construction, of the multitude of intellectual and affective workers.

Commenting on this, Anne Herla remarks:

Immaterial labor is biopolitical labor *par excellence*, since it is not satisfied with creating material goods, but also produces relations and social life itself. Its modes of functioning are information, communication, cooperation. Its organization is typically post-Fordist: putting the stress on the flexibility of work time and mobility, it functions in smaller decentralized units that collaborate in the form of a network.[30]

The thesis maintained by Hardt and Negri is that this form of labor cannot be controlled or exploited as was done with earlier industrial labor, for it requires the free deployment of creative subjectivities and the spontaneous cooperation of workers beyond national borders. Immaterial labor is already situated beyond capitalism, since it has the capacity to realize its own value without being purchased by Capital, which amounts to saying that living labor can in the end create value without Capital's intervention: "What distinguishes immaterial labor is that its products are themselves in many respects immediately social and common" (*M.*, 141). In immaterial labor, surplus labor extracted from labor power is hard to translate into surplus value, and tends on the contrary to present itself as a "revolutionary excess." Decentralized and deterritorialized, but also cooperative and creative of shared value, immaterial labor develops by means of horizontal connections that tend to escape the Empire's vertical control. It is in all this that its liberatory potential resides.

---

[30] Anne Herla, "Empire et Multitude: la démocratie selon Antonio Negri" ["Empire and Multitude: Democracy According to Antonio Negri"], lecture for PhiloCité, January 23–25, 2007.

Hardt and Negri conclude first that immaterial labor also involves freedom of thought, which is bold to say the least,[31] but
above all the necessity of admitting that henceforward the deployment of Capital's guardianship across new forms of activity
is also what creates the possibility of escaping from it. As Thomas
Coutrot writes, "Its organization in collaborative networks allows the multitude not only to retake control of social production from Capital, but to seize control of society and radically
democratize it in spite of the Empire."[32] Biopower thus comes
down to the biopotential of subjects, a potential itself bioproduc-
tive.

In such a context, exploitation by Capital is no longer a certain relation between the quantity of necessary labor and the
quantity of surplus labor generative of surplus value, but is defined as "expropriation of what is in common" (*M.*, 184). Now,
as Perre Dardot observes:

> Such a redefinition is less innocent than it appears, inso-
> far as it rests on the idea that the wealth (in common)
> produced by immaterial labor is produced *outside* the
> control of capital. . . . This amounts to saying it is entirely
> impossible for capital to privatize the whole of the com-
> mon, that expropriation is condemned to remain *partial*,

---

[31] The more immaterial labor there is, Negri assures us, "the more
freedom of thought is necessary to be productive" (interview in *Philosophie Magazine*, 60). This is to blind oneself to the compatibility of immaterial labor with mass conformism. As Slavoj Žižek writes, "Today,
freedom of thought signifies the freedom to question the predominant
liberal-democratic 'post-ideological' consensus — or else it does not signify anything" (*Que veut l'Europe? Réflexions sur une nécessaire réappro-
priation* [*What Does Europe Want? Reflections on a Necessary Reappropriation*] [Castelnau-le-Lez: Climats, 2005], 98). Cf. also Slavoj Žižek, "Have
Michael Hardt and Toni Negri Rewritten the *Communist Manifesto* for
the Twenty-First Century?," *Rethinking Marxism*, 2001, nos. 3–4.

[32] Thomas Coutrot, "'Multitude' et démocratie: le saut périlleux"
["'Multitude' and Democracy: The Dangerous Leap"], in Alain Caillé,
ed., *Quelle démocratie voulons-nous? Pièces pour un débat* [*What Democracy
Do We Want? Pieces for a Debate*] (Paris: La Découverte, 2006), 50.

and, consequently, that a "common surplus" is thus constituted upon which the multitude increasingly draws to produce ever more common wealth.[33]

This is in fact what Hardt and Negri maintain. "Cognitive labor is extremely difficult for Capital to digest," Negri assures us.[34] Once immaterial labor generalizes reproducible and shared property, exclusive and privatized property "becomes a fetter for the capitalist mode of reproduction," adds Michael Hardt.[35] Here again, Hardt and Negri, starting from a correct observation (with Bill Gates, "private property in the means of production" no longer means much), draw a conclusion that is both dubious and optimistic, to say the least. By proclaiming that Capital is henceforth "in people's brains" (in immaterial labor, the instrument of labor is the brain, instruments of production themselves becoming prostheses of brains), Hardt and Negri state contrary to all reality, that Capital has ceased to impose itself as a social relation.

Here again, Hardt and Negri think themselves able to appeal to Marx in alleging the Marxian concept of "*general intellect*" to analyze the phenomenon of the Internet and immaterial labor more generally in a direction scarcely different from the discourse of the theorists of the "web economy" and "fortunate globalization." In his *Grundrisse* (1857–1858), Marx in fact announced, by means of his considerations on the "*general intellect*," the massive integration of intellectual-cognitive labor into productive labor. But he saw in this only an element aggravating the contradictions inherent in the law of value. If he was one of

---

[33] Pierre Dardot, "À propos de la multitude" ["As Regards the Multitude"], *Mouvement*, March–April 2005, 146.

[34] Toni Negri, "Communisme: quelques réflexions sur le concept et la critique" ["Communism: Some Reflections on the Concept and the Critique"], in Alain Badiou and Slavoj Žižek, eds., *L'Idée du communisme* [*The Idea of Communism*] (Paris: Nouvelles éditions Lignes, 2010), 224.

[35] Michael Hardt, "Le commun dans le communisme" ["The Common in Communism"], *L'Idée du communisme*, 164. Cf. also *M.*, 147: "In immaterial production the creation of cooperation has become internal to labor and thus external to Capital."

the first to observe that "science, a product of the general intellect of the development of society, also appears directly incorporated into Capital," it was to add immediately that "its application to the process of material production [is] independent of the knowledge and capacity of the individual worker."[36] Under these conditions, it seems rather abusive to appeal to Marx to support the idea that immaterial labor largely escapes the grasp of Form-Capital. In speaking of "immaterial labor" as a synonym for "intellectual labor power" or "general intellect," Hardt and Negri are clearly guilty of misinterpretation.

Moreover, the way Hardt and Negri speak of knowledge as the principal source of value and profit in "immaterial labor" often falls into a sort of fetishism of knowledge or intelligence (without taking into account individual inequalities in cognitive capacities, of course). Jacques Guigou and Jacques Wajnsztejn write on this subject that "the pretention to reduce what has been defined as general intellect to the individual capacity of self-valorization allowed by the development of science and technology is ridiculous. These intelligences are subjected to the machine with an inversion of the prosthetic function, which makes its vehicles reproducers of what exists."[37]

The very concept of "immaterial labor" must be examined more closely. Even without subscribing to Michel Husson's opinion according to which, as concerns the organization of labor, "we uncover no tendency toward a rise in the power of the cognitive model sufficient to supplant today's dominant model, which can be described as neo-Taylorist,"[38] it must first be

---

[36] Karl Marx, *Un chapitre inédit du "Capital"* [*An Unpublished Chapter of "Capital"*] (Paris: UGE/10–18, 1971), 249.

[37] Jacques Guigou and Jacques Wajnsztejn, *L'Évanescence de la valeur. Une presentation critique du groupe Krisis* [*The Evanescence of Value: A Critical Presentation of the Krisis Group*] (Paris: L'Harmattan, 2004), 134.

[38] Michel Husson, "Sommes-nous entrés dans le capitalisme cognitif?" ["Have We Entered the Era of Cognitive Capitalism?"], *Critique communiste*, Summer–Autumn 2003. "What happens in a South Korean automobile factory remains at least as important as what is exchanged between two flexible and nomadic computer users," writes Serge Quadruppani ("Notes critiques sur le livre de Toni Negri et Michael

remarked that, strictly speaking, immaterial *labor* quite simply does *not* exist. What exists is immaterial *production*, which in fact is tending to increase today, but which nonetheless most often remains the result of quite concrete labor. (And there is also, of course, an immaterial capital that likewise continues to develop by means of financial capitalism.) To confuse an activity — productive labor — with its result — the nature of the thing produced — is already clumsy. To draw from the rise in immaterial *production* the conclusion that "immaterial *labor*" has intrinsic emancipatory virtues amounts to setting little value on the concrete working conditions of those who participate in that production, whether in developed countries or the Third World. In fact, cognitive capitalism tends rather to *reinforce* the constraints imposed on workers, and not to lighten them, since henceforward the production of Capital demands the domination of every social form: "The upheaval brought by information and communication technology allows capitalism to seize the worker's time for living not only during his working hour but also outside them."[39] "Technological transformations," adds Michel Husson, "are taken advantage of the better to control workers. The constraints they undergo have never been so heavy, and the new technologies are taken advantage of to exercise an increasingly tight and individualized form of control."[40] This is what Thomas Coutrot established through a whole series of field studies.[41]

But it is an even more serious matter to confound this "immaterial labor" with the "abstract labor" mentioned by Marx, by writing, for example, that "through the computerization of production, work tends toward the position of an abstract form of labor" (*E.*, 357). It is true, on the one hand, that "concrete labor is

---

Hardt" ["Critical Notes on the Book of Toni Negri and Michael Hardt"], *No Pasarán* [2001]).

[39] Jean-Marie Harribey, "Le cognitivisme, nouvelle société ou impasse théorique et politique" ["Cognitivism: A New Society or a Theoretical and Political Impass?"], *Actuel Marx*, September 2004, 151–80.

[40] Husson, "Sommes-nous entrés dans le capitalisme cognitif?"

[41] Cf. Thomas Coutrot, *Critique de l'organisation du travail* [*Critique of Work Organization*] (Paris: La Découverte, 1999).

an act, a deed, which is always material, i.e., an expense of energy and time, fatigue, stress; and whether it is predominantly
manual, intellectual, or relational does not change this."[42] On the
other hand, in speaking of abstract labor, Marx in no way al-
ludes to the growing degree of labor's or production's "immate-
riality." He merely wants to say that labor of whatever sort always has an abstract dimension because of its social character, or
more precisely because the market validates a fraction of its social character through the exchange of merchandise, thus allowing the particular character of singular labor carried out by the
producers to be forgotten:

> Under capitalist conditions, *all* labor—even in mines or
> workshops—has an abstract aspect, because it represents a
> certain quantity of time necessary for its production.
> Computerization does not render labor more abstract than
> it was before. The labor that creates merchandise is always
> at once abstract *and* concrete.[43]

In fact, Hardt and Negri's considerations on immaterial labor
fit into the framework of what has been written for the past
twenty years on "cognitive capitalism," a concept first spread by
Yann Moulier-Boutang[44] but that has also been studied by André Gorz.[45] This concept is fairly close to the "computing capitalism" of which Manuel Castells speaks in the first volume of
his trilogy on time in networks,[46] or indeed to certain ideas of

---

[42] Harribey, "Le cognitivisme, nouvelle société ou impasse
théorique et politique."

[43] Jappe, "Les habits neufs du marxisme traditionnel," 30.

[44] Yann Moulier-Boutang, *Le Capitalisme cognitif. La nouvelle grande
transformation* [*Cognitive Capitalism: The New Great Transformation*], 2nd
ed. (Paris: Amsterdam, 2008). Cf. also Christian Azais, Antonella
Corsani, and Patrick Dieuaide, eds., *Vers un capitalisme cognitive* [*Toward
a Cognitive Capitalism*] (Paris: L'Harmattan, 2000).

[45] André Gorz, *L'Immatériel. Connaissance, valeur et capital* [*The Immaterial: Knowledge, Value, and Capital*] (Paris: Galilée, 2003).

[46] Manuel Castells, *La Société en réseaux*, vol. 1: *L'Ère de l'information*,
[*The Network Society*, vol. 1: *The Era of Information*], trans. Philippe

Bernard Stiegler.[47] As for the idea of an opposition between the old vertical hierarchies and the self-regulating networks functioning in a horizontal way, it is similar to what Pierre Lévy has written on the "collective intelligence" that would result from the "interconnection between computers and brains on a planetary scale."[48]

"Cognitive capitalism" refers to the new regime of Capital accumulation that is today tending to substitute itself for the Fordist and Taylorist capitalism of old mass production. Its theorists also connect it to the rise of an "immaterial economy," defined as one in which knowledge becomes the principal productive force. This economy is naturally associated with the development of new computing and communication technologies, beginning with computer science (the Internet), and, at the social level, with the rise of networks. The free software movement is paradigmatic of this "brain cooperation." Just as immaterial labor tends to supplant industrial labor, cognitive capitalism is called upon to succeed industrial capitalism in the same way the latter (in part) succeeded the original commercial capitalism. Yann Moulier-Boutang speaks in this context of a "third sort" of capitalism whose emergence will amount—alluding to the famous book by Karl Polyani—to a new "Great Transformation." Studying this development, the "cognitivists" assure us that it will involve not merely feedback between consumption and production, but also an "autonomization of the sphere of knowledge production as a sphere of capitalist accumulation unto itself" (Antonella Corsani).

Marx said that the real subject of the capitalist economy is *value* itself (the "automatic subject"). Now, according to the "cognitivists," a fundamental trait of cognitive capitalism is that it involves a questioning of the concept of value, whether one thinks living labor is no longer a source of value or whether one

---

Delamare (Paris: Fayard, 1999).

[47] Bernard Stiegler, *Pour une nouvelle critique de l'économie politique* [*For a New Critique of Political Economy*] (Paris: Galilée, 2009).

[48] Pierre Lévy, *L'Intelligence collective* [*Collective Intelligence*] (Paris: La Découverte, 1997).

thinks every instant of life must be included in living labor, which amounts to saying that everything is productive of value, that value is everywhere. Affirming that time today no longer simply measures value, certain writers, such as Yann Moulier-Boutang and Antonella Corsani, conclude that the law of value has disappeared. Others, like Hardt and Negri, tend to say that, since value is no longer measurable, one can just as well say it is everywhere—another way of saying that it is nowhere. In any case, since capitalism's grasp can no longer be calculated in terms of labor time and surplus value, the Marxian theory of value must be abandoned, for it would be impossible today to distinguish between productive labor, reproductive labor, and unproductive labor. (The "cognitivists" do not go so far as to reject the distinction between living and dead labor.)

Negri thus writes that the law of value "has become useless," that it has lost "all meaning in view of boundless social accumulation, since the most important form of fixed Capital is henceforth found in the brain."[49] The rise of immaterial labor, we also read in *Multitude*, supposedly has the consequence that "exploitation no longer amounts merely to the extraction of surplus value measured by individual or collective labor-time, but that it is above all the capture of a value produced by cooperative labor and that tends, by circulating within social networks, to become common value" (*M.*, 141). Carlo Vercellone similarly states that the rise in knowledge calls into question

> the theory according to which unmediated labor-time devoted to an activity of material production is the principal productive source of human labor. . . . At the theoretical level, escaping industrial capitalism would toll the funeral bell of the law of labor-value. And on the political level, the only way out would be to accompany the evolution of

---

[49] The critique made by Hardt and Negri of the Marxian theory of value had already been developed by a neo-workerist such as Maurizio Lazzarato. Cf. Maurizio Lazzarato and Antonio Negri, "Travail immatériel et subjectivité" ["Immaterial Labor and Subjectivity"], *Futur antérieur*, no. 6, Summer 1991.

this form of capitalism . . . which promises to each worker the chance to "produce himself."[50]

This obviously poses the question of whether the production of value remains the goal of capitalist production or not. If the exchange value of merchandise is no longer determined by the quantity of general labor they contain but by their content in information and knowledge, and if crystallized knowledge has replaced crystalized labor, what becomes of the very concept of value and the possibility of measuring it? And above all, what about value as *social relation*?

Like a number of other "cognitivists," Hardt and Negri once again appeal to certain Marxian texts, in particular the passage where he envisages a mutation such that the creation of real wealth comes to depend "less on labor-time and the quantum of labor employed than on the power of the agents set in motion in the course of labor-time": "As soon as labor in its immediate form has ceased being the great source of wealth," writes Marx, "labor-time ceases necessarily to be its measure, and consequently, exchange value ceases to be the measure of use value."[51] But Hardt and Negri read this passage wrongly. Marx in fact is speaking of the growing gap between living labor and the use value of the wealth created, not of a growing gap between labor and value. This is why he notes, quite correctly, that Capital's tendency "is always to create disposable time on the one hand, and on the other to convert it into surplus labor."[52] Marx, in other words, is indicating the contradiction between merchandise and the socialization of productive forces—by expressly emphasizing that, to resolve it, "it must be the working masses themselves which appropriate their own surplus labor"—whereas the theoreticians of cognitive capitalism refer to this socialization to make it the principle of a new form of capitalism.

---

[50] Harribey, "Le cognitivisme, nouvelle société ou impasse théorique et politique."

[51] Karl Marx, *Manuscrits de 1857–1858. Grundrisse*, trans. Jean-Pierre Lefevre, vol. 2 (Paris: Éditions Sociales, 1980), 192–93.

[52] Marx, *Manuscrits de 1857–1858*, 196.

The "cognitivists," in the end, think that the creation of wealth no longer fundamentally rests on labor-time, but on the level attained by science and information technology. "It is increasingly upstream from the sphere of 'salaried work and the commercial world' in society, and especially in the system of education and research, that the key to productivity and the development of social wealth is found."[53] From this they conclude that "with respect to the emergence of knowledge, the Marxian theory of value no longer holds," because "labor is no longer the source of value, and labor-time is ceasing to be its measure."[54] In reaching this conclusion, and even though their initial observation is not incorrect, they are making at least three mistakes.

The first consists in confusing wealth and value (as exchange value, monetary and commercial), unlike Marx, who emphasized the difference between the two concepts, specifying that labor is not the only source of wealth, but the only source of value.[55] It was even the dissociation between value and wealth that allowed Marx to point out one of the major contradictions in Capital's logic, since it is indeed Capital that confines the economy to the sphere of exchange value, where wealth is merely a means. It is clear that, if we do not take that distinction into account, it is impossible to understand why the enormous gains in productivity recorded by capitalism have not resulted in proportionate levels of abundance, nor to any fundamental restructuring of social labor.

Their second mistake is to confuse value and the law of value, or, if you prefer, the creation of value by productive forces and

---

[53] "Table ronde sur le capitalisme cognitif" ["Roundtable Discussion of Cognitive Capitalism"], *Regards*, April 2003, 260.

[54] Antonella Corsani, "Le capitalisme cognitif: les impasses de l'économie politique" ["Cognitive Capitalism: The Impasses of Political Economy"], in Carlo Vercellone, ed., *Sommes-nous sortis du capitalisme industriel?* [*Have We Exited from Industrial Capitalism?*] (Paris: La Dispute, 2002), 65.

[55] David Ricardo had noted this before him: "The labour of a million of men in manufactures, will always produce the same value, but will not always produce the same riches" (Chapter 20, 320, of *Principles of Political Economy and Taxation*, third ed. [London: John Murray, 1821]).

the conditions of that creation, i.e., the social relations within which they operate. As Jean-Marie Harribey writes:

> The development of productive forces leads to the gradual exclusion of living labor from the process of production and, in the long run, the value of merchandise, a development that reinforces the incorporation of increasingly greater knowledge. This exclusion does not constitute a negation of the law of value as a tendency, but is its strict application. . . . The law of value is not "obsolete" in the field of economy; it has never been more valid.[56]

In cognitive capitalism we behold a degeneration of value, but not a degeneration of social labor within the law of value.

The third mistake, finally, is to confound, starting from an observation of feedback effects between production and consumption in the domain of computing, the irreducible difference between use value and exchange value, forgetting that the former is of a practical or symbolic order, while only the latter is of an economic order.

In reality, Hardt and Negri never seriously question the concept of value. As Robert Kurz notes:

> For them, form-value (that fetishized form that makes a product a commodity) is simply an ontological given in which humanity realizes itself. . . . In this regard, Hardt and Negri are not equal to their ambitions, for to want to make a critique of capitalism without taking the form of value and its valorization into account is similar to wanting to make a critique of religion without taking the concept of divinity into account.[57]

Indeed, the ultimate goal of capitalism is still to augment surplus

---

[56] Harribey, "Le cognitivisme, nouvelle société ou impasse théorique et politique."

[57] Kurz, "L'Empire et ses théoriciens" ["The Empire and Its Theoreticians"], in Jappe and Kurz, Les Habits neufs de l'Empire, 86–87.

value (profit) and not the quantity of goods. Growth in the quantity of goods is merely the consequence of the constant attempt to augment surplus value. (In other words, it is not because we sell more commodities that profits increase, but it is because we want profits to increase that we sell ever more commodities, which amounts to saying that capital is a process of creating surplus value by way of producing commodities, and this process permanently transforms living labor into dead labor.) This is why we can conclude that, today as formerly, capitalist production is founded on value tied to the extraction of surplus labor, and that the knowledge of which Hardt and Negri make so much is merely the current form of living labor that Form-Capital tends to transform into dead labor.

Some Marxist economists have, of course, reacted with a certain harshness against Hardt and Negri's distortions of Marx's thought. Michel Husson, for example, thinks that modern forms of commodity, far from leading to the obsolescence of the law of value alleged by the advocates of "cognitivism," allow us to rediscover "the absolutely classic contradiction between the form assumed by the development of productive forces and capitalist relations of production."[58] The fact is that Hardt and Negri entirely forget Marx's pages devoted to commodity reification (*Verdinglichung*) and commodity fetishism. Anselm Jappe even goes so far as to say that categories as central as commodity, labor, and money are not the object of any particular analysis in

---

[58] Michel Husson, "Le capitalisme contemporain et Marx" ["Contemporary Capitalism and Marx"], *Droit social*, 2008, 2, 238. The same author writes elsewhere:

> The thesis concerning the passage from labor value to "knowledge value" must be rejected for the following reasons: knowledge value does not exist within the field of capitalist social relations; capitalism integrates the workers' knowledge with their productive power as it has always done; and the law of value continues to hold, with renewed brutality and breadth, "thanks" to generalized commodification. ("Notes critiques sur le capitalism cognitif" ["Critical Notes on Cognitive Capitalism"], *Contretemps*, February 2007).

Hardt and Negri—any more than they criticize labor as a form of social life and sphere separate from life:

> The authors of *Empire* accept these categories in their appearance as natural, ontological, anthropological categories exactly as does bourgeois science. . . . In their eyes, labor and Capital stand in the same relation as the plenum and the void. . . . For them, the multitude is an absolute and ontological positivity, whereas the "Empire" is a mere void, the absence of being and production. This is naturally incompatible with any analysis of fetishism or alienation.[59]

At the practical level, the whole question is whether "cognitive capitalism" is better or worse than the forms of capitalism that preceded it. There are clearly some reasons for considering it to be worse, since it results in a generalized alienation of the totality of social life, but Hardt and Negri resolutely adopt the contrary view, as we have seen. They maintain that cognitive capitalism, far from representing a new form of domination, opens previously unknown paths of liberation.

Hardt and Negri's thesis rests, let us remember, on the debatable idea that "cooperative networks of production" can henceforth emancipate themselves from the tutelage of capital by way of the "absolutely democratic" character of the network form (insofar as, in a network, the "immaterial laborers" can freely compare their creativity and their subjectivity). The rise in unemployment, and the diminution of the fraction of surplus value taken up by salaries, are not therefore the objects of any particular consideration for them. Flexibility and precariousness, which

---

[59] Jappe, "Les habits neufs du marxisme traditionnel," 16 and 25. For a critical view of "cognitive capitalism," cf. also Michel Husson, *Un pur capitalisme* [*A Pure Capitalism*] (Lausanne: Page Deux, 2008) and David Forest, "De quoi le 'capitalisme cognitif' est-il le nom?" ["Of What Is Cognitive Capitalism the Name?"], *Quaderni*, Winter 2009–2010, 1–5. Cf. also Pierre Dardot, Christian Laval, and El Mouhoub Mouhoud, *Sauver Marx? Empire, multitude, travail immatériel* [*Saving Marx? Empire, Multitude, Immaterial Labor*] (Paris: La Découverte, 2007).

allow an increase in the levels of labor-power's exploitation, are positively evaluated. Far from interpreting the rise of immaterial labor as the emergence of a sinister system for the domestication of bodies, aggravated by the mobility and "flexibility" of employment, Hardt and Negri celebrate its virtues to the point of singing paeans to social precariousness,[60] opposing the rhizomatic example of the excluded, the nomad, the precarious worker to the enslaved rootedness of the worker with stable employment. The exclusion suffered is thus magically transformed into a voluntary and liberating exile, the flexibility of employment into a promising form of nomadism!

The facts in no way confirm immaterial labor's intrinsically liberating virtues. "Nothing allows us to affirm that the individualized labor of a telemarketer, a part-time advertising agent, someone who runs a business from his home, is more liberating than labor power's collective organization," observes Daniel Bensaïd.[61] André Gorz, moreover, was able to maintain the exact opposite thesis, emphasizing that labor's loss of material substance is expressed by increased alienation. Thomas Coutrot for his part observes that

> the neo-liberal enterprise in the form of a network in fact articulates, in a very hierarchical manner, quite heterogeneous forms of organization. . . . These forms are articulated not thanks to intersubjectivity and affective communication, but by fearful disciplinary processes: the fixing of goals, competition, a permanent process of selection. The mobility of Capital, in contrast with the relative immobility of labor, gives it the social power to orient workers' productive activity in a manner that suits it, and to appropriate gains in efficiency. . . . To claim that organization in the form of a network naturally gives actors, independently of their position within the network, control over their

---

[60] Cf. Toni Negri, "Refonder la gauche italienne" ["Refounding the Italian Left"], *Le Monde diplomatique*, August 2002.

[61] Daniel Bensaïd, *Éloge de la politique profane* [*In Praise of Profane Politics*] (Paris: Albin Michel, 2008), 288.

activity and over the network is absurd. In current forms of business organization one need only examine the concentration of income to the benefit of the holders of Capital and the insecurity imposed on workers to convince oneself of this: "collaborative networks" are in no way a guarantee of greater power or autonomy for the workers, even if they are "immaterial."[62]

Neither are the connections between the decentralization of decision-making and democracy obvious. Here, Hardt and Negri's error consists in "hypostatizing a technical or organizational form, attributing to it an intrinsically liberating content, reducing the complex dialectic between technology, organization, and social relations to an unequivocal determinism."[63] In reality, relations of production cannot be escaped *en masse*. "One does not collectively desert the system of exploitation and domination. One must either undergo it or confront it in order to break it."[64] Far from uncovering or manifesting great emancipatory potential, "cognitive capital" marks above all the entry of Form-Capital into an era where it tends to rid itself of all "rigidities" and "archaisms" that still hamper it, and of all regulations imposed on it by a century of social struggles.

*

Intellectual labor, say Hardt and Negri, is intrinsically associated with sharing and common production. This "common," consisting in information, knowledge, and emotional and affective relations, is both the condition for and the result of today's predominant form of labor—but of course it has nothing to do with what is generally understood under this term. It does not found a community, for it has neither unity nor identity. The "being in common," for Hardt and Negri, is merely the activity of producing what is common. The Communism of singularities is thus rigorously opposed to the communitarianism of identity. Besides, the common is "the incarnation, production,

---

[62] Coutrot, "'Multitude' et démocratie: le saut périlleux," 51–52.
[63] Coutrot, "'Multitude' et démocratie: le saut périlleux,"53.
[64] Bensaïd, *Éloge de la politique profane*, 301.

and liberation of the multitude" (*E.*, 303). The stronger the hegemony of immaterial labor, the more the power of the "multitude" is supposed to grow.

Thus we arrive at the key concept of *multitude*, which Hardt and Negri make the new historical subject of our age. The "plural multitude of subjectivities productive and creative of globalization," they affirm, constitutes the "other head of the imperial eagle." It is supposedly the "living alternative growing within the Empire itself" (*M.*, 7). So it must be examined in detail.

Negri defines multitude as the "desire to construct the common," in which respect it is the ontological foundation of all society. But in reality, this concept of multitude is never defined clearly or analytically with reference to given sociopolitical categories. Hardt and Negri are content to say that it constitutes an "ensemble of singularities" forming an imminent collective body.[65] The important point is to see that it must not on any account be perceived as a "totality" in the fashion of a people, but as an "open multiplicity," i.e., a mere collection of individuals endowed with the attributes of power. Here we come back to the liberal definition of collectivities. "The multitude," write Hardt and Negri, "is a multiple subject, differentiated within, which is not constructed and does not act from any principle of identity or unity (and still less of indifference), but from what is common to it" (*M.*, 126). Michael Hardt adds that "the multitude is multiplicity rendered powerful."[66] Thus it is a social body without organs; a community of interested behavior, desires, and needs; an ensemble of singularities preserving their differences, but able to think and act in common without the least mediation. This, moreover, is why the multitude, borrowing its form from immaterial labor, is today organizing itself in networks. This is clearly a definition that leaves one wondering—as Didier Muguet has noted, for whom "this term which recurs on almost

---

[65] From this one can deduce that "every body is already a multitude" (*sic*). Negri also says that "the multitude's flesh wants to transform itself into the body of the general intellect," *Multitudes*, June 2002.

[66] Michael Hardt, *Gilles Deleuze: An Apprenticeship in Philosophy* (Minneapolis: University of Minnesota Press, 1993), 110.

every page of the book and which serves as the basis of its argument is in fact a sort of chameleon signifier, a rather inconsistent evocation: in fact, a real catch-all."[67] Still more radically, Daniel Bensaïd writes that the concept of multitude is at once "theoretically confused, sociologically inexact, philosophically obscure, and strategically empty."[68]

As we have just seen, rather than "subject" (a Cartesian concept), Negri systematically speaks of "singularity" (a Spinozian concept) to designate the individual. An important and significant reference: the term "multitude" (*multitudo*) is in fact taken from Spinoza, whom Negri considers the first philosopher to have given a materialist framework to human existence. More precisely, the author of the *Ethics*, read here in light of Deleuze and Guattari's "materialistic ontology," is perceived not merely as one of the first philosophers to have deconstructed the central concept of *subject*, but also as one of the first to have opposed multitude (singularities) to the people and inscribed the democratic aspiration within the horizon of immanence, i.e., as a thinker of the power of a multitude of singularities acting in co-operation. This line of reasoning, let us note in passing, is part of a larger "back to Spinoza" movement affecting a number of authors such as Étienne Balibar, Giorgio Agamben, Pierre Macherey, Jacques Bidet, Frédéric Lordon, Alexandre Matheron, etc.[69] For Hardt and Negri, it is Spinoza's "prophetic desire" that "must be reactivated so that the multitude can sabotage the parasitic power of the Empire and reappropriate the fruit of

[67] Didier Muguet, *EcoRev: Revue critique d'écologie politique*, Spring 2005. The author concludes that "Hardt and Negri's analysis can only lead to catastrophic political results."

[68] Bensaïd, *Un monde à changer* [*A World to Be Changed*] (Paris: Textuel, 2003), 68–89, and *Éloge de la politique profane*, 279.

[69] Cf. Céline Spector, "Le spinozisme politique aujourd'hui: Toni Negri, Étienne Balibar . . ." ["Political Spinozism Today: Toni Negri, Étienne Balibar . . ."], *Esprit*, May 2007, 27–45. Cf. also André Tosel, "Des usages 'marxistes' de Spinoza. Leçons de méthode" ["Some 'Marxist' Uses of Spinoza: Lessons in Method"], in Olivier Bloch, ed., *Spinoza au XXe siècle* [*Spinoza in the Twentieth Century*] (Paris: PUF, 1993), 515–25.

the cooperation of living labor — its productive force within the biopolitical mode of production."[70] But we must recall here that Spinoza is generally considered one of the great ancestors of liberalism precisely insofar as he was the first to proclaim the autonomy of subjectivity's internal space in politics.[71] The rereading of Spinoza by the two authors is therefore often forced. Negri, for example, passes over in complete silence that for Spinoza the multitude must be led "as if by a single mind." "Spinoza is indeed the thinker of the power constitutive of the multitude; is he really the thinker of its self-organization without mediation or representation?" asks Céline Spector.[72]

Inasmuch as the Empire, understood ontologically, is supposed to produce subjectivities capable of resisting it, Hardt and Negri affirm that a new theory of subjectivity is necessary. "After a new theory of surplus value," they write, "a new theory of subjectivity must be formulated that fundamentally functions *via* knowledge, communication, and language." The goal is nothing less than to transform the multitude into a mass of intelligent productivity, which would create the conditions for absolute democracy! In fact, one may ask, along with David Sherman, whether this theory does not fall back into the logic of identity peculiar to the Enlightenment dialectic by limiting itself to invoking a perfectly empty subjectivity founded on an "artificial positivity" that characterizes one of the worst aspects of current "imperial" domination.[73]

---

[70] Spector, "La multitude ou le peuple?," 31.

[71] Cf. Carl Schmitt, *Le Léviathan dans la doctrine de l'État de Thomas Hobbes* [*The Leviathan in the State Theory of Thomas Hobbes*], trans. Denis Trierweiler (Paris: Seuil, 2002), 117–18. Cf. also Manfred Walther, "Carl Schmitt et Baruch Spinoza ou les aventures du concept du politique" ["Carl Schmitt and Baruch Spinoza or the Adventures of the Concept of the Political"], in Bloch, ed., *Spinoza au XXe siècle*, 361–74.

[72] Spector, "Le spinozisme politique aujourd'hui," 38. Cf. also François Zourabichvili, *Le Conservatisme paradoxal de Spinoza* [*The Paradoxical Conservatism of Spinoza*] (Paris: PUF, 2002).

[73] Cf. Sherman, "The Ontological Need: Positing Subjectivity and Resistance in Hardt and Negri's *Empire*." Cf. also Sergio Bologna, "Proletari e Stato di Antonio Negri" ["Proletarians and State in Antonio

Hardt and Negri, it is true, also say that we must not so much ask ourselves what the multitude is as what it "can become" (*M.*, 131). The multitude, in other words, is mainly of value as a tendency or process that reveals a socio-historical subject already at work in the present, and at the same time pregnant with the future. The multitude is supposed to be "the tendency by which the social subject that already exists seeks to affirm itself as the political subject that it still is not."[74] The question becomes: What renders this "social subject" especially apt to constitute itself as a political subject?

In fact, thanks to the concept of multitude, it is mainly a matter of warding off any temptation to hypostatize a historical subject in a unified manner, whether this subject is the people, class, revolution, or proletariat. The opposition between *multitude* and *people* is especially marked, which justified Céline Spector's remark that "the concept of multitude, at first glance, appears as an obvious substitute for the concept of the people, discredited because of its structural connection with the genesis of modern sovereignty in the form of the nation state."[75] Besides, Negri explicitly defines the concept of multitude as opposed to that of people: "As opposed to the concept of people, the concept of multitude is that of a singular multiplicity, a concrete universal. The people constitutes a social body; the multitude does not, for the multitude is the flesh of life."[76]

So let us take up this issue. For most political theorists, the people is fundamentally distinct from the multitude in that it is endowed with particularities proper to it and that make it a sort of person at once moral and socio-historical, while the multitude is merely an anonymous multiplicity, an undifferentiated mass. In this context, the multitude receives a pejorative sense: it marks the limit beyond which or short of which politics sinks

---

Negri"], in *Primo Maggio*, quoted by Steven Wright in *Storming Heaven: Class Composition and Struggle in Italian Autonomist Marxism* (London: Pluto Press, 2002), 170.

[74] Dardot, "À propos de la multitude," 144.

[75] Spector, "La multitude ou le peuple?," 886.

[76] Negri, "Pour une définition ontologique de la multitude."

into formlessness or chaos. This is the sense Plato gives to *okhlos*, the "multitude," and also which Cicero attributes to *multitudino effrenata*, the "unchained multitude." In the best case, as in Hobbes, the multitude refers back to the pre-political state preceding the institution of the social contract. The multitude, says Hobbes, has no political being. It partakes of the state of nature or civil war, while the people is "something unified, having a will, and to which an action can be attributed." This is why "we give the public person the name of people rather than that of multitude."[77] Besides, in the history of political science, whether in Hobbes, Hegel, or Rousseau, the concept of people is produced from the transcendence of the sovereign. It is by positing itself as a transcendent power that the state was able to construct the people and identify itself with them, even as it imposed its sovereignty upon them. National identity thus associated itself with popular sovereignty, which produced it as the final representation of itself. The people is therefore a correlate of sovereignty.

Spinoza, on the other hand, presents an image of the multitude that directly breaks with all these classic political theories. While they put the stress on an external power's necessary mediation on society in order to reconcile the contradictory aspirations of which it is the locus, Spinoza believes in the spontaneous development of collective forces that require no state mediation to harmonize with one another (we are not very far here from the liberal theory of the "invisible hand"). This is why Hardt and Negri appeal to him.

The leading trait of the "absolute democracy" the authors advocate is to reject any form of sovereignty, whether national, statist, or popular. "The multitude cannot be sovereign," they say explicitly (*M.*, 375). Even better, it "banishes" sovereignty "from politics" (*M.*, 386). "If the multitude must form a body, this must remain an open, plural composition without ever becoming a unitary entity divided as a function of hierarchized organs" (*M.*, 226). Making the *transcendence of the one* the condition of the social bond, political sovereignty inevitably engenders a form of

---

[77] Thomas Hobbes, *De Cive* (1642), XII, 8.

domination.[78] Now, continue Hardt and Negri, from the moment individuals produce social relations autonomously, thus constituting themselves as a multitude, any form of unitary sovereignty becomes superfluous. The multitude is a multiple that cannot be reduced to the one: "The people is one; the multitude, by contrast, is multiple" (M., 8). Since any form of sovereignty implies transcendence, and therefore domination, Hardt and Negri mean to break with such transcendence by returning to the concepts of subjectivity, immanence, and multitude. Since multitude is just as immanent as "imperial" power, Negri deduces from it that its "ontological power can eliminate the relation of sovereignty today." The relation between imperial biopower and the multitude does not, therefore, have a dialectical character.[79] Instead, it configures a "sequence of events" produced by the creative activity of new forms of subjectivity.

All that remains is to dissociate the concept of power from that of sovereignty. This is what Hardt and Negri do by taking up the old dichotomy between *potentia* and *potestas*. The potentiality of being in Spinoza is constituted spontaneously as a movement of emancipation. In his *Political Treatise*, Spinoza emphasizes that the holders of *potestas* never have anything more than the *potentia* accorded them by the multitude. Negri takes from this the idea that the "expression of potentiality" can never signify "the institution of power." It is in this sense that he too speaks of the "power of the multitude" (*potentia multitudinis*): power involving no sovereignty, but which resides in the teeming and multiform creativity continually produced by the "common."

---

[78] We note that Hardt and Negri do not manage to conceive of sovereignty except on the model of Jean Bodin, who defines it as indivisible. The concept of divided sovereignty completely escapes them.

[79] Antonio Negri is abandoning here the dialectic he still defended a few years ago. Another great merit of Spinoza is supposedly to have escaped any consideration of a dialectical character: if God is confounded with the world's substance, there is no reason to make humanity's final redemption depend on any "reconciliation" with an alienated nature.

Hardt and Negri are thus proposing a "new science of democracy" (*M.*, 394) rid of everything that suggests politics, beginning with popular sovereignty. The sovereign in their eyes is necessarily an oppressor. The "destruction of sovereignty" is explicitly cited as a precondition for the "construction of democracy" (*M.*, 399). This negation of politics is said to be all the more justified in that cooperative networks of production are supposed to engender a "new institutional structure" (*M.*, 396). In the end, the alternative "sovereignty or democracy" is called upon to replace the alternative "sovereignty or anarchy." This allows democracy to be redefined as something other than the popular sovereignty with which it has always been identified. After this Hardt and Negri once again emphasize that, in contrast to the people, the multitude tends towards a play of differences that is not the vehicle of any identity (*M.*, 125). It is precisely in this that its intrinsic value lies: "The people's identity is replaced by mobility, flexibility, and the permanent differentiation of universal multiplicity" (*E.*, 416). Then it becomes possible to "dissolve the concept of people at the same time as that of nation." We come to understand that recourse to the "multitude" is in fact a means for denying the autonomy of politics and getting the people (and peoples) out of the way.

"The concepts people, proletariat, and social classes are henceforward obsolete," affirms Antonio Negri.[80] But this does not prevent him from saying that the multitude is a "class concept" (*M.*, 129) and that it is simply a new name for the proletariat, or even that it incarnates the "new subjective figure of the proletariat." Obviously, this is only possible by completely redefining what is to be understood by "social class" and "proletariat." As is well-known, it has been a long time since Marxist theoreticians themselves have identified the proletariat exclusively with the working class. Hardt and Negri are thus breaking down an open door when they write: "We understand the proletariat as a vast category including all those whose labor is directly or indirectly exploited by the capitalist norms of production and reproduction to which it is subject" (*E.*, 27). The problem is

---

[80] Negri, interview in *Philosophie Magazine*, 59.

that by claiming "all forms of labor tend to proletarianize themselves" (*E.*, 315), they end by including everybody and anybody
in the proletariat. Whereas social class is obviously an exclusive
concept, the multitude is an inclusive concept, meaning that
nearly everybody can be put into it: "If we posit the multitude as
a class concept, the concept of exploitation will be defined as the
exploitation of cooperation: cooperation not between individuals, but between singularities, exploitation of the totality of singularities, of the networks that compose the totality, and of the
totality that includes the networks."[81] Being composed "of all
the different figures of social production" (*M.*, 9) and of "the totality of those who work under the guardianship of capital," the
"cooperating multitude" can then be posited as a "universal
class force." Since the distinction between productive labor, reproductive labor, and unproductive labor has become elusive,
everyone (or very nearly) can be considered as a "proletarian."
Unlike class, multitude does not presuppose any primacy of salaried over unsalaried labor, nor even of labor over non-labor.
"What determines the belonging of the multitude," observes
Pierre Dardot, "is, in the end, participation in production understood as the production of scientific and practical knowledge
and information."[82] Negri himself goes so far as to speak of a
"new cognitive proletariat." This "cognitariat" will replace the
proletariat, unless they are Internet users . . . or consumers.[83]

Hardt and Negri in fact have all the less difficulty affirming
the classic social classes' disappearance in that they have posited
from the beginning the vanishing of the law of value in "cognitive capitalism." This is what allows them to reject both the people and the proletariat in the traditional sense of the term. The
spontaneous movement of the desiring masses, the defense of
the constitutive power of the free play of subjectivities, the
"power to act upon bodies," and the cooperation of "swarms of

---

[81] Negri, "Pour une définition ontologique de la multitude."

[82] Dardot, "À propos de la multitude," 144–45.

[83] The same idea is supported by Alexander Bard and Jan
Soderqvist (*Netocracy: The New Power Elite and Life After Capitalism*
[London: Reuters, 2002]).

intelligence" replace the class struggle. It is no longer a class point of view, but the "multitude's" point of view that must be adopted to judge politics and the state.

So what remains of Marxist theory in their work? Not a lot, as we have already seen regarding the question of value. Marx is in fact systematically revised in light of Spinoza and Deleuze. When they write, for example, that "real revolutionary praxis refers to the level of production" (*E.*, 201), Hardt and Negri immediately redefine "production" not as economic production, but also as "production of the desiring machine" or "production of subjectivity," since classic industrial production today is tending to give way to the computing model of the rhizome or the network. The opposition between dominant and possessing classes and dominated classes is also totally transformed. Not only is there no more working class, but power can no longer be defined in terms of economic relations of production. Finally, the old dialectic no longer lets us grasp the reality of social relations, nor the deployment of material processes of production, since "imperial sovereignty is no longer organized around a central conflict, but around a mobile network of micro-conflicts and evanescent contradictions, proliferating, impossible to locate."[84] Hardt and Negri thus only take up Marx's ambitions by denaturing them, their redefinition of the concept of social class having the particular advantage of letting us scrap that of class struggle.

*

Biopolitics, in this context, is defined as that force immanent to the social realm that creates relations and forms of life through a cooperative form of production. "When the multitude works," write Hardt and Negri, "it produces in an autonomous fashion and reproduces the entire world of life. To produce and reproduce in an autonomous fashion means to construct a new ontological reality" (*E.*, 475). The problem with a procedure founded on "ontology" is obviously that it is not of much practical use for knowing what must be done to arrive at the emancipation sought. What about ontological praxis? In the third part

---

[84] Spector, "La multitude ou le peuple?," 884.

of *Empire*, Hardt and Negri inquire how the multitude could establish itself as a political subject. Their answer is vague, at the very least, if it does not result in utopian demands of considerable banality. We learn here that it is by producing its own life that the multitude appropriates its power, that this production is identical to the appropriation of language and communication, and that the multitude's political coming-to-be is carried out on the grounds of exodus, nomadism, and flight and desertion. But what does this mean, concretely?

The only thing fairly clear is the general strategy, for it follows directly from the initial analysis. The basic idea, as we have seen, is that the evolution of Capital itself furnishes the instruments for liberating oneself from it, since it favors the "autonomy that has accrued to the common." By provoking a deterritorialization and a generalized dissolution of traditional social relations and bonds, globalization at the same time liberates potentially centrifugal forces that the dominant system does not have the means to control. That is how we can explain the "proximity between the idea of Communism and capitalist production" (*sic*): "The idea is not that capitalist development creates Communism or that biopolitical production brings liberation directly or immediately. In fact, it is through the centrality that has accrued to the common in capitalist production—the production of ideas, affects, social relations, and forms of life—that the conditions and weapons for a Communist project emerge. In other words, capitalism creates its own gravediggers."[85] Paradoxically, this statement takes on the character of a new dialectics: "The deterritorialized power of the multitude is the productive force that supports the Empire, and is at the same time the force that calls for and makes necessary its destruction." "We know," say Hardt and Negri, "that capitalist production and the life (itself productive as well) of the multitude are bound ever more closely and mutually determine one another" (*M.*, 116).

Capitalism is already functioning in the fashion of the networked multitude, so it is no longer a matter of combatting or

---

[85] Hardt, "Le commun dans le communisme," in Badiou and Žižek, eds., *L'Idée du communisme*, 174.

even resisting it, but only of reorganizing and reorienting it toward new ends. The multitude will not take "power" by revolution, or by violence, or by a general strike, but by redirecting to its own profit the new social characteristics it owes to the Empire: "The forces of the multitude that support the Empire are just as capable of constructing a counter-Empire, i.e., a substitute political organization for exchange and global currents" (*E.*, 20). We must "theorize and act both *within* and *against* the Empire" (*E.*, 21). This is why Negri rejects any frontal attack, or any idea of political action conceived on the friend-enemy model: "In no case is it a matter of returning to an opposition between power and the multitude, but of allowing the multitude to liberate itself from power by means of the immense networks that constitute it and the finite strategic determinations that it produces."[86]

In the age of the Empire, the "revolutionaries" no longer need to reason in terms of strategy and tactics, maneuver and position, strong points and weak points. It is enough for them to give way to a spontaneous desire for change that will be realized under the influence of the free cooperation of their subjectivities.[87] Revolution is no longer necessary, since to change the world, it is enough to delegitimize "the power of institutions and of the potentialities that hold it by removing growing autonomous spaces from Capital's planetary grasp." The example they cite is "freeware," or even financial capital: "Insofar as [financial capital] is oriented toward the future, we can, paradoxically, discern in it the emerging face of the multitude, even if it takes on an inverted and distorted form [*sic*]" (*M.*, 324). So there is "no contradiction between reform and revolution": "The historic transformation we are witnessing is so radical that reformist propositions can be enough to lead to revolutionary changes!" We note that, in passing, Hardt and Negri recommend an "ontological break with the workers' movement's

---

[86] Negri, "Pour une définition ontologique de la multitude."

[87] "It is indeed a question," notes Céline Spector, "of favoring the spontaneity of social movements over the organization of revolution by betting on productivist ontology more than on historical determinism" ("Le spinozisme politique aujourd'hui," 32).

ideological traditions" (*M.*, 258) . . .

Imperial power draws its vitality from the multitude, but the multitude draws its own from the very existence of this power. In this context, imperial power becomes, at its limit, "the negative residue, the retreat of the multitude's operation; it is a parasite that draws its vitality from the multitude's capacity to create ever new sources of energy and value" (*E.*, 436). In short, the best way to struggle against the Empire is to accelerate its establishment—or, if you prefer, to consider that succumbing to imperial logic is the best way to resist it! This is what Hardt and Negri quite seriously maintain when they write, for example, that "the Empire creates and governs a truly global society whose autonomy grows in proportion to the Empire's dependence on it" (*M.*, 381), or that "the more Capital extends its global networks of production, the more each particular point of revolt is—perhaps—powerful" (*E.*, 89). The statements become truly Orwellian at this point: the best way to struggle against capitalism is . . . to help it become more powerful. Total alienation is the key to emancipation!

We cannot be surprised, under these conditions, that authors such as Takis Fotopoulos and Alexandros Gezerlis have been able to see in *Empire* a "reformist message welcoming neoliberal globalization."[88] With Hardt and Negri it is no longer a matter of saying, as Marx did, that the system in place is destined to destroy itself through its own power, to ruin the political forms that allowed it to secure its domination, or to succumb to its own internal contradictions, but to state outright that the system is intrinsically the vehicle of positive virtualities insofar as the model that allows us to resist it is the same one that allowed its emergence. Instead of postulating the idea of a necessary break, Hardt and Negri, convinced that the conditions of emancipation flow from premises already existing in the dominant ideology, limit themselves to defining the "counter-Empire" as a

---

[88] Takis Fotopoulos and Alexandros Gezerlis, "Hardt and Negri's *Empire*: A New Communist Manifesto or a Reformist Welcome to Neoliberal Globalization?," *Democracy and Nature: The International Journal of Inclusive Democracy*, July 2002.

"substitute political organization for global exchanges and currents." This strategy has been described very well by Bruno Bosteels:

> Power is not a monstrous Leviathan . . . and resistance must not depend on the weakest link as the struggle's external articulation point. Power and resistance appear rather like the front and back of a Möbius strip. The idea is merely to push far enough that one surreptitiously transforms into the other.[89]

The advent of the Internet has played a considerable role in this way of looking at things, which explains Hardt and Negri's tendency to conceive global society on the model of the *network society* (Manuel Castells). Since the Web has become the very model of the social field, the "multitude" is supposed to appropriate the dominant imperial tendencies positively in the same way Internet users make use of the rhizomatic structure with neither center nor hierarchy to reappropriate knowledge and diffuse a form of counter-information. Thus the two authors write: "We can get an idea of the multitude's capacity for decision-making from the example of cooperative software development and the innovations that see the light of day in the Open Source movement. One can see the democracy of the multitude as an Open Source society" (*M.*, 385). "Communism will be realized by an army of software microentrepreneurs," observes Anselm Jappe ironically.

It is all the more striking to observe that Hardt and Negri never question the nature of technology and technoscience, nor even the content of the productive forces whose emergence they salute. While their entire theory is based on the development of new technologies, especially those of communication, we never see them take into account the ambivalence of technologies, or make the least substantive criticism of mechanization and

---

[89] Bosteels, "L'hypothese gauchiste: le communisme à l'âge de la terreur" ["The Leftist Hypothesis: Communism in the Age of Terror"], in Badiou and Žižek, eds., *L'Idée du communisme*, 68–69.

productivism (computers are *also* machines). "They do not say a word about the fact that, for at least sixty years, science and technology have declared war on human beings."[90] Quite the contrary, the technomorphism that surrounds us is for them eminently positive: "Not only do the multitude use machines for production, but it itself becomes increasingly mechanical, with the means of production continually better integrated into the multitude's minds and bodies" (*E.*, 488). "We know, however," observes Serge Quadruppani, "that there is no innocent form of technology, that a technology is always the product of given social relations, and that it is deeply marked and oriented by the needs of the dominant social form that produced it."[91]

As soon as it is a question of *organizing* the multitude, Hardt and Negri run into innumerable logical difficulties. How are we to imagine a politics with none of the characteristics of politics? A *potentia* without *potestas*? A decision without sovereignty? How do we get an institutional form to follow from the idea of the rhizome? How do we institute a "universal society" without putting international institutions in place? "The possible forces of disaggregation present in the 'multitudinous' society will be controlled and possibly sanctioned by a specific court of appeal," declares Negri.[92] But what will such a court of appeal consist of, who will establish it, and how can it, deprived of power, "control" or "sanction" anything? "The crucial question remains undecided: How do we make the multitude emerge as a political subject?"[93]

Convinced that modernity's political philosophy is finished, Hardt and Negri say they want to "invent a new grammar of politics."[94] But what sort? In an earlier work, Antonio Negri,

---

[90] Jappe, "Les habits neufs du marxisme traditionnel," in Jappe and Kurz, *Les Habits neufs de l'Empire*, 40.

[91] Quadruppani, "Notes critiques sur le livre de Toni Negri et Michael Hardt."

[92] Toni Negri, interview in *Philosophie Magazine*, 40.

[93] Spector, "La multitude ou le peuple?," 894.

[94] Cf. Antonio Negri, *Fabrique de porcelaine. Pour une nouvelle grammaire du politique* [*The Porcelain Workshop: For a New Grammar of Politics*], trans. Judith Revel (Paris: Stock, 2006).

rejecting any "constitutional" solution to the political problem, was already at pains to redefine constituent power as an irruptive force tied to "living labor," an "absolute procedure, all-powerful and expansive, without limit and without a preexisting goal,"[95] with no relation to its traditional procedural definition aimed at giving a basis of legitimation to constituted power. In this context, constitutive power becomes a mere synonym for "liberating" force, strictly anti-institutional and foreign to any form of sovereignty. But how do we reconcile constitutive power's *decisive* character with the simultaneous will to remove it from any logic of sovereignty? To do this, Hardt and Negri must have recourse to the idea of a decision that is not sovereign, but which imposes itself *qua* decision. So does the act of constitutive power arise from any process, or does it represent an event?

> Hence the theoretical confusion that comes through in *Multitude*'s last pages, all the way down to the vocabulary, in connection with the crossing of two lines of thought difficult to harmonize. On the one hand, the multitude's constitutive act is inscribed in the *continuity* of social production. . . . But on the other, it is said to "emerge from the multitude" or "from the ontological and social process of productive labor" (385, 397). Now, the concept "emergence" expresses the *arising of the new* in terms of qualitative *discontinuity*, and puts the emphasis on the irreducibility of what emerges to that from which it emerges, which is hard to reconcile with the idea of a preexistence of the decision itself in the common social being.[96]

Moreover, Negri has come out against participative democracy, which he describes as a "very hypocritical model."[97] But he also contests representative democracy—not without reason—

---

95 Antonio Negri, *Le Pouvoir constituant. Essai sur les alternatives de la modernité* [*Constituent Power: Essay on the Alternatives of Modernity*], trans. Étienne Balibar and François Matheron (Paris: PUF, 1997), 20

96 Dardot, "À propos de la multitude," 147.

97 Negri, interview in *Philosophie Magazine*, 40.

because it gives its blessing to the domination of representatives over those represented ("We must bury the concept of representation" [*M.*, 294]). He advocates a democracy based on the generalization of voting, but apparently without state or parliament. He adds that "if the multitude wins out over the Empire, we cannot, however, say that it will be in power, because the multitude is essentially the dissolution of power and the establishment of new institutions." Institutions without power, then. Here we are veering straight into an anti-political utopia.

To describe the new course of things, Hardt and Negri remain equally vague. It is supposedly a matter of "actually imposing everyone's freedom and equality, without exception," and of setting in motion a "redistribution of property." Negri also speaks of a "repartition of all goods, and of values tied to these goods" on the basis of a "principle of equality in common,"[98] without of course specifying who would take charge of this "repartition," what criteria shall govern it, and how it will be possible to impose it (and prevent it from being contested) without appealing to an authority, and therefore—inevitably— to a power. He also says that "the institutional figure who will assume management of what is in common will not necessarily be part of any state, the central thing being no longer to nationalize wealth but, on the contrary, to divide it into equal parts." To describe this ideal of integral egalitarian privatization, he specifies that "it will not be a matter of Communism imposed from above, but of something in common managed from below." Managed, of course, without the institutional figure charged with this task holding the least power. . . . *Wishful thinking.* As Daniel Bensaïd has noted, the "spontaneous" coinciding of singularities and of the common allows "evasion of the question how the multitude can transform its vital capacity to act in common into a political subject,"[99] the stress placed on the "common" allowing the pulverization of the classic distinction between public and private—to the benefit, of course, of the private sphere.

---

98 Negri, interview in *Philosophie Magazine*, 40.
99 Bensaïd, *Éloge de la politique profane*, 284.

"Only absolute democracy is capable of allowing and giving an account of the multiplicity of singularities that proliferate in the common," states Negri further.[100] Since "democracy of the multitude" is merely a fog without substance, we can never know what the "multitude in power" might look like. "Absolute democracy" is simply supposed to take the place of the classless society. "In this restored teleological historicism, the 'absolute concept of democracy' replaces the Hegelian absolute spirit, bringing back in its wake the temptation of preannounced ends of history."[101] In the end, what suits Hardt and Negri is a radical elimination of politics as a dimension proper to the public sphere productive of norms and legitimacy. In *Empire* as in *Multitude*, observes Judith Balso, "the thesis of the—absolutely contrived—possibility of finding support in the development of capitalism as an emancipatory figure gets transformed into the plain and simple annulment of politics as a separate, singular project."[102]

For the moment, everything "deterritorialized" is *ipso facto* considered potentially "democratic." Whence the importance Hardt and Negri give to communication, presented as the "central element that establishes relations of production, piloting capitalist development and thereby transforming the productive forces as well" (*E.*, 420). Because of its deterritorialized autonomy, they write, "the multitude's biopolitical existence has the potential to be transformed into an autonomous mass of intelligent productivity, i.e., into an absolute democratic power, as Spinoza would have said" (*E.*, 416). According to this line of reasoning, we must obviously congratulate ourselves on the disappearance of rooted ways of life, on the abstraction of political issues from the particular territories where they arise, and on the growing mobility of Capital—all tendencies that the "multitude"

---

[100] Antonio Negri, *Du retour. Abécédaire biopolitique. Entretiens avec Anne Dufourmantelle* [*Back Again: ABC of Biopolitics. Interviews with Anne Dufourmantelle*] (Paris: Calmann-Lévy, 2002).

[101] Bensaïd, *Éloge de la politique profane*, 310.

[102] Balso, "Être présent au présent" ["Being Present in the Present"], in Badiou and Žižek, eds., *L'Idée du communisme*, 38.

can use to its own profit in order to undermine the current beneficiaries of the imperial order's power. It is by rallying to the ideal of nomadism, exodus, or desertion that this multitude, rediscovering its constitutive power, will end by giving birth to the "hybrid" humanity supposed to represent its ideal: "By crossing within the multitude, by crossing multitude with multitude, bodies join, mix, hybridize, and transform themselves. They are like the waves of the sea in perpetual movement, in perpetual reciprocal transformation" (!)[103] Hardt and Negri thus advocate a cosmopolitanism "of desertion and lines converging at a vanishing point" (Alain Brossat), as Deleuze and Guattari do in *A Thousand Plateaus*. Here we are involved in a logic of mixture and flow that could rightly be called "maritime" ("like the waves of the sea"), by opposition to the telluric logic organized around the concept of border. This logic of the sea is immediately in harmony with "liquid" postmodern society.[104] The taste for hybridization here goes as far as madness, for example when Hardt and Negri maintain that "there are no fixed frontiers between man and animal, man and machine, male and female, and so on" (*E.*, 269). Unless it does not veer off into mere burlesque, as when the "kiss-ins organized by Queer

---

[103] Toni Negri, "Pour une définition ontologique de la multitude."

[104] On late modernity's "liquid" character, cf. Zygmunt Bauman, *Liquid Modernity* (London: Polity Press, 2000). On the opposition between sea and land logic, which is also an opposition between commercial and political logic, cf. Carl Schmitt, *Terre et Mer: Un point de vue sur l'histoire mondiale* [*Land and Sea: A World-Historical Meditation*], trans. Jean-Louis Pesteil (Paris: Le Labyrinthe, 1985). Negri, of course, is at the opposite extreme from Carl Schmitt, whose anti-universalist and anti-normativist positions, favorable to the emergence and maintenance of a "*pluriversum*" (as opposed to the "*universum*"), have been taken up again in the domain of international relations by the distant heirs of Grotius such as Martin Wight and Hedley Bull, defenders of great power equilibrium, preventive diplomacy, and multilateral negotiations between states. Cf. Martin Wight, "Why There Is No International Theory," in Herbert Butterfield and Martin Wight, eds., *Diplomatic Investigations: Essays in the Theory of International Politics* (London: Allen & Unwin, 1969) and Hedley Bull, *The Anarchical Society: A Study of Order in World Politics* (London: Macmillan, 1977).

Nation, during which men kiss one another and women kiss one another in a public place in order to shock the homophobes" are given as an example of "new weapons for democracy."

So concretely, the two works merely propose paths to follow. This is said quite clearly in *Multitude*'s closing pages: "This work cannot answer the question: What is to be done?" (*M.*, 403). It is true that Marx himself, who was not very eloquent on how the Communism to come was to be realized, was not interested in writing "recipes for the cookbooks of the future."[105] Nevertheless, the fourth part of *Empire* outlines three supposedly practical propositions: the right to a universal basic income, the right to reappropriate the means of production and communication, and the right to world citizenship. This list already makes it clear that we are not transcending the logic of *rights*, even as Hardt and Negri declare themselves hostile to legalism.[106] But by the same token, a classic question is posed once again: What is the value of law without the force to apply it, and without the means of coercion necessary to guarantee it concretely? Céline Spector asks:

> Who shall grant these "rights" within the legal constitution of imperial sovereignty? If such economic and social rights must be applicable at the level of the world community, don't they imply reinforcement by the international structures the authors condemn under the very name of Empire? Doesn't the very invocation of "law" . . . imply the reorganization of the despised structures of the rule of law, with no solution of continuity?[107]

The same point was made more strongly by Slavoj Žižek:

> It is paradoxical that Hardt and Negri, the poets of mobility, variety, and hybridization, formulate three demands by

---

[105] Karl Marx, *Le Capital* (Paris: Maurice Lachâtre, 1872), 349.

[106] He is following Spinoza on this point, who rejected the legal concept of the State that we find in Descartes as much as Rousseau or Hegel.

[107] Spector, "La multitude ou le peuple?," 895.

having recourse to the terminology of universal human rights. The problem with these demands is that they oscillate between empty formulas and impossible radicalization.[108]

The establishment of a "world citizenship" that Hardt and Negri define as a "reappropriation of space by the mobile multitude" (*sic*), is not the same in their eyes as the old cosmopolitan dream of a universal state, since any statist perspective is here rejected. It is to be understood rather as a matter of proclaiming a universal right of "mobility":

> Global space's virtual character constituted the first determination of the multitude's movements—a virtual character that must mutate into the real. . . . Circulation must become freedom. In other words, the multitude must arrive at world citizenship. (*E.*, 436).
>
> The general right to control one's own movements is the multitude's final demand concerning world citizenship. (*E.*, 481)

All migration is thus interpreted as a factor of emancipation:

> Autonomy of movement is what defines the place proper to the multitude. . . . The cities of the Earth are going to become at once great repositories of cooperating humanity and engines of circulation, temporary residences and distribution networks for living humanity. By way of circulation, the multitude reappropriates space and constitutes itself as an active subject. (*E.*, 477–78)

Laissez faire, laissez passer! But here again, how do we go beyond begging the question? There can obviously be no world citizenship where there is neither a world state nor world sovereignty. The "equal right of citizenship for all" is in this respect merely a pretense.

---

[108] Žižek, *Que veut l'Europe?*, 93.

The call to world citizenship in fact amounts to a call to suppress borders, which today in developed countries would have the effect of accelerating the installation of masses of low-salary workers from the Third World or the developing world—with consequences easy to imagine. That most migrants today owe their uprootedness to the endless dislocations brought about by the logic of the global market, that this uprootedness is precisely what capitalism seeks in order to adapt man more fully to the market, and finally, secondarily, that territoriality is part of natural human motivations does not bother Hardt and Negri in the least. On the contrary, they note with satisfaction that "Capital itself has demanded increasing mobility from its workers and continual migrations across national borders" (*E.*, 481). The world market therefore constitutes the natural framework of "world citizenship": "The ideology of the world market has always been the anti-essentialist discourse *par excellence*. Circulation, mobility, diversity, and mixture are the very conditions of its possibility" (*E.*, 194–95). Because it "demands a smooth space of non-coded and deterritorialized currents" (*E.*, 403–404), the world market is supposed to serve the multitude's interests, for mobility involves a price to be paid for capital, viz., an increased desire for liberation (*E.*, 312).

The drawback to this defense of uprootedness (and artificiality) considered as the first condition of a liberating "nomadism" is that it rests on a completely unrealistic view of the concrete situation of migrants and displaced persons. As Jacques Guigou and Jacques Wajnsztejn write:

> Hardt and Negri are deluding themselves about the capacity of immigration to be both the source of a new opportunity to valorize capital and the basis for an enrichment of the multitude's perspectives. Migration is in fact nothing more than a [Hegelian] moment of a universal competition. Migration *per se* is no more liberating that staying home. The "nomadic" subject is no more inclined to critique and revolt that the sedentary subject.[109]

---

[109] Guigou and Wajnsztejn, *L'Évanescence de la valeur*, 126.

Robert Kurz adds:

> As long as men leave their neighbors and go, even at risk
> of their lives, to look for work elsewhere—to be ground up
> by the capitalist mill, in the end—they will no more be ve-
> hicles of emancipation than the West's postmodern self-
> valorizers. They will merely be the poor version.[110]

All this discourse is part of an egalitarian project of the classic
type, with nothing new (or particularly postmodern) about it:

> In the common, there will exist neither proprietors nor
> discrimination tied to criteria of race, sex, gender, national-
> ity, religion. . . . All identities will have the right to exist as
> such while freely mixing, articulating themselves, and in-
> terlacing in a relation that will never become negative be-
> cause it will never involve the effacement of the singulari-
> ties thus placed in relation to one another. The multitude
> is not the effacement of differences; it is their permanence,
> including in experiments of miscegenation and mutual en-
> richment. . . . The institution of the family will only be le-
> gitimate in case it is freely chosen. . . . The community will
> take responsibility for the education of children; there will
> be no restrictions or taboos concerning gender preferences,
> the cultural models proper to this or that world, the domi-
> nant representations; it will be enough that the principles
> of equality, freedom, and respect can be verified.[111]

Once again, we are awash in the purest liberalism.

The other two propositions—the right to a minimum salary
and the right to reappropriate the means of production and
communication—also fail to convince because they are part of a
"universal" perspective that renders them inapplicable. Anselm
Jappe summarizes Hardt and Negri's program as follows:

---

[110] Kurz, "L'Empire et ses théoriciens," in Jappe and Kurz, *Les Habits
neufs de l'Empire*, 114–15.

[111] Negri, interview in *Philosophie Magazine*, 41.

This enumeration of pious wishes within the framework of a mushy utopia gives one the impression of a schoolboy rattling off a summary of every petty-bourgeois and proletarian illusion regarding an "equitable capitalism" of the past two centuries; it amounts to the two authors' intellectual suicide.[112]

It must also be remarked that Hardt and Negri, not content to cleanse the United States of any suspicion of imperialist practice, do not conceal that for them there is, in certain respects, an American *model*. "The American Revolution," they think, "represents a moment of great innovation and a break in the genealogy of modern sovereignty" (*E.*, 160). America's Founding Fathers in fact understood that "the order of the multitude should not emerge from a transfer of title in respect of power and law, but from an arrangement intrinsic to the multitude, from a democratic interaction of powers connected in a network." In this sense, the creation of the United States was a fortunate event: "From our point of view, the fact that a new Empire was formed against the old powers of Europe can only have been good news" (*E.*, 454). In the American Constitution, Hardt and Negri see the beneficent primer of the imperial Constitution because of "its concept of a frontier of unlimited freedom and its definition of an open spatiality and temporality celebrated in a constitutive power" (*E.*, 488). What they define as "Empire" would in any case be born of the "global expansion of the American constitutional project" (*E.*, 182)—a project rather close to Hans Kelsen's theses in legal matters. American sovereignty in fact makes no distinction between interior and exterior, inside and outside. Like Capital, the horizon of its deployment in potentially infinite.

This pro-American position comports oddly—or significantly—with certain references relying on Christianity. For Antonio Negri, who got his early experience with Catholic Action, this is a recurring temptation. His book on Job, written in prison, was

---

[112] Kurz, "L'Empire et ses théoriciens," 120–21.

already heavily impregnated with Christian dolorism.[113] To "clarify the future life of Communist militancy," Hardt and Negri do not hesitate to summon the figure of St. Francis of Assisi: "In postmodernity we will find ourselves in the same situation as St. Francis, opposing the joy of being to the poverty of power" (*E.*, 496). Moreover, Negri sees in the poor man both the "biopolitical subject *par excellence*" and the "foundation of the multitude" (*sic*).[114] The inspired rhetoric of the beatitudes is especially present in *Multitude*, whose last pages make clear the way in which, for Hardt and Negri, Communism is finally folded back into the Christian conception of love—i.e., *agape*. The two authors are in fact at pains to raise *love* once again to the level of a "political" concept:

> We must recover the public and political concept of love proper to pre-modern traditions. Christianity and Judaism, for example, both conceive love as a political act that constructs the multitude. . . . Divine love for humanity and human love for God are expressed and incarnated in the common material project of the multitude. (*M.*, 397)

Nor do they hesitate to compare today's potential revolutionaries to the Christians of the late Roman Empire: "We can take inspiration from St. Augustine's vision of a project destined to combat the declining Roman Empire" (*E.*, 259).[115] But surely not in the fashion of Georges Sorel . . .

This line of reasoning has not failed to contribute to the

---

[113] Toni Negri, *Job, la force de l'esclave* [*Job: The Strength of the Slave*], trans. Judith Revel (Paris: Hachette-Littératures, 2002).

[114] On Negri's ideas concerning poverty and the role of Franciscan ideology in his thought, cf. Daniel Barber and Anthony Paul Smith, "On 'Poverty' in Negri," European Consortium for Political Research, University of Pisa, September 2007, and Daniel Colucciello Barber and Anthony Paul Smith, "Too Poor for Measure: Working with Negri on Poverty and Fabulation," *Journal for Cultural and Religious Theory*, Summer 2010, 1–15.

[115] Cf. also Toni Negri, "Ainsi commença la chute de l'Empire" ["Thus Began the Empire's Fall"], *Multitudes*, 7, 17.

renewed interest in political theology observed in recent years,[116] although it remains a rather meager illustration of it. Daniel Bensaïd thinks that in Hardt and Negri:

> Recourse to theological jargon ends by serving as a stopgap that poorly conceals the disproportion between the promised philosophical revolution and the (quite real) poverty of their political answers. The perspective tends, in fact, to reduce itself to the double theme of exodus and miracle. . . . To escape the sorcery of the commodity, it is enough to flee, without trying to conquer any sort of power. . . . As for that long march of exile and exodus across the deserts, it amounts to a political event transfigured into a theological miracle.[117]

The analysis concludes with a fairly logical prophetic vision: "When the moment arrives, an event will propel us like an arrow into that living future. This will be the true act of political love" (*M.*, 404). In the end — an old dream — it is a matter of forming a "new race, i.e., a subjectivity politically coordinated and produced by the multitude," and "of giving birth to a new humanity" (*M.*, 401). In this performative declaration one may well see a mere theorization of powerlessness — or more simply, an interiorization of defeat.

*

Michael Hardt and Antonio Negri's line of reasoning aims finally at reconciling a sugary form of Marxism with certain postmodern currents, as well as with Spinoza's ideas — or, if you prefer, the ideology of progress with the postmodern idea

---

[116] Cf. especially Creston Davis, ed., *The Continental Shift*, special issue of the journal *Political Theology*, March 2010; in particular the articles by Daniel M. Bell, Jr., "The Fragile Brilliance of Glass: Empire, Multitude, and the Coming Community," 61–76; and Mary-Jane Rubinstein, "Capital Shares: The Way Back into the With of Christianity," 103–19. The second article examines the possible relation between Christian universalism and the emergence of global capitalism.

[117] Bensaïd, *Éloge de la politique profane*, 308–309.

that there is no historical "objectivity." Hardt and Negri are certainly not wrong to say we are living in the postmodern age of "Empire" and that a society of surveillance and control has been substituted for the old disciplinary society, with this new society essentially functioning thanks to a form of social control increasingly internalized by individuals. But their mistake is in finding nothing to criticize about this, and to imagine the change opens the way to forms of resistance capable of re-launching the project of liberation. Nor do Hardt and Negri limit themselves to observing the rising power of cognitive capitalism, which has already been described by many other authors. Their originality consists rather in presenting the Empire as an adversary even as they celebrate its intrinsic qualities, to the point where it would be harmful and "reactionary" to attack it. "Turbo-capitalism" is not perceived as even worse than the old industrial or commercial capitalism, but as better because it bears an emancipatory potential. "The historic metamorphoses from which Hardt and Negri deduce the Empire's emergence proceed in fact from a double determinism: technological (the effect of new technologies on labor's content and organization) and sociological (the irresistible rise of the multitude marching toward its fabulous destiny)."[118] "The very latest thing in point of social technology and management that capitalism uses in the management of the crisis," adds Robert Kurz, "thus advances to the rank of liberating forces."[119]

Denouncing the dominant system even as they celebrate its fundamental characteristics (fluidity, mobility, deterritorialization, etc.), Hardt and Negri come to deny Capitalism's crisis situation even as it develops before our very eyes. Capitalism today is supposedly "miraculously healthy, and its accumulation more vigorous than ever" (E., 330). Where many see nothing but an enormous rise in conformism and total alienation, these two authors maintain that globalization is instead engendering a man irreducibly rebellious against any form of authority. They do not see that today, it is society as a whole which is

---

[118] Bensaïd, *Éloge de la politique profane*, 296.
[119] Kurz, "L'Empire et ses théoriciens," 89.

subordinate to the logic of Capital—or rather, when they do perceive this, it is to celebrate it, letting it be understood that the "Communism" to come will in some sense be liberal globalization's natural child.[120] Their central affirmation according to which the Empire's emergence increases the potential for the multitude's liberation is never really proven, even though the whole theory rests on it. Nor does any concrete experience provide confirmation of it.

As for the concept of "multitude" on which both authors continuously harp, it obviously has no real content. In their books, and in spite of all their efforts, it appears above all as a chaotic fog. One can only be struck in this regard by how the concepts employed by Hardt and Negri transform themselves over the course of their writings into so many mental categories. As Daniel Bensaïd has written: "The world scene then becomes a shadow theater where an abstraction called the Multitude confronts another abstraction called the Empire." The watchwords "nomadism," "deterritorialization," and "liberation of hybridization" are unable to replace definite political commands, either. Finally, against the generalized effects of reification and commercial alienation, "we cannot remain content with formulas opposing the multitude to the people, the elusive gush of desire to the grasp of power, deterritorialized currents to the grid of national boundaries, biopolitical reproduction to economic production."[121] Deprived of its theoretical references, the enterprise looks like a reverie content to recycle classic mental attitudes: naïve egalitarianism, hostility to any form of power, the predominance of the prophetic over the political, etc.

---

[120] Hardt and Negri are also among the authors who criticize capitalism while taking care not to question the liberal heritage historically associated with it, on the grounds that the latter has today become sufficiently "autonomous" for a critique of capitalism to rely upon it. This line of reasoning has been criticized many times, notably by Slavoj Žižek and Jean-Claude Michéa.

[121] Daniel Bensaïd, "Antonio Negri et Michael Hardt analysent le nouveau dispositif du capitalisme mondial" ["Antonio Negri and Michael Hardt Analyze the New System of Global Capitalism"], *Le Monde des livres*, March 22, 2001.

In the final analysis, it is not a critique of capitalism that Hardt and Negri are proposing, but a kind of critical defense of that same capitalism, in other words, an alternative capitalism. In any case, it is as "Left-wing" theorists of cognitive capitalism and the new finance capital that they have often been perceived. Hardt and Negri's writings, notes Philippe Raynaud, "combine the revolutionary project with a hopeless admiration for the capitalist imagination in both its productivist and individualist components."[122] Slavoj Žižek even went so far as to speak of their work as a "celebration of capitalism."[123] Others have spoken of "a somewhat magical Christmas tale,"[124] or even of "the final masquerade of traditional Marxism."[125] "No one needs to refute Negri-ism. The facts themselves will take care of that," we have read in the journal *Tiqqun*, which is close to a certain autonomous and neo-Situationist tendency.[126] Such citations could be multiplied.[127]

In the end, Hardt and Negri's work recycles an old illusion of the workers' movement: that of a capitalism without capitalists, of a capitalism that could be placed in the service of the

---

[122] Raynaud, *L'Extrême gauche plurielle*, 169.

[123] Slavoj Žižek, interview in *L'Humanité*, September 25, 2007.

[124] Philippe Corcuff, "Antonio Negri, la multitude contre l'Empire" ["Antonio Negri, the Multitude contra the Empire"], *Sciences humaines*, May 2005.

[125] Jappe, *Les Aventures de la marchandise*.

[126] "Réfutation du négrisme" ["Refutation of Negrism"], *Tiqqun*, October 2001, 266. The journal continues by alluding to the "incestuous relation between political Negrism and imperial pacification: he wants its reality, but not its realism. He wants biopower without the police, communication without the Spectacle, peace without having to make war for it." Cf. also Tiqqun, *Tout a failli. Vive le communisme!* [*Everything Has Failed: Long Live Communism!*] (Paris: La Fabrique, 2009), 101.

[127] Let us also cite a violent anarchist caricature: Crisso and Odoteo, *Barbari. L'insorgenza disordinata* (Turin: NN, 2002) (English translation: *Barbarian: The Disordered Insurgence* [Los Angeles: Venomous Butterfly Publ., 2003]). The work especially criticizes Hardt and Negri's technicist position and interprets their books as a call to accelerate the planetary homogenization of ways of life.

workers without fundamentally changing its nature. It is in this respect that, even apart from its philosophy of nomadism and chaos, it reveals itself upon examination as a pathetic mystification.

LIBERTY — EQUALITY — FRATERNITY
(ON THE POLITICAL MEANING OF A
REPUBLICAN SLOGAN)

As is well-known, the republican slogan "Liberty — Equality — Fraternity" was first invoked during the French Revolution.[1] At the time it was merely one slogan among many. Falling into disuse under the Empire, and frequently called into question thereafter, it reappeared during the Revolution of 1848 when it was inscribed as a "principle" of the Republic in the Constitution of February 27, 1848. We run into it again in many socialist theorists of that time, such as Pierre Leroux and Louis Blanc. But it only finally succeeded in imposing itself in the age of the Third Republic. For the July 14 celebration of 1880, it was decided to inscribe the slogan on the pediments of public buildings. It was thereafter inserted into the Constitution of 1946 (the Fourth Republic), as well as that of 1958 (the Fifth Republic).

For two centuries, these three concepts have never ceased being the object of intense debate.

The compatibility of liberty and equality were not at first contested. Under the Revolution, liberty was often perceived as a perfectly natural means of assuring equality, the latter conversely being considered as engendering liberty thanks to the power of the law. Later, an author such as Pierre Leroux — who coined the term "socialism" — tried to evade difficulties by making liberty a

---

[1] It was in December 1790, in his "Speech on the Organization of the National Guards," which was never delivered but widely distributed throughout France, that Robespierre demanded the words "Liberty, Equality, Fraternity" be inscribed on uniforms and flags. This project was never adopted, however. The following year, in May 1791, we find the same triad in a proposal made at the Cordeliers Club by the Marquis de Guichardin. Cf. Mona Ozouf, "Liberté, égalité, fraternité," in Pierre Nora, ed., *Lieux de mémoire*, vol. 3: *La France. De l'archive à l'emblème* [*Places of Memory*, vol. 3: *France from Archive to Emblem*] (Paris: Gallimard, 1997), *Quarto* series, 4353–89; and Michel Borgetto, *"Liberté, Égalité, Fraternité"* (Paris: PUF, 1997).

goal of which equality was the principle and fraternity the means. These conclusions were soon questioned, however. Equality and liberty were posited as relatively antagonistic to one another. This opposition increased when equality was redefined not as equality of rights but as equality of results; the idea then spread that such equality involved a certain coercion limiting liberty (whence liberals' distrust of equality). Conversely, liberty was regarded as susceptible of giving birth to new inequalities (whence socialists' distrust of liberty).

A whole dialectic was then established between the two concepts. Some authors, for example, made each of these two terms the means for preventing the other's excesses. Liberty would limit the tendency towards levelling implied by equality, while equality would limit an excess of liberty leading towards intolerable hierarchies. But from a different point of view, it is the slogan's third term, fraternity, that appeared as a means of reconciling the other two, and secondarily of reconciling their respective defenders as well. In other words, to fraternity was entrusted the means of conciliating, and at the same time transcending, equality and liberty. This transcendence could be compared to a Hegelian *Aufhebung*, with fraternity playing the role of synthesis in relation to the thesis liberty and the antithesis equality.

The three concepts have also been placed in chronological order. Men at first demanded liberty, then equality, after which their aspirations turned to fraternity. Victor Hugo made of fraternity the "final step" that could only be attained once the other two had been reached. This interpretation corresponds to the slogan's formulation, in which fraternity does in fact come last. But some authors proceed in the opposite direction, defining fraternity as the necessary condition for the establishment of liberty and equality within a political society.

*

If we want to speak coherently about the republican slogan "Liberty, Equality, Fraternity," the first thing we must understand is that it is a political slogan. This means that it is the *political* (and not the general, symbolic, moral, etc.) meaning of each of these concepts that must be taken into account: political liberty, political equality, political fraternity. To pass from political

freedom to economic freedom, for example, or to confound political equality with natural equality, or political fraternity with
moral fraternity, represents a serious misinterpretation.

Here we shall limit ourselves to equality and fraternity, for it
is regarding these two concepts that most misunderstandings
occur.

The equality between A and B (A = B) means either that A is
similar or identical to B — i.e., not different from it — or that they
are equivalent according to a specific criterion and in a determinate relation. Then one must specify this criterion or identify this
relation. "If there is only equality in a determinate relation,"
writes Julien Freund, "the same beings and the same things can
be different or unequal in other relations." It follows that equality is never an absolute given, and does not refer to an intrinsic
relation, but depends on a convention — in fact, on the criterion
used or the relation chosen. Stated as a self-sufficient principle, it
is empty, for there is no equality or inequality except in a given
context and in relation to criteria allowing it to be concretely
posited or appreciated. The concepts of equality and inequality
have thus always been relative and, by definition, are never
without their arbitrary aspect.

As for democratic equality, so poorly understood for various
reasons on both the Left and Right, it must be understood first of
all as an intrinsically political concept. Political equality no longer signifies merely that in a democracy the law is the same for
all, independent of distinctions of birth or origin. It is above all a
characteristic, a prerogative shared by all the citizens. All citizens are politically equal not because they are similar or "naturally" equal, but because they are all equally citizens.

Democracy thus implies the political equality of citizens and
not at all their "natural" equality. As Carl Schmitt remarks:

The equality of everything "with a human face" cannot issue in a state, or a form of government, or a governmental
form. We can draw from it no distinctions or limitations. . .
. From the fact that all men are men we cannot deduce anything specific, neither in morality, nor in religion, nor in
politics, nor in economics. . . . The idea of human equality

furnishes no legal, political, or economic criterion. . . . An equality that has no other content than the common equality *per se* of all men would be an apolitical equality, for its lacks the corollary of a possible inequality. Every form of equality draws its importance and meaning from its correlation with a possible inequality. It is all the more intense the more significant is the inequality with respect to those who are not among the equals. An equality without possibility of inequality, an equality one possesses intrinsically and can never lose, is without value and a matter of indifference.[2]

Like any political concept, democratic equality refers to the possibility of a distinction. It sanctions a common belonging to a particular political entity. The citizens of a democratic country enjoy equal political rights not because they have the same competences but because they are equally citizens of their country. Similarly, universal suffrage is not the sanction of an intrinsic equality of the voters. The real democratic principle is not "one man, one vote" but "one citizen, one vote." As we have already said, it is the logical consequence of the voters all being citizens, and its function is to express their preferences and to permit their disagreement or consent to be recorded. Political equality, the condition for all the other forms (in democracy the people represent the constitutive power), is in no way abstract; it is altogether substantial. Already among the Greeks, *isonomia* did not mean that the citizens were equal in terms of competence, but that all had the same right to participate in public life. Democratic equality thus implies a common belonging, and thereby contributes to define an identity. This term "identity" refers both to that which distinguishes (singularity) and to that which allows those who share this singularity to identify with one another collectively.

The first consequence of this is that "the essential concept of democracy is the people and not humanity. If democracy is to

---

[2] Carl Schmitt, *Théorie de la Constitution* [*Constitutional Theory*], trans. Lilyane Deroche (Paris: PUF, 1993), 364–65.

remain a political form, there are only democracies of the people, and no democracy of humanity."[3] The second consequence is that the corollary of the equality of citizens resides in their non-equality to those who are not citizens. Carl Schmitt writes:

> Political democracy cannot rest on the absence of distinc-
> tion between all men, but only on belonging to a specific
> people; such belonging can be determined by quite diverse
> factors. . . . The equality that is part of the very essence of
> democracy thus only applies within a state and not out-
> side it: within a democratic state, all citizens are equals. A
> consequence for politics and public law is that he who is
> not a citizen has nothing to do with that democratic equal-
> ity.[4]

It is in this respect that "democracy as a principle of political form is opposed to the liberal ideas of liberty and the equality of each individual with every other individual. If a democratic state recognized universal human equality in the domain of public life and law down to its ultimate consequences, it would rid itself of its own substance."[5]

What about the concept of fraternity?

Fraternity, from the Latin *frater*, "brother," originally designated a natural — not to say biological — bond. The term *fraternitas* did not appear, however, until the second century and in Christian authors. But its political meaning is quite different; in certain respects, even opposed. In the political sense, fraternity refers to an existing bond (or a bond one wishes to see exist) between the members of a single organization or a single community of reference, between those who share the same ideal or defend the same cause, and by extension between those who belong to the same political entity. Thus it appears that fraternity cannot be disassociated from citizenship. In the political sense, it expresses the bond that ought to unite all citizens.

---

[3] Schmitt, *Théorie de la Constitution*, 371.

[4] Schmitt, *Théorie de la Constitution*, 365.

[5] Schmitt, *Théorie de la Constitution*, 371.

If the term fraternity has often appeared problematic, this is precisely because people have wanted to give it a universal character or moral scope ("all men are brothers") that directly contradicts its political usage.

Political fraternity has nothing natural about it. Not only does it not consist in considering all men brothers and members of the same family, but it is an elective solidarity: it consists in recognizing as brothers people who do not belong to our family, and doing so merely because they are fellow citizens. Fraternity is not the same as siblinghood, as Régis Debray rightly noted when he wrote: "Fraternity is the contrary of consanguinity; it is the remedy for siblinghood. . . . For me, there is fraternity from the moment one breaks the circle of the family, the prison of natural communities, and gives oneself an elective family, which is a transnatured, if not denatured, family."[6] In political fraternity, one is only born a brother because one was born in the same political society. And this fraternity extends to all temporal dimensions: it associates the dead and the living. Let us cite Régis Debray once more: "Since peoples, like individuals, are composed as much of the dead as of the living, how can the living be respected if one is not the dead's younger brother?"[7]

Fraternity is not identical with friendship. While friendship is a durable sentiment, a permanent bond that is in some sense static, fraternity asserts itself mainly in reference to a context, an event, a struggle. Like solidarity (which it transcends by adding the affirmation of a principle), it is a response to a situation. It asserts itself by way of opposition. It transforms occupation into resistance, humiliation into pride. It thus possesses a more dynamic character. It is also more collective, more "popular" than friendship which, because of its personal character, rather favors elitism. It is in this sense that Régis Debray was able to describe fraternity as a "modern and democratic sentiment," also emphasizing that fraternity cannot be defined as a

---

[6] Régis Debray, "Les miens et les nôtres" ["My People and Ours"], *Le Nouvel Observateur*, April 16, 2009, 90.

[7] Régis Debray, *Le Moment fraternité* [*The Moment of Fraternity*] (Paris: Gallimard, 2009), 351.

pure sentiment insofar as it is often indissociable from *praxis*, from action ("friendship lulls, fraternity shakes").

But this is also the reason fraternity separates as much as it joins. It has indeed been said that political fraternity does not associate all men. On the contrary, it establishes a dichotomy between those who are regarded as brothers and those who are not, integrating the former while excluding the latter. Fraternity, in other words, defines a collective *us* by way of opposition to those who do not belong to this *us*, and whom it keeps at a distance or places apart. It gives this *us* the possibility of forming a single body. But there is no *us* without a *them*. Régis Debray declares in principle that "fraternal communities, born of adversity, have difficulty doing without adversaries."[8] The best proof is that one never fraternizes so well as when one fraternizes against a common enemy. This is also what Robespierre said:

> Fraternity is the union of hearts, it is the union of principles: the patriot can only ally himself to a patriot. . . . When a people has established its liberty . . . when its enemies are reduced to an inability to harm it, the moment of fraternity has arrived.

Here we must also remark that there exist certain differences between the nature of fraternity and that of the other two concepts of the republican triad, equality and liberty. The first difference is that liberty and equality can be posited as rights to conquer: we have a "right to liberty," a "right to equality." Liberty and equality can be specified as well: liberty of expression, equality of opportunity, etc. Fraternity has no genitive case. It is less a right than an imperative; indeed, an obligation. One fights for or against liberty and equality, which explains why they can be separated from one another when their defenders and opponents enter into confrontation. Fraternity, on the other hand, reconciles. It unites insofar as it constitutes an obligation of all to all, of each to another.

Another important difference is that equality and liberty can

---

[8] Debray, *Le Moment fraternité*, 324.

be posited as prerogatives applicable only to individuals. They can for this reason become individual values. Fraternity, on the contrary, by definition implies a community or collectivity. It is an encompassing concept by the same title as Aristotelian "friendship," which it closely resembles, and also by the same title as the ancient concept of the common good. Fraternity, in other words, cannot be distributed. It is an indivisible good all the citizens enjoy in common and immediately, in an almost fusional manner. This good is an attribute not of the individual, but of the social and of sociability. There is no fraternity of a single person. It is significant in this respect that a number of liberal authors have accepted the concepts of liberty (transposed into individual autonomy) and equality (limited to equality of rights) while professing a certain distrust of the "collectivist," "socialist," or "holistic" concept of fraternity.

In his speech of November 15, 1941, General de Gaulle declared: "We say Liberty-Equality-Fraternity because our will is to remain faithful to the democratic principles that our ancestors drew from the genius of our race and that are at stake in this war for life or death." We might add that at a time when we are witnessing an increasing disaggregation of the social bond, only the concept of fraternity can allow the recreation of a collective *us* and reanimate a collective project abandoned by the *me*. In the past, popular democracies appealed to equality, liberal democracies to liberty. Organic democracy, founded on the participation of the greatest possible number of citizens in public affairs, should above all be based on fraternity.

INDEX

Numbers in bold refer to a whole chapter or section devoted to a particular topic.

ABOUT THE AUTHOR

Alain de Benoist (b. 1943) is a political philosopher and historian of ideas. The author of a hundred books and thousands of articles, his recent books in English include *Ernst Jünger: Between the Gods & the Titans* (Middle Europe Books, 2022) and *Against Liberalism: Society Is Not a Market* (Middle Europe Books, 2024).